MERCEDES-BENZ
280SL
280SEL
280S
280SE
1968-1972
WORKSHOP
MANUAL

A Floyd CLYMER Publication by:
www.VelocePress.com
Copyright 2024 Veloce Enterprises

PREFACE

TRADEMARKS & COPYRIGHT

Mercedes-Benz ® is the registered trademark of Mercedes-Benz AG. This publication is not sponsored by or endorsed by the trademark owner. We recognize that some words, model names and designations, for example, mentioned herein are the property of the trademark holder. We use them for identification purposes only. This is not an official publication however; it may include non-copyright works of the trademark holder.

INTRODUCTION

Welcome to the world of digital publishing ~ the book you now hold in your hand was printed using the latest state of the art digital technology. The advent of print-on-demand has forever changed the publishing process, never has information been so accessible and it is our hope that this book serves your informational needs for years to come. If this is your first exposure to digital publishing, we hope that you are pleased with the results. Many more titles of interest to the classic automobile and motorcycle enthusiast, collector and restorer are available via our website at www.VelocePress.com. We hope that you find this title as interesting as we do.

NOTE FROM THE PUBLISHER

The information presented is true and complete to the best of our knowledge. All recommendations are made without any guarantees on the part of the author or the publisher, who also disclaim all liability incurred with the use of this information.

INFORMATION ON THE USE OF THIS PUBLICATION

This manual is an invaluable resource for those interested in performing their own maintenance. However, in today's information age we are constantly subject to changes in common practice, new technology, availability of improved materials and increased awareness of chemical toxicity. As such, it is advised that the user consult with an experienced professional prior to undertaking any procedure described herein. While every care has been taken to ensure correctness of information, it is obviously not possible to guarantee complete freedom from errors or omissions or to accept liability arising from such errors or omissions. Therefore, any individual that uses the information contained within, or elects to perform or participate in do-it-yourself repairs or modifications acknowledges that there is a risk factor involved and that the publisher or its associates cannot be held responsible for personal injury or property damage resulting from the use of the information or the outcome of such procedures.

WARNING!

One final word of advice, this publication is intended to be used as a reference guide, and when in doubt the reader should consult with a qualified technician.

CONTENTS

Basic troubleshooting & tools	5
Engine	17
Fuel	39
Ignition	57
Cooling	65
Clutch	71
Manual gearbox	79
Automatic transmission	95
Prop-shaft, rear axle & suspension	109
Front suspension & hubs	123
Steering	133
Brakes	145
Electrical	161
Body	171
Technical data	181
Conversion chart	188
Torque wrench settings	189
Lubrication Charts	192
Wiring Diagrams	196

BASIC TROUBLESHOOTING AND TOOLS

(NOTE: Detailed troubleshooting can be found at the end of each appropriate chapter)

Troubleshooting can be relatively simple if done logically. The first step is to define symptoms as closely as possible. Subsequent steps involve testing and analyzing areas which could cause the symptoms.

Procedures in this chapter are not the only ones possible. There may be several approaches to solving a problem, but all methods must have one thing in common—a logical, systematic approach.

TROUBLESHOOTING EQUIPMENT

The following equipment is necessary to properly troubleshoot the engine and its components.

1. Voltmeter, ammeter, and ohmmeter
2. Hydrometer
3. Compression tester
4. Vacuum gauge
5. Tachometer
6. Dwell meter
7. Timing light
8. Exhaust gas analyzer

Items 1 through 7 are essential. Item 8 is necessary for exhaust emission control compliance. The following is a brief description of the function of each instrument.

Voltmeter, Ammeter, and Ohmmeter

For testing the ignition and electrical systems, a good voltmeter is required. The range of the meter should cover from 0 to 20 volts, and have an accuracy of $\pm \frac{1}{2}$ volt.

The ohmmeter measures electrical resistance and is required to check continuity (open- and short-circuits), and to test fuses and lights.

The ammeter measures electrical current. One for automotive use should cover 0-10 amperes and 0-100 amperes. An ammeter is useful for checking battery charging and starting current. The starter and generator procedures use an ammeter to check for shorted windings.

Hydrometer

A hydrometer gives an indication of battery condition and charge by measuring the specific gravity of the electrolyte in each cell.

Compression Tester

The compression tester measures pressure buildup in each cylinder. The results, when properly interpreted, can indicate general cylinder and valve condition. To perform the compression check, proceed as follows:

1. Run the engine until normal operating temperature is reached.
2. Block the choke and throttle in the wide open position.
3. Remove all spark plugs.
4. Connect compression tester to one cylinder, following manufacturer's instructions.
5. Have an assistant crank the engine for at least 4 turns.
6. Remove the tester and record the reading.
7. Repeat the above steps for each cylinder.

If the compression readings fall within the appropriate range shown in the Technical Data specifications, and do not differ from each other by more than 20 psi (40 psi for diesel engines), the rings and valves are in good condition. If all cylinders are uniformly low or high, the compression tester may be inaccurate. The important point is the difference between the readings.

Compression Defects

1. *Low Compression in One Cylinder.* If a low reading (see above) is obtained on one cylinder, this indicates valve or ring trouble. To determine which, pour about a teaspoon of engine oil through the spark plug hole onto the top of the piston. Turn the engine over once to clear some of the excess oil, then take another compression test and record the reading. If the compression returns to normal, the valves are good but the rings are defective on that cylinder. If compression does not increase, the valves require servicing.

2. *Low Compression in Two Adjacent Cylinders.* This may indicate that the head gasket has blown between the cylinders and that gases are leaking from one cylinder to the other. Replace the head gasket as described in Chapter One.

To isolate the trouble more closely, compare the compression readings with vacuum gauge readings as described below.

Vacuum Gauge

The vacuum gauge is easy to use, but difficult for an inexperienced mechanic to interpret. The results, when considered with other findings, can provide valuable clues to possible trouble.

Connect the vacuum gauge with a T-connector in the hose from the carburetor to the vacuum advance on the distributor. Vacuum reading should be steady at 18-22 in. Subtract 1 in. from reading for every 1,000 feet of altitude. **Figure 1** shows numerous typical readings with interpretations. Results are not conclusive without comparing to other test results, such as compression readings.

Fuel Pressure Gauge

This instrument is vital for evaluating fuel pump performance. Often a vacuum gauge and fuel pressure gauge are combined into one instrument.

Tachometer

A tachometer is essential for tuning engines with exhaust emission control systems. Ignition timing and carburetor adjustments must be performed at specified idle speeds. The best instrument for this purpose is one with a range of 0-1,000 or 0-2,000 rpm. Extended range (0-6,000) instruments lack accuracy at lower speeds. The instrument should be capable of detecting changes of 25 rpm.

Dwell Meter

A dwell meter measures the distance in degrees of cam rotation that the distributor breaker points remain closed while the engine is running. Since this angle is determined by breaker point gap, dwell angle is an accurate indication of point

①

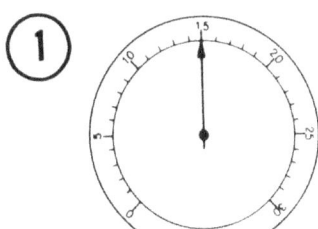

1. NORMAL READING
Reads 15 in. at idle.

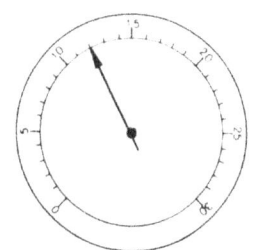

2. LATE IGNITION TIMING
About 2 inches too low at idle.

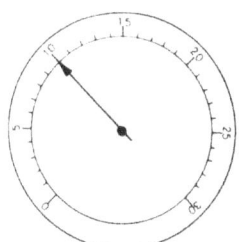

3. LATE VALVE TIMING
About 4 to 8 inches low at idle.

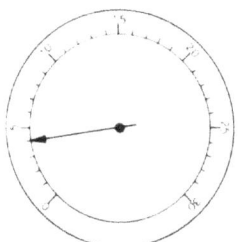

4. INTAKE LEAK
Low steady reading.

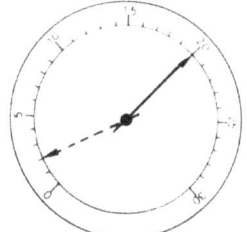

5. NORMAL READING
Drops to 2, then rises to 25 when accelerator is rapidly depressed and released.

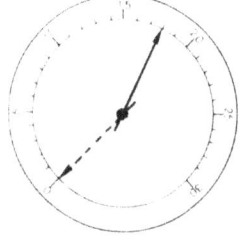

6. WORN RINGS, DILUTED OIL
Drops to 0, then rises to 18 when accelerator is rapidly depressed and released.

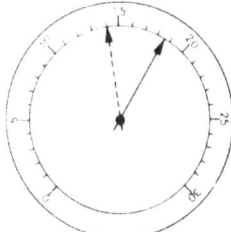

7. STICKING VALVE(S)
Normally steady. Intermittently flicks downward about 4 in.

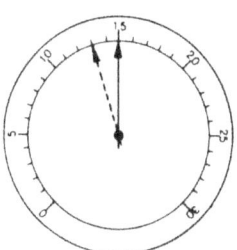

8. LEAKY VALVE
Regular drop about 2 inches.

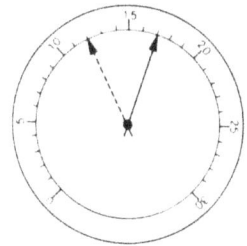

9. BURNED OR WARPED VALVE
Regular, evenly spaced down-scale flick about 4 in.

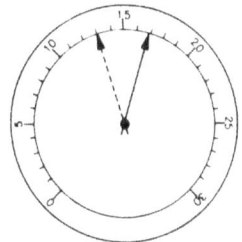

10. WORN VALVE GUIDES
Oscillates about 4 in.

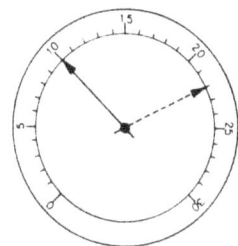

11. WEAK VALVE SPRINGS
Violent oscillation (about 10 in.) as rpm increases. Often steady at idle.

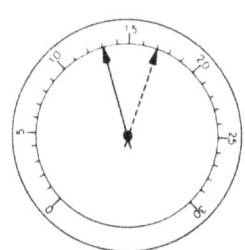

12. IMPROPER IDLE MIXTURE
Floats slowly between 13-17 in.

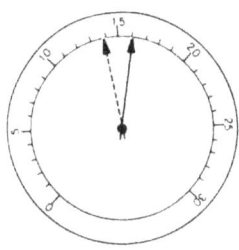

13. SMALL SPARK GAP or DEFECTIVE POINTS
Slight float between 14-16 in.

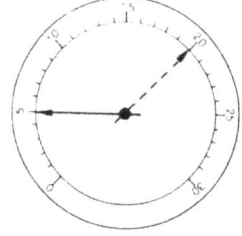

14. HEAD GASKET LEAK
Gauge floats between 5-19 in.

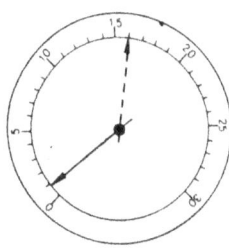

15. RESTRICTED EXHAUST SYSTEM
Normal when first started. Drops to 0 as rpm increases. May eventually rise to about 16.

gap. Many tachometers incorporate a dwell meter as well. Follow the instrument manufacturer's instructions to measure dwell.

Stroboscopic Timing Light

This instrument permits accurate engine timing. By flashing a light at the precise instant that cylinder No. 1 fires, the position of the crankshaft pulley at that instant can be seen. Marks on the pulley are lined up with the crankcase pointer to time the engine.

Suitable lights are neon bulb and xenon strobe types. Neon bulb timing lights are difficult to see and must be used in dimly lit areas. Xenon strobe timing lights can be used in bright sunlight. Use the light according to the manufacturer's instructions.

Exhaust Analyzer

Of all instruments, this is the least likely to be owned by an amateur mechanic. The most common type samples exhaust gases from the tailpipe and measures thermal conductivity. Since different gases conduct heat at varying rates, thermal conductivity is a good indication of gases present.

STARTER TROUBLESHOOTING

Starter system troubles are relatively easy to isolate. The following are common symptoms.

Engine Cranks Very Slowly or Not At All

Turn on the headlights; if the lights are very dim, the battery or connecting wires most likely are at fault. Check the battery with hydrometer. Check wiring for breaks, shorts, and dirty connections. If the battery and wires are all right, turn the headlights on and crank the engine. If the lights dim drastically, the starter is probably shorted to ground.

If the lights remain bright or dim slightly when cranking, the trouble may be in the starter, solenoid or wiring. If the starter spins, check the solenoid and wiring to the ignition switch. To isolate the trouble, short the large battery solenoid terminal to the small solenoid ignition lead (not to ground). If the starter still fails to crank properly, refer the problem to a dealer or automotive electrical specialist.

Starter Turns, But Does Not Engage With Engine

Usually caused by defective pinion or solenoid shifting fork. The teeth on the pinion, flywheel ring gear, or both may be worn too far to engage properly.

Starter Engages, But Will Not Disengage When Ignition Switch Is Released

Usually caused by sticking solenoid, but occasionally the pinion may jam on the flywheel. The pinion can be temporarily freed by rocking the car in fourth gear.

Loud Grinding Noises When Starter Runs

The teeth on the pinion and/or flywheel are not meshing properly or the overrunning clutch mechanism is broken. Remove the starter and examine gear teeth and pinion drive assembly.

CHARGING SYSTEM TROUBLESHOOTING

Charging system troubles may be in the generator (alternator), voltage regulator, or drive belt. The following symptoms are typical.

Dashboard Indicator Shows Continuous Discharge

This usually means that battery charging is not taking place. Check drive belt tension. Check battery condition with hydrometer and electrical connections in the charging system. Finally, check the alternator and/or voltage regulator.

Dashboard Indicator Shows Intermittent Discharge

Check drive belt tension and electrical connection. Trouble may be traced to worn alternator brushes or bad slip rings.

Battery Requires Frequent Addition of Water or Lamps Require Frequent Replacement

Alternator may be overcharging the battery or the voltage regulator is faulty.

Excessive Noise from the Alternator

Check for loose mountings and/or worn bearings.

ENGINE TROUBLESHOOTING

These procedures assume the starter cranks the engine over normally. If not, refer to the *Starter* section.

Engine Won't Start

Could be caused by the ignition system or fuel system. First, determine if high voltage to spark plugs occurs. To do this, disconnect one of the spark plug wires. Hold the exposed wire terminal about ¼ to ½ in. from ground (any metal in the engine compartment) with an insulated screwdriver. Crank the engine. If sparks don't jump to ground or the sparks are very weak, the trouble may be in the ignition system. If sparks occur properly, the trouble may be in the fuel system.

Engine Misses Steadily

Remove one spark plug wire at a time and ground the wire. If engine miss increases, that cylinder is working properly. Reconnect the wire and check the other. When a wire is disconnected and engine miss remains the same, that cylinder is not firing. Check spark as described above. If no spark occurs for one cylinder only, check distributor cap, wire, and spark plug. If spark occurs properly, check compression and intake manifold vacuum.

Engine Misses Erratically at All Speeds

Intermittent trouble can be difficult to find. It could be in the ignition system, intake system, or fuel system. Follow troubleshooting procedures for these systems to isolate the trouble.

Engine Misses at Idle Only

Trouble could be in ignition or carburetor idle adjustment. Check idle mixture adjustment and check for restrictions in the idle circuit. Check for inlet manifold and vacuum leaks.

Engine Misses at High Speed Only

Trouble is in the fuel system or ignition system. Check accelerator pump operation, fuel pump delivery, fuel line, etc. Check spark plugs and wires.

Low Performance at All Speeds, Poor Acceleration

Trouble usually exists in ignition, fuel system, or exhaust system.

Excessive Fuel Consumption

Could be caused by a number of seemingly unrelated factors. Check for clutch slippage, brake drag, defective wheel bearings, poor front end alignment, faulty ignition, leaky gas tank or lines, and carburetor condition.

Low Oil Pressure Indicated by Oil Pressure Gauge

If the oil pressure gauge shows low oil pressure with the engine running, stop the engine immediately. Coast to a stop with the clutch disengaged. The trouble may be caused by low oil level, blockage in the an oil line, defective oil pump, overheated engine, or defective oil pressure gauge. Check the oil level and drive belt tension. Remove and clean the oil pressure relief valve. Do not re-start the engine until you know why the low indication was given and are sure the problem has been corrected.

Engine Overheats

Usually caused by trouble in the cooling system. Check the level of coolant in the radiator, condition of the drive belt, and water hoses for leaks and loose connections. Check the operation of the electric cooling fan. Can also be caused by late ignition or valve timing.

Engine Stalls As It Warms Up

The choke valve may be stuck closed, the manifold heat control valve may be stuck, the engine idling speed may be set too low, or the emission control (PCV) valve may be faulty.

Engine Stalls After Idling or Slow-Speed Driving

Can be caused by defective fuel pump, overheated engine, high carburetor float level, incorrect idle adjustment, or defective emission control valve.

Engine Stalls After High-Speed Driving

Vapor lock within the fuel lines caused by an overheated engine is usually the cause of this trouble. Inspect and service the cooling system. If the trouble persists, changing to a different fuel or shielding the fuel line from engine heat may prove helpful.

Engine Backfires

Several causes can be suspected; ignition timing, overheating, excessive carbon, wrong heat range spark plugs, hot or sticking valves, cracked distributor cap, a hole in the exhaust system, excessively rich fuel/air mixture.

Smoky Exhaust

Blue smoke indicates excessive oil consumption usually caused by worn rings or valve guides. Black smoke indicates an excessively rich fuel mixture.

Excessive Oil Consumption

Can be caused by external leaks through broken seals or gaskets, or by burning oil in the combustion chamber. Check the oil pan and the front and rear of the engine for oil leaks. If the oil is not leaking externally, valve stem-to-guide clearances may be excessive, piston rings may be worn, cylinder walls may be scored, PCV may be plugged.

Engine Is Noisy

1. *Regular Clicking Sound*—Valves and/or tappets out of adjustment.

2. *Ping or Chatter on Load or Acceleration*—Spark knock due to low octane fuel, carbon buildup, overly advanced ignition timing, and causes mentioned under engine backfire.

3. *Light Knock or Pound With Engine Not Under Load*—Indicates worn connecting rod bearings, worn camshaft bearings, misaligned crankpin, and/or lack of engine oil.

4. *Light Metallic Double Knock, Usually Heard During Idle*—Worn or loose piston pin or bushing and/or lack of oil.

5. *Chattering or Rattling During Acceleration*—Worn rings, cylinder walls, low ring tension, and/or broken rings.

6. *Hollow, Bell-like Muffled Sound When Engine Is Cold*—Piston slap due to worn pistons, cylinder walls, collapsed piston skirts, excessive clearances, misaligned connecting rods, and/or lack of oil.

7. *Dull, Heavy Metallic Knock Under Load or Acceleration, Especially When Cold*—Regular noise: worn main bearings; irregular noise: worn thrust bearings.

IGNITION SYSTEM TROUBLESHOOTING

The following procedures assume the battery is in good enough condition to crank the engine at a normal rate.

No Spark to One Plug

The only causes are defective distributor cap or spark plug wire. Examine the distributor cap for moisture, dirt, carbon tracking caused by flashover, and cracks. Check spark plug wire for breaks or loose connectors.

No Spark to Any Plug

This could indicate trouble in the primary or secondary ignition circuits. First, remove the coil wire from the center post of the distributor. Hold the wire end about ¼ in. from ground with an insulated screwdriver. Crank the engine. If sparks are produced, the trouble is in the rotor or distributor cap. Remove the cap and check for burns, moisture, dirt, carbon tracking, cracks, etc. Check rotor for excessive burning, pitting, and cracks, and check its continuity with a test light.

If the coil does not produce any spark, check the secondary wire for a break. If the wire is good, turn the engine over so the breaker points are open. Examine them for excessive gap, burning, pitting, or loose connections. With the points open, check voltage from the coil to ground with a voltmeter or test lamp. If voltage is present, the coil is probably defective. Have it checked or substitute a coil known to be good.

If voltage is not present, check wire connections to coil and distributor. Disconnect the wire leading from the coil to the distributor and measure from the coil terminal to ground. If voltage is present, the distributor is shorted. Examine breaker points and connecting wires carefully. If voltage is still not present, measure the other coil terminal. Voltage on the other terminal indicates a defective coil. No voltage indicates a broken wire between the coil and battery.

Weak Spark

If the spark is so small it cannot jump from the wire to ground, check the battery. Other causes are bad breaker points, condenser, incorrect point gap, dirty or loose connection in the primary circuit, or dirty or burned rotor or distributor. Check for worn cam lobes in the distributor.

Missing

This is usually caused by fouled or damaged plugs, plugs of the wrong heat range, or incorrect plug gap.

FUEL SYSTEM TROUBLESHOOTING

Fuel system troubles must be isolated to the carburetor, fuel pump, or fuel lines. The following procedures assume the ignition system has been checked and is in proper working order.

Engine Will Not Start

First, determine that fuel is being delivered to the carburetor. If fuel is delivered to the carburetor, check the carburetor and choke system for dirt and/or defects.

Engine Runs at Fast Idle

Misadjustment of fast idle screw or defective carburetor, vacuum leak, intake manifold leak, carburetor gasket leak.

EXHAUST EMISSION CONTROL TROUBLESHOOTING

Failure of the emission control system to maintain exhaust output within acceptable limits is usually due to a defective carburetor, general engine condition, or defective exhaust control valves.

CLUTCH TROUBLESHOOTING

Several clutch troubles may be experienced. Usually the trouble is quite obvious and will fall into one of the following categories:

1. Slipping, chattering, or grabbing when engaging.

2. Spinning or dragging when disengaged.

3. Clutch noises, clutch pedal pulsations, and rapid clutch disc facing wear.

Clutch Slips While Engaged

Improper adjustment of clutch linkage, weak or broken pressure spring, worn friction disc facings, and grease or oil on clutch disc.

Clutch Chatters or Grabs When Engaging

Usually caused by misadjustment of clutch linkage, dirt or grease on the friction disc facings, or broken, worn clutch parts, warped or burned flywheel.

Clutch Spins or Drags When Disengaged

The clutch friction disc normally spins briefly after disengagement and takes a moment to come to rest. This sound should not be confused with drag. Drag is caused by the friction disc not being fully released from the flywheel or pressure plate as the clutch pedal is depressed. The trouble can be caused by clutch linkage misadjustment, defective or worn clutch parts, or a warped flywheel.

Clutch Noises

Clutch noises are usually most noticeable when he engine is idling. First, note whether the noise is heard when the clutch is engaged or disengaged. Clutch noises when engaged could be due to a loose friction disc hub, loose friction disc springs, and misalignment or looseness of engine or transmission mountings. When disengaged, noises can be due to a worn release bearings, defective pilot bearing, or misaligned release lever.

Clutch Pedal Pulsates

Usually noticed when slight pressure is applied to the clutch pedal with the engine running. As pedal pressure is increased, the pulsation ceases. Possible causes include misalignment of engine and transmission, bent crankshaft flange, distortion or shifting of the clutch housing, release lever misalignment, warped friction disc, damaged pressure plate, or warped flywheel.

Rapid Friction Disc Facing Wear

This trouble is caused by any condition that permits slippage between facings and the flywheel or pressure plate. Probable causes are "riding" the clutch, slow releasing of the clutch after disengagement, weak or broken pressure spings, pedal linkage misadjustment, warped clutch disc or pressure plate, faulty master or slave cylinders, blocked cap vent or flex hose.

TRANSMISSION TROUBLESHOOTING

Hard Shifting Into Gear

Common causes are the clutch not releasing, misadjustment of linkage, linkage needing lubrication, detent ball stuck, or gears tight on shaft splines.

Transmission Slips Out of First or Reverse Gear

Causes are gearshift linkage out of adjustment, gear loose on main shaft, gear teeth worn, excessive play, insufficient shift lever spring tension, or worn bearings.

Transmission Slips Out of Second, Third, Fourth, or Fifth Gear

Gearshift linkage is out of adjustment, misalignment between engine and transmission, excessive main shaft end play, worn gear teeth, insufficient shift lever spring tension, worn bearings, or defective synchronizer. Gear may be loose on main shaft.

No Power Through Transmission

May be caused by clutch slipping, stripped gear teeth, damaged shifter fork linkage, broken gear or shaft, and stripped drive key.

Transmission Noisy in Neutral

Transmission misaligned, bearings worn or dry, worn gears, worn or bent countershaft, and excessive countershaft end play.

Transmission Noisy in Gear

Defective clutch disc, worn bearings, loose gears, worn gear teeth, and faults listed above.

Gears Clash During Shifting

Caused by the clutch not releasing, defective synchronizer, or gears sticking on main shaft.

Oil Leaks

Most common causes are foaming due to wrong lubricant, lubricant level too high, broken gaskets, damaged oil seals, loose drain plug, and cracked transmission case.

DIFFERENTIAL TROUBLESHOOTING

Usually, it is noise that draws attention to trouble in the differential. It is not always easy to diagnose the trouble by determining the source of noise and the operating conditions that produce the noise. Defective conditions in the universal joints, wheel bearings, muffler, or tires may be wrongly diagnosed as trouble in the differential or axles.

Some clue as to the cause of trouble may be gained by noting whether the noise is a hum, growl, or knock; whether it is produced when the car is accelerating under load or coasting; and whether it is heard when the car is going straight or making a turn.

1. *Noise during acceleration*—May be caused by shortage of lubricant, incorrect tooth contact between drive gear and drive pinion, damaged or misadjusted bearings in axles or side bearings, or damaged gears.

2. *Noise during coasting*—May be caused by incorrect backlash between drive gear and drive pinion gear or incorrect adjustment of drive pinion bearing.

3. *Noise during turn*—This noise is usually caused by loose or worn axle shaft bearing, pinion gear too tight on shafts, side gear jammed in differential case, or worn side gear thrust washer and pinion thrust washer.

4. *Broken differential parts*—Breaking of differential parts can be caused by insufficient lubricant, improper use of clutch, excessive loading, misadjusted bearings and gears, excessive backlash, damage to case, or loose bolts.

A humming noise in the differential is often caused by improper drive pinion or ring gear adjustment which prevents normal tooth contact between gears. If ignored, rapid tooth wear will take place and the noise will become more like a growl. Repair as soon as the humming is heard so that new gears will not be required. Tire noise will vary considerably, depending on the type of road surface. Differential noises will be the same regardless of road surface. If noises are heard, listen carefully to the noise over different road surfaces to help isolate the problem.

BRAKE SYSTEM TROUBLESHOOTING

Brake Pedal Goes to Floor

Worn linings or pads, air in the hydraulic system, leaky brake lines, leaky wheel cylinders, or leaky or worn master cylinder may be the cause. Check for leaks and worn brake linings or pads. Bleed and adjust the brakes. Rebuild wheel cylinders and/or master cylinder.

Spongy Pedal

Usually caused by air in the brake system. Bleed and adjust brakes.

Brakes Pull

Check brake adjustment and wear on linings and disc pads. Check for contaminated linings, leaky wheel cylinders, loose calipers, lines, or hoses. Check front end alignment and suspension damage such as broken front or rear springs and shock absorbers. Tires also affect braking; check tire pressures and tire condition.

Brakes Squeal or Chatter

Check brake and pad lining thickness and brake drum and rotor condition. Ensure that shoes are not loose. Clean away all dirt on shoes, drums, rotors, and pads.

Brakes Drag

Check brake adjustment, including handbrake. Check for broken or weak shoe return springs, swollen rubber parts due to improper brake fluid or contamination. Check for defective master cylinder. Also check the brake pedal-to-master cylinder clearance.

Hard Pedal

Check brake linings for contamination. Check for brake line restrictions and frozen wheel cylinders and calipers.

High Speed Fade

Check for distorted or out-of-round drums and rotors and contaminated linings or pads.

Pulsating Pedal

Check for distorted or out-of-round brake drums or rotors. Check for excessive disc runout.

COOLING SYSTEM TROUBLESHOOTING

Engine Overheats

May be caused by insufficient coolant, loose or defective drive belt, defective thermostat, defective water pump, clogged water lines, incorrect ignition timing, and/or defective or loose hoses, defective thermoswitch or fan motor. Inspect radiator and all parts for leaks.

Engine Does Not Warm Up

Usually caused by defective thermostat or extremely cold weather.

Loss of Coolant

Radiator leaks, loose or defective hoses, defective water pump, leaks in cylinder head gasket, cracked cylinder head or engine block, or defective radiator cap may be the cause.

Noisy Cooling System

Usually caused by defective water pump bearings, loose or bent fan blades, or defective drive belt.

STEERING AND SUSPENSION TROUBLESHOOTING

Trouble in the suspension or steering is evident when any of the following occur:

1. Hard steering
2. Car pulls to one side
3. Car wanders or front wheels wobble
4. Excessive play in steering
5. Abnormal tire wear

Unusual steering, pulling, or wandering is usually caused by bent or misaligned suspension parts. If the trouble seems to be excessive play, check wheel bearing adjustment first. Next, check steering free-play and kingpins and balljoints. Finally, check tie rod ends by shaking each wheel.

Tire Wear Analysis

Abnormal tire wear should always be analyzed to determine the cause. The most common are incorrect tire pressure, improper driving, overloading, and incorrect wheel alignment. **Figure 2** identifies wear patterns and their most probable causes.

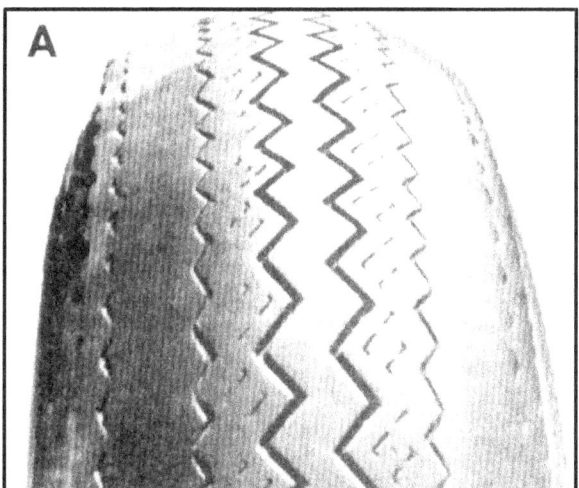

Underinflation — Worn more on sides than in center.

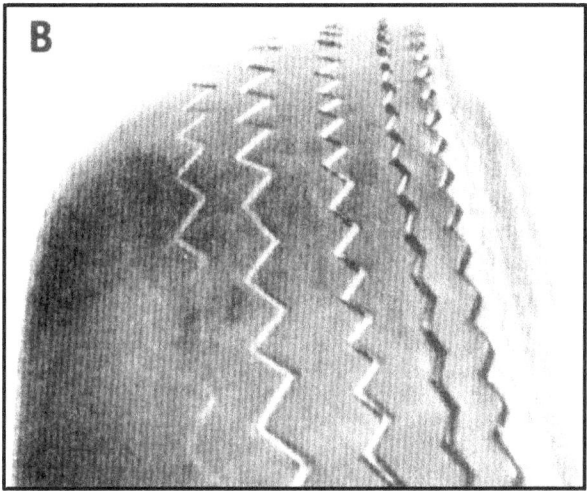

Wheel Alignment — Worn more on one side than the other. Edges of tread feathered.

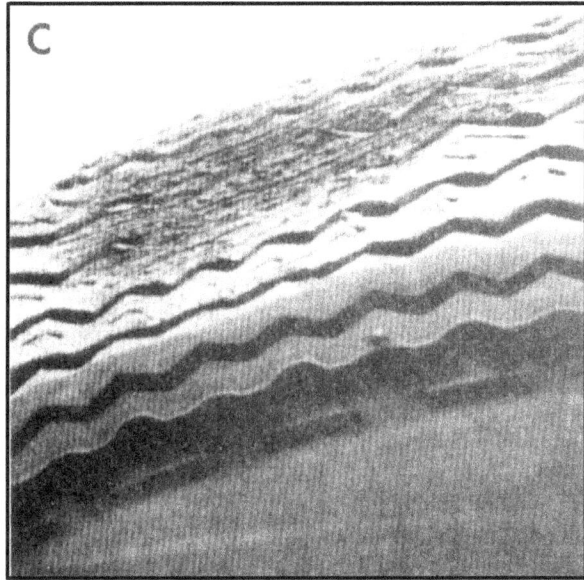

Road Abrasion — Rough wear on entire tire or in patches.

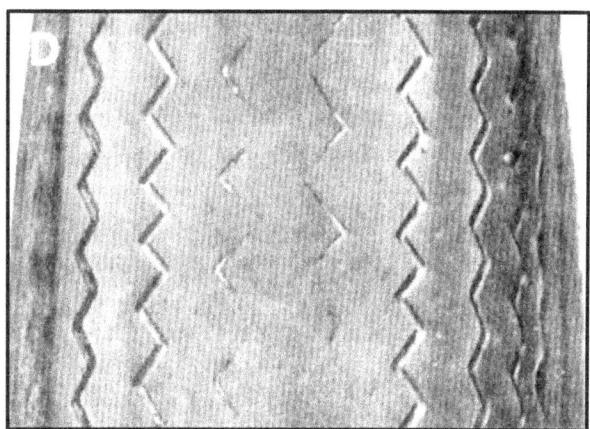

Overinflation — Worn more in center than on sides.

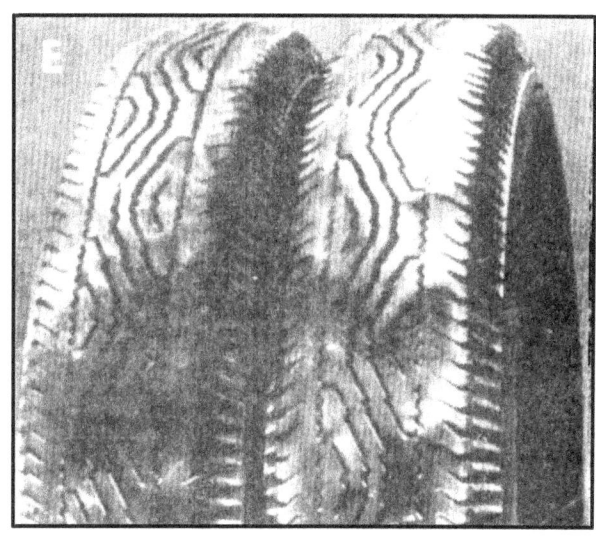

Wheel Balance — Scalloped edges indicate wheel wobble or tramp due to wheel unbalance.

Combination — Most tires exhibit a combination of the above. This tire was overinflated (center worn) and the toe-in was incorrect (feathering). The driver cornered hard at high speed (feathering, rounded shoulders) and braked rapidly (worn spots). The scaly roughness indicates a rough road surface.

Wheel Balancing

All 4 wheels and tires must be in balance along 2 axes. To be in static balance (**Figure 3**), weight must be evenly distributed around the axis of rotation. (A) shows a statically unbalanced wheel. (B) shows the result—wheel tramp or hopping. (C) shows proper static balance.

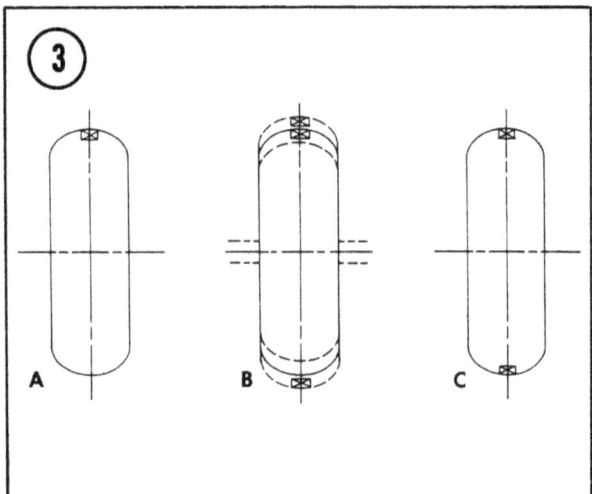

To be in dynamic balance (**Figure 4**), the centerline of the weight must coincide with the centerline of the wheel. (A) shows a dynamically unbalanced wheel. (B) shows the result—wheel wobble or shimmy. (C) shows proper dynamic balance.

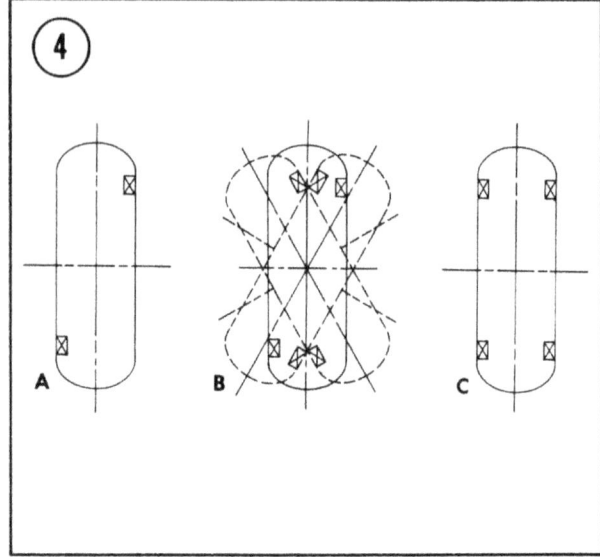

CHAPTER 1 - THE ENGINE

1 Description
2 Engine removal
3 Cylinder head removal
4 The camshaft
5 The valves and valve clearances
6 Decarbonizing
7 The valve timing and distributor gear
8 The sump, oil pump and oil filter
9 The clutch and flywheel
10 The crankshaft damper and front oil seal
11 The crankshaft and bearings
12 The pistons and connecting rods
13 Reassembling a stripped engine
14 Emission control
15 Fault diagnosis

1 Description

The engine follows the general design of the Mercedes series. Extensive use is made of light-alloy castings and the valve train bears the unmistakable Mercedes stamp. All the engines are six-cylinder in-line, water-cooled and of conventional design. The design will vary slightly depending on whether fuel injection or carburetters are fitted. Exterior views of the 280 S/8 engine are shown in **FIG 1** and a sectioned view of an engine fitted with fuel injection is shown in **FIG 2**. **FIG 2** also shows the path of the air for ventilating the crankcase. Fumes are drawn out of the rocker cover through a calibrated orifice 1 and then into the venturi control unit 2. On carburetter models the fumes are drawn directly into the intake manifold.

The engine is conventional in that the crankshaft is supported in seven main bearings and all crankshaft bearings are fitted with renewable steel-backed bearing inserts. The gudgeon pins are fully floating and secured in the pistons by circlips. Lubrication is by a gear pump drawing oil from the sump and passing it through a full-flow oil filter to the oil gallery. Oil pressure relief valves limit the maximum oil pressure when the engine is cold. From the oil gallery, internal passages lead the oil to the main components. Further internal passages in the crankshaft lead the oil from the main bearings to the big-end bearings. Those parts not directly lubricated are lubricated by the splash thrown from the bearings.

The design of the valve gear is typical Mercedes, using an overhead camshaft mounted in bearing pedestals on the cylinder head, shown typically in **FIG 3**. The camshaft is driven at half engine speed by a timing chain and sprockets. The timing chain also supplies the drive to the distributor, and the oil pump and typical parts are shown in **FIG 4**. The shafts 10 in the figure supply the drive for distributor and oil pump. An idler sprocket 56 is fitted to a swinging arm 55 and this arm is held so as to tension the chain by a hydraulic chain tensioner 40. Individual rocker arms 90 transmit the motion of the cams on the camshaft 1 to thrust pieces 83 on top of the valve stems so that the valves open. Each rocker arm 90 is mounted on an adjustable ball stud 92 which screws into a special holder 91 on the cylinder head. Double valve springs 75 and 76 are fitted to each valve 70 or 71. Valve seals 78 and 79 are fitted to the guides to prevent excess oil from leaking down into the combustion chambers. All the valves are fitted with rotators 81 which allow the valve to rotate as it opens. This action helps to remove deposits from the sealing faces and also extends their life. A sectioned view of the valve train is shown in **FIG 5**. The exhaust valves have hollow stems partially filled with sodium. At operating temperatures the sodium melts and transfers heat from the hot head to the cooler stem, by sloshing backwards and forwards as the valve opens and closes. **Great care must be taken in disposing of old exhaust valves. Sodium will burn vigorously in**

FIG 1 External views of the 280 S/8 engine

air and may spontaneously ignite on contact with water. The positioning of the valves and the firing order are shown in **FIG 6**.

Because light-alloy is used extensively throughout the engine, great care must be taken when tightening attachments otherwise threads can easily be stripped. Torque loadings for all important attachments are given throughout the manual and in the **Technical Data** as well and if these are adhered to the chance of damage is practically negligible. If the worst does occur and a thread strips, special metal thread inserts can be fitted by a service agent so as to repair the casting.

General details of the engine are given in **Technical Data**.

2 Engine removal

All top overhaul operations can be carried out with the engine fitted to the car. The sump is made up of two parts and only the pressed steel portion can be removed with the engine in the car, so that work on the crankshaft or its bearing will require the engine to be removed from the car.

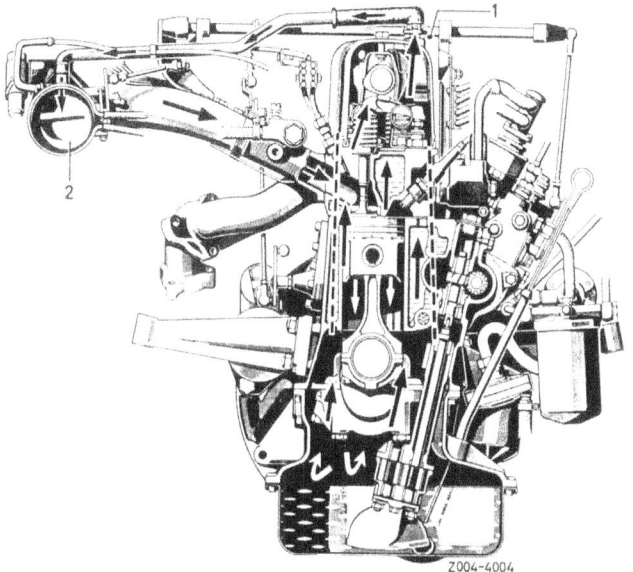

FIG 2 Sectioned view of engine with fuel injection

1 Connection 13 mm ID   2 Venturi control unit

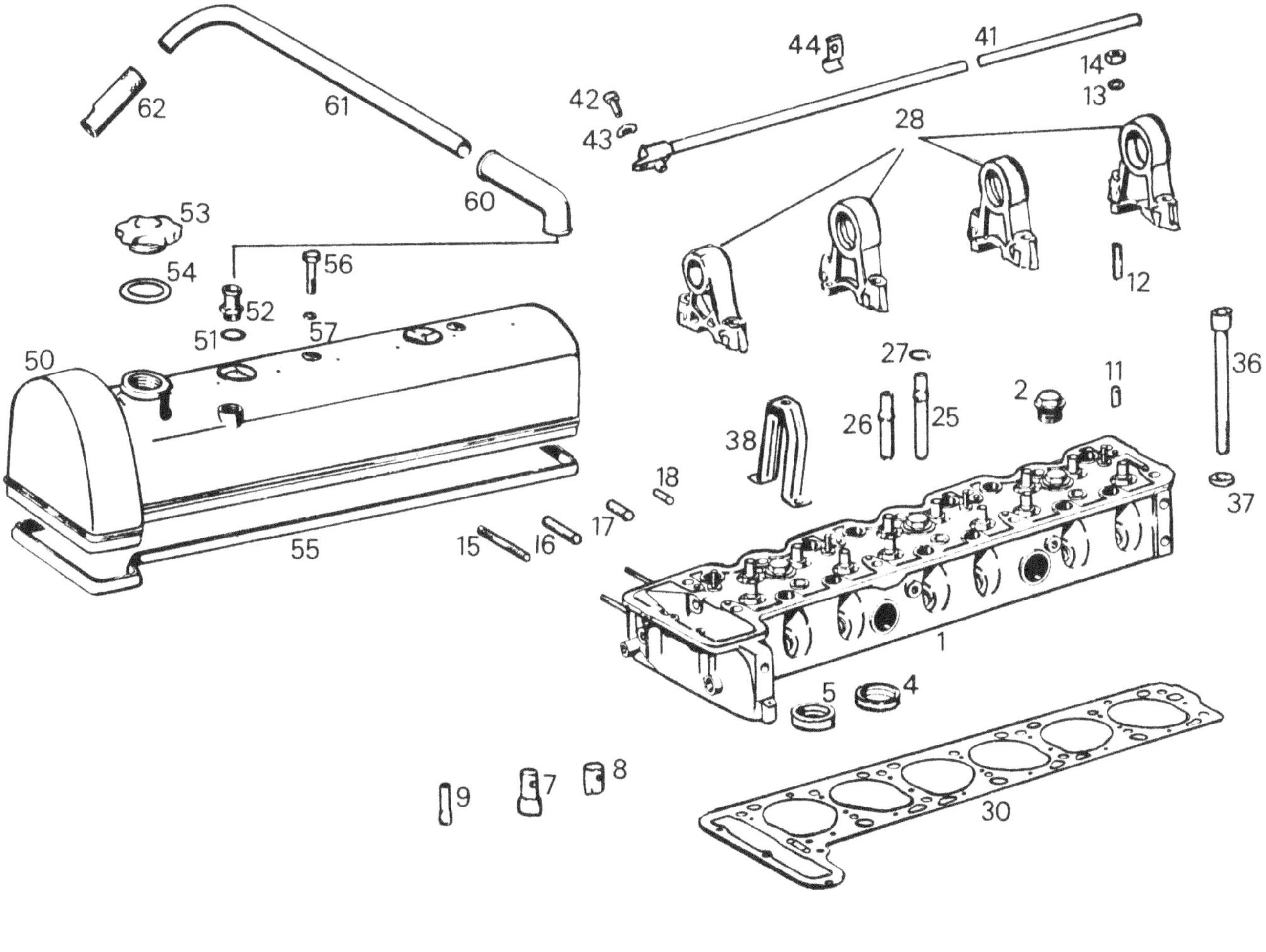

FIG 3 Typical cylinder head parts

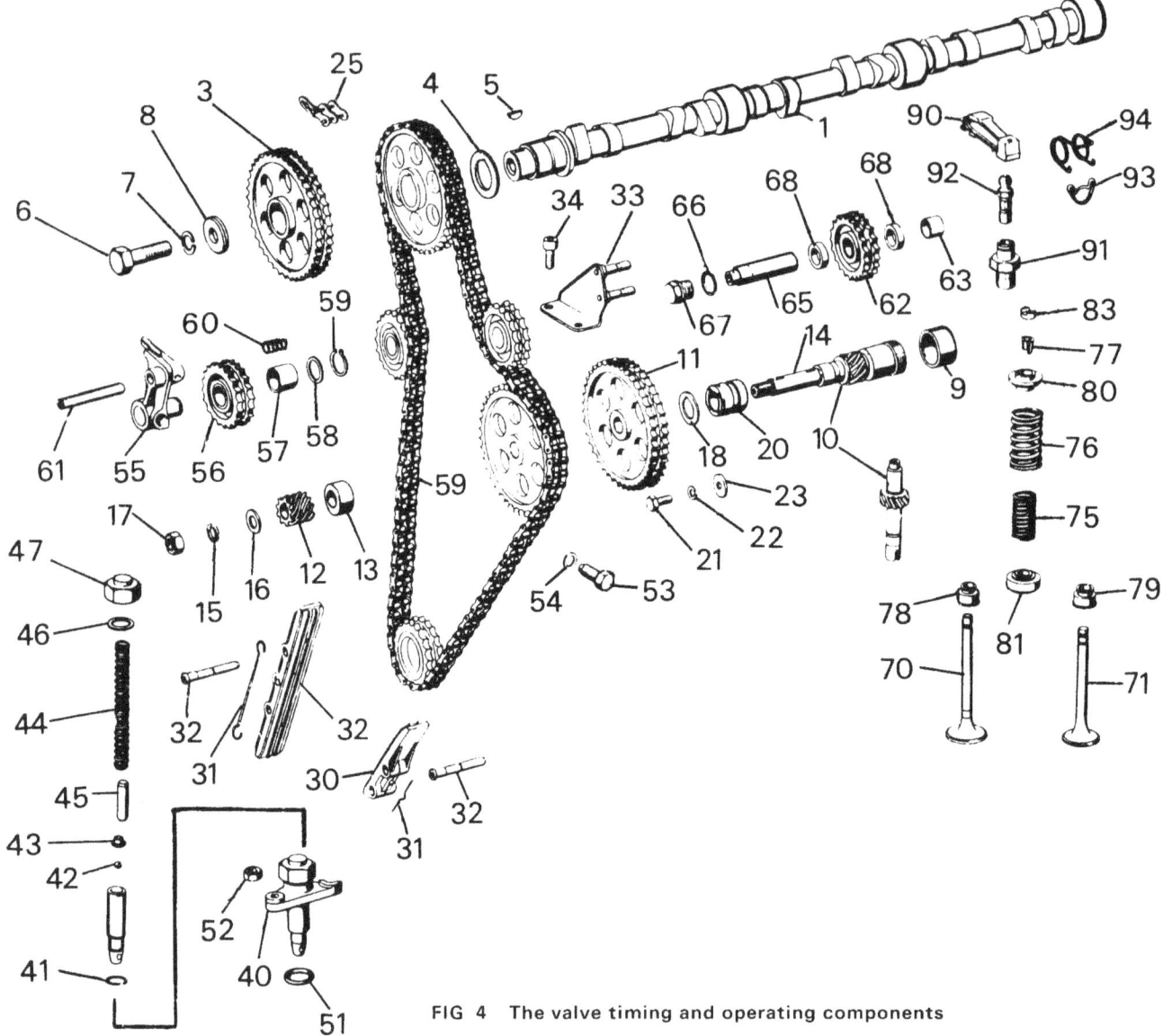

FIG 4 The valve timing and operating components

When removing the engine the transmissions must also be taken out so make sure that any slings and supports are strong enough to take the weight. Be sure that all safety precautions for raising the car and working on the air conditioning (if fitted) are complied with. Failure to observe safety precautions can result in serious injury to the operator.

1 Remove the engine hood (see **Chapter 13**). Disconnect the battery. Drain the cooling system and disconnect the radiator and oil cooler hoses. Plug the oil cooler lines and remove the radiator from the car. Remove the cooling fan. Fuller details are given in **Chapter 4**. Disconnect the heater hoses.

2 On 280/S models remove the air cleaner and on all other models disconnect the hoses for the air cleaner and idling speed. Disconnect the controls from the fuel system, including any electrical leads. Disconnect the vacuum hose for the brake servo from the inlet manifold. Disconnect the fuel inlet and return lines. Fuller details are given in **Chapter 2**.

3 Disconnect the oil pressure gauge line. Move the bag for the screen washer out of the way. If power steering is fitted, draw out the fluid from the reservoir with a syringe and disconnect the lines from the body of the pump. Unscrew the fastening bolt 2 for the telethermometer using the valve adjusting spanner SW.14 as shown in **FIG 7**. Loosen the distributor cap and remove the distributor finger.

4 Disconnect all electrical leads to the engine and transmission, including the engine ground cable, starter motor leads, alternator leads, ignition high-tension and low-tension leads between coil and distributor. Label the leads if there is any danger of forgetting the correct connections or if the colours on the leads have faded.

5 Free the exhaust pipes from the exhaust manifold. Free the bracket for the exhaust pipe from the transmission,

slacken the U-bolt and allow the bracket to hang down from the pipe. The bracket for models with manual-shift transmission is shown in **FIG 8** and that for automatic transmissions in **FIG 9**. Disconnect the speedometer drive cable, shift linkage and propeller shaft from the transmission as well as the clutch pipe on manual transmission. The propeller shaft is dealt with fully in **Chapter 8**. Support the transmission with a jack and pad of wood underneath it. Mark the rear carrier and frame with aligning marks and remove the rear carrier by removing the nuts arrowed in **FIG 9**.

6 Remove the spray shield. Take out the bolts for the front mountings and free the attachments of the engine mounting damper. Support the weight of the engine with a sling, take great care to **check that there are no connections between engine or transmission and car**. Raise the power unit slightly to free it from the mountings. Tilt the unit to approximately 45 degrees and hoist it out of the car. If the cooling fan is still fitted, take great care to prevent it from catching in the radiator mounting shell.

Installation:

The engine is installed in the reverse order of removal. Check all engine mountings and renew them if the rubber has worn, perished, or is permanently distorted.

The hexagonal socket bolt on the rear support should be left slack until after the engine has been run and the clamp nut on the propeller shaft should not be tightened until after the car has been rolled backwards and forwards several times to settle the suspension.

Fill all systems correctly and check the levels after the engine has been run. Adjust the clutch and transmission linkages as well as the fuel system as required.

3 Cylinder head removal

The cylinder head must only be removed when the engine is cold otherwise the parts are liable to distortion.

1 Drain the cooling system and disconnect the battery. On 280 S/8 models remove the air cleaner and on all other models disconnect the air cleaner and idling hoses. Disconnect the controls to the fuel system and pipes as required (see **Chapter 2**). Disconnect the HT leads from the sparking plugs and remove the distributor complete. Remove the valve rocker cover. Take out the hydraulic chain tensioner shown at 40 in **FIG 4**.

2 Remove all the rocker arms as shown in **FIG 10**. When cranking the engine, do so at the crankshaft damper, using either a rod in the holes in the periphery or a socket wrench on the damper securing bolt. **Do not crank the engine by using a wrench on the camshaft sprocket securing bolt.** Cranking the engine by hand will be easier if the sparking plugs are removed. Turn the engine until the base circle of the appropriate cam is against the sliding surface of the rocker arm and the valve is fully closed. Lift the spring clamp 2 out of the slot in the rocker 3 and pull the spring outwards to free it. Insert the special tool 4 (No. 112.589.08.61.00) as shown in the figure and use the tool to press the valve open. The rocker arm 3

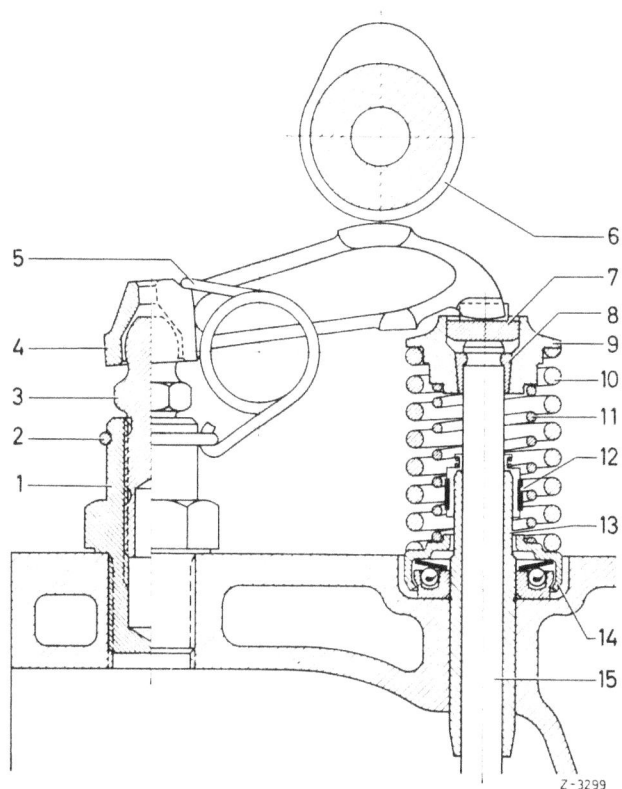

FIG 5 Sectioned view of the valve train

1 Kamax threaded bolt
2 Annular spring
3 Adjusting screw with ball for mounting rocker arm
4 Rocker arm
5 Clamping spring
6 Camshaft
7 Thrust piece
8 Valve cone half
9 Valve spring retainer
10 Outer valve spring
11 Inner valve spring
12 Valve sealing ring
13 Valve guide
14 Valve rotator
15 Valve

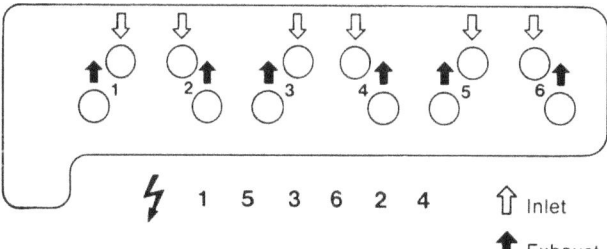

FIG 6 The valve positions and the firing order

FIG 7 Removing the tele-thermometer
1 Valve adjusting spanner   2 Fastening bolt tele-thermometer

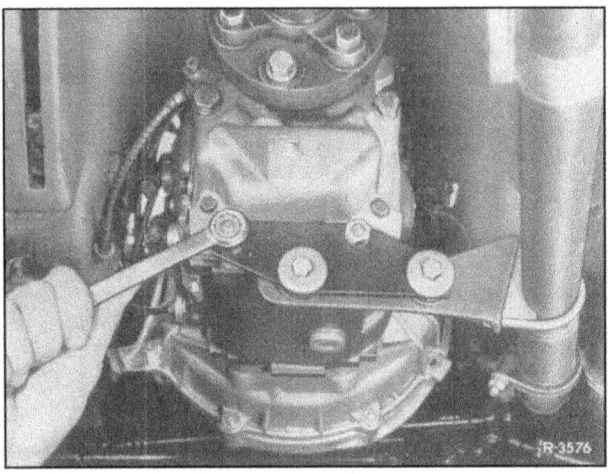

FIG 8 The manual-shift transmission exhaust clamp

FIG 9 The automatic transmission exhaust clamp

1 Rear engine carrier
2 Engine mount
3 Exhaust pipe support with automatic transmission

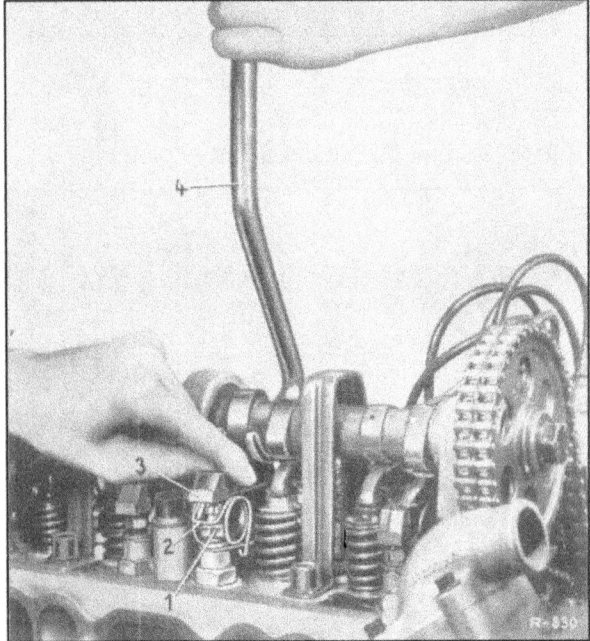

FIG 10 Removing a rocker arm

1 Ball pin top
2 Clamping spring
3 Rocker arm
4 Removal and installation tool

can then be lifted off the ball stud 1 and removed Store the arms in their correct order as they must be refitted to their original positions.

3 Remove the bolt 6 and washers 7 and 8 that secure the camshaft sprocket 3 to the camshaft 1, shown in **FIG 4**. Withdraw the camshaft sprocket 3 from the camshaft using a suitable two-legged extractor and collect the compensating washer 4 fitted behind the sprocket. Remove the key 5 for safe keeping. In some cases this key may be cranked to adjust the valve timing and **the direction of the crank must then be carefully noted so that the key can be correctly installed.** Installing the key with the crank in the wrong direction will seriously alter the valve timing. **Do not attempt to remove the camshaft or its bearing pedestals.**

4 Slacken the four bolts **a** and then progressively slacken the remainder of the cylinder head bolts, in the reverse sequence to the one shown in **FIG 11**. When all the bolts are slack, take them out and remove the cylinder head. If the head sticks, tap it up using a wooden drift and as a final resort install the sparking plugs and crank the engine with the starter motor to break the seal. Discard the old cylinder head gasket.

Installation:

Decarbonize the head and remove the parts for servicing as described in the sections that follow. When all the parts have been cleaned, examined, and serviced as required again clean them to remove any traces of dirt, abrasive, or sealing material. Old gaskets and sealing compound should be softened with trichlorethylene or suitable solvent and then scraped off with a piece of wood or perspex. Clean the threads of the bolts and check that they turn freely in their threaded holes.

If the cylinder head gasket has blown, check the cylinder head for distortion. A steel straightedge and feeler gauges can be used or the head can be gently rubbed on a surface table or piece of plate glass lightly smeared with engineer's blue. High spots will show up dark while hollows will be light. High spots, nicks and burrs can be smoothed down by careful use of a scraper or smooth file. A slight amount of distortion can be cured by lapping the head on plate glass lightly smeared with fine-grade grinding paste—followed by metal polish if desired. Larger amounts of distortion must be removed by specialist machining, noting that a maximum of 1.0 mm (.039 inch) of stock may be removed.

1 Lay a new cylinder head gasket into place, making sure that any marks (such as TOP or FRONT) are correctly positioned. A light smear of grease may be used as a sealer, provided that a composition type

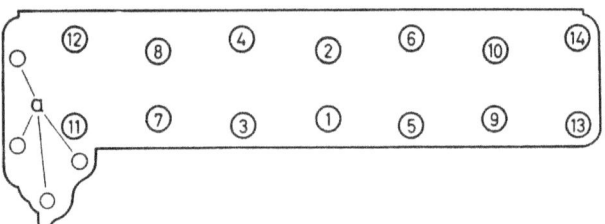

FIG 11 The sequence for tightening the cylinder head bolts

gasket is not used. Lower the cylinder head into place, using removable guide studs. Fit all the cylinder head bolts fingertight, after lubricating their threads and the undersides of their heads with clean oil.

2 The cylinder head bolts must be tightened in stages following the sequence shown in **FIG 11**. The bolts **a** are tightened to 2.5 mkp (18 lbs ft). Tighten the remainder of the bolts in sequence first to 4 mkp (29 lb ft) then to 7 mkp (50 lb ft) and finally to 10 mkp (72 lb ft) with the engine cold. After sufficient parts have been installed to allow the engine to run safely and without splashing oil, the engine is run until the coolant temperature has reached 80°C and the main bolts are tightened to 11 mkp (79 lb ft).

3 Crank the engine until the No. 1 (front piston) is at TDC, carefully guiding the timing chain, using the timing marks on the crankshaft damper. Install the compensating washer and key to the camshaft. Turn the camshaft until the sprocket, encircled with the timing chain, can be fitted back so that the valve timing marks on the compensating washer and front pedestal are in line, as shown in **FIG 12**. Secure the sprocket with the bolt and two washers. If the valve timing is thought to be incorrect or there is a possibility of a cranked key having been installed the wrong way round, take the car to a service agent who will have the necessary tools and gauges for checking the valve timing.

3 Be sure that the timing chain tensioner is empty of oil and in good condition. Install the tensioner. Fill the recess in the cylinder head with warm engine oil and operate the tensioner by applying pressure with a screwdriver as shown in **FIG 13**. At first the tensioner will move easily and oil will be drawn into it as it is released, so keep the recess topped up with warm oil to prevent air being drawn into the tensioner. When the unit is bled, it will require very heavy pressure to move the arm and there will be no free movement. The tensioner must be fitted empty otherwise the pressure will damage the attachments as it is being installed.

4 Set the correct valve clearances (see **Section 5**). Temporarily install the rocker cover and connect the fuel and injection systems so that the engine can be

FIG 13 Bleeding the chain tensioner

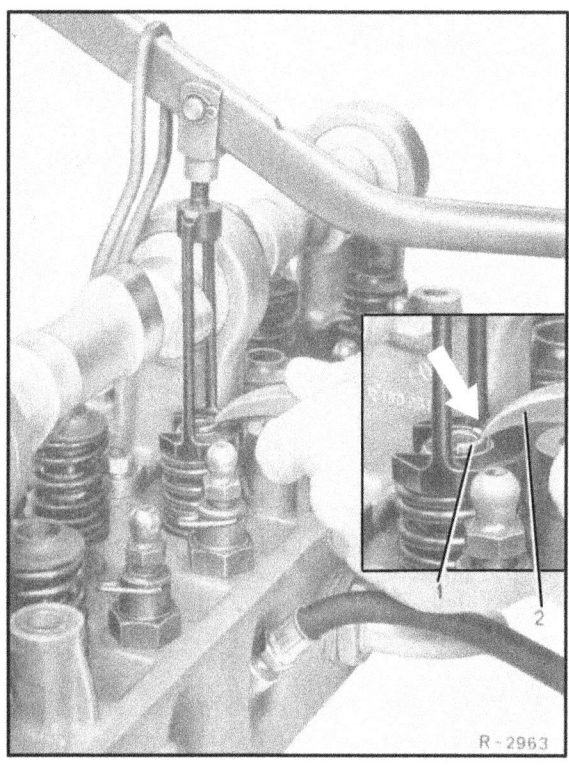

FIG 14 Removing the valve springs with the cylinder head fitted

1 Valve cone half   2 Magnetic lifter 108 589 09 63 00

FIG 12 The valve timing marks and the correct method of fitting a jointing link to the chain

1 Spring lock   2 Connector link (chain lock)

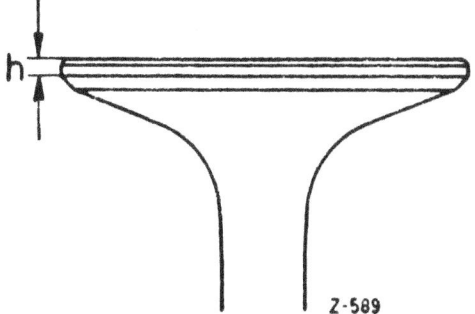

FIG 15 The minimum height of the valve head

safely run. When the coolant temperature has reached 80°C run for five more minutes then stop the engine and remove the rocker cover. Tighten the cylinder head bolts in the sequence shown in **FIG 11** to a torque load of 11 mkp (79 lb ft). Install the remainder of the parts in the reverse order of removal. Start the engine and check for leaks as well as making any adjustments required to the ignition and fuel systems.

5 When the car has been used for approximately 600 kilometres (500 miles) check the torque on the cylinder head bolts. The engine should have been run until the coolant had reached 80°C. The bolts are checked in sequence but before each bolt is checked it should be slackened back slightly and then tightened to the correct torque. If a torque spanner set to the correct figure is used without slackening the bolt then the bolt may already be too tight or it may be slightly loose and 'stiction' may prevent it from moving.

4 The camshaft

The camshaft mounting pedestals should not be removed from the cylinder head unless parts are worn or damaged. This means that in order to remove the camshaft, with the engine installed, it will be necessary to remove the cylinder head. Once the head has been removed, the camshaft can be slid out rearwards from the bearing pedestals.

If the bearing pedestals do have to be removed, such as for repair or machining, be sure that the mating surfaces of head and pedestals are scrupulously clean. Secure the pedestals fairly firmly and install the camshaft. Check that the camshaft rotates freely before fully tightening the pedestal attachments. If the camshaft is stiff to turn, align the pedestals by tapping their bases with a rubber mallet. Check that the camshaft still rotates freely after the cylinder head has been installed.

End float:

This is measured, using feeler gauges, between the compensating washer and front face of the bearing pedestal. If the end float is outside specification, the camshaft must be removed and its front face precision reground. The approximate limits are .05 to .128 mm (.002 to .005 inch).

At the same time use a DTI (Dial Test Indicator) to check the radial play on the bearings. If the radial play exceeds .057 mm (.002 inch) remove the camshaft for examination and measurement of bearings and journals. Undersize bearing pedestals are available so that the journals can be ground undersize and new pedestals fitted to take up wear.

Examination:

Examination of the journals and bearings has already been dealt with. Check the cams themselves for wear or scorings. Light pitting may be expected on the lobes of the cams after long service. Light damage can be smoothed down with an oil stone. Cams can be reground but usually it is better to fit a new camshaft if the wear or damage is extensive.

5 The valves and valve clearances

A sectioned view of a valve and operating gear is shown in **FIG 5**. The valve springs and seals can be renewed

FIG 16 Setting the valve clearances

A Position of cam when adjusting valve clearance
1 Valve gauge holder with tolerance strip
2 Valve clearance adjusting spanner
3 Torque spanner

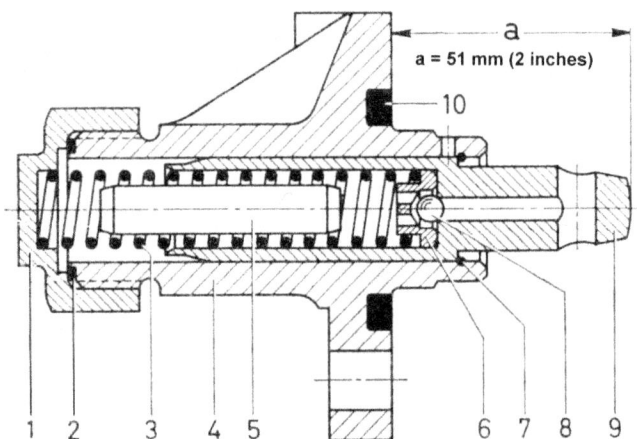

FIG 17 Section of the chain tensioner

1 Closing nut
2 Sealing ring
3 Compression spring
4 Housing
5 Pin
6 Ball cage
7 Circlip
8 Ball
9 Thrust bolt
10 O-ring

with the cylinder head still fitted to the engine but for removal of the valves, guides or seats the cylinder head must be taken off.

Removal:

If the cylinder head has been removed from the engine, a conventional valve spring compressor can be used to compress the valve springs so that the thrust pieces and valve cone halves can be removed. Release the tool slowly and take off the retainer so that the springs can be removed and the valves slid out from the combustion chamber.

The valves must be stored in order and installed back into their original positions. The best method of storing the valves is to take a cardboard box and punch twelve holes in the base so that the valve stems can be slid into the holes.

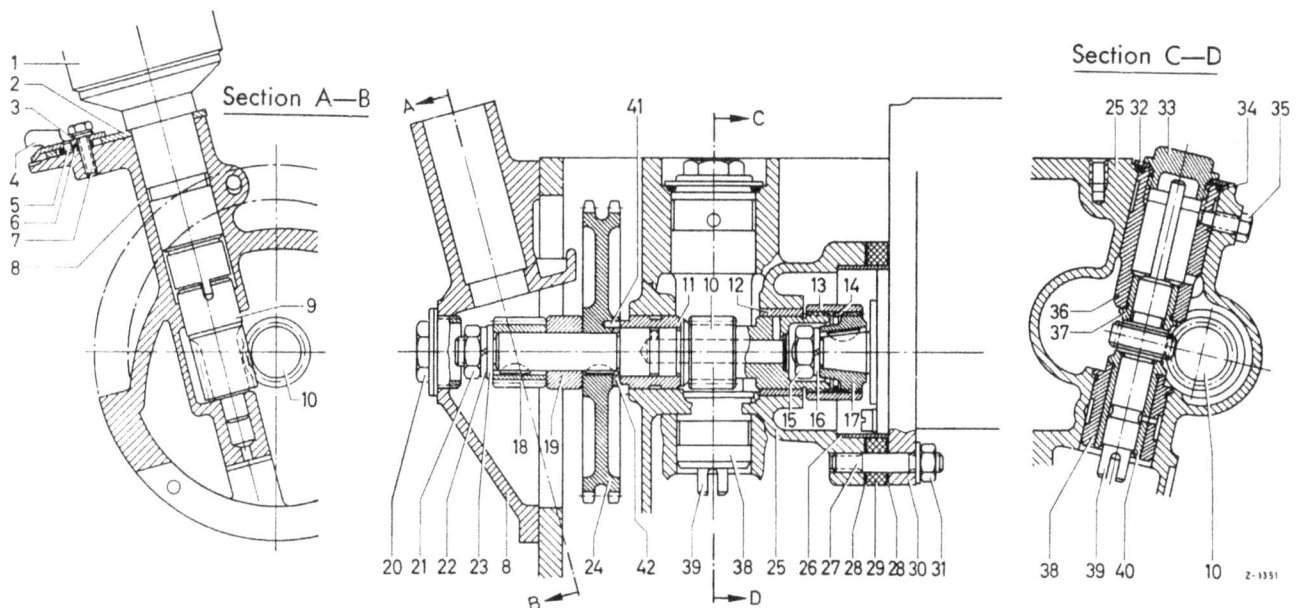

FIG 18 Sectioned views of the distributor and oil pump drive on engines fitted with fuel injection. The tachometer drive parts replace the plug 33 if a tachometer is fitted

1 Distributor
2 Timing lever
3 Spring washer
4 Hand lever
5 Cylindrical pin
6 Eccentric disk
7 Hexagon screw
8 Distributor bearing
9 Helical gear
10 Idling gear shaft
11 Bearing bushing front
12 Bearing bushing rear
13 Coupling sleeve
14 Snap ring
15 Hexagon nut
16 Lock washer
17 Follower
18 Drive sleeve
19 Spacer sleeve
20 Screw plug and seal
21 Hexagon nut
22 Lock washer
23 Washer
24 Idling gear
25 Crankcase
26 Bearing bushing
27 Stud bolt
28 Sealing flange
29 Insulating flange
30 Injection pump
31 Hexagon nut and washer
32 Cover disk
33 Screw plug
34 Rubber ring
35 Hexagon screw
36 Pressure piece
37 Bearing bushing
38 Bearing assembly
39 Helical gear
40 Bearing bushing
41 Notched pin
42 Stop ring

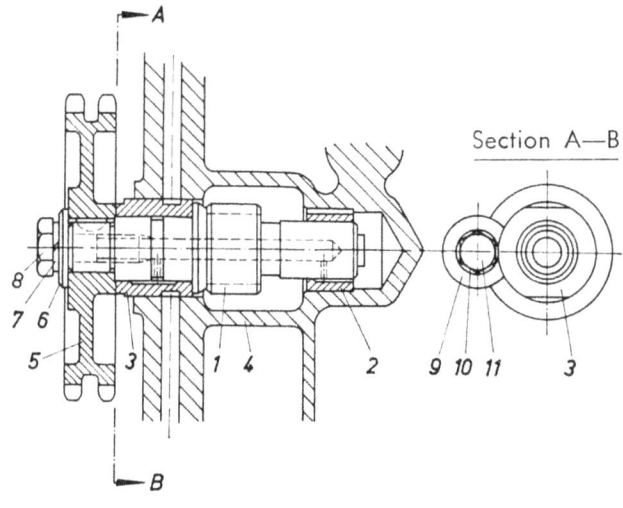
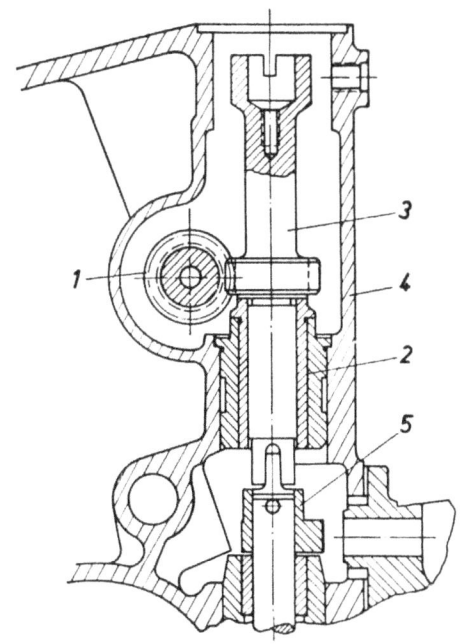

FIG 19 Sectioned views of the distributor and oil pump drive on engines fitted with carburetters

1 Idling gear shaft
  with Woodruff key
2 Rear bearing bushing
3 Front bearing bushing
4 Crankcase
5 Idling gear
6 Washer
7 Lock washer
8 Hexagon screw
9 Retaining disk
10 Lock washer
11 Hexagon screw

1 Idling gear shaft
2 Bearing with bushing
3 Helical gear
4 Crankcase
5 Oil pump drive shaft with
  cam for fuel feed pump

Valve seals:

Teflon sealing rings are fitted to the valve guides to prevent excessive oil from leaking into the combustion chambers. New seals should be fitted when servicing the cylinder head. Lever off the old seals and discard them. Press the new seals into position, using the arbor 116.589.00.43.00 to install the seals on the inlet valve guides and the arbor 116.589.01.43.00 for the exhaust valve seals.

Valve rotators:

A defective valve rotator cannot be repaired and a new one must be fitted in its place. A defective rotator can cause an otherwise satisfactory valve to leak so try fitting a new rotator if a valve does leak. If the rotator was the cause the fault will cure itself within 3000 kilometres (2000 miles).

Examining valves:

Leave the valves fitted until the combustion chambers have been cleaned as the valves will protect the seats from damage.

Clean the deposits from the valve head, using a suitable scraper or wire brush. **Take great care not to damage or mark the seat face or the ground portion of the valve stem.** Any gum on the valve stem can be cleaned off using a suitable harsh solvent, such as trichlorethylene.

Discard any valves that have badly burnt heads and deeply pitted seat faces. Check the stems with a steel straightedge and discard valves with bent or scored stems. Similarly discard any valves where the seat face is so wide that it makes a sharp edge with the face of the valve.

The exhaust valves are sodium filled so great care must be taken in their disposal. Do not saw them open and do not leave them where they may be a future hazard.

Seats and guides:

These are a shrink fit in the cylinder head and can be renewed when excessively worn. The work should be left to a service agent as accurate machining of the head is required. The head must be carefully heated and the inserts chilled. If new guides are fitted, the seats must be recut to ensure concentricity.

Grinding-in valves:

The most effective method is to have the valves and seats recut at a service garage, where they will use special cutters or grinders. Grinding-in paste may be used by the owner, though if a valve or seat is pitted excessively it is advisable to have that face recut as the use of grinding paste will remove excessive metal from the mating surface.

If grinding paste is to be used, fit the valve back into its guide with a light spring between it and the cylinder head. Smear a little grinding paste evenly around the sealing faces. Normally medium-grade paste should be used but if the faces are in good condition, fine-grade may be used immediately. Press the valve down onto its seat with a suction tool and grind with a semi-rotary motion, spinning the tool between the palms of the hands. To prevent scores from forming, regularly allow the valve

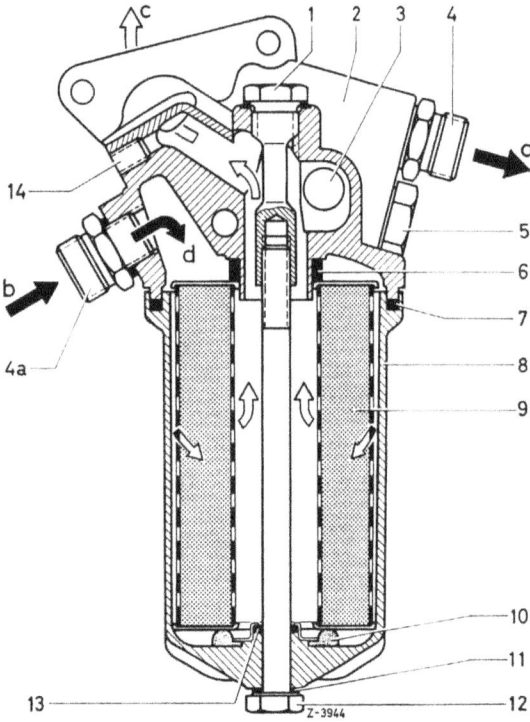

FIG 20 Sectioned oil filter

1 Holding screw
2 Oil filter top
3 Duct for overflow valve
  opening pressure 3.5 kp/cm²
4 Screw connection
4a Screw connection
5 Bypass valve–oil cooler
  opening pressure 1.5 kp/cm²
6 Sealing ring
7 Sealing ring
8 Oil filter bottom
9 Paper filter insert
10 Sealing ring
11 Sealing ring
12 Hex. screw for attaching oil filter bottom
13 Sealing ring
14 Oil pressure gauge connection

The method of removing the springs and seals with the head fitted is shown in **FIG 14**. Remove the rocker arms, as shown in **FIG 10** and take out the sparking plug. Install an adaptor and apply air pressure into the combustion chamber. Air pressure of 5 kg/sq cm (75 lb/sq in) will act on the heads of the valves and keep the valves closed when the springs are compressed so that the valve cone halves can be lifted out with a magnetic tool. The engine may rotate until the piston is at BDC when air pressure is applied. **If the air pressure is cut off once the valve springs have been removed, wrap the valve stems with elastic bands or adhesive tape to prevent the valves from dropping down into the engine.**

Valve springs:

The dimensions and test data are given in **Technical Data**. The extension against load is best measured on a special rig but a modified spring balance and steel rule can be used instead. A new set of springs should be fitted if the old ones are more than 10 per cent beyond specification.

As a rough and ready test, mount an old spring end on to a new one and compress the pair between the jaws of a vice. If the old spring is more than 10% shorter than the new one a new set should be fitted.

The spring must be fitted so that the blue dot or word UNTEN is downwards and the narrow windings of the spring are also downwards.

to rise off its seat and turn it through a quarter turn before pressing it down again and continuing grinding. When pits have been removed, wipe away the old paste and change to fine-grade. Continuing grinding until the seats are even and matt-grey with no pits or scores.

When the valves have been ground, check the depth of metal above the seat face, shown as h in **FIG 15**. If the height is less than 1 mm (.04 inch) for inlet valves or less than 2 mm (.08 inch) for exhaust valves then a new valve must be fitted. The valve seats are cut to an angle of 45 degrees.

Check the width of the seat faces in the cylinder head. The width of the seats should lie between 1.25 and 2.0 mm (.05 to .08 inch) and if the width is excessive cutters should be used to reduce the seat width. Use large and small angled cutters to reduce the seat to specification so that it meets the seating face on the valve centrally. The seats are cut to 45 degrees.

Adjusting the valve clearances:

The positions of the inlet and exhaust valves are shown in **FIG 6**, and a sectioned view through the valve train in **FIG 5**. The clearance is set between the sliding portion of the rocker arm and the base circle of the cam, as shown in **FIG 16**.

The correct clearance for inlet valves is .08 mm (.003 inch) and that for exhaust valves of .20 mm (.008 inch).

Crank the engine until the base circle of the appropriate cam is against the rocker arm and the lobe of the cam is pointing directly away from the arm, as shown at **A**. Rough settings can be made with the starter motor but fine settings must only be made at the crankshaft damper. The adjustment is made by altering the ball stud in the Kamax seat. The valve adjustment can be made with an ordinary spanner but a torque wrench is essential for checking on the ball stud and Kamax seat. If the torque required to turn the ball stud is outside the limits of 2.0 to 3.5 mkp (15 to 26 lb ft), try renewing the ball stud and if this does not bring the torque within limits then a new Kamax base must also be fitted.

Insert a feeler gauge of the correct thickness between the cam and arm. Adjust the ball stud until the feeler gauge can be slid through the gap with slight drag on it.

When all the valve clearances have been set, install the parts removed and check for leaks or noise with the engine running.

6 Decarbonizing

Do not use sharp metal tools or rotary wire brushes as they will cause damage to the cylinder head.

Remove the cylinder head as described in **Section 3** and draw the camshaft out of its bearings. **Do not remove the bearing pedestals.** Leave the valves fitted until after the combustion chambers have been cleaned.

Insert pieces of rag into oil and waterways of the cylinder block, making sure that the pieces are large enough not to be forgotten on reassembly or pushed into the block. Smear a little grease around the top of each bore to trap dirt. Clean the crowns of the pistons with a tool of soft material. A piece of wood, perspex or solder sharpened to a chisel point will do admirably. Do not use any form of abrasive as particles will remain to score the cylinder bores. The pistons will be easiest to clean if the engine is cranked so that they are at TDC. When

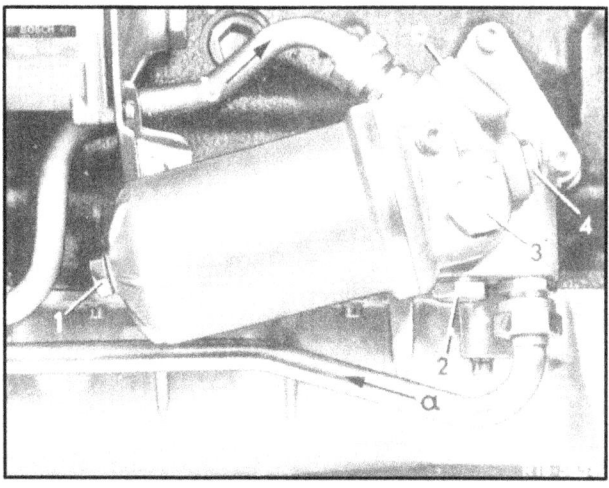

FIG 21   Oil filter attachments
1 Fastening bolt for oil filter base
2 Bypass valve oil cooler
3 Overflow valve filter insert
4 Holding screw (glued-in, do not loosen)
a Line to oil cooler
b Line from oil cooler
c Connection oil pressure gauge

all the pistons have been cleaned, blow away all loose dust and dirt. Crank the engine for a few turns so that the piston rings scrape the dirt and grease to the tops of the bores where they can easily be wiped out. Remove the pieces of rag.

Clean the combustion chambers in a similar manner to the piston crowns, though in this case old emerycloth dipped in paraffin can be used to give a light polish as all abrasive particles can be washed off afterwards. Remove the manifolds and valves so that the ports can be cleaned, **taking great care not to damage the valve seats or valve guides.** If an afterburner system is fitted, do not forget to clean the nozzles and passages. The valve guides are best cleaned using special wire brushes made for the purpose, but if these are not available pull strips of clean rag soaked in fuel through the guides to clean them.

When all the parts have been serviced, clean them again to make sure that no dirt or abrasive particles remain. Assemble the parts using fresh oil on all bearing and pivot surfaces.

7 The valve timing gear and distributor drive

On manufacture, an endless timing chain is used and this is the type of chain that should be used on major overhaul. A split type of chain is available and this chain can be fitted without dismantling the engine. The parts of the system are shown in **FIG 4** and **FIG 12**.

Timing chain renewal:

1 Remove sufficient parts and take off the rocker cover. Remove all the sparking plugs so that the engine will be easier to turn. Remove all the rocker arms. Removal of the rocker arms is not strictly essential but it will make the camshaft easier to turn and if the timing slips there is no danger of the valves hitting the piston crowns.

2 Turn the engine by hand until the valve timing marks, shown in **FIG 12**, are in alignment. Remove the chain tensioner. Lay rags into the aperture to catch filings and file off two rivets on the chain so that a

link can be removed. **Do not allow the chain to slip off the camshaft sprocket.** Attach the new timing chain to the trailing end of the old one, so that the spring clip is at the rear and its open end is in the trailing direction.

3 Slowly crank the engine by hand while guiding the chains on the sprocket. Keep cranking until all the old chain is off the sprockets and the new chain is on them. Free the jointing link and use it to secure the new chain to the sprocket. The spring clip of the link must be fitted at the rear so that its open end faces in the trailing direction.

4 Set the engine so that No. 1 (front) cylinder piston is at TDC after the compression stroke. TDC is found by the timing marks on the crankshaft damper and the correct position is when the rotor arm of the distributor is pointing towards the position of the electrode in the cap connected to No. 1 sparking plug. The position can also be found by blocking the sparking plug hole with a thumb so that a pressure rise will be felt as the piston moves up on the compression stroke. When the engine is correctly set, the valve timing marks should be accurately aligned.

5 Install the empty timing chain tensioner and fill and bleed it once it is in place. Install the rocker cover and remainder of parts removed.

Timing sprockets:

Worn timing sprockets will be apparent from the hooked appearance of their teeth. Worn sprockets must be renewed otherwise they will quickly ruin a new chain.

The sprockets must be kept in alignment otherwise undue stresses will be put on the timing chain. The compensating washer behind the camshaft sprocket is used to set the alignment.

Chain tensioner:

Special test equipment is required for fully checking the tensioner. The unit can be dismantled for cleaning and checking but if parts are found to be defective a complete new tensioner must be fitted, as the parts are mated on manufacture.

As a rough check, immerse the tensioner in a bath of warm oil and exercise it until all air has been bled out. When all the air is out, very heavy pressure will be required to move the thrust bolt and there should be no free movement.

A sectioned view of the tensioner is shown in **FIG 17**. Remove the cap nut 1, against the pressure of the spring 3, and withdraw the spring and pin 5. Remove and discard the sealing ring 2 from the cap nut 1. Shake out the ball cage 6, taking care not to lose the ball 8, and slide out the thrust bolt 9 from the open end, without removing the circlip 7 from the other end.

Clean the parts and examine them for wear or scoring. Trichlorethylene should be used to remove gum and deposits from the parts. Lay the ball 8 into place in the thrust bolt 9 and tap the ball gently with a copper drift to seat it, so as to reform the seat.

Assemble the unit in the reverse order of dismantling, using new sealing rings 2 and 10. When the unit is assembled, check that the free length **a** is correct at 51 mm (2 inch).

To avoid straining the attachments, install the unit empty. The unit is then filled and bled by filling the recess in the cylinder head with warm oil and exercising it, as shown in **FIG 13**, until all air is driven out. The slots in the thrust bolt ensure that the unit is self-bleeding is use.

Distributor drive:

The typical parts for the 280 S/8 are shown in **FIG 18**. The typical parts for other models are shown in **FIG 19**. The parts can be removed or installed after the cylinder head has been removed. **Pack the recess with clean rags to prevent any small parts or tools from dropping down into the engine sump.**

Once the parts have been installed and the valve timing correctly set, check the positioning of the distributor. With the valve timing marks aligned, check the position of the distributor rotor arm relative to the body. The arm should be pointing to the position of the electrode connected to No. 1 cylinder sparking plug. If the ignition is not correct, slip the timing chain, a tooth at a time, over the drive sprocket until the rotor arm is correctly set. The final accurate adjustment of the ignition is made by rotating the distributor body as described in **Chapter 3**.

8 The sump, oil pump and oil filter

Oil filter:

A sectioned view of the oil filter showing the normal path of the oil through it is shown in **FIG 20**. The dirty oil direct from the oil pump passes through the filter top to the oil cooler in the direction 'a'. From the oil cooler the oil enters the unit at the arrow 'b' and then passes through the filter element before passing to the engine in the direction 'c'. If the oil cooler is clogged, or the oil in it is so cold as to offer large resistance to flow, the bypass valve 5 opens so that the oil does not pass through the oil cooler in the radiator but passes directly to the oil filter element. If the paper element 9 is so dirty that it causes a pressure drop of more than 3.5 kg/sq cm across it the overflow valve 3 opens allowing the oil to bypass the filter element. This is a precaution against complete oil starvation if the element is choked but the oil will pass unfiltered to the engine.

The holding screw 1 is glued to the filter top and must never be removed or turned.

Oil change:

The engine oil and filter element should be changed at intervals of 6000 kilometres (5000 miles) under normal conditions. If the car is used in arduous or very cold conditions the interval between oil changes should be reduced.

Before changing the oil, the engine should be run for a short while to warm the oil and lift dirt into suspension. If the oil is changed after a long run the oil may be hot enough to cause serious scalding. Slide suitable containers under the sump and radiator (oil cooler) and remove the drain plugs. One drain plug is fitted to the rear of the pressed-steel portion of the sump while the oil cooler drain plug is fitted to the lefthand bottom side of the radiator assembly.

The attachments of the oil filter are shown in **FIG 21**. Unscrew the bolt 1, preferably with a drip tray underneath to catch spillage, and remove the oil filter base assembly. **Do not unscrew or turn the bolt 4 which is glued into place.** Pour out the old oil and remove the filter element so that it can be discarded. If there are excessive amounts of sludge in the oil filter it is likely that coolant is leaking into the engine. Wash out the base with clean fuel. Remove the old sealing ring from around the top of the base and install the new one supplied, making sure that it is fully and squarely seated with no air trapped under it. Install the new element and fit the base back to the top, after checking all other seals. Tighten the bolt 1 finger tight and rotate the base slightly to ensure that it is fully and squarely seated. Fully tighten the bolt to a torque of 4 kg m (29 lb ft).

Install the drain plugs, using new sealing rings. Fill the engine with 5.5 litres (9.7 Imp. pints) of fresh oil. Start the engine and check for oil leaks. Park the car on level ground and switch off the engine. Leave the level to settle for at least five minutes and then top up with approximately 1 litre (2 pints) more of oil. The extra oil will be required to replace the oil drawn into the oil filter and oil cooler. Do not fill above the top mark on the dipstick.

If the engine has had a major overhaul or a reconditioned engine has been installed, a special fine pored filter element should be used for the first 600 kilometres (500 miles).

Oil pump:

The oil pump is driven by the same gears as the distributor and is accessible after the pressed-steel portion of the sump has been removed (which is possible with the engine fitted in the car). The inlet strainer to the oil pump should be cleaned and checked every time that the pressed-steel portion of the sump is removed, for whatever reason.

The oil pump can be removed after taking out the bolts that secure it to the block. Install the pump in the reverse order of removal, making sure that the drive tang on its shaft aligns with the slot in the drive gear.

The full flow of oil passes through the pump and therefore it will give a long and satisfactory life. Failing to change the engine oil and filter element within the recommended interval, so that the oil is dirty, will be the main cause of oil pump wear. A defective pump is best discarded and a new one fitted in its place. The pump can be dismantled by removing the screws that secure its cover.

After cleaning the pump and examining its parts for wear assemble the unit and liberally lubricate it with fresh oil. No precautions need to be taken to prime the pump after it has been fitted.

Relief valves:

Two relief valves are fitted, one in the pump and the other in the main oil gallery. The valve in the gallery releases at 5 kg/sq cm (60 lb/sq in) while the one in the pump releases at 12 kg/sq cm (170 lb/sq in) and the valve in the pump is identified by the number 12 stamped on it at the face end of the hexagon head.

If low oil pressure is thought to be caused by a leaking valve, remove the valve and clean it. If the valve is found to be defective replace it with the latest type, which is identified by a ring groove around the body housing.

FIG 22 The clutch attachments

Sump:

The main cast portion of the sump can only be removed from the engine with the engine out of the car.

Before installing a part of the sump clean it thoroughly, both inside and outside, and check it for damage. Small burrs or chips on the cast portion can be smoothed down with a fine file and distortion of the pressed portion should be dressed out.

9 The clutch and flywheel

The full details of the clutch and its servicing are given in **Chapter 5**. This section deals only with the removal and installation of the clutch.

The clutch and flywheel (or drive plate) are only accessible after the transmission has been removed. Removal of the manual-shift transmission is dealt with in **Chapter 6** and that of the automatic transmission in **Chapter 7**.

Clutch removal:

The attachments of the clutch are shown in **FIG 22**. The arbor 1 shown in the figure is not a part of the clutch but is used for centralizing the driven plate when installing the clutch.

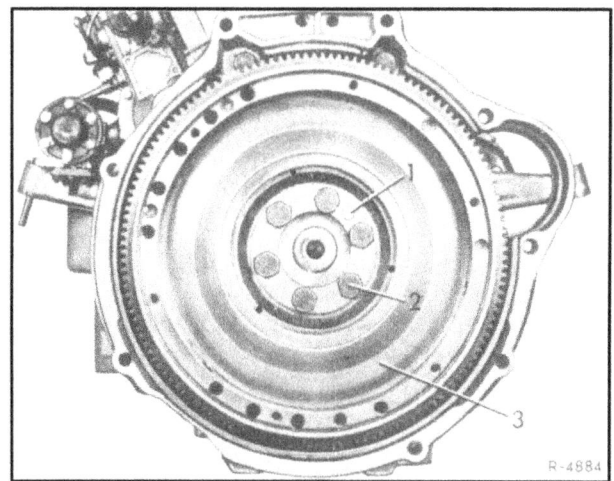

FIG 23 The flywheel attachments
1 Set pin   2 Expanding screw   3 Flywheel

Remove the transmission. Make aligning marks on the cover and flywheel so that the clutch will be installed back into its original position. Progressively slacken all the bolts 1 to 1½ turns at a time until they are all free. **If the bolts are not slackened progressively the pressure of the clutch spring will distort the clutch cover.** Support the cover and remove the bolts. Lift off the cover taking care not to allow the driven plate to fall. **Handle the parts with care and do not drop them or allow grease or oil onto them.**

Install the parts in the reverse order of removal. Support the driven plate on the arbor 136 589 00 61 and fit the cover back so that the marks again align. **It is essential that the driven plate is centralized otherwise it will be impossible to insert the input shaft of the transmission when installing the transmission.** Lightly secure the cover and then tighten all the bolts progressively by 1 to 1½ turns until they are all tight.

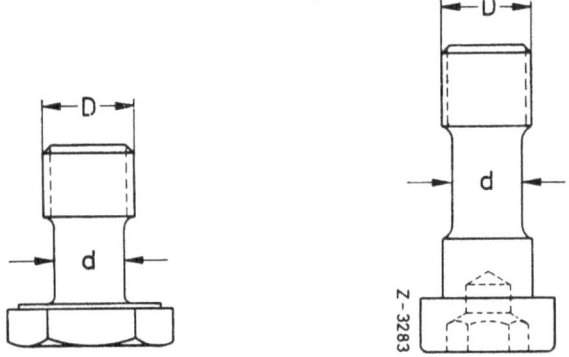

FIG 24 The flywheel attachment bolts

Flywheel:

The flywheel is attached to the crankshaft by anti-fatigue bolts and its attachments are shown in **FIG 23**. **It is essential to use well fitting, unworn tools as high torque loads are used and worn tools may slip causing serious injury to the operator.**

The anti-fatigue bolts distort slightly every time that they are used. Typical attachment bolts are shown in **FIG 24**. Measure the diameter d with a sharp edged vernier and renew the bolts when the diameter reaches a minimum of 8.8 mm (.35 inch). Slacken the bolts and remove the flywheel, taking care not to drop it as it comes free from the set pin 1.

Before installing the flywheel, make sure that the mating surfaces are scrupulously clean and free from particles of dirt. Install the flywheel and use a suitable torque wrench to tighten all the bolts to a torque of $3+1$ kg m ($22+7$ lb ft). Each bolt must now be tightened by a further angle of $90+10$ deg. Use a solid bar and well fitting socket. Position the flywheel so that the bolt can be fully tightened in one movement. Estimate the angle, noting that it must not be less than 90 deg. but that it can go up to 100 deg.

Flywheel repairs:

If the clutch face of the flywheel is lightly scored or has burn marks on it the damage can be removed by specialist machining. A sectioned view of the flywheel is shown in **FIG 25**. When the flywheel is being machined, equal amounts of stock must be removed from the mounting face **B** as the operating face **A** in order to keep the dimension a constant ($19.4+.1$ mm). If the dimension b is less than 17.5 mm (.689 inch) after machining then a new flywheel must be fitted.

When ordering a new flywheel the old one must be handed in to the dealer. This is so that the new flywheel can be balanced to the same setting as the old one. The two flywheels are mounted 180 deg. out of phase on a balancing arbor and the assembly is then statically balanced by drilling holes in the new flywheel.

Clutch spigot bearing:

This should be examined whenever the clutch is removed. If the bearing is worn, prise out the cover and take out the bearing with a suitable extractor. Press a new bearing into the end of the crankshaft and install a new cover. The bearing is item 11 in **FIG 26** and the cover is item 12.

Flywheel ring gear:

If the teeth on the ring are broken or worn a new ring 15 must be fitted. Drill nearly through at the root of a tooth and then split the ring at the weak point using a cold chisel. **Take great care not to damage or mark the flywheel itself.**

Thoroughly clean the periphery of the flywheel, using a wire brush to remove dirt and scale and emerycloth to smooth down burrs or high spots. Lay the flywheel, clutch face downwards, onto hardwood blocks.

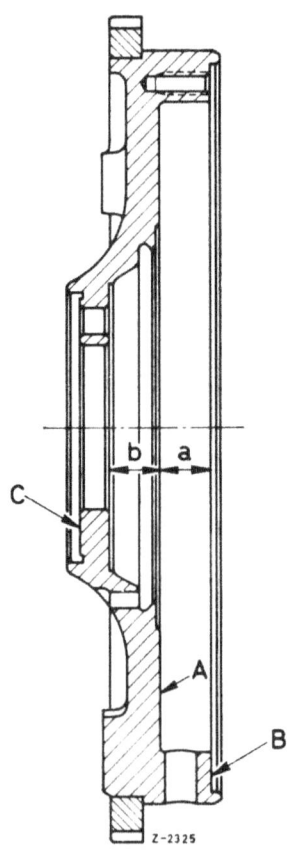

FIG 25 Section through the flywheel

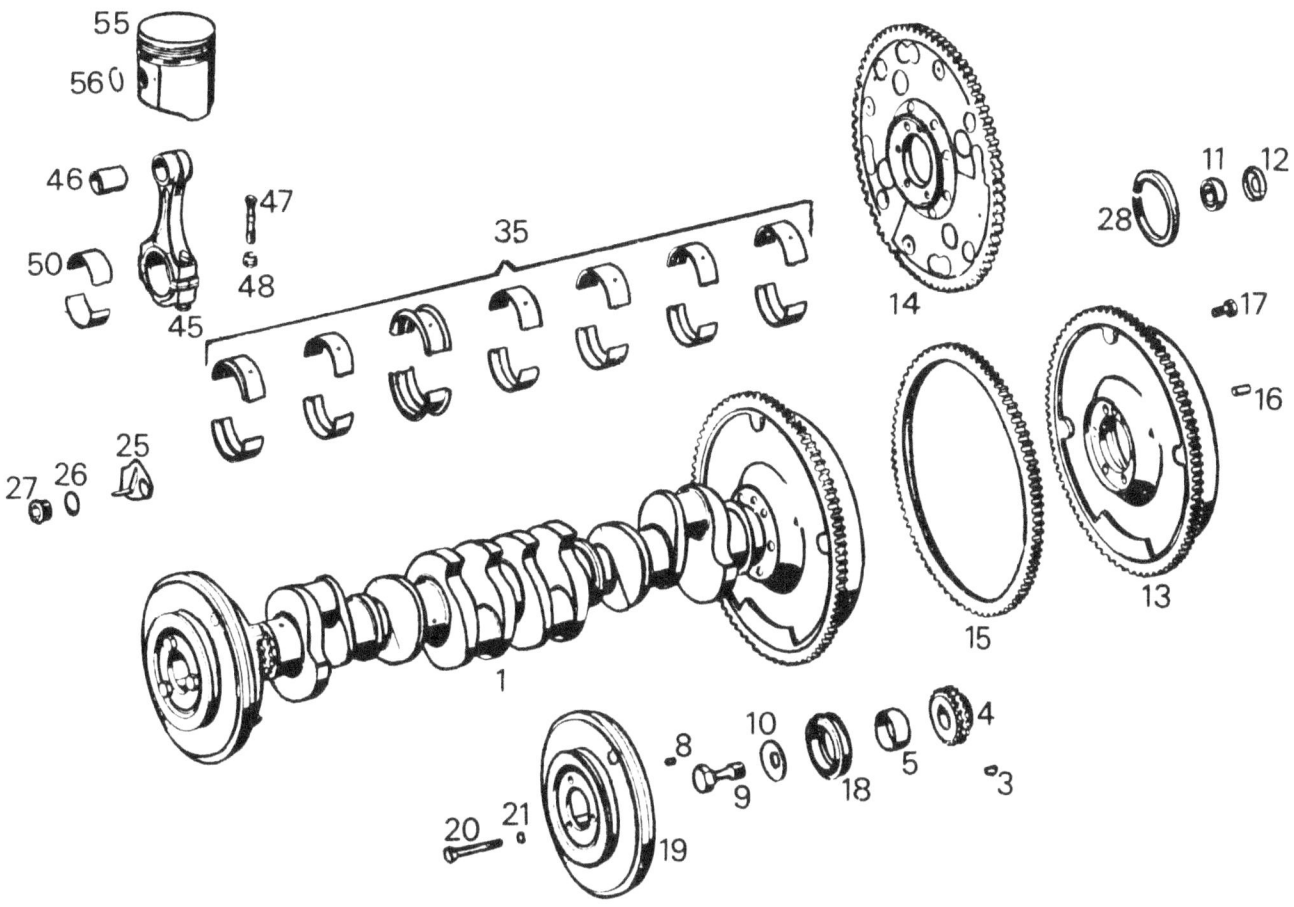

FIG 26 The camshaft and typical associated parts

Heat the new ring to a temperature of 200°C, preferably in an oil bath or oven. If flame is used, have more than one blowlamp and keep the flame playing around the ring to avoid localized overheating. Overheating will ruin the temper of the metal.

When the ring is hot, use tongs to lay it into place on the flywheel, with the chamfered edge of the teeth uppermost. Tap the ring fully into position with soft metal drifts and leave it to cool naturally before moving the flywheel.

10 The crankshaft damper and front oil seal

A sectioned view of the assembly is shown in **FIG 27**. The assembly can be removed with the engine fitted to the car but parts must be removed to gain access. Drain the cooling system and remove the radiator. Take off all drive belts (see **Chapter 4**). For vehicles fitted with power steering or air conditioning, remove the additional pulley fitted to the damper. For vehicles fitted with power steering it will also be necessary to remove the high pressure pump, complete with its carrier, after emptying the reservoir.

The damper 5 can be removed separately but if the balancing disc 6 requires removal it is best to remove the disc and damper together and then separate the two. To remove the complete assembly, hold the damper and remove the bolt 1 with its plate springs 2. Pull off the assembly with the extractor 112 589 07 33 00 as shown in **FIG 28**. The extractor is secured using two of the fastening bolts 3. If a new balancing disc is to be fitted it must be balanced to the same state as the old one.

The assembly is pulled into place using the installation tool 186 589 07 61 00, shown in **FIG 28a**, with a supplementary sleeve fitted to it as shown. locating holes of the cylinder pins 7 **FIG 27**, are slightly offset so that the assembly can only be mounted in one position. Take care to accurately align the holes. Tighten the bolt 1 which secures the assembly to a torque of 21+1 kg m (150 lb ft).

Oil seal:

Remove the damper assembly as just described and then prise out the old sealing ring using two screwdrivers, taking great care not to damage or mark the crankshaft or seal housing. Smooth off burrs from the edge of the casting with fine grade emerycloth. Renew the sealing ring if it is scored.

Moisten the lips of the new sealing ring with oil and carefully press it back into position using the installation bushing No. 111 589 17 61 00.

Install the damper and balance disc assembly in the reverse order of removal and then fit the remainder of the parts removed. Set the drive belt tensions as described in **Chapter 4**.

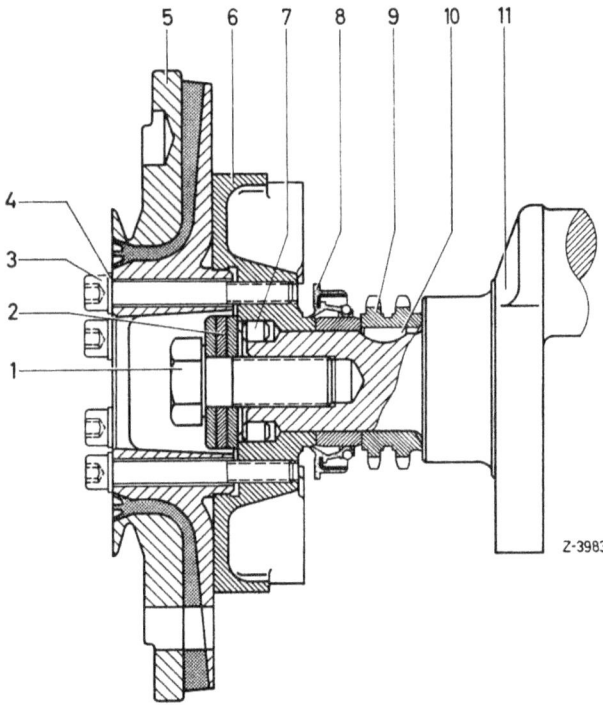

FIG 27 The crankshaft damper, balance and oil seal

1 Hex. bolt
2 Plate springs
3 Hex. socket bolt
4 Washer
5 Vibration damper
6 Balancing disc
7 Cylinder pin
8 Sealing ring
9 Sprocket
10 Key
11 Crankshaft

11 The crankshaft and bearings

Typical components are shown in **FIG 26**. As the cast portion of the sump cannot be removed with the engine installed it will be necessary to remove the engine from the car before work can be carried out on the crankshaft or its bearings. Because of the amount of work required, all the crankshaft bearings should be examined at the same time.

Bearings:

Remove the engine from the car (see **Section 2**). Take off the transmission and remove the clutch and flywheel. Remove the rocker cover, chain tensioner and camshaft sprocket. Invert the engine on a suitable stand or in such a way that components are not damaged and remove both parts of the sump as well as the oil pump. Remove the crankshaft damper assembly and discard the old oil seal. If required, the crankshaft sprocket can be removed using a suitable extractor, after lifting up the chain from it.

1 Check that all the bearing caps and connecting rods are numbered in order. The numbers on the big-ends must all face the lefthand side of the engine. If the parts are not marked, code them with light punch marks so that they can be installed in their original positions.
2 Evenly slacken the nuts that secure the big-end caps to the connecting rods. Pull off the nuts when the caps have been removed and lay the caps out in order. Press the connecting rods into the cylinder bores so that they free from the crankshaft throws.
3 Evenly slacken the bolts that secure the main bearing caps, remove the caps and lay them out in order. Lift the crankshaft out of the engine and discard the rear oil seal parts from the cap and crankcase.
4 Remove all the bearing caps from their caps and mountings, laying the inserts out in order. Renew the complete set if any one shell insert shows signs of cracking, wearing scores or other damage. New inserts are fitted as received, apart from cleaning off dirt and protective, and do not require scraping or boring.
5 Thoroughly clean the crankshaft, blowing through oilways with paraffin followed by compressed air. This is particularly important if the crankshaft has been reground, otherwise swarf may remain in the oilways and be forced into the bearings when the engine is running. Clean the mountings for the inserts thoroughly as well. Leather should be used for wiping the parts as this leaves no fibres, otherwise use lint-free cloth (such as old sheets).
6 Measure each crankpin and journal at several points to determine the wear, out of round, and taper. If the shaft is excessively worn or scored it must be sent away for specialist regrinding and new undersized bearings inserts fitted on reassembly.
7 The bolts in the connecting rods are of the antifatigue type and should therefore be checked as shown in **FIG 29**. If the minimum diameter of the neck has reached 7.8 mm (.307 inch) then the bolt must be driven out and a new bolt installed. **Do not remove the bolts from the connecting rods for any other reason than renewal.**
8 Bearing inserts are available in different grades so that the correct diametrical clearance of the bearing can be selectively made. The best method of checking the clearance is to use a Plastigage on the clean and dry bearings. Fit the inserts and secure the bearing by tightening the cap attachments to the correct torque, with a strip of Plastigage laid parallel to the crankshaft. Do not turn the crankshaft and remove the cap after it has been tightened. The clearance can then be read off by measuring the spread of the strip with the gauge provided. Selectively fit inserts until all bearings are at the correct clearance and then store the inserts in their correct order. Before removing the crankshaft from the main bearings, mount a DTI on the crankcase so that its stylus rests vertically on the end of the

FIG 28 Removing the damper assembly

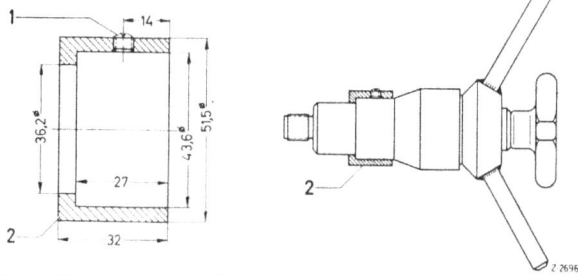

FIG 28a Installation tool and supplementary sleeve

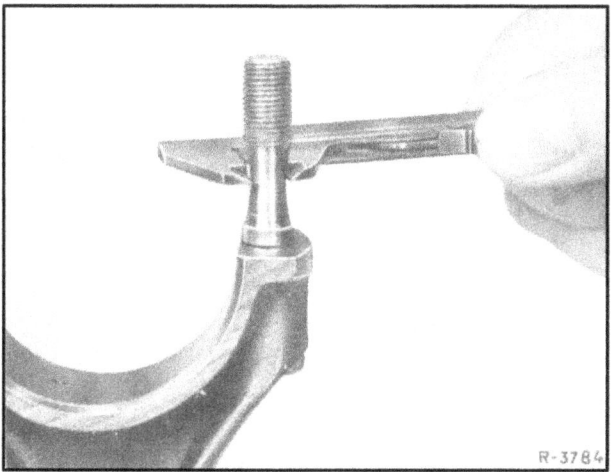

FIG 29 Checking connecting rod bolts

FIG 30 Installing a rear crankshaft oil seal

crankshaft. Lever the crankshaft backwards and forwards so that the end float can be measured. If the end play exceeds the wear limit of .3 mm (.012 inch) fit new thrust bearing inserts. Check that the crankshaft rotates freely in the main bearings before removing it again. **Do not file connecting rods on bearing caps in an attempt to take up excessive clearance or wear.**

9 Install the new rear oil seal. Taper pins are fitted, one in the crankcase and the other in the cap to secure the seal. Make sure that these pins are not broken and that the seal is pressed firmly down onto them. Press the seal in by hand first and then smooth it down fully with a hammer handle smeared lightly with oil, as shown in **FIG 30**. When the seal is fully in place, with no high spots, cut off the ends so that there is .6 mm (.025 inch) of seal protruding squarely above the parting faces. A tool for ensuring the correct protrusion is shown in **FIG 31**. Lay the tool in place and cut the seal with a very sharp knife. Install the seal in the rear main cap in the same manner.

10 Check that all the bearing inserts are correctly located and secured by their tags. Oil holes in the inserts must align with the oil holes in the crankcase. Lubricate the main bearings liberally with fresh oil and lay the crankshaft back into place, not forgetting to fit the timing chain over it. Install the bearing caps in their correct positions. Clean the threads of the bolts and dip them in oil. Secure the caps with the bolts and progressively tighten all the bolts to a torque load of 8 kg m (58 lb ft). Check that the crankshaft rotates freely. Binding at this stage will most likely be caused by an incorrectly fitted rear oil seal.

11 Attach each connecting rod in turn to the crankpins. Pull the connecting rod out of the bore until it fits onto the crankpin and lubricate liberally with fresh oil. Install the cap correctly and tighten the nuts, after lubricating the threads with oil, to a torque of 4+1 kg m (29+7 lb ft). The nuts must now be tightened through a further angle of 90+10 deg. Use a solid bar, which will not bend or yield, and tighten through the estimated angle in one movement. The angle must not be less than 90 deg. but it may safely go up to a 100 deg.

12 When all the connecting rods have been installed check that the engine rotates freely. Install the remainder of the parts in the reverse order of removal.

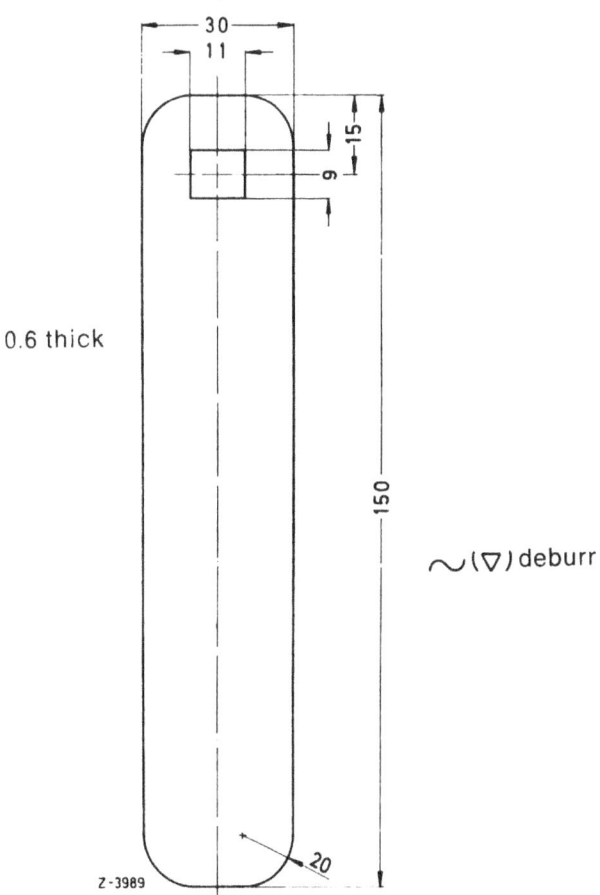

FIG 31 Tool used to cut the rear crankshaft oil seal

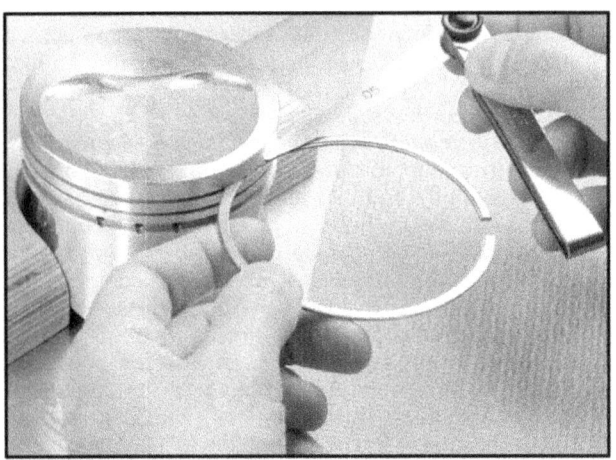

FIG 32 Checking the ring clearance in the piston

12 The pistons and connecting rods

These are removed from the engine after the cylinder head has been taken off and the big-ends disconnected, with the engine removed from the car.

Before removing the assemblies it is advisable to have the unworn ridge and ring of carbon around the top of the bores removed with garage cutters. This ring may well damage the piston rings as they pass over it on removal. When the big-ends have been disconnected, push the connecting rods right up the bores so that the pistons emerge and the assemblies can be drawn out. Store them in order as the pistons and connecting rods must be installed back into their original bores.

Pistons:

Remove and discard the circlips that secure the gudgeon pins in the pistons. Immerse the piston in very hot or boiling water and when the piston is hot, press the gudgeon pin out with hand pressure.

Remove the piston rings so that the piston can be cleaned and checked. A granular etched surface on the piston crown is indicative of pre-ignition and in severe cases the edge of the piston may be eroded away. Lacquering and blackening on the side of the piston is usually caused by gases blowing past the rings. If the piston is badly eroded or scored a new one should be fitted in its place.

The crown of the piston can be lightly polished with worn emerycloth dipped in paraffin, after scraping deposits with a soft tool, as all abrasive can be washed off afterwards.

The sides of the pistons must not have any abrasive used on them. Lacquering or deposits should be removed using a suitable harsh solvent, such as trichlorethylene.

Clean out the ring grooves using an old broken piston ring. **Take great care to remove only carbon and not metal from the piston.** Clean out the return holes behind the oil control ring with a blunt-ended piece of wire.

Fit a new piston ring into the groove, as shown in **FIG 32**, and use feeler gauges to check the side clearance. Fit a new piston if the clearance is excessive otherwise there will be a high oil consumption.

Piston rings:

The safest method of removing or installing piston rings is to use a special ring expander. The tool grips the ring by its ends and then gently parts them so that the ring can pass up or down over the piston.

Failing the correct tool, use three shims such as discarded feeler gauges. Carefully lift one end of the ring out of its groove and slide a shim under it. Work the shim around under the ring while pressing the ring as it comes free onto the piston land above it. When all the ring is on the land, slide the other two shims under the ring so that the three shims are equally spaced around the piston. Gently part the ends of the ring with the thumb nails and slide it up and off the piston, taking great care not to allow the back of the ring to score the piston. Install the rings in the reverse order of removal.

Before installing new rings, check their gaps when fitted. Spring each ring in turn into the bore and press it down squarely with an inverted piston until it is approximately 3 cm (1 inch) from the top of the bore. Measure the gap between the ends with feeler gauges. If the gap is not to specification, remove the ring and file the ends carefully and squarely with a fine file until the gap is correct when fitted.

If new rings are being fitted it is essential to remove the unworn ridge around the top of the bore with garage cutters or honing equipment. The ridge and old top ring will have worn together but the new ring, being unworn, will hit the ridge at every stroke and rapidly break up.

Connecting rods:

The bushes for the gudgeon pins in the connecting rods are renewable. New bushes must be jig-reamed after installation so the work should be left to a service agent.

If it is suspected that the connecting rods are bent or twisted (from the wear pattern on the big-end bearings or bore) they should be checked with suitable mandrels, V-blocks and a DTI on a surface table.

Clean the connecting rods thoroughly, using a stiff brush and clean fuel and then dry them with compressed air or lint-free cloth.

Cylinder bores:

For an accurate assessment of the wear, remove the pistons and measure the bores at several points with a special dial gauge. However, a reasonable estimate of the wear can be made by judging the depth of the unworn ridge around the top of each bore. The block must be rebored if the wear exceeds .12 mm (.005 inch).

If the bore has been worn or scored by seized rings or a loose gudgeon pin, check the depth of the damage visually. If the honing structure of the bore has been removed then the bore must be rebored. If the honing structure is still visible then the bore is fit for further service.

New rings can be fitted if the oil consumption warrants it but the wear does not warrant a full rebore and oversized piston.

Installation:

Heat the piston in very hot or boiling water. **The piston must be installed with the arrow or word VORN facing towards the front of the engine and the connecting rod must be fitted with its identification mark facing the left side of the engine**, so take care to fit the piston to the gudgeon pin correctly. When the piston is hot, press the gudgeon pin into place through the piston and connecting rod. Secure the gudgeon pin using new circlips, making sure that the circlips are fully and squarely seated in their recesses in the piston.

Install the piston rings and lightly oil them and the piston skirt. Turn the rings so that their gaps are evenly spaced around the piston and no gap is in line with the gudgeon pin. Compress the rings into their grooves with a suitable ring clamp. If a clamp is not available a worm-driven hose clip may be used but more care will be required.

Lower the connecting rod down its correct bore, with the mark facing to the left of the engine and the mark on the piston crown forwards. Enter the skirt of the piston into the bore and gently press down the piston, allowing the clamp to slide off the rings as they enter. Do not allow the rings to escape from the clamp before they are in the bore and do not try to force the rings. The piston rings are very brittle and will snap if mishandled.

Once the piston and connecting rod are in place, correctly connect the big-end as described in the previous section.

13 Reassembling a stripped engine

All operations have been dealt with in detail in the relevant sections so reassembly is merely a question of tackling the task in the best order.

Cleanliness is essential. The parts should have been washed on dismantling. Bright metal parts should be wiped over with an oily rag to prevent corrosion. Small parts, nuts and bolts should be put into bags and tied to the main component after cleaning.

Before starting assembly, clean the parts again to remove any protective or dirt picked up in storage. Covers and plugs should be removed so that oilways and passages can be cleaned out. Typical block and sump parts are shown in **FIG 33**.

All old seals and gaskets should be discarded, using new ones on reassembly. Old gaskets or sealing compound should be softened with trichlorethylene and then

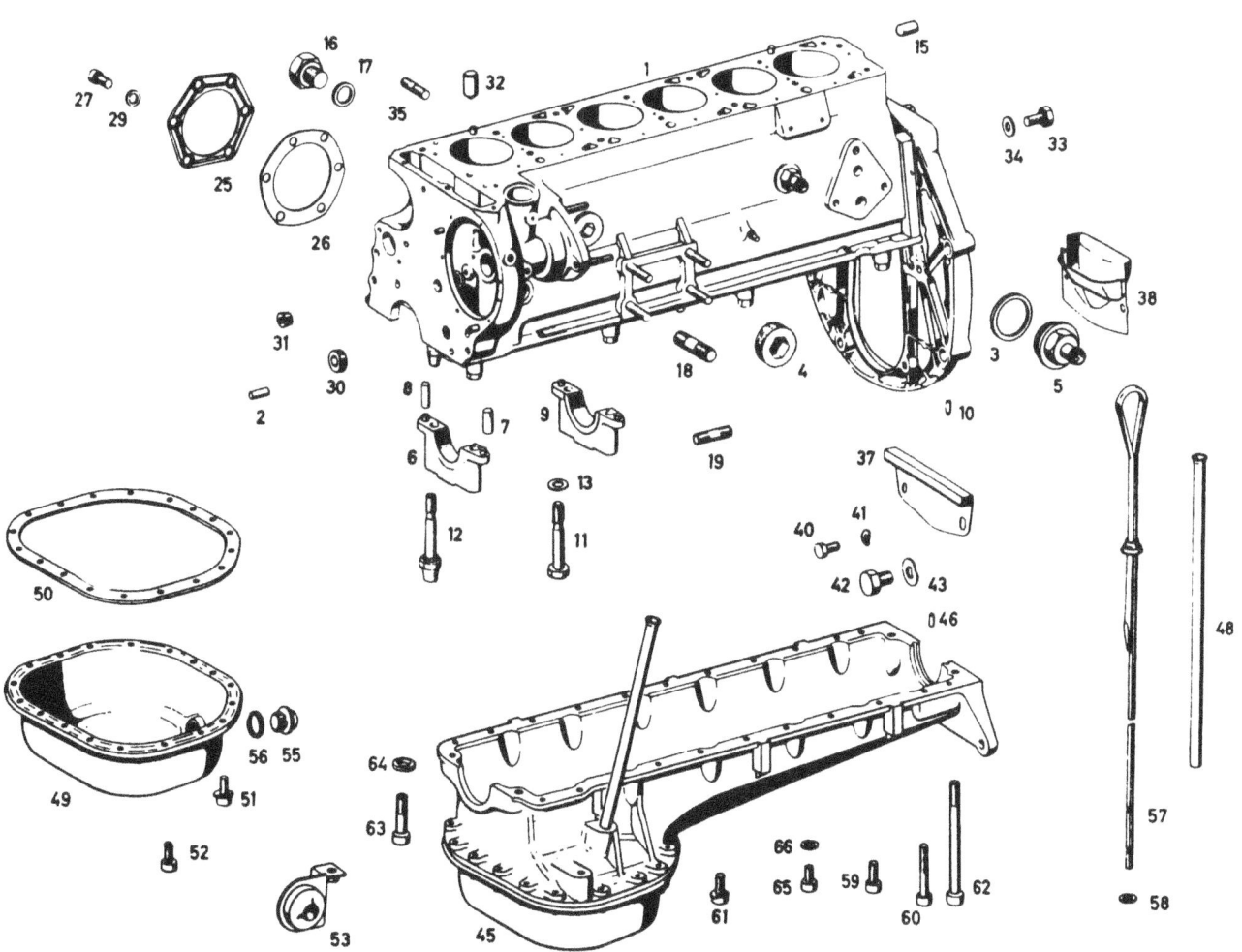

FIG 33 Typical cylinder block and associated parts

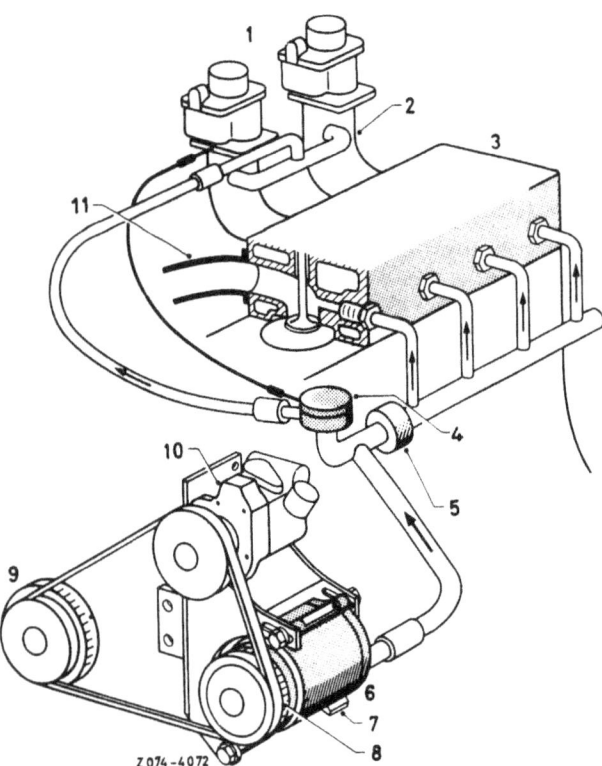

FIG 34 Schematic layout of the afterburner emission control system

1 Carburetor
2 Intake manifold
3 Cylinder head
4 Rochester valve
5 Check valve
6 Saginaw pump
7 Pressure relief valve
8 Air inlet
9 Crankshaft
10 Vickers pump
11 Exhaust line

scraped off using a piece of wood or perspex. Light damage, nicks or burrs should be smoothed down with a fine file or oilstone.

Start by installing the crankshaft and follow this with the pistons and connecting rods. If the intermediate flange has been removed, install this before fitting the flywheel and clutch. Fit the distributor drive parts followed by the front oil seal and damper assembly. Install the oil pump and sump parts so that the engine can be stood upright and the cylinder head fitted. Set the valve clearances with the engine out as it will be easier. Leave external accessories until last to avoid any danger of damaging them.

When all the parts have been installed check that the engine rotates freely before installing it. Remove the sparking plugs and crank the engine on the starter motor after installation, as a further check and to assist in priming the fuel and oil systems.

14 Emission control

On models destined for the North American market an afterburner system is installed to reduce the emissions from the engine. The schematic layout of the system is shown in **FIG 34**. The air pump 6 is driven by a belt from the engine crankshaft pulley 9. If power steering is fitted the pump 10 is driven by the same belt as the air pump. The air from the pump is injected through ports into the exhaust ports of the cylinder head 3. The excess air mixes with the hot exhaust gases to burn the hydrocarbons and convert any carbon monoxide into carbon dioxide, as the mixture passes down the exhaust pipes 11. A check valve 5 prevents exhaust gases from blowing back through the system.

An anti-backfire valve 4 is fitted to prevent backfiring and emissions on deceleration. Under normal running a thin film of neat fuel builds up on the walls of the inlet manifold 2. On deceleration the high vacuum causes the fuel to evaporate rapidly and be gulped into the engine. The rich mixture caused by this would allow unburnt fuel to pass through into the exhaust pipe where it would react explosively with the air from the pump, causing backfiring. The valve is operated by the suction from the carburettor and diverts the air from the exhaust ports to the inlet manifold when the engine decelerates. The excess air going into the engine burns the surplus fuel from the manifold walls and so reduces emissions while at the same time preventing backfiring.

Air pump:

The air pump is not repairable and a new unit must be fitted if the old one is defective. A maintenance-free centrifugal filter 8 is fitted to the inlet of the pump. When washing the engine, cover the filter to prevent water, dirt or solvents from entering the pump.

A renewable relief valve 7 is fitted to the pump to limit the maximum pressure in the system. If the valve sticks in the closed position, undesirably high temperatures will be developed in the exhaust system.

To check the pump, start the engine and leave it running at idling. Disconnect the hose from the pump and check that air is blowing out. At idle the relief valve should be quiet with no air coming from it. Block the outlet from the pump with a hand and check that the relief valve blows air. Take care to avoid the moving drive belts with the hands, clothing or tools.

Check valve:

Disconnect the air inlet hose from the valve, and check that no exhaust gases are blowing out from the valve with the engine at idle. Install a new valve if the old one leaks.

Anti-backfire valve:

Check the vacuum line to the valve for leaks, kinks or splits. Start the engine and check the valve for air being drawn through it. A very small leak, insufficient to alter the idling, is acceptable but if there is a large leak a new valve must be fitted.

Briefly operate the throttle and allow it to return to idle. The valve should continue to draw air for approximately 1 second after the throttle has closed. If the valve does not operate correctly it must be renewed.

15 Fault diagnosis

(a) Engine will not start

1 Defective ignition coil
2 Dirty or incorrectly set ignition points
3 Ignition wires loose or insulation faulty
4 Water or dirt on HT leads
5 Faulty capacitor in distributor
6 Faulty or jammed starter motor
7 Battery discharged or terminals dirty
8 Vapour locks in fuel lines
9 Defective fuel pump
10 Incorrect use of choke or defective automatic choke
11 Blocked fuel filters
12 Leaking valves
13 Sticking valves
14 Valve timing incorrect
15 Ignition timing incorrect
16 HT leads incorrectly connected

(b) Engine stalls

1 Check 1, 2, 3, 5, 10, 11, 12, 13 and 16 in (a)
2 Sparking plugs defective or incorrectly gapped
3 Retarded ignition
4 Weak mixture
5 Water in fuel
6 Fuel tank vent blocked
7 Incorrect valve clearances

(c) Engine idles badly

1 Check 2 and 7 in (b)
2 Air leaks at intake manifold
3 Fuel system incorrectly adjusted
4 Worn piston rings
5 Worn valve guides or valve stems
6 Weak exhaust valve springs

(d) Engine misfires

1 Check 1, 2, 3, 4, 5, 9, 11, 12, 13 and 16 in (a) and also check 2, 3, 4 and 7 in (b)
2 Weak or broken valve springs
3 Defective HT lead

(e) Engine overheats (see Chapter 4)

(f) Compression low

1 Check 12, 13 and 14 in (a); 4 and 5 in (c) and 2 in (d)
2 Worn piston ring grooves
3 Scored or worn cylinder bores

(g) Engine lacks power

1 Check 2, 11, 12, 13, 14 and 15 in (a); 2, 3, 4 and 7 in (b); 4 and 5 in (c); 2 and 3 in (f) and also (e)
2 Defective cylinder head gasket
3 Badly fouled or worn out sparking plugs
4 Automatic advance not operating

(h) Burnt valves or seats

1 Check 12, 13 and 14 in (a); 4 in (b) and 2 in (d). Also check (e)
2 Excessive carbon in combustion chamber

(j) Sticking valves

1 Check 2 in (d)
2 Bent valve stem
3 Scored valve stem or guide
4 Incorrect valve clearances
5 Gummy deposits on valve stem

(k) Excessive cylinder wear

1 Check 10 in (a) and also check (e)
2 Lack of oil
3 Dirty oil
4 Piston rings gummed or broken
5 Connecting rod bent or twisted

(l) Excessive oil consumption

1 Check 4 and 5 in (c) and also check (e) and (k)
2 Oil return holes in piston blocked
3 Oil level too high in sump
4 External oil leaks

(m) Main or big-end bearing failure

1 Check 2, 3 and 5 in (k)
2 Restricted oilways
3 Worn journals or crankpins
4 Loose bearing caps
5 Extremely low oil pressure

(n) Low oil pressure

1 Check 2 and 3 in (k) and 2, 3 and 4 in (m)
2 Choked oil filter
3 Weak relief valve spring or dirt under seat
4 Faulty gauge or connections

(o) Internal water leakage (see Chapter 4)

(p) Poor coolant circulation (see Chapter 4)

(q) Corrosion (see Chapter 4)

(r) High fuel consumption (see Chapter 2)

NOTES

CHAPTER 2 – THE FUEL SYSTEM

1 Description
2 The air cleaner
3 The fuel tank

PART 1 CARBURETTER

4 The fuel pump
5 Operation of the carburetter
6 Idling adjustments
7 Carburetter adjustments
8 Carburetter faults
9 Hot spot
10 Emission control
11 Fault diagnosis

PART 2 FUEL INJECTION

12 The fuel pump
13 Filters
14 Operation of the system
15 Adjustments
16 Servicing
17 Fault diagnosis

1 Description

The 280 S/8 model is fitted with twin Zenith carburetters while all the other models covered by this manual are fitted with a mechanical fuel injection system. Models for the USA market are fitted with various devices to reduce the emissions from the engine. The two systems are totally different in design and operation, even to the extent of having completely differing fuel supply pumps. To avoid confusion between the two systems, Part 1 will deal exclusively with the 280 S/8 model fitted with twin carburetters and Part 2 will deal with the injection system.

The air cleaners and fuel tanks are similar enough to be grouped into their own sections following.

2 The air cleaner

The standard air cleaners are fitted with renewable paper elements which should be cleaned at intervals of 10,000 kilometres (6000 miles) and renewed at intervals of 50,000 kilometres (30,000 miles) under normal conditions. If the car is used in dusty or dirty conditions the intervals between servicing should be reduced.

The air cleaner on the 280 S/8 models is shown in **FIG 1**. To remove the air cleaner or change the element 3, pull off the hot air and vent hoses. Undo the fasteners 2 and remove the unit from the engine. To remove the element, undo the clips and take off the cover so that the element 3 can be taken out.

When fitting the cover align the red marks on cover 1 and body 4. Check that the rubber rings 8 are in position on the carburetters and when installing the assembly make sure that the water separator 5 fits into the rubber sleeve 7.

The air cleaner fitted to the other models is shown in **FIG 2**. To remove the element, free the clip 5 and turn the top to the left so that it can be removed. Withdraw the element 2 from the base 1. Install the element in the reverse order of removal.

To clean the paper element, blow through it from the inside to the outside with air under fairly low pressure then blow obliquely across the outside to remove the dirt. If an airline or tyre pump are not available, stand the element vertical and tap around on the outside onto a firm surface so as to dislodge loose dirt. **Do not wash the element in water or any form of solvent or oil.** Before installing the element, wipe out the air cleaner with a piece of lint-free cloth moistened with fuel.

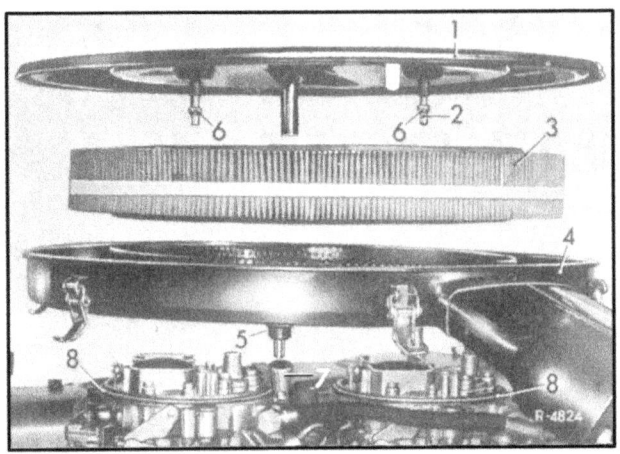

FIG 1 The air cleaner fitted to 280 S/8 models

1 Air cleaner top
2 Fastening screws
3 Air cleaner insert
4 Air cleaner base
5 Water separator
6 Collar nut
7 Rubber sleeve
8 Rubber ring

The 280 S/8 air cleaner is fitted with a thermostatically controlled intake duct shown in **FIG 3**. The flap on the shaft 8 is operated by the thermostat 1 so that in cold conditions warm air is drawn into the engine from around the exhaust. Before 1971 the warm air flap is in the full hot position below +15°C and in the full cold position above +28°C. In the beginning of 1971 a larger warm air scoop was installed and also a new thermostat which disconnects the warm air supply approximately 10°C sooner. To remove the parts, take off the clips 7 to free the operating rod 6 from the flap shaft 8. Compress the spring 5 until the guide sleeve 4 is free from the pin of the thermostat. Push the operating rod 6 rearwards to free it from the eye. The thermostat 1 can then be unscrewed, from inside the duct, out of the plastic nut 2 after slackening the nut 3. Install the parts in the reverse order of removal and set the dimension **a** to 8+0−1 mm (.3+0−.04 inch).

An optional oil bath air cleaner can be installed and the parts are shown in **FIG 4**. Remove the air cleaner top 1 and withdraw the insert 2. Clean the filter insert 2 with paraffin or diesel fuel. Drain out the old oil and sludge from the base 3 and wipe the inside of the base and top clean. With the base in a level position, pour in fresh oil up to the marks shown. Install the insert after having allowed it to drain dry and refit the top.

3 The fuel tank

Before 1970 the fuel system was fitted with a compensating tank only and the main and compensating tanks are shown in **FIG 5**. Any overflow from the main tank passes up either of the lines to the compensating tank 35 where liquid fuel is trapped. Vapour alone then passes out of the third line through the vent 43, hidden behind the rear bumper on the side, to atmosphere. As fuel is used in the main tank, any liquid fuel in the compensating tank returns down the lines to the main tank. Air to replace the fuel as it is used is drawn in through the vent 43. A combined fuel filter and drain plug 12 is fitted under the tank. If there is a blockage in the fuel lines, drain the tank and check the filter. If the filter is damaged or torn, make sure that the correct replacement marked BENZIN is installed.

As from 1970, models for the USA market are fitted with an evaporative control system, shown in **FIG 6**. A larger compensating tank 2 is fitted and the vent for the tanks is taken from the top of the compensating tank. A valve system 3 is fitted for guiding the air or fumes. Normally fumes and air pass through the valve **a** to the chain case on the engine and they are then drawn into the intake manifold and burnt with the fumes from the engine. In case excessive pressure does build up, with the engine stopped, a relief valve **c** is fitted which opens at its set pressure and allows the fumes to vent to atmosphere. As fuel is used in the system, air is drawn in through the valve **b** to replace it and to prevent a vacuum forming. The components fitted are shown in **FIG 7**.

On all models the design of the fuel tank is very similar and the tank is removed from underneath the car. If there are excessive amounts of water or dirt in the tank, try draining and filling with fresh fuel but if necessary remove the tank and swill it out before refitting it.

PART 1 CARBURETTER

4 The fuel pump

A mechanical fuel pump mounted on the engine and operated by a cam on the oil pump drive is used in conjunction with the twin carburetters on the 280 S/8 models. The parts of the pump are shown in **FIG 8**. The filter 15 should be unscrewed and cleaned at intervals of 50,000 km (30,000 miles) and once the filter has been installed the pump should be tested with gauges for suction and pressure.

Testing:

As a brief functional test, disconnect the fuel line at the carburetters and point it into any suitable container. Crank the engine over on the starter motor and if the pump is functioning there will be a good spurt of fuel from the hose at every other revolution of the engine (the oil pump being driven at half engine speed).

Disconnect both fuel lines from the fuel pump and connect a vacuum gauge to the inlet of the pump. Remove the rotor arm to prevent the engine from starting on the fuel in the float chambers. Crank the engine over on the starter motor and note the reading on the gauge. If the pump is satisfactory the reading will be .3 to .4 kg/sq cm (4.3 to 5.7 lb/sq in) or 230 to 320 mm Hg (9.1 to 12.6 inch Hg).

Remove the vacuum gauge from the inlet and fit a pressure gauge to the outlet. Again crank the engine and note the reading. The pump is satisfactory if the pressure reading is .12 to .18 kg/sq cm (1$\frac{3}{4}$ to 2$\frac{1}{2}$ lb/sq in).

High fuel pressure will only be caused by hardening of the diaphragm or an incorrect spring being fitted under the diaphragm.

Dismantling:

Evenly and in a diagonal sequence take out the screws 91 and remove the top 1. Wash the filter and top in clean fuel. Check the plate valves in the top, both visually and by blowing and sucking through them. If the valves leak or are distorted, fit a new top assembly. Unhook the diaphragm rod and remove the assembly 41. Fit a

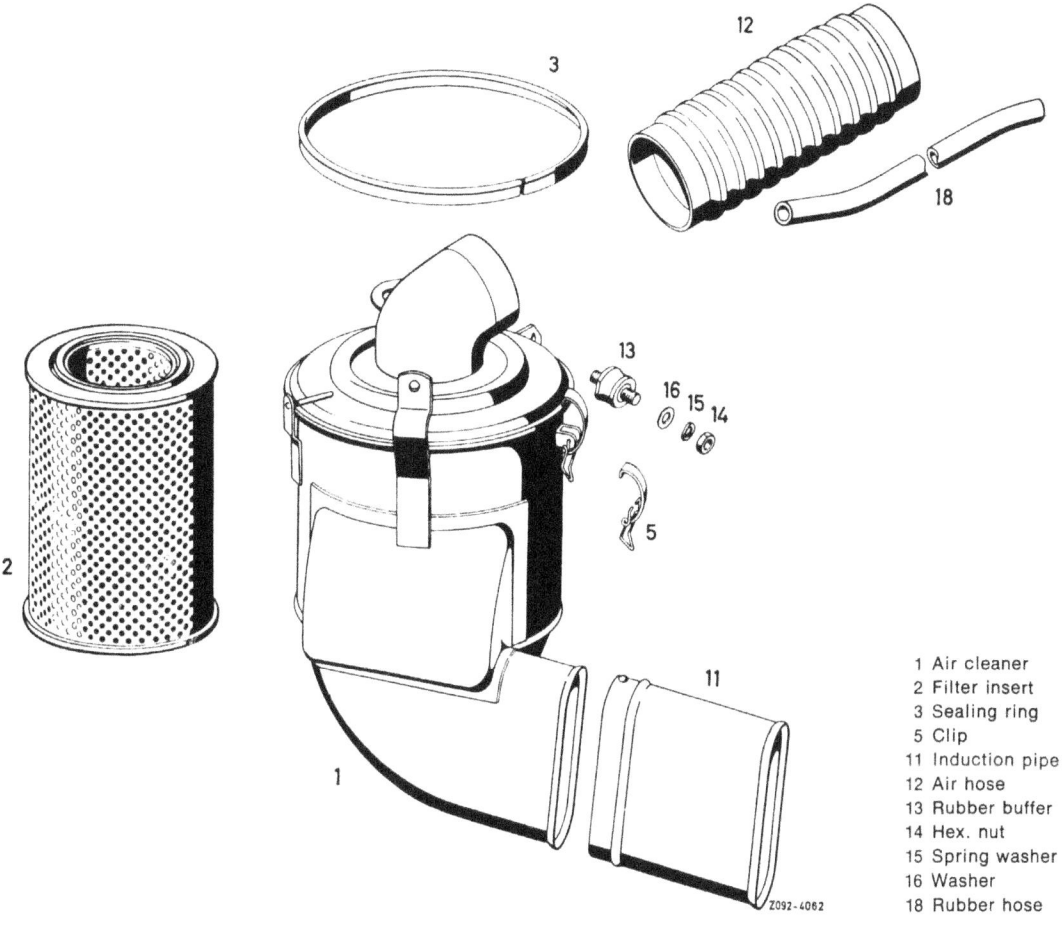

FIG 2 The air cleaner

1 Air cleaner
2 Filter insert
3 Sealing ring
5 Clip
11 Induction pipe
12 Air hose
13 Rubber buffer
14 Hex. nut
15 Spring washer
16 Washer
18 Rubber hose

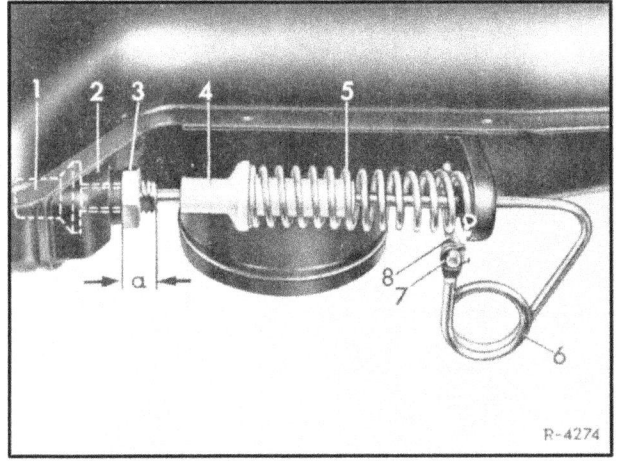

$a = 9.0 - 1$ mm

1 Thermostat
2 Plastic fastening nut
3 Hex. nut
4 Guide sleeve
5 Compression spring
6 Actuating lever
7 Locking ring
8 Flap shaft

FIG 3 The air cleaner duct fitted to the 280 S/8

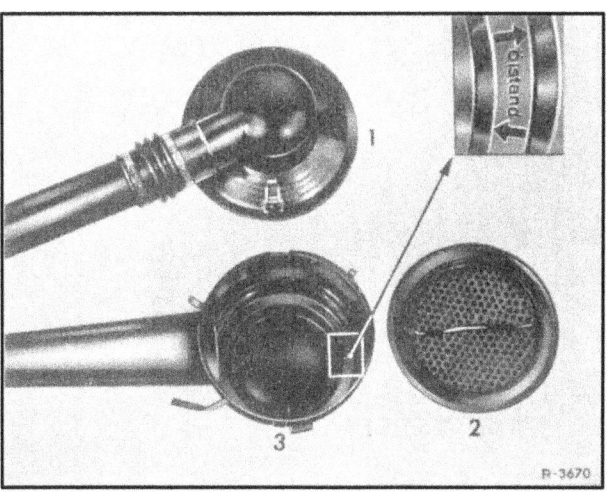

1 Top   2 Insert   3 Base

FIG 4 Optional oil bath air cleaner

41

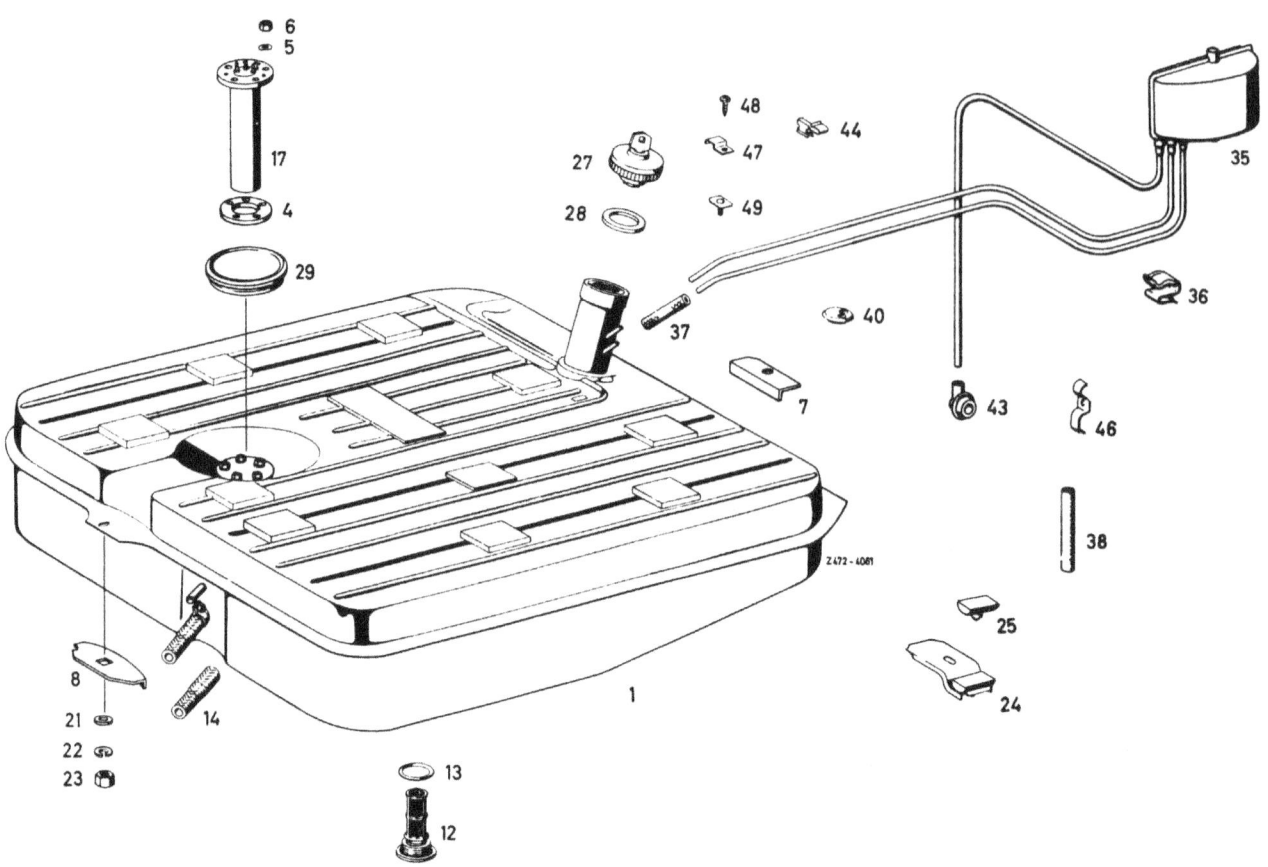

FIG 5 Early fuel tank and compensating tank

1 Fuel tank	13 Sealing ring	25 Rubber buffer	38 Fuel hose
4 Sealing ring	14 Connecting hose	27 Tank lock	40 Rubber sleeve
5 Spring washer	17 Indicator	28 Sealing ring	43 Sleeve
6 Hex. nut	21 Washer	29 Cover	44 Clip
7 Reinforcing member	22 Snap ring	35 Compensating tank	46 Fastening clip
8 Reinforcing member	23 Hex. nut	36 Fastening clip	48 Oval head screw
12 Fuel filter	24 Holder	37 Fuel hose	49 Trim strip screw

FIG 6 Later type of fuel tank and vent system

1 Fuel tank	3 Valve system	a Venting air inlet valve	c Pressure relief valve
2 Compensating tank	4 Connection on crankcase	b Venting air outlet valve	

new assembly if the diaphragm has hardened, has slits or pinholes in it, or if the spring is corroded or damaged. The arm 71 and spring 76 can be removed if required, after taking off the clips 75 and withdrawing the pin 74.

Assemble the pump in the reverse order of dismantling. Before fitting the top, slightly pre-tension the diaphragm so that it rests against the pump bottom 61. Tighten the screws 91 evenly and in a diagonal sequence.

5 Operation of the carburetter

The carburetter is of the twin-barrelled type. The primary barrel operates for cold starts, acceleration, and part throttle openings, and its throttle valve is linked directly to the accelerator pedal. The second barrel only comes into operation at large throttle openings and its throttle valve is operated by a vacuum unit. This ensures high efficiency and good economy, as at low speeds there is sufficient airflow through the primary barrel to ensure effective metering and vaporisation, while at high speeds the secondary barrel comes into operation so that the flow through the primary barrel does not become too great for efficiency.

A sectioned view through the carburetter is shown in **FIG 9**. At idling speeds there is insufficient airflow to draw the mixture out through the exit arms 18 and the main suction in the carburetter takes place beside the throttle valve 17. A mixture of fuel and air for slow running is drawn out through the port controlled by the idle mixture screw 6. The fuel is metered by the jet 10 and air by the bore 25. Transition ports are fitted above the idling port to smooth the changeover from idling to main jets.

At running speeds the fuel mixture is drawn out through the exit arm 18 and the fuel is metered by the main jet 11. Air is bled into the fuel for correction and emulsifying through the jet 24. The secondary barrel operates on similar principles and mixture, controlled by the jet 14 and air bleed 22, is drawn in by the throttle valve 16 to smooth the transition from primary to secondary barrel.

The vent valve 4 is operated by the throttle linkage and allows the float chamber to vent directly into the air intake when the engine is running faster than idle.

The front carburetter is fitted with a fuel return valve which is open until the engine reaches a speed of 2000 rev/min. The valve ensures that there is a rapid circulation of fuel through the pump and lines even when the engine is running at idle. In hot weather the heat under the hood could raise the temperature of the fuel, if it moved slowly, sufficiently to cause it to vaporize and form vapour locks in the lines. By having a rapid circulation from the comparatively cool tank the chances of vapour locks are minimized, and if they do occur the bubbles of vapour will be passed back into the fuel tank and not into the carburetters.

On acceleration the fuel flow, because of its greater inertia, will lag behind the airflow and cause a temporary weak mixture. To compensate for this an acceleration pump, operated by the throttle linkage, is fitted. On acceleration the pump injects extra fuel into the airstream through the injection nozzle.

An automatic choke is fitted. The choke valve is held closed by a bimetallic spring. When the ignition is switched on, a heater coil warms a ceramic insert and the bimetallic spring. As the spring warms up it weakens

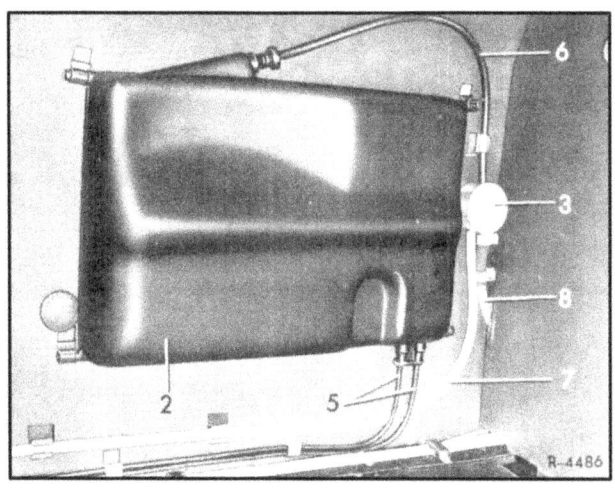

FIG 7 Later type of tank vent system installed

2 Compensating tank
3 Valve system
5 Forward flow and return flow line
6 Venting line
7 Venting line for ambient air
8 Venting line to engine

and allows the choke valve to be opened by the combined action of the airflow over the offset plate valve and the manifold suction acting on the starter valve.

6 Idling adjustments

The installation of the carburetters is shown in **FIG 10**. On later models destined for the USA market, special carburetters are fitted and these are manufactured to very close tolerances. On this type of carburetter the idle mixture screws 7 are not of the type shown in the figure but recessed into brass cones or fitted with limiters so that only a limited amount of adjustment can be made, ensuring that the engine will not be set outside the emission limits laid down by law.

Start the engine and run it until it has reached its normal operating temperature of 80°C. If the engine is overheated after a long run, leave it to idle until it has cooled down to normal. Remove the air cleaner. On 1970 emission control models, disconnect the plug from the 100°C temperature switch on the engine (see **Section 10**). Disconnect the connecting rod 12 and the regulating rod 17 so that the carburetters are isolated. Check that all the throttle valves operate freely and easily.

Check that both actuating levers 8 are resting against their idle stops 4 and if necessary back off the bolt 6 on the vacuum regulator to allow the actuating lever of the rear carburetter to rest against its stop.

It is also advisable to check the setting of the vent valves at this point.

Adjust the idle speed to 800 to 900 rev/min using the two idle speed adjusting screws 1 so that the airflow through both carburetters is the same. A balance meter will simplify the synchronization of the air flows but they can be balanced by listening to each intake in turn with a short piece of hose, and adjusting until the idle speed is correct and the hiss in both carburetters is equal.

The idle mixture screws 7 should now be set using an exhaust gas analyser. **This is particularly important in Sweden and the USA.** Failing an exhaust gas analyser set the mixture screws to give the fastest idle consistent with smooth running and an even exhaust

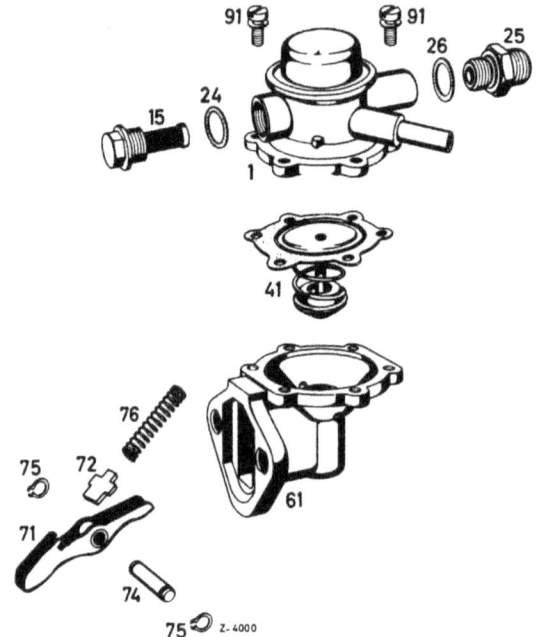

FIG 8 The mechanical fuel pump

1 Pump top
15 Fuel strainer
24 Sealing ring
25 Screw connection
26 Sealing ring
41 Pump diaphragm
61 Pump bottom
71 Pump lever
72 Spring countersupport
74 Shaft
75 Locking ring
76 Compression spring
91 Fillister-head screw

beat. A vacuum tester can be used, in which case the mixture screws should be set to give the highest vacuum. Adjustments will be required to bring the idle back to specification, using the screws 1 and checking the balance.

Refit the connecting rod 12 so that it slips back into place without tension or altering the settings. Check the balance of the carburetters at 1200 to 1500 rev/min and make any adjustments required to the length of the rod 12 to keep the carburetters in balance at this speed. Set the fast speed by levering up the actuating lever 8 of the front carburetter.

The progressive idle linkage is shown in **FIG 11**. On models fitted with a manual-shift transmission or automatic transmission with two planetary gear sets, adjust the length of the rod 17 using the nut 18 so that the roller 21 nestles in the end of its slot without tension.

The linkage for models fitted with a three planetary gear set automatic transmission is shown in **FIG 12**. Disconnect the pullrod 23 from the adjusting lever 15. Slacken the clamping screws 16 and move the adjusting lever 15 until the rod 23 can be refitted free of tension or pressure. Tighten the clamping screws 16. Start the engine and adjust the length of the rod 17, see **FIG 10**, using the ball head 13, so that the rod 17 can be refitted free of tension and fully extended with the idling lever 8 resting against the idling speed stop screw 4.

Install the air cleaner and make any small adjustments necessary to set the correct idle with a smooth exhaust beat and minimum emission.

Switch off the engine and floor the accelerator pedal. The pedal should rest against the full throttle stop at the same time as the throttle flap lever of the front carburetter. If necessary make adjustments to the regulating shaft of the pedal assembly.

Vent valve:

The vent valve is shown as 5 in **FIG 10**. The opening of the vent valve is adjusted on manufacture by setting the idling speed stop screw 4 and this screw should not be altered by the owner. The setting of the vent valve can be checked. Make sure that the choke is fully open and turn the actuating lever to the position where the vent valve will not open any further. Use a twist drill or gauge of 2.3 mm diameter and if this just fits neatly between the end of the idling stop screw 4 and the edge of the lever 8 then the adjustment is correct and has not been accidentally altered.

Fuel return valve:

Start the engine and use a tachometer to set a steady running speed of 2000 rev/min. At this speed the fuel return valve 27 should be fully closed. If necessary, adjust using the screw 25.

Vacuum regulator:

With the idle correctly set and the engine stopped, unscrew the bolt 6 until the vent valve 5 has lifted .5 to 1.0 mm (.02 to .04 inch) via the actuating lever 8. On USA versions from 1970 onwards it will be necessary to slacken the nut 9 and hold the nut 10 while adjusting the bolt 6. Turn the adjusting nut 10 until there is a gap of approximately .1 mm (.004 inch) between the adjusting bolt 6 and actuating lever 8.

7 Carburetter adjustments

The idling adjustments of the carburetters have been dealt with in the previous section.

Automatic starting device:

Check that the choke valves move smoothly and freely. Switch on the ignition and check that the valves open after a few minutes as the heaters operate. On USA versions from 1969 onwards the chokes are operated via the temperature switches. One switch measures coolant temperature and operates at 65°C while the other measures from the crankcase and operates at 55°C. Check the adjustment on the cover of the automatic starter. The index marks on the housing and cover should be in line for the correct operation of the chokes.

Start and run the engine, either warm or cold, and open the throttle linkage slightly. Insert a small screwdriver as shown in **FIG 13** and push the transmission rod up to a noticeable stop against the diaphragm rod. Do not lever against the holding clip 6. This operation sets the linkage to the fast-idle position shown in **FIG 14**. Note that the cover has only been removed for illustrative purposes. With the linkage set, measure the gap between the choke plate valve and carburetter body as shown in **FIG 15**. On standard models the gap should be 2.4 mm (.09 inch) and on USA models the gap should be 2.2 mm (.086 inch). If the gap is incorrect,

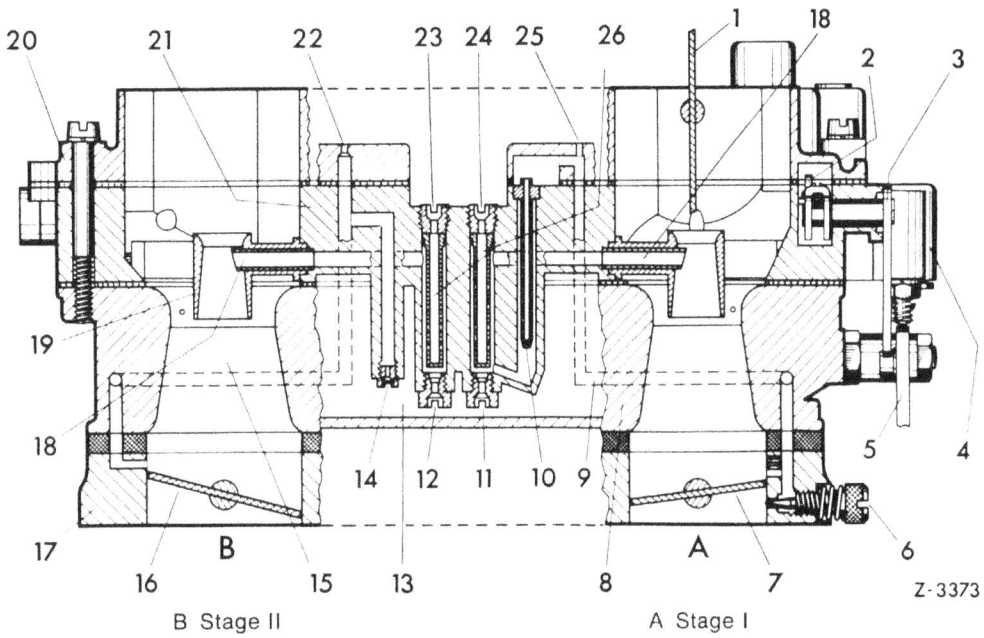

FIG 9   Sectional view of the carburetter

1 Choke
2 Inner pump lever
3 Outer pump lever
4 Float chamber venting valve
5 Actuating lever
6 Idling speed mixture regulating screw
7 Throttle valve
8 Float housing
9 Duct
10 Idling speed fuel jet
11 Main jet Stage I
12 Main jet Stage II
13 Float chamber
14 Transition fuel jet
15 Venturi Stage II
16 Throttle valve Stage II
17 Throttle valve section
18 Outlet arm
19 Preatomizer
20 Carburetor cover
21 Bedplate
22 Transition air hole
23 Air correction jet Stage II
24 Air correction jet Stage I
25 Idling speed air hole
26 Mixing tube

FIG 10   The carburetters installed

1 Idling speed adjusting screw
2 Throttle valve lever
3 Test connection
4 Idling speed stop screw
5 Float housing venting valve
6 Adjusting screw
7 Idling speed mixture screw
8 Actuating lever
9 Counter nut
10 Adjusting nut
11 Compression spring
12 Connecting rod
13 Ball head
17 Regulating rod
25 Adjusting screw fuel return valve
26 Actuating lever fuel return valve
27 Fuel return valve

FIG 11 The progressive linkage

8 Actuating lever
17 Regulating rod
18 Adjusting nut
19 Bell crank
20 Cam lever
21 Roller
22 Bearing bracket

fit a gauge or drill shank of the correct size into place and use the adjusting screw 5 on the starter valve 4 to adjust the gap to specification.

Reset the linkage to fast idle on one carburetter as shown in **FIG 13**. On the USA versions from 1970 onwards, remove the vacuum hose for the ignition changeover from the carburetter and adjust on the front carburetter only. Keep the engine running and measure the fast idle speed. For standard versions the speed should be 2400 to 2600 rev/min but for USA versions it should be 2500 to 2700 rev/min. Release the choke linkage and adjust the fast idle by the screw 3 **FIG 14**. With the linkage released the screw will protrude through the side of the housing, when full throttle is applied.

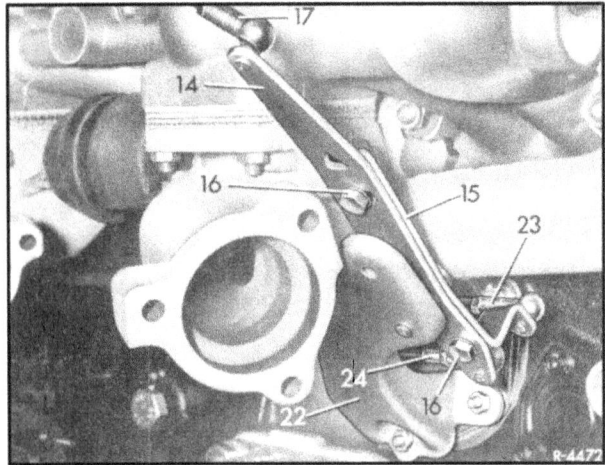

FIG 12 The progressive linkage fitted with automatic transmissions

14 Intermediate lever
15 Adjusting lever
16 Clamping screws
17 Regulating rod
22 Bearing bracket
23 Pull rod automatic transmission
24 Pull rod regulating shaft

Turning the screw by a $\frac{1}{2}$ turn will alter the speed approximately 200 to 300 rev/min, screwing it out to reduce speed and to increase. On standard models adjust the other carburetter in the same manner.

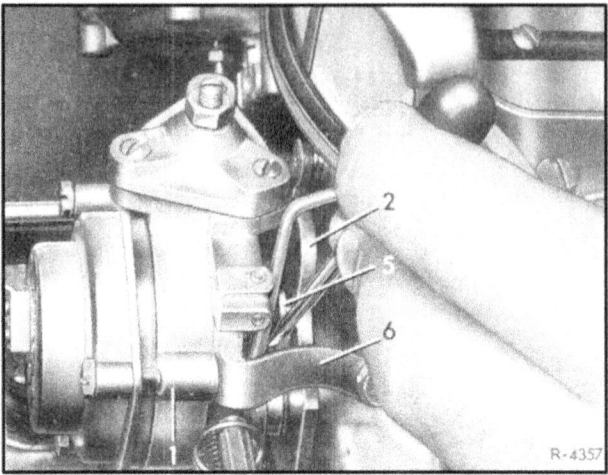

FIG 13 Setting the choke linkage to fast idle

1 Starter housing
2 Throttle lever
5 Transmission lever
6 Holding clip

Acceleration pump:

Remove the air cleaner so that the jet from the injection nozzle can be observed. The jet should hit the wall of the venturi approximately 10 to 15 mm from the top of the bedplate, as shown in **FIG 16**. On models with manual-shift transmission, the spray may be adjusted so that it sprays directly into the throttle valve gap to give harder acceleration. If the jet is incorrect, very carefully bend the nozzle to correct.

If it is suspected that the injection quantity is incorrect, remove the pre-atomizer for the barrel after taking out the pressure screw that secures it. The special measuring container 111 589 17 21 00 can then be fitted into the barrel under the nozzle and used to measure the quantity injected by the pump. The pump should inject .7 to 1.0 cc per stroke and the injection should start immediately the throttle moves. If the amount injected is incorrect, check the nozzle and pump plunger for defects. The nozzle is a

FIG 14 The choke linkage set to fast idle

1 Driving lever
2 Stop lever
3 Adjusting screw
4 Step disc
5 Stop diaphragm rod
6 Restoring spring

push fit into the bedplate and can therefore be twisted and pulled out using a pair of pliers. Drive the new nozzle into place by tapping with a blunt screwdriver against the brass sleeve. If the nozzle and plunger are satisfactory, adjust the injection quantity by carefully bending the internal lever as shown in **FIG 17**.

8 Carburetter faults

The components of the carburetter are shown in **FIG 18**. The most likely cause of poor operation, other than incorrect adjustments, will be dirt in the jets or needle valve. A punctured or defective float 83 will cause too high a fuel level in the carburetter, leading to very rich mixture strength of flooding. Similarly dirt under the needle valve 81 can cause it to jam open and flood the carburetter, as can wear on the needle itself, while a needle that is jammed shut will cut off the fuel supply.

Poor idling can be caused by wear. If difficulty is found in setting the idle mixture strength, remove the adjusting screw 14 and check the tapered end for wear or damage. Renew the screw if the tapered portion has a step worn in it. **Do not tighten the screw firmly into its seat as this is the main cause of wear.**

To gain access to the float, jets and needle valve remove the cover and bedplate. Free the articulated member 124 of the connecting rod 73 from the shaft of the choke plate valve. On some models a closing cap will have to be prised out before the parts are accessible. Take out the screws securing the cover and prise the cover up so that it can be lifted off. Remove the remaining two screws and lift off the bedplate.

The float is secured to the bedplate by a retainer and screw. Renew the float if it is punctured or damaged. With the float off, unscrew the needle valve assembly 81 and its sealing ring 82. Renew the assembly if it leaks when blown through with the needle held closed or if

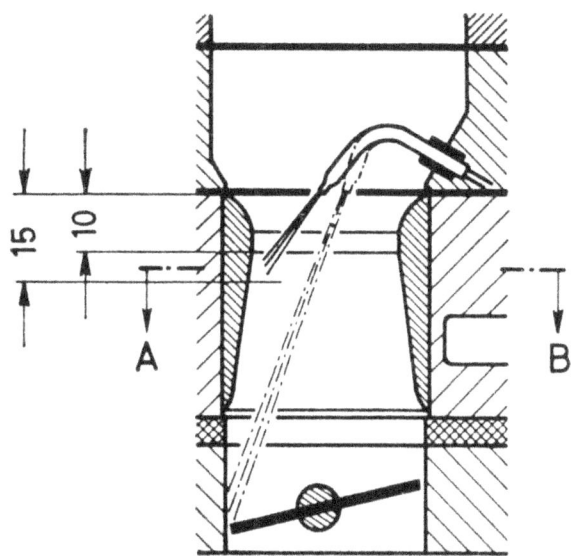

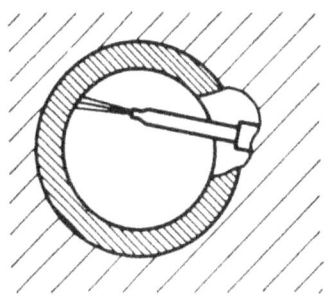

FIG 16 The correct setting of the injection spray from the acceleration pump

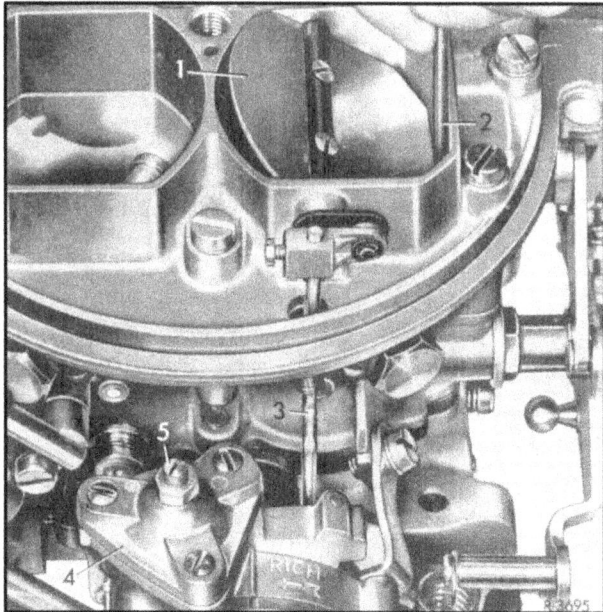

FIG 15 Checking the choke valve adjustment

1 Choke
2 Measuring gauge
3 Connecting rod
4 Starter valve
5 Adjusting screw

FIG 17 Adjusting the acceleration pump delivery quantity

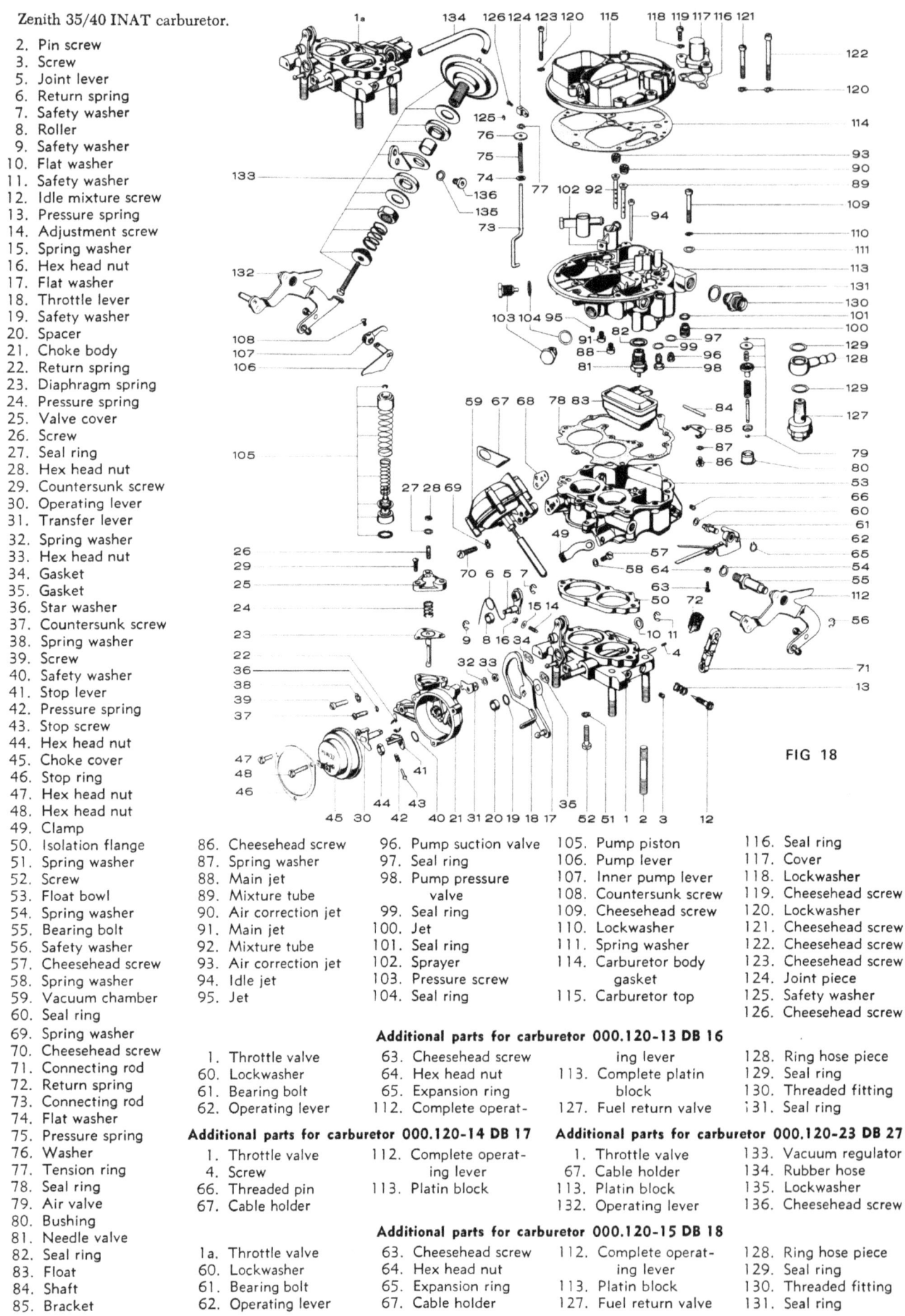

Zenith 35/40 INAT carburetor.

2. Pin screw
3. Screw
5. Joint lever
6. Return spring
7. Safety washer
8. Roller
9. Safety washer
10. Flat washer
11. Safety washer
12. Idle mixture screw
13. Pressure spring
14. Adjustment screw
15. Spring washer
16. Hex head nut
17. Flat washer
18. Throttle lever
19. Safety washer
20. Spacer
21. Choke body
22. Return spring
23. Diaphragm spring
24. Pressure spring
25. Valve cover
26. Screw
27. Seal ring
28. Hex head nut
29. Countersunk screw
30. Operating lever
31. Transfer lever
32. Spring washer
33. Hex head nut
34. Gasket
35. Gasket
36. Star washer
37. Countersunk screw
38. Spring washer
39. Screw
40. Safety washer
41. Stop lever
42. Pressure spring
43. Stop screw
44. Hex head nut
45. Choke cover
46. Stop ring
47. Hex head nut
48. Hex head nut
49. Clamp
50. Isolation flange
51. Spring washer
52. Screw
53. Float bowl
54. Spring washer
55. Bearing bolt
56. Safety washer
57. Cheesehead screw
58. Spring washer
59. Vacuum chamber
60. Seal ring
69. Spring washer
70. Cheesehead screw
71. Connecting rod
72. Return spring
73. Connecting rod
74. Flat washer
75. Pressure spring
76. Washer
77. Tension ring
78. Seal ring
79. Air valve
80. Bushing
81. Needle valve
82. Seal ring
83. Float
84. Shaft
85. Bracket

86. Cheesehead screw
87. Spring washer
88. Main jet
89. Mixture tube
90. Air correction jet
91. Main jet
92. Mixture tube
93. Air correction jet
94. Idle jet
95. Jet
96. Pump suction valve
97. Seal ring
98. Pump pressure valve
99. Seal ring
100. Jet
101. Seal ring
102. Sprayer
103. Pressure screw
104. Seal ring
105. Pump piston
106. Pump lever
107. Inner pump lever
108. Countersunk screw
109. Cheesehead screw
110. Lockwasher
111. Spring washer
114. Carburetor body gasket
115. Carburetor top
116. Seal ring
117. Cover
118. Lockwasher
119. Cheesehead screw
120. Lockwasher
121. Cheesehead screw
122. Cheesehead screw
123. Cheesehead screw
124. Joint piece
125. Safety washer
126. Cheesehead screw

Additional parts for carburetor 000.120-13 DB 16

1. Throttle valve
60. Lockwasher
61. Bearing bolt
62. Operating lever
63. Cheesehead screw
64. Hex head nut
65. Expansion ring
112. Complete operating lever
113. Complete platin block
127. Fuel return valve
128. Ring hose piece
129. Seal ring
130. Threaded fitting
131. Seal ring

Additional parts for carburetor 000.120-14 DB 17

1. Throttle valve
4. Screw
66. Threaded pin
67. Cable holder
112. Complete operating lever
113. Platin block

Additional parts for carburetor 000.120-15 DB 18

1a. Throttle valve
60. Lockwasher
61. Bearing bolt
62. Operating lever
63. Cheesehead screw
64. Hex head nut
65. Expansion ring
67. Cable holder
112. Complete operating lever
113. Platin block
127. Fuel return valve

Additional parts for carburetor 000.120-23 DB 27

1. Throttle valve
67. Cable holder
113. Platin block
132. Operating lever
133. Vacuum regulator
134. Rubber hose
135. Lockwasher
136. Cheesehead screw
128. Ring hose piece
129. Seal ring
130. Threaded fitting
131. Seal ring

FIG 18

the needle sticks in the closed position. With the float installed and the bedplate inverted, use a depth gauge to measure the height of the float, with the gasket removed, as shown in **FIG 19**. The height should be 21 to 23 mm (.8 to .9 inch). If the float is incorrectly set, selectively fit sealing washers under the needle valve assembly to bring the height within specification.

The positions of the jets are shown in **FIGS 20** and **21. When removing the jets themselves use well fitting tools, as badly fitting tools will damage them. The idle speed jet and mixing tubes should be drawn out with a sharpened piece of wood if they stick in place.** Wash the jets in clean fuel and blow through them to clear blockages. **Do not poke through the jets with wire or bristles as this will wear the accurately calibrated jets.** Blow through passages, preferably in a reverse direction to normal flow, to clear and clean them. When installing the jets, take great care not to confuse them and fit them back into their original locations.

Reassemble the parts in the reverse order of dismantling.

9 Hot spot

A thermostatically controlled hot spot is fitted under each carburetter to allow the exhaust gases to heat the inlet manifold when the engine is cold. The valve is operated by a bimetallic spring. The bimetallic spring should be renewed if it burns out or fails. If the valve itself sticks, lubricate the pivots with Caramba oil, crude oil or penetrating oil. If the valve cannot be freed it will be necessary to take the manifold to a service agent for installation of a new valve, as the parts must be accurately welded in.

10 Emission control

The vacuum lines for the system are shown in **FIG 22** and the electrical wires and components in **FIG 23**. The temperature switches 8 and 23 sense the temperature of the engine and cylinder head while the speed relay 4 senses the engine speed. At normal temperatures if the engine speed drops below 2200 rev/min the system energizes the three-way valve 11 so that vacuum is switched to the retard side of the distributor and the ignition is retarded. If the engine temperatures are outside the limits then the speed relay is isolated by one or other of the temperature sensors and the three-way valve 11 is not actuated. The two-way valve is similarly controlled to operate the vacuum unit on the carburetter. Faults in the system are best checked by a service agent.

11 Fault diagnosis

(a) Poor fuel delivery

1. Fuel filters choked
2. Fuel lines blocked
3. Needle valve stuck closed
4. Defective fuel pump
5. Bad air leak on suction side of pump
6. Incorrectly set or defective fuel return valve

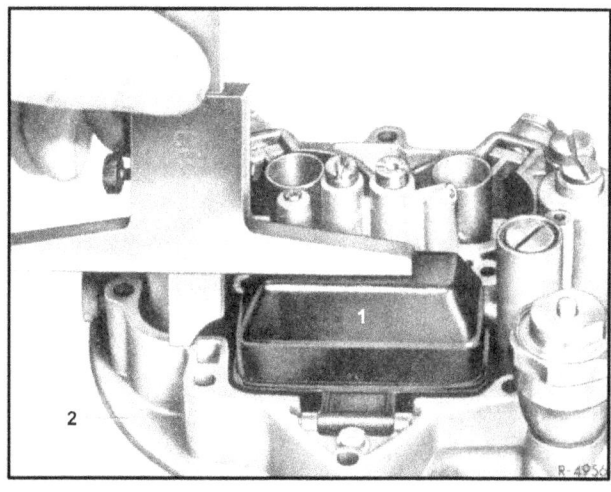

FIG 19 Checking the float setting

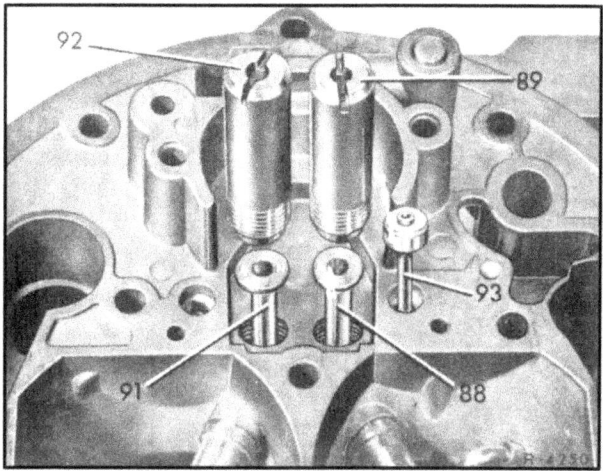

FIG 20 Jet positions

88 Mixing tube Stage I
89 Air correction jet Stage I (USA version)
91 Mixing tube Stage II
92 Air correction nozzle Stage II (USA version)
93 Idling speed fuel jet

FIG 21 Jet positions

87 Main jet Stage I
90 Main jet Stage II
94 Transition jet
95 Pump intake valve
97 Pump pressure valve

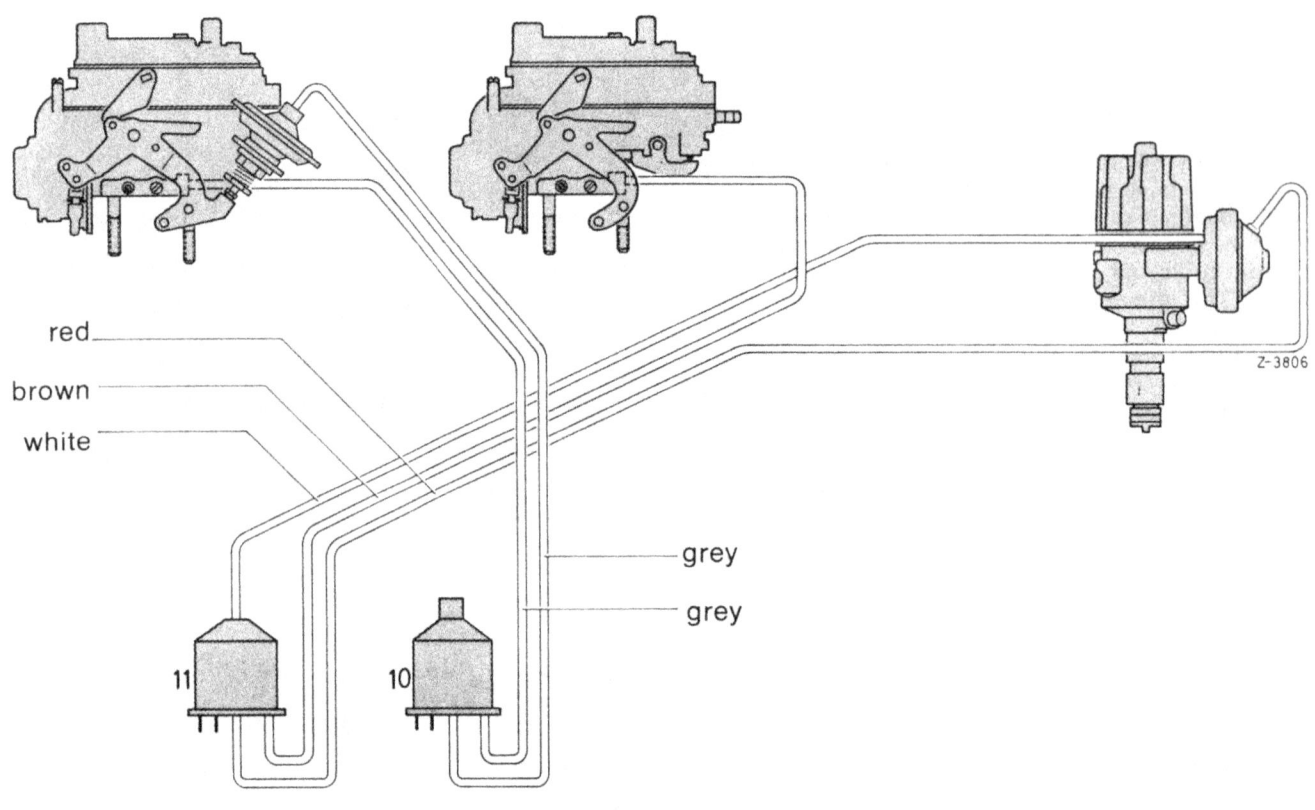

FIG 22 The vacuum lines for the emission control system

10 Two-way valve   11 Three-way valve

(b) High fuel consumption

1 Leaking float needle valve
2 Defective float
3 Incorrectly set float height
4 Incorrect acceleration pump settings
5 Defective automatic choke
6 Dirty air cleaner
7 Excessive engine temperature
8 Brakes binding
9 Tyres under-inflated
10 Idling speed too high
11 Car overloaded
12 Worn carburetters

(c) Idling speed too high

1 Linkage sticking
2 Vent valves sticking
3 Vacuum control incorrectly adjusted
4 Carburetters incorrectly adjusted

(e) Poor idle

1 Check 3 and 4 in (a)
2 Damaged idle mixture screw
3 Air leaks around carburetter and manifold
4 Dirt in jets or canals

PART 2 FUEL INJECTION

12 The fuel pump

An electrically-driven vane-type pump is fitted to all the models and the pump supplies fuel under pressure to the fuel injection pump. The attachments of the later type pump are shown in **FIG 24**. The later smaller type of pump is shown in the figure and this type has a bypass system which returns fuel vapour bubbles to the tank. The later type of pump can be recognized by the connections for the electrical leads being on the main casting and not on the cover of the pump as for the earlier motors. **When installing the pump, be sure that the correct polarity is observed as the pump will not supply fuel if the leads are crossed.** The positive terminal has a red plastic plate and the negative terminal a brown plastic one. When installing the pump, also check that the suction line does not sag—cutting it shorter if required.

The electrical portion of the pump must not be dismantled, or worked on in any way by the owner. Faults in the electrical portion, including renewal of brushes, must only be carried out by an authorized agent. The vane portion can be drawn out after the cover has been taken off but if scores or other damage are found then it is best to fit a new pump.

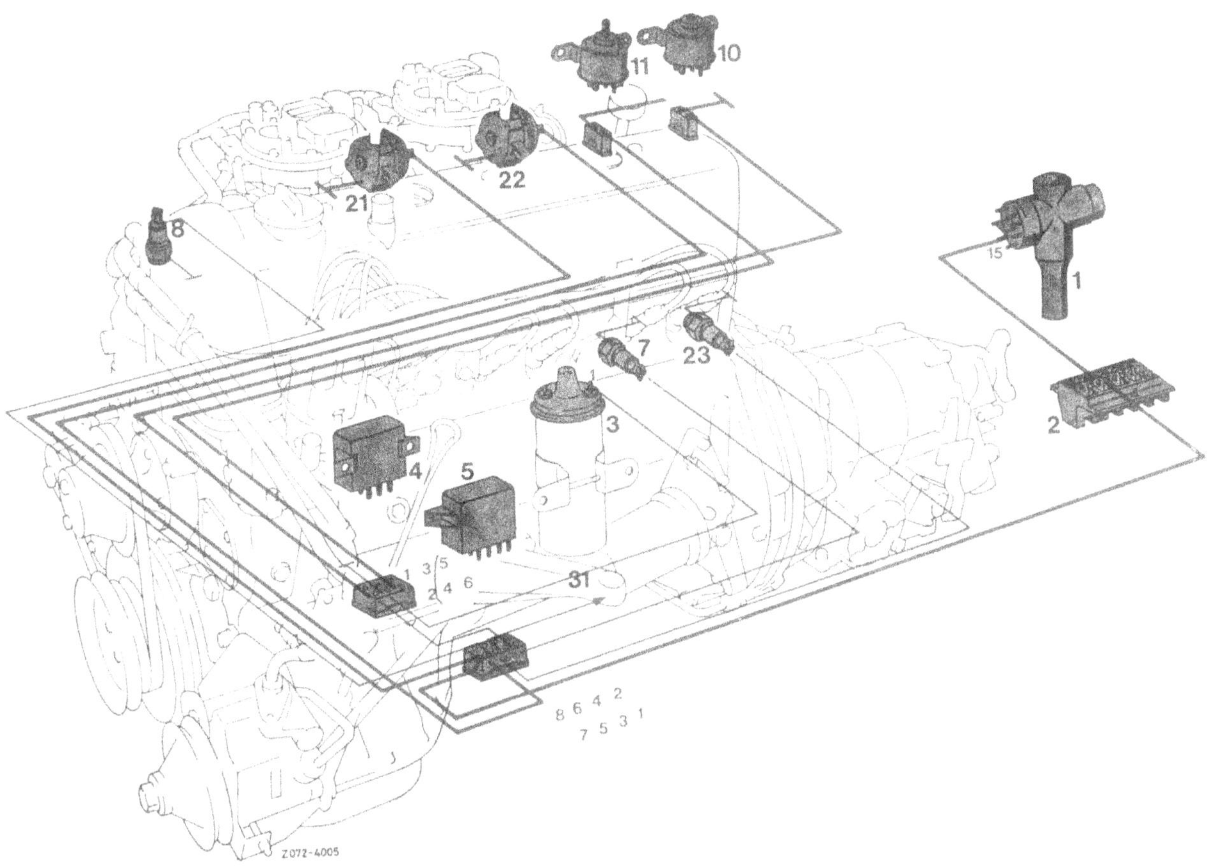

FIG 23   The electrical leads and components for the emission control system

1 Ignition starting switch
2 Fusebox
3 Ignition coil
4 Speed relay
5 Relay box
7 Temperature switch 17°C
8 Temperature switch 100°C
10 Two-way valve
11 Three-way valve
21 Front starter cover
22 Rear starter cover
23 Temperature switch 65°C
31 To relay for supplementary fan

13 Filters

The elements in the fuel filter and air filter on the injection pump should be renewed at regular intervals. Be sure that the correct replacement parts are obtained.

14 Operation of the system

Each cylinder of the engine has its own small pump consisting of a piston operating in an accurately machined cylinder. The pistons are machined with spiral grooves and the groove aligns with a port in the side of the cylinder so that fuel can be drawn in. On the compression stroke, the piston forces the metered amount of fuel out through the pipe and through an injector into the inlet port of the cylinder head. The fuel is sprayed in the form of a cone and rapidly breaks up into tiny droplets which mix with the air. By rotating the piston in its cylinder the port will be aligned with a different portion of the spiral on the piston and the amount of fuel will therefore be accurately metered. Each piston of the pump is accurately set by the movement of the control bar 34 shown in **FIG 25**. The position of the rod is controlled by a three dimensional cam. The governor controls the axial position of the cam and the load controls the rotational position of the cam.

FIG 24   The mountings of the electrical fuel pump

1 Fuel pressure line
2 Fuel bypass line
3 Fuel suction line
7 Vibration damper
6 Holding bracket
8 Fastening plate

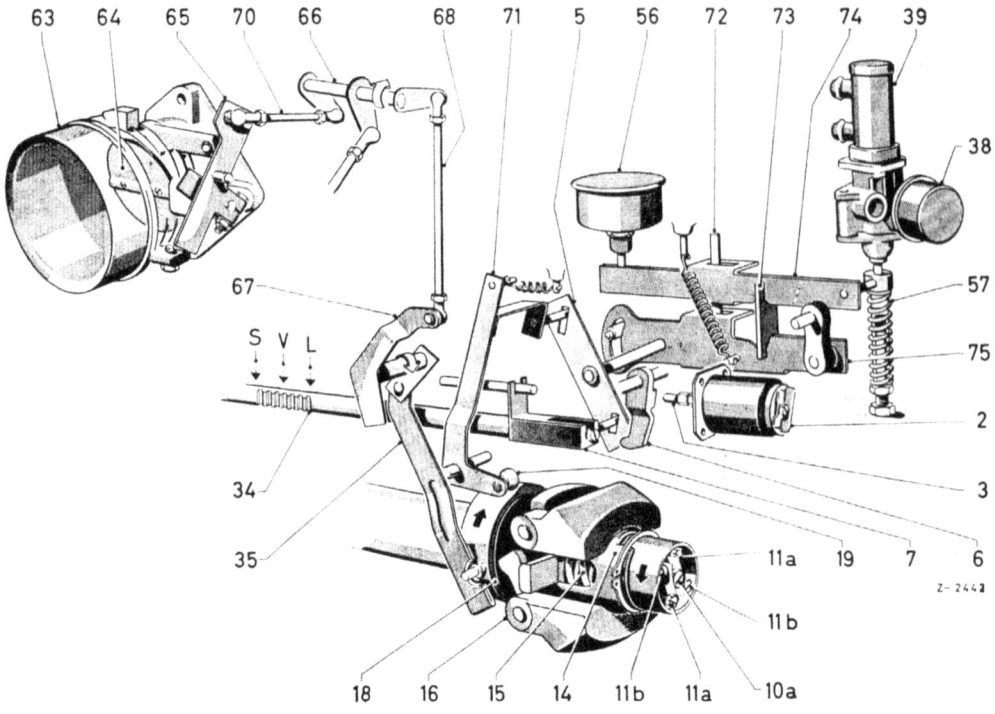

FIG 25 The mixture regulator components in the injection pump

S = Starting position of control rod
V = Full load position
L = Idling speed position

2 Solenoid switch
3 Actuating rod
5 Guide lever
6 Start lever
7 Control rod head
10a Idling speed adjustment screw
11a Partial load adjusting screw (black)
11b Adjusting screw (white, top speed range)
14 Joint
15 Regulator springs

16 Flyweight
18 Three-dimensional cam
19 Feeler roller
34 Control rod
35 Adjusting lever
38 Air cleaner
39 Cooling water heat feeler
56 Altitude corrector
57 Guide pin
63 Venturi control unit

64 Throttle valve
65 Throttle valve lever
66 Regulating shaft
67 Adjusting lever
68 Regulating rod
70 Regulating rod
71 Roller lever
72 Guide pin
73 Support
74 Rocker
75 Correcting lever

FIG 26 The fuel system installed

1 Throttle valve lever
2 Full load stop
3 Idling speed stop screw
4 Regulating rod
5 Regulating lever
6 Regulating rod
7 Regulating shaft
8 Regulating rod
9 Adjusting lever
10 Idling speed and full load stop

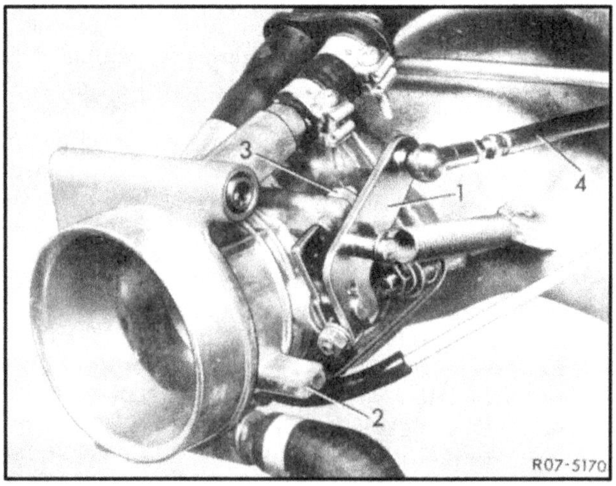

FIG 27 The venturi unit

1 Throttle valve lever
2 Full load stop
3 Idling speed stop screw
4 Regulating rod

A solenoid 2 is fitted for cold starts and the sensing device 39 measures the temperature of the coolant and adjusts the linkage accordingly. An altitude sensor 56 is fitted to weaken the mixture with increasing height as well as allowing extra air for cold starts—to give a higher idling speed.

The air for the system is controlled by the venturi unit 63 and the throttle valve 64. The throttle valve is linked to the accelerator pedal, as is the fuel injection pump, and the engine speed is therefore controlled from the accelerator pedal. A venturi is used so that suction is produced to operate the advance and retard on the ignition distributor and draw fumes from the crankcase.

The injection pump is made to extremely close tolerances as the amount injected per stroke is very small and must be measured with extreme accuracy. Special equipment is essential for accurately setting the system and the owner should not attempt random adjustments.

The installation of the components is shown in **FIG 26**.

15 Adjustments

The position of the throttle valve in the venturi unit must be accurately set in relation to the adjusting lever of the injection pump. If parts have been distorted or damaged then the car should be taken to a service agent for full checks using special graduated discs fitted to the controls.

1 Disconnect the regulating rod 6 (see **FIG 26**) and check the linkage for absence of play, distortions and easy operation. Renew ball heads on the rods if they are defective. The adjusting lever on the pump itself may not always return to the idle stop on the pump when the linkage is released but the linkage is satisfactory if the lever jumps back to the stop when the engine is briefly cranked on the starter motor. **Do not alter the position of the full load/idle stop on the pump.**

2 Views of the venturi unit are shown in **FIGS 27** and **28**. Disconnect the control rod 4 from the venturi. Check that the throttle valve moves fully and freely through its range of movement. When the throttle valve lever 1 is pressed tightly against the idle stop 3, the throttle valve should be slightly gripped in the bore without actually binding. If necessary adjust the idle stop 3 to bring about this condition, air for idling being passed through a separate hose. Coasting surge and other faults can be caused by the throttle valve closing off the port for suction when the valve is shut. If the valve blocks the port as shown at detail **X** in **FIG 29**, apply a slight chamfer to the edge of the valve so that the port is clear as shown in the figure. Note that dirt in the bore or port will give the same effect as the valve blocking the port.

3 Disconnect the connecting rod 8 (see **FIG 26**) and adjust the rod until it can be fitted back without tension with the adjusting lever of the pump resting against the idle stop. For models without a fitted hole for the centering bolt, adjust the length of the rod 8 to 233 mm. Similarly adjust the rod 4, making sure that the throttle valve lever rests against the idle stop on the venturi.

4 Slowly operate the mechanism from the central regulating lever and check that both regulating levers,

FIG 28 The venturi unit

1 Throttle valve lever
2 Full load stop screw
3 Idling speed stop screw
4 Regulating rod
14 Idling speed air screw

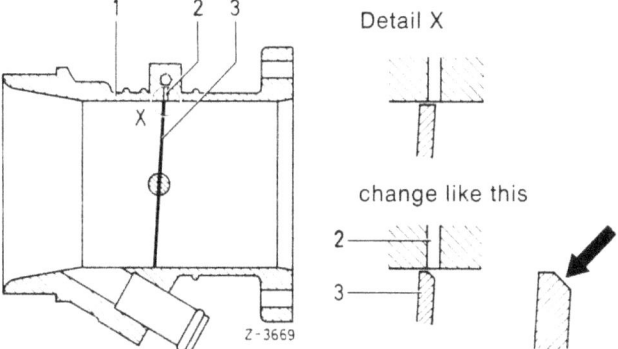

FIG 29 Modifying the throttle valve to clear the vacuum port, if required

1 Venturi control unit
2 Bore
3 Throttle valve

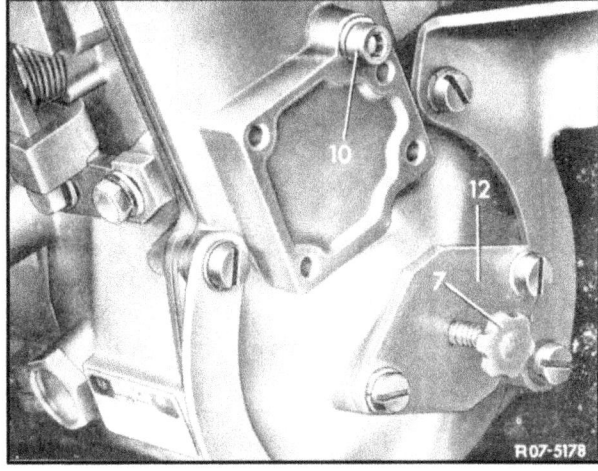

FIG 30 The idle mixture strength adjustment point

7 Idling speed adjusting screw
10 Closing screw—full load adjustment
12 Closing flange partial load adjustment

the one on the injection pump and the other on the venturi, lift simultaneously from their idle stops. When the pump lever is against its full load stop there should be a clearance of 1 mm between the venturi lever and its full load stop.

5 Adjust and install the connecting rod 6. If a progressive linkage is fitted, the rods should be so adjusted that the roller nestles comfortably against the end stop of the slot in the lever without the rods being under tension. On models with a closing damper, adjust the linkage until the lever just barely lifts off the end of the damper pin and set the damper so that its stroke is 4 to 5 mm (.16 to .20 inch).

Idling adjustments:

Start the engine and run it until it has reached the normal operating temperature of 80°C. If the engine is overheated, after a long fast run, it should be allowed to run until it has settled down to its normal operating temperature. Check that the linkage is correctly adjusted and operating freely as described previously.

An exhaust gas analyser should be used for setting the mixture strength of the system. This is particularly important for cars used in North America or Sweden. A vacuum gauge can be used for adjusting the mixture strength. A tachometer should be used to set the correct speed.

Adjust the engine idle speed to 750 to 800 rev/min using the idling speed adjustment screw on the venturi. Read the amount of carbon monoxide in the exhaust gases and adjust the mixture strength using the screw 7 on the pump, shown in **FIG 30**. The screw is pressed in and then makes contact with the governor. **As the governor rotates when the engine is running the engine must be stopped every time an adjustment is made to the mixture strength.** Turn the screw to the left to make the mixture weaker and to the right to make it richer.

If an exhaust gas analyser is not available, connect a vacuum tester to the venturi, as shown in **FIG 31**. Start the engine and open the idling adjustment screw until the vacuum collapses. Close the screw again until the vacuum again collapses. From the second position, open the adjusting screw until the fastest idling speed is obtained and note the speed. If the idle speed is too fast the mixture is too rich and if it is too slow the mixture is too weak. Adjust the mixture at the screw on the pump, **after stopping the engine**, and again check the adjustment.

Some models are fitted with a constant speed system to prevent the idle speed from dropping when the air conditioning is in use or gear selected when automatic transmission is fitted. Set the adjusting screw 2 on the solenoid, shown in **FIG 32**, so that the minimum idle speed is 700 rev/min with air conditioning on or gear selected.

On the 1970 and onwards models for the USA market a vacuum box 3, shown in **FIG 33**, is fitted to the venturi. Check that with the engine idling and special features out of operation the adjusting screw 10 is just resting on the contact surface of the clamping bolt 8. Select drive and check that the throttle is opened by 1.0 to 1.5 mm (.04 to .06 inch), adjusting the screw 10 and nut 12 as required. The main settings of the unit are shown in **FIG 34**.

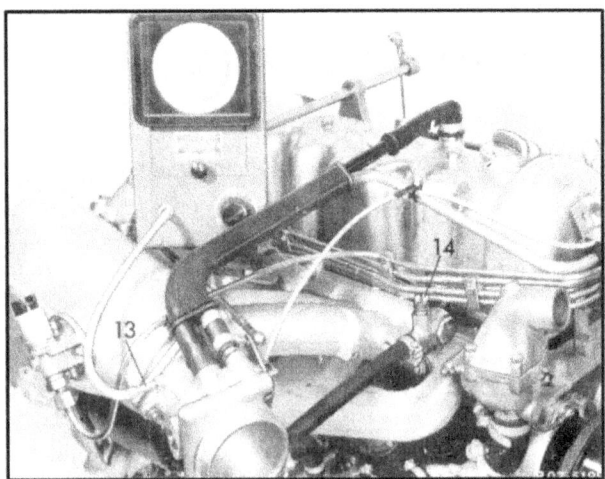

FIG 31 Checking the idle mixture strength without an exhaust gas analyser

13 Test connection 14 Idling speed air screw

FIG 32 The constant speed solenoid
1 Hex. nut 2 Adjusting nut 3 Actuating lever

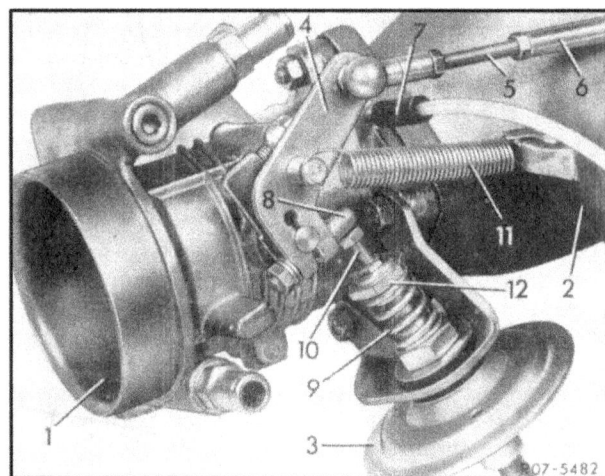

FIG 33 The vacuum governor (USA models from 1970)

1 Venturi control unit 7 Vacuum tap
2 Intake manifold 8 Clamping bolt
3 Vacuum box 9 Compression spring
4 Throttle valve lever 10 Adjusting screw
5 Sliding rod 11 Return spring
6 Sliding sleeve 12 Adjusting nut

16 Servicing

Injectors:

These are sealed units that cannot be cleaned or repaired and must be renewed when defective. An agent can check the spray pattern of the injectors using a modified diesel injector tester if it is suspected that an injector is defective.

Injection pump:

The temperature sensing unit and the ball valves for each operating cylinder can be renewed with the unit fitted to the vehicle. Any other repairs require that the unit be mounted on a Bosch stand and work carried out using special tools and equipment. Such work should only be entrusted to an authorized agent.

The pump is lubricated from the engine and requires no topping up.

Injection pump removal:

The attachments of the pump are shown in **FIG 35**. Disconnect the battery cables and drain the cooling system. Disconnect the coolant hoses 1 and 2, supplementary air hose 4, as well as fuel lines 9, 10 and 11, from the unit. Free the connection at the oil line 7. Disconnect the electrical wires to the cold start and stopping solenoids (as fitted).

Take out the bolts and socket headed screws 6 and 8. Withdraw the pump in a rearward direction and remove the drive coupling.

Before installing the pump, check that the regulating rod moves freely. Usually a long M5 bolt can be screwed into the operating rod and the rod moved on this bolt. If threads are not fitted to the operating rod, push it rearwards and check that it returns on its own.

If the operating rod is stiff to move or sticks, pour a little perfectly clean fuel into the return or forward flow of the suction chamber and leave the fuel to act for a short while. Push the operating rod backwards and forwards while rotating the pump on the drive to free the parts.

Crank the engine until No. 1 cylinder piston is 20 deg. after TDC of the firing stroke. It will be easier to crank the engine if all the sparking plugs are taken out. Remove the distributor cap and crank the engine until the firing marks on the body and rotor arm are aligned (see **Chapter 3**) and then crank the engine until the 20 deg. ATDC mark on the crankshaft damper is aligned with the timing pointer. Position the pump itself so that the marks shown in **FIG 36** are all in line and install the pump in the reverse order of removal. Make sure that the injection lines are connected to the correct injectors.

The lines will be empty so connect the **W** terminal on the thermal time switch to ground and keep cranking until the engine keeps running. No other precautions need be taken to prime the system.

FIG 35 The attachments of the injection pump

1 Cooling water hose
2 Cooling water hose
3 Cooling water heat feeler
4 Supplementary air line
5 Regulating rod
6 Hex. screws
7 Oil line
8 Hex. socket screws
9 Fuel line (feed)
10 Fuel line (return)
11 Injection lines

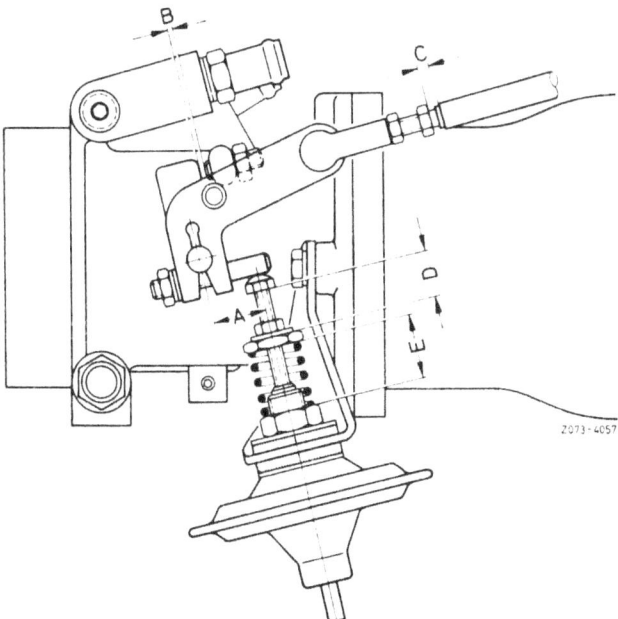

FIG 34 The setting of the vacuum governor

A Shaft distance = 17 mm (± 0.5 mm)
B Throttle valve opening = 1.0–1.5 mm with gear engaged
C Idle travel of sliding rod
D Length of thrust bolt = 14.5–15.5 mm
E Spring length = 19.5 mm

FIG 36 The timing marks on the injection pump

12 Cheesehead screws

17 Fault diagnosis

(a) Engine fails to start

1 Current not reaching pump motor
2 Defective fuel pump
3 Fuel pump electrical leads incorrectly connected
4 Badly fouled fuel filter
5 Blocked or incorrectly routed fuel lines

(b) Poor cold start

1 Defective cold start components
2 Pump control rod binding
3 Incorrect control rod travel

(c) Engine stalls after cold start

1 Check 2 and 3 in (a)
2 Blocked supplementary air filter or defective control valve

(d) Poor starting when warm

1 Check 4 and 5 in (a) and 2 in (b)
2 Injector lines or valves leak fuel

(e) Poor idle

1 Throttle valve not correctly set in venturi
2 Air leaks into system or manifolds

(f) Engine sputters under thrust load or surges on coast

1 Blocked or covered vacuum bore in venturi unit

CHAPTER 3 – IGNITION SYSTEM

1 Description
2 Maintenance
3 The breaker points
4 Ignition faults
5 Removing the distributor
6 Servicing the distributor
7 Setting the ignition timing
8 The sparking plugs
9 The transistorized ignition
10 Fault diagnosis

1 Description

The ignition system consists of the following components: distributor, ignition coil and sparking plugs. A low-tension circuit, supplied from the battery, flows through the ignition coil primary windings and the distributor. Ordinary wiring is used for the low-tension circuit. The high-tension circuit comes from the ignition coil, passes through the distributor cap and rotor arm and from there to the appropriate sparking plug. Special leads are used for the high-tension circuit.

The distributor is mounted on the engine and driven at half engine speed. The distributor shaft carries the cam for operating the contact breakers and it also carries a slot for mounting the rotor arm. The shaft is synchronized with the engine and the body of the distributor carefully adjusted about the shaft so that the operations take place at the correct instant.

When the contacts in the distributor are closed, current flows in the low-tension circuit and a magnetic field is set up around the primary coils of the ignition coil. At the correct moment the contacts are opened by the cam and the current cut off. Rapid cut-off of the current is ensured by the action of the capacitor fitted to the distributor. This action leads to a very rapid collapse of the magnetic field around the primary coils, and as the field collapses a very high voltage is induced in the many windings of the secondary coil in the ignition coil. This HT voltage is led out through the well insulated top of the coil, through an HT lead to the central electrode of the distributor cap. A carbon brush leads the voltage to the rotor arm and from there it jumps the small gap to the correct side electrode in the distributor cap. Another HT lead carries the high voltage to the appropriate sparking plug where it jumps across the electrode and ignites the mixture. As all the parts are synchronized the spark occurs in the correct cylinder at the correct time.

The exact ignition point for optimum performance will vary with engine speed and load. Combustion takes a finite time so if it is initiated at the correct time when the engine is turning slowly combustion will be taking place too late when the engine is rotating fast. The distributor shaft is fitted with a centrifugal advance mechanism to compensate for engine speed. Spring loaded weights are fitted between the shaft and cam in such a way that, as they move outwards, they advance the cam in relation to the shaft. As the engine speeds up, centrifugal force moves the weights outwards against the pull of the calibrated springs to advance the ignition. The time taken for combustion will vary with the pressure of the mixture in the cylinder (more mixture being drawn in under load and therefore a higher pressure being reached on the compression stroke) and adjustment must be made for this. The suction in the carburetter or intake manifold is proportional to the throttle opening and load on the engine, so a vacuum unit is connected to measure the suction. The vacuum unit rotates the baseplate of

FIG 1 The distributor and timing marks

A Contact breaker set (contact closed)
1 TDC mark or degree scale on counterweight of crankshaft
2 Pointer for degree scale on crankshaft
3 Ignition distributor rotor
4 Cheesehead screw for fastening contact holder
5 Contact holder with adjusting slot
6 Lugs on contact breaker plate
7 Cable of contact breaker lever
8 Marking for cylinder 1 on ignition distributor housing
9 Holding angle with pin on contact breaker plate
10 Pull rod for vacuum adjustment (adjusting possibility of entire adjusting range)
11 Cheesehead screw for attaching holding angle and ground connection cable to contact breaker plate
12 Vacuum adjuster
13 Closing screw
14 Connection for vacuum line

the contact breaker about the cam to alter the ignition point. On some emission-controlled models a dual vacuum unit is fitted where the ignition is advanced normally with increasing suction but on deceleration the vacuum is switched to the other portion so that the ignition is fully retarded.

On some models a transistorized ignition system is fitted in place of the conventional system. The transistorized system is dealt with fully in **Section 9**.

2 Maintenance

Regularly wipe the top of the ignition coil, distributor cap and HT leads with a soft clean cloth to remove any dampness, oil or dirt from them.

The sparking plugs should be cleaned and tested at intervals of 8000 kilometres (6000 miles) and renewed at intervals of 16,000 kilometres (12,000 miles) as described in **Section 8**.

At fairly long intervals the distributor should be lubricated and the contact points checked and cleaned. **Avoid excessive lubrication on the distributor.**

Lubrication:

Free the clips and lift off the distributor cap, still attached to its leads. The distributor will then appear as shown in **FIG 1**. Grasp the rotor arm 3 and pull it firmly but squarely off from the distributor shaft. Pour in a few drops of oil through the points arrowed on the distributor shown in **FIG 2**. Use a clean finger to smear a little grease around the lobes of the cam at the point arrowed. **Do not allow any lubricant onto the contact points themselves and wipe away any surplus that is spilled.** Wipe the rotor arm and inside of the distributor cap clean before installing them in the reverse order of removal. Make sure that the lug in the arm aligns with the slot in the shaft and push the rotor arm fully down into position. Lugs and slots also align the distributor cap correctly.

3 The breaker points

Cleaning:

The points should have a frosted slate-grey colour for efficient operation. Oil or grease on the points will blacken them and may also show up as a thin smudgy line on the baseplate under the contacts. Cleaning in such cases should be carried out using a small stiff brush and chloroform or methylated spirits to remove all traces of lubricant from the points. If the contact points are badly blackened or burnt, the set should be renewed.

In the course of normal use metal will be transferred from one contact to the other, leaving a pit in one and forming a crater on the other. **No action need be taken over this until the build-up of metal has reached the same dimension as the correct contact gap.** When the build-up reaches this amount, discard the old points and install a new set. Only in an emergency should the points ever be cleaned by filing or grinding them down.

Spring tension:

The tension of the spring on the moving contact should be checked with a suitable spring gauge. Apply the load so that it is at right angles to the contact faces and pull until the points just open. Renew the contact set if the spring is weak.

Renewing contacts:

Refer to **FIG 1**. Remove the distributor cap and rotor arm. Take out the two screws 4 and 11 and remove the angle bracket 9. Slacken the nuts of the primary terminal and pull out the cable shoe 7. Remove the snap ring on the bearing pin and lift out the contact assembly holder 5.

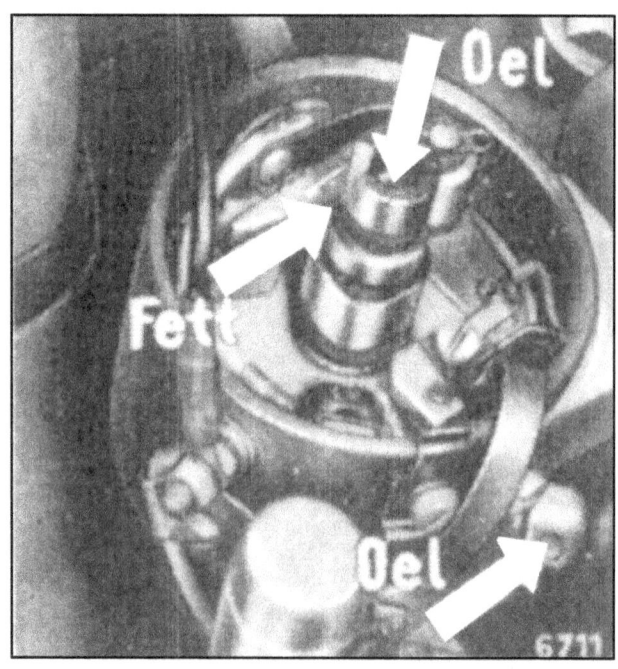

FIG 2 The distributor lubrication points

Oel = Oil   Fett = Grease

Wipe out dirt from the baseplate. Before installing a new set of contacts, wipe them over with a piece of cloth moistened in methylated spirits to remove any dirt or protective. Spread a clean film of grease over the cam surfaces and install the new set in the reverse order of removal. Check that the moving contact pivots freely about the bearing post. If the contact tends to stick, remove the contacts and lightly polish the bearing post with a very fine grade of emerycloth. Once the points have been installed, set the correct contact gap.

Adjusting the gap:

The most accurate method of setting the gap is to use a dwell meter with the engine running (or the distributor on a test stand).

Feeler gauges can be used to set the gap. On new contacts the gauge can be slid fully between the contacts but if the contacts have been in use for some time make sure that the gauge acts only between the unworn portions of the contacts, as shown in **FIG 3**, otherwise the gauge will bridge the gap and give a false reading. The correct gap is .3 to .4 mm (.012 to .016 inch) and .4 to .5 mm (.016 to .020 inch) for models fitted with transistorized ignition.

To alter the gap, slacken the screw 4 that secures the fixed contact and insert a screwdriver between the lugs 6 and slot in the end of the carrier 5. The gap can then be altered by twisting the screwdriver.

Crank the engine until the foot of the moving contact is free from the cam and the contacts are closed. Check that the contacts meet squarely and fully, adjusting as required by carefully bending the support of the fixed contact as required. Crank the engine further until the foot of the moving contact is against the lobe of the cam and the contacts are fully open. Fit a feeler gauge of the correct thickness between the contacts and adjust them until they lightly nip the gauge. Tighten the securing screw and check that the gap has not altered. It is advisable to crank the engine and check that the gap is correct at the other lobes of the cam.

If a dwell meter is used, the gap must be physically checked and a new set of contacts installed if the gap is below the minimum when the dwell angle is correct. Always set the gap to the upper limit to allow for wear in the moving foot, particularly when a new set of contacts have been fitted.

4 Ignition faults

Serious damage can be caused to the transistorized system if the checks are not carried out in accordance with **Section 9**.

A persistent misfire in the engine can be caused by defective ignition. The quickest way to pinpoint faults is to connect the engine to electronic test equipment, preferably with an oscilloscope, and the fault can then be readily and quickly identified.

Before checking the ignition, check the fuel system settings and also make sure that the contact points are clean and correctly set.

Start the engine and set it to a fast-idle. The best way is to prop down the accelerator pedal slightly with a weight. Allow the engine to run until it is warm.

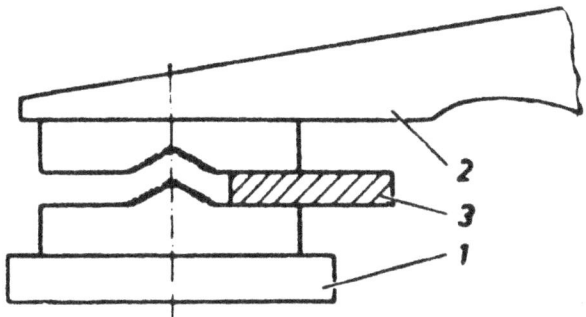

FIG 3 The correct positioning of the feeler gauge when setting the contacts gap

Use rags, gloves or specially insulated tongs and disconnect each HT lead in turn from its sparking plug while listening to the note of the engine. If the cylinder is not firing there will be no difference in the engine note or speed while if the cylinder is firing the speed will drop slightly. Check all the cylinders in turn in case more than one is defective.

When the faulty cylinder(s) have been found, stop the engine and fit an old sparking plug to the lead, after stopping the engine. Restart the engine and hold the lead so that the electrode of the sparking plug is approximately 5 mm ($\frac{3}{16}$ inch) away from a convenient grounded metal part, but not near the fuel system. If the lead and ignition are satisfactory there will be a regular stream of fat blue sparks. If it is found that all cylinders have poor sparks, disconnect the HT lead from the central electrode of the distributor cap and hold it 5 mm away from a grounded part. Crank the engine over on the starter motor and if the sparks are weak or poor either the ignition coil or central HT lead is defective.

If the sparks are satisfactory, remove and clean or renew the sparking plug. If the sparking plug is found to be satisfactory on pressure test but the engine still misfires, first try fitting a brand new sparking plug and if the defect is still present then it is caused by an engine defect.

If the spark to a cylinder is poor, examine the HT lead and renew it if it shows signs of burning, perishing or cracking. If the lead is satisfactory or the spark is still poor after renewing the lead, check the distributor cap and rotor arm. Wash them both with chloroform or methylated spirits, brushing out dirt from crevices with a small stiff brush. Check them both for cracks and renew if defective. A careful examination should be made of the distributor cap as hidden hairline cracks may be the cause of the trouble. Also check the cap for signs of 'tracking'. 'Tracking' shows up as thin black lines between electrodes or an electrode and the edge of the cap and again renewal is the only cure. Check that the carbon brush in the cap is undamaged and makes good contact with the brass on the rotor arm.

Testing the primary circuit:

Remove the distributor cap and crank the engine until the contact points are closed. Switch on the ignition and flick the points apart with a fingernail. If current is flowing there will be a small low-voltage spark across them.

A more accurate test can be carried out with the aid of a low-wattage test lamp. Disconnect the primary lead from between distributor and ignition coil and reconnect it with the test lamp in series. Slowly crank the engine over. The engine will be easier to turn if all the sparking plugs are removed and it should be cranked using the crankshaft damper. If the system is satisfactory, the test lamp will come on as the points close and then go out again as they open. If the lamp fails to come on at all, check that the points are closing fully and that they are clean. If the points are satisfactory, trace back through the wiring system until the fault or break is found and can be repaired.

If the lamp lights but does not go out at all there is a short circuit in the distributor. Check the contact points to make sure that they are opening and that they are correctly installed with all insulating washers in place. Check the wires in the distributor for breaks or frayed insulation. If the points and internal wires are satisfactory, repeat the test with the capacitor disconnected and if the lamp now operates correctly there is a short circuit in the distributor.

Capacitor:

Capacitor failure is usually rare. If the paper insulation in the unit fails, the spark in the area usually erodes away the foil so that the capacitor is self-healing for short circuits. A short-circuited capacitor can easily be found as described just previously.

An open circuit in the capacitor is more difficult to detect without special test equipment, though it may be suspected if the points are excessively 'blued' and starting is difficult. The best check is to fit a new capacitor and see if it cures the fault.

5 Removing the distributor

Free the clips and lift off the distributor cap, leaving it attached to the HT leads. If the cap is to be removed, label the leads before disconnecting them at either end so that they can be installed in the correct order.

Turn the engine until it is at TDC on No. 1 cylinder and the piston is at the end of the compression stroke. The engine timing marks are on the crankshaft damper and when the setting is correct the marks 8 on the rotor arm and distributor case, shown in **FIG 1**, will also be in line. To save having to reset the timing make aligning marks on the distributor body and engine. Free the clamp bolt and withdraw the distributor from the engine.

The distributor is installed in the reverse order of removal. The setting of the distributor drive gear has been dealt with in **Chapter 1**. If the marks 8 and the previously made marks on engine and distributor are aligned again, provided that the engine has not been cranked, then the ignition timing will not be lost. If the engine has been cranked, rotate it back to the correct position. The TDC marks are set on the crankshaft damper and the compression stroke of No. 1 cylinder is found by blocking the sparking plug hole with a thumb while cranking the engine slowly. There will be a pressure rise in the cylinder as the piston comes up on the compression stroke. If the rocker cover is removed the position can also be found as the valves on No. 1 cylinder will both be fully closed at the correct TDC.

6 Servicing the distributor

Typical distributor components are shown in **FIG 4**. It may be difficult to obtain spare parts if the distributor is worn and generally it will be found easier, and better, to install a new distributor rather than trying to repair a defective one.

1 Remove the distributor and take off the rotor arm 11. Take out the screws that secure the distributor clips, vacuum unit and capacitor. Free the connecting rod of the vacuum unit and remove the vacuum unit. Slacken the primary terminal nuts and free the capacitor lead so that the capacitor can be removed. The contact breaker assembly complete can then be lifted out from the distributor and serviced separately. Normally this is sufficient dismantling for cleaning and checking of the distributor parts.

2 **If further dismantling is required, carefully note the relation of the slot in the cam 6 to the offset of the drive dog 7.** Drive out the pin 16 so that the drive dog can be removed together with its thrust washers. Check the end of the shaft for burrs or damage, cleaning it by polishing with emerycloth, before pushing it out of the body.

3 The centrifugal mechanism can be dismantled by carefully freeing the calibrated springs 5 and removing the spring clips 4. Do not stretch or distort the calibrated springs when removing or installing them.

4 If the bushings 1a, 1b and 2 are worn, they can be pressed out with a suitable mandrel. New bushes must only be pressed in with a mandrel that has a highly polished spigot longer than the bush and of exactly the same diameter as the distributor or shaft. Lubricate the shaft liberally with oil and check that it rotates freely in the bushes, then run it in using a test stand.

The distributor is reassembled in the reverse order of dismantling, taking great care to ensure that all the parts are in their original alignments and that the cam slot is in the correct relation to the drive dog.

Before assembling the distributor, wash all the metal parts and felt pads in clean fuel. Lubricate the distributor as described in **Section 2** and also lightly lubricate the pivot and bearing points on the centrifugal advance mechanism with oil.

7 Setting the ignition timing

The timing data is given in Technical Data at the end of the manual.

Static setting:

1 Disconnect the low-tension lead from between the distributor and ignition coil and then reconnect it with a low-wattage test lamp in series. Take out the sparking plugs so that the engine will be easier to crank.

2 Crank the engine, in a forwards direction, until it is at TDC at the end of the compression stroke on No. 1 cylinder. When the engine is correctly set the pointer 2 should be on the 0 deg. mark on the damper 1 and the marks 8 on the distributor should be in line. If the marks 8 are not in line, reset the distributor drive as described in **Chapter 1**.

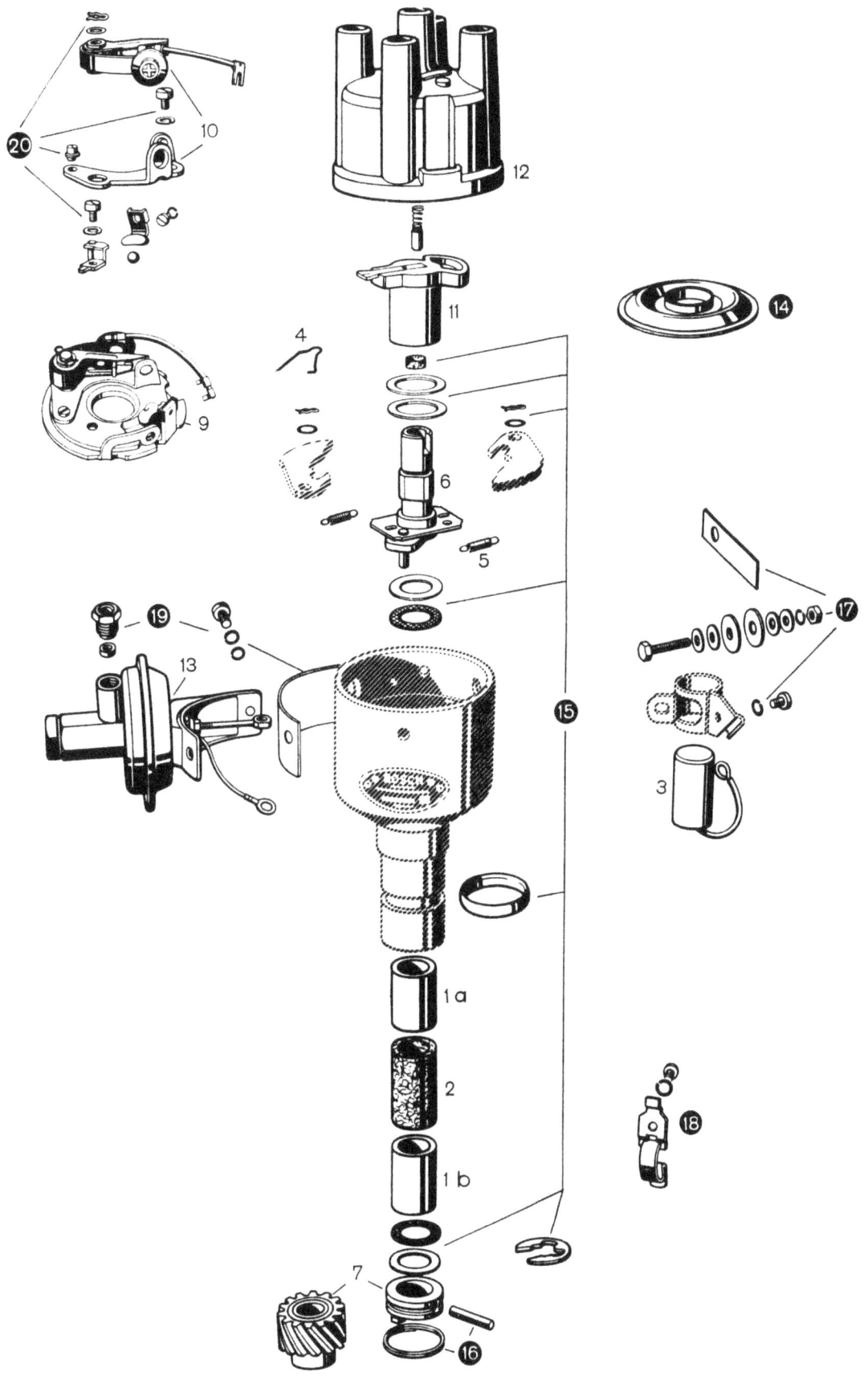

FIG 4 Typical distributor components

3 Crank the engine in a forwards direction for two turns and align the pointer 2 exactly to the correct timing mark on the damper. **If, at any time, the correct timing point is overshot turn the engine forwards for two more revolutions to ensure that all backlash is taken up.** If the engine is rotated backwards the backlash will not be taken up.

4 Slacken the distributor clamp bolt and switch on the ignition. On models fitted with fuel injection it is advisable to remove the fuse so that the fuel pump is not continuously running. Rotate the distributor body slightly in either direction until the point is found where the test lamp has just gone out, indicating that the contact points have just opened. Tighten the distributor clamp bolt to secure the distributor body in this position.

5 As a check, crank the engine forwards for two further revolutions, slowing down the rate of turning at the end of the second revolution. Stop turning the instant that the test lamp goes out, noting that it will have come on and gone out again each time that the contacts close and open, and if the timing is correct the pointer will again align with the correct timing mark on the damper.

6 Remove the test lamp and reconnect the low-tension lead. Install the distributor cap correctly.

Stroboscopic timing:

This is the most accurate method of setting the timing and is carried out with the engine running. The static timing must be set with reasonable accuracy to allow the engine to be started, warmed up and run safely. Run the engine until it has reached its normal operating temperature.

On the 280 S/8 models fitted with emission control and a double-cell vacuum unit on the distributor, disconnect the cable plug from the 100°C temperature switch in the thermostat housing. After adjustment, connect the lead to ground and check that the idle speed increases to between 1300 and 1500 rev/min before connecting the cable back to the temperature switch.

When the engine is hot, stop it and connect the stroboscopic lamp to the ignition circuit. Mark the edge of the pointer and the correct timing mark on the damper with thin white lines so that they can be easily seen. Restart the engine and set it to run at the correct speed. **Take great care to keep hands, tools or clothing well clear of the moving drive belts and cooling fan.** Set the lamp to shine on the timing marks and slightly slacken the clamp bolt on the distributor. Rotate the distributor body slightly in either direction until the timing mark line and edge of the pointer appear exactly in alignment. Tighten the distributor clamp bolt and restore the circuit to normal.

8 The sparking plugs

Removal:

Slacken each plug in turn with a well fitting box spanner or special wrench. Use an air line or tyre pump to blow away all loose dust and dirt from around the plugs and then unscrew them by hand. If the sparking plug is stiff, take great care not to strip the threads in the cylinder head. First try carefully unscrewing it with the wrench but stop trying as soon as the pressure required becomes heavy. Try screwing the plug in and out several times to the point where it is stiff before attempting to unscrew it further. If the plug does not yield to this treatment, wrap a piece of cloth around the base and soak it in paraffin, penetrating oil or even old hydraulic oil and leave it overnight to soften.

As the sparking plugs are removed they should be stored in order so that their firing ends can be examined.

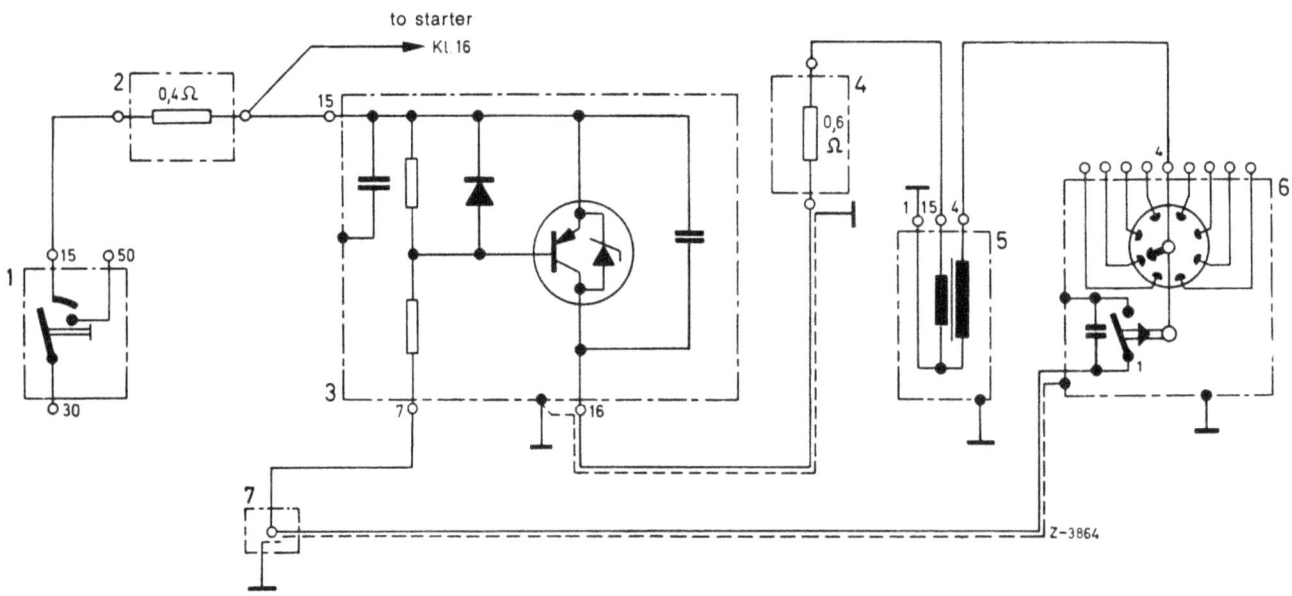

FIG 5 The transistorized ignition circuit

1 Ignition starting switch 3 Switchgear 5 Ignition coil 7 Cable connector (terminal 7
2 Series resistance 0.4 Ω 4 Series resistance 0.6 Ω 6 Ignition distributor switchgear ignition distributor)

Examination:

The colour and condition of the deposits on the firing ends of the sparking plugs will give a good guide to the conditions inside the combustion chambers. After examining the plugs, throw away any that have cracked insulators or badly burnt electrodes without bothering to have them cleaned and tested.

A light powdery deposit ranging in colour from brown to greyish tan, coupled with light wear on the electrodes, indicates that the conditions are normal. Much constant-speed or city driving will leave the deposits white or yellowish though in all cases cleaning and testing are all that is required.

If the deposits are wet and black they are caused by oil entering the combustion chamber, either up past worn rings and pistons or down past worn valves and guides. In some cases renewal of the valve stem seals (see **Chapter 1**) may provide a partial cure but usually an engine overhaul is the only full cure. Fitting a hotter-running grade of sparking plug may help to alleviate the problem.

If the deposits are black but dry and fluffy looking they are caused by incomplete combustion. This may be caused by excessive idling—particularly if all plugs are similarly affected—but it may be caused by defective ignition, defective sparking plug, or running with too rich a mixture.

Overheated sparking plugs have a white blistered look about the central insulator coupled with excessive burning of the electrodes. If lead-based fuels are used there may be glints of metal on the central electrode and insulator. Some possible causes are: engine overheating, very weak mixture, incorrectly set ignition timing, incorrect grade of plug, or running at high-speeds with the car overloaded.

Cleaning, adjusting and testing:

Wash oily plugs in fuel before attempting to clean them further. Have the plugs cleaned on an abrasive-blasting machine and pressure tested after attention to the electrodes.

Trim the electrodes square with a fine file and then adjust them to the correct gap by bending the side electrode only. **Do not bend the central electrode as this will crack the insulator.**

Check that the plugs spark under pressure. While still applying pressure to the firing ends, drip a little oil onto the junction of the insulator with the body. Reject any plugs that have air bubbles forming in the oil.

Scrub the threads of the plug with a wire brush to remove any deposits left after abrasive-blasting and clean the external portion of the insulator with tri-chlorethylene, methylated spirits or unleaded fuel.

Installation:

If the threads in the cylinder head are dirty, clean them using a well greased tap. Failing a tap use an old sparking plug with crosscuts down the threads.

Graphite grease only may be used on the threads of the sparking plugs as any other grease will bake hard and may lock the plugs to the cylinder head.

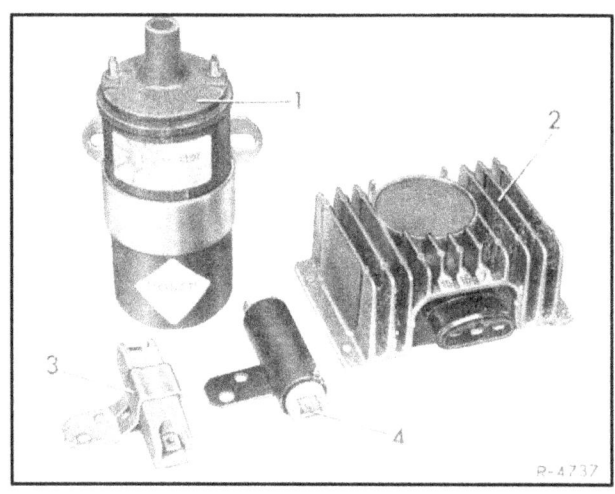

FIG 6 The components of the transistorized ignition

1 Ignition coil   3 Series resistance 0.6 Ω
2 Switchgear   4 Series resistance 0.4 Ω

Screw the plugs in by hand until they bottom and then tighten them using a torque spanner to a torque of 3 to 3.5 kg m. If a torque spanner is not available, tighten them by a maximum of half-a-turn from the handtight position. Leaks are cured by installing new gaskets to the plugs and tightening them to the correct load, not by wringing down the plugs until they almost shear.

9 The transistorized ignition

The wiring circuit for the system is shown in **FIG 5**. The contact breaker is similar to the one installed in conventional systems but instead of taking the full primary current it only acts as a trigger for the transistor system. This means that there are lower operating currents through the contacts and there are no induced back voltages from the primary coils of the coil so that contact life is greatly extended and the likelihood of trouble reduced. When the contacts are closed the transistor conducts and current passes through the primary coils of the ignition coil. As soon as the points open the transistor locks and cuts the current through the primary coils. A Zener diode is fitted to protect the transistor against overvoltage and capacitors are installed to prevent the entry of induced voltages from the car electrical system. The components are shown in **FIG 6**.

Testing:

An accurate voltmeter should be used for the tests. With the ignition switched off, crank the engine until the contact points in the distributor are closed. Connect the voltmeter between the ignition coil and ground so that the red lead is connected to terminal 15 and the black lead to ground. Switch on the ignition and the voltmeter should read 2.6 to 3.5 volt.

The resistances and the ignition coil should be tested using a conventional resistance measuring bridge, and the temperature noted, as normal resistance meters and multi-reading instruments are not sufficiently accurate.

For full checks and diagnosis it is advisable to take the car to a service agent equipped with electronic test units, and this includes diagnosis for misfiring. When setting the ignition timing it is advisable to use a voltmeter rather than a test lamp to determine the exact points at which the points open, as the system can be overloaded by the use of a test lamp.

Not all dwell meters or stroboscopic lamps can be connected to the system.

10 Fault diagnosis

(a) Engine will not fire

1 Battery discharged
2 Distributor points dirty or out of adjustment
3 Distributor cap defective
4 Defective low-tension circuit
5 Defective rotor arm (or arm omitted on reassembly)
6 Broken contact spring or points stuck open
7 Water on HT leads
8 Defective ignition coil
9 Defective HT lead between coil and distributor

(b) Engine misfires

1 Check 2, 3, 4, 8 and 9 in (a)
2 Weak contact breaker spring
3 Defective HT lead
4 Sparking plug defective, fouled, loose or incorrectly gapped
5 Ignition too far advanced

(c) Points excessively blued or burnt

1 Defective capacitor or radio suppressor
2 Incorrectly installed radio suppressor
3 Incorrect alignment of the points
4 Charging system at too high a voltage
5 Extended operation at high speeds

CHAPTER 4 – THE COOLING SYSTEM

1 Description
2 Maintenance
3 The radiator
4 The thermostat
5 The water pump
6 The drive belts
7 The cooling fan
8 Frost precautions
9 Fault diagnosis

1 Description

The normal thermo-syphonic flow of coolant around the cooling system is boosted by the action of a centrifugal engine-driven pump. The coolant is pumped into the engine and then rises through the water jackets around the cylinders and through the passages in the cylinder head, taking away excess heat. The coolant passes out through an elbow on the cylinder head and into the top tank of the radiator. Air passing outside the radiator core cools the coolant as it passes through the tubes and the coolant is then drawn from the bottom tank of the radiator by the action of the water pump. The passage of air over the radiator core is usually caused by the motion of the car but a cooling fan is fitted to the water pump to ensure movement of air even when the car is stationary or travelling slowly.

A thermostat is fitted into the outlet elbow from the engine to ensure a rapid warm up and to keep the engine temperature up within the operating range even in very cold weather. A wax filled element is used and when the coolant is cold the wax is solid and keeps the valve closed. The coolant is diverted back through a bypass hose directly to the water pump and from there returns into the engine. There are no heat losses from the radiator and, as not all the coolant is heated, a rapid warm up is assured. When the coolant reaches its normal operating temperature, the wax expands and allows the valve to open. The coolant then passes normally to the radiator where it is cooled before returning to the engine.

The system is sealed apart from the filler to the radiator and this has a special cap fitted to it, shown sectioned in **FIG 1**. The cap is secured by a double acting bayonet type fitting, the first part of the turn allowing the cap to lift without coming free and the second part of the turn freeing the cap. The outer valve seats against the filler neck when the cap is fully closed and is held down by the spring. When the internal pressure reaches 1 kg/sq cm (approximately 15 lb/sq in) the outer valve lifts off its seat and allows surplus coolant or air to escape down the overflow pipe. By pressurizing the system it raises the boiling point of the coolant and ensures that boiling will not occur at localized hot spots in the engine. It also allows the engine to be run at a higher temperature which makes it more efficient and allows the use of a smaller radiator for the same rate of heat loss. The inner valve of the filler cap opens at a suction of .1 kg/sq cm (1.5 lb/sq in) to prevent a vacuum from forming and collapsing the hoses as the system cools down. **Never attempt to remove the radiator filler cap when the engine temperature is above 90°C, or boiling coolant will be forced out over the operator's hand.**

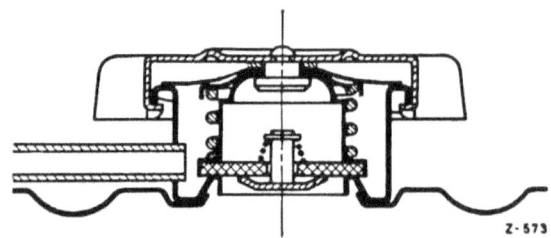

FIG 1 A sectioned view of the radiator filler cap

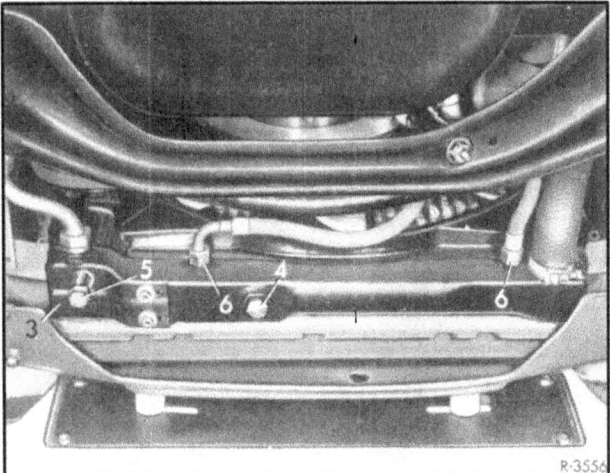

FIG 2 The radiator and oil coolers

3 Air oil cooler
4 Drain plug coolant
5 Drain plug air oil cooler
6 Transmission fluid cooler connections

On models fitted with automatic transmission an oil cooler is fitted into the bottom tank of the radiator so that the transmission fluid will be cooled by the coolant. An air/oil cooler is also fitted to the lefthand side of the radiator for engine oil cooling.

As the engine contains large amounts of light-alloy it is essential that some form of corrosion inhibitor is added to the coolant. Antifreeze contains its own inhibitors, which last effectively for a year, so no other inhibitor need be added with antifreeze. In temperate climates it is best to leave the antifreeze in all year round and discard it at the beginning of winter, filling up with fresh antifreeze after flushing the system. A list of generally available inhibitors is given in Technical Data and these should be added at the rate of 2.5 to 5 cc per litre of water in the system.

2 Maintenance

There are no lubrication points in the system.

Draining:

If this is being carried out for repairs or other work to the engine or ancilliaries, complete draining is not essential and it is sufficient to remove the filler cap and drain plug from the radiator. A typical radiator is shown from underneath in **FIG 2**. The oil cooler lines 6 are only fitted on models with automatic transmission.

If the system is only being drained for repairs, collect the coolant into a clean container so that it can be returned to the system after the repairs have been completed.

If complete draining is required, set the heater controls to HOT. Take off the filler cap from the radiator and remove the drain plug 4 from under the radiator. Remove drain plug from the engine. If the flow from the drains is sluggish, carefully poke them clear with a short piece of wire.

Filling:

Refit the drain plugs, using new sealing washers if fitted, and tighten engine plug to 2 to 2.5 kg m (14.5 to 17 lb ft) and the radiator plug to .6 to 1 kg m (4 to 7 lb ft). Set the heater controls to hot. Mix up the antifreeze or inhibitor with soft clean water to make a volume slightly less than required by the cooling system. Pour the coolant in slowly through the filler neck until it reaches the tag in the neck indicating the correct cold level. Start the engine and allow it to idle for a few minutes to disperse the air in the system. Top up to the correct level.

When the system is hot the level will be approximately 1.5 cm ($\frac{1}{2}$ inch) above the normal cold level. Overfilling is wasteful as the surplus will be vented overboard through the overflow pipe. Hot water can be added at any time to the cooling system but if cold water is to be added when the engine is hot the engine should be left running.

Flushing:

The system should be flushed out at yearly intervals when renewing the antifreeze. The system can be flushed through by running water in through the filler and allowing it to run out of the drains until it comes out clean. This method will be more effective if the thermostat is removed.

FIG 3 The radiator attachments

1 Sealing strip   2 Rubber loop   3 Air oil cooler

Pressure flushing in a reverse direction can be carried out by an agent to free and remove obstinate deposits of sludge.

A more effective way is to degrease and then descale the system. Drain the system and refill it with a 5 per cent solution of P-3 (Henkel degreasing solution) and then use the car normally for 24 hours, making sure that long enough runs are carried out to ensure that the coolant reaches its normal operating temperature. At the end of the period drain out the degreasing solution and flush through with clean water. Refill the system with a 5 per cent soda solution and leave this in the system for 24 hours. During this time take the car for as long a run as possible as the descaling action is more effective the hotter the system. At the end of the second 24 hours, drain out the soda solution and flush through thoroughly with clean water. In extreme cases it may be necessary to remove the radiator, invert it and flush through with clean water to remove scale from the tubes. Even if the radiator is not removed, blow through from the engine side with an airline or hosepipe to remove accumulations of dirt and dead insects. Again in extreme cases the radiator will have to be removed so that the fins can be soaked and scrubbed in a very hot weak detergent solution.

Fill the system correctly with fresh coolant.

Hoses:

At regular intervals, especially when the cooling system is empty, examine the hoses. Squeeze them gently between the fingers to check for hardening, softening, collapsing, perishing or cracking. Check that the hose clips are tight but not so tight that they are cutting into the hoses.

Renew any hoses or hose clips that are defective before they have a chance to burst or leak. After slackening the clip, pull the hose off its connector with a twisting motion. Press the new hose on so that it and the hose clip are well beyond the annular bead around the connector. Water or soft soap may be used as a lubricant for tight hoses but under no circumstances use oil or grease as they will perish the material of the hose.

3 The radiator

The cleaning of the radiator has been dealt with in the previous section.

Removal:

Drain the cooling system. The attachments are shown in **FIG 3**. Drain the oil cooler for the engine through the drain plug 5 shown in **FIG 2**. Disconnect the oil cooler lines for both the engine and transmission if automatic transmission is fitted. The lines should be blanked and the adaptors to the coolers blanked to prevent the ingress of dirt. Remove the radiator guard and disconnect the coolant hoses from the radiator. Support the radiator and disconnect the rubber loops 2 shown in **FIG 3** and lift the radiator out of the car, collecting the radiator guard.

Install the radiator in the reverse order of removal. After the radiator has been fitted, check the engine oil level and automatic transmission fluid level (see **Chapter 7**) as well as making sure that the cooling system is correctly filled.

Oil coolers should be flushed through with paraffin or fuel and then allowed to dry in air to clean them out. A special spray gun can be used as this will assist in flushing out any dirt. The transmission oil cooler should be cleaned whenever the transmission fluid is changed.

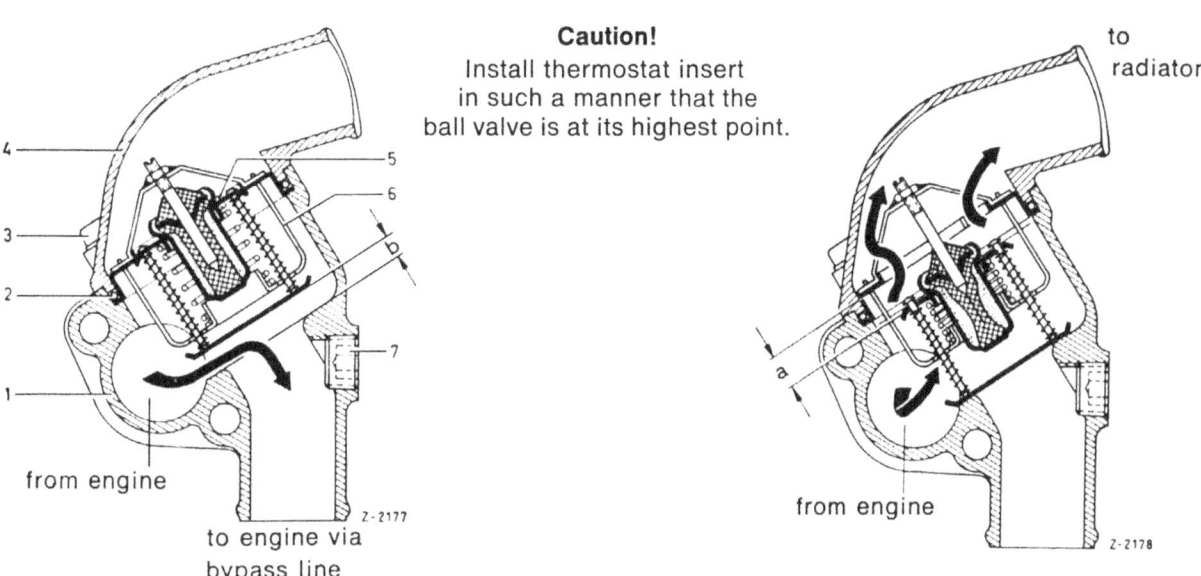

FIG 4   The operation of the thermostat valve

Main valve closed
Bypass valve fully opened
Stroke b = 6–7.5 mm
at 0 to approx. 78° C

1 Thermostat
2 Sealing ring
3 Hex. screw
4 Cover

5 Ball valve
6 Thermostat insert
7 Closing plug

Main valve opened
Bypass line closed
Stroke a = 8 mm
at approx. 91–94° C

4 The thermostat

The operation of the thermostat valve is shown in **FIG 4**.

Removal:

Drain the cooling system so that the level is below that of the thermostat. Remove the bolts 3 that secure the cover 4 and ease off the cover. The water hose should be sufficiently flexible to allow the cover to be moved out of the way without having to disconnect the hose. Remove the sealing ring 2 and withdraw the element 6.

Install the valve in the reverse order of removal. The ball valve 5 must be fitted to the highest point and the seal 2 only installed after the element 6 is in place. Evenly tighten all four bolts 3 when the cover is in place and refill the cooling system.

Grades:

A thermostat with a higher opening temperature can be fitted in winter to ensure a shorter warm-up period as well as making the heater more efficient. **The winter grade should not be used in summer conditions as it may lead to overheating of the engine.**

FIG 5 The drive belts installed

1 Tensioning roller
A V-belt high-pressure pump
B V-belt refrigerator compressor
C V-belt alternator and water pump

FIG 6 The installation of the steering pump

Testing:

As a rough check, feel the top tank of the radiator as the engine warms up. There should be a sudden warming of the tank as the thermostat opens.

For accurate testing the thermostat must be removed from the engine. Suspend, not lay, the thermostat into a container of water over a heater. Stir the water with a thermometer while slowly heating the water and note the temperature at which the valve begins to open. The standard grade of thermostat should start to open within a few degrees of 78 to 79°C and the winter grade near 87°C. If the valve does not start to open within a few degrees of the correct temperature or if the valve sticks in any position then the thermostat is defective and must be renewed. No repairs can be carried out to a defective thermostat.

5 The water pump

The water pump can be removed from the engine after removal of the drive belts and the cooling fan assembly. Bolts secure the pump but the actual attachments may vary slightly through the range. On some earlier models there may be a small copper bleed pipe leading from the pump to the cylinder head, and this pipe will be secured by two banjo bolts. Drain the cooling system before starting to remove the pump.

Install the pump in the reverse order of removal, using new seals and gaskets.

In some cases the water pump can be dismantled and repaired, but special tools and a press are essential. Some parts are also heated before installation so that they form a shrink fit. For these reasons the old water pump should be taken to a service agent for repair or exchange, as required.

6 The drive belts

The runs of the various belts are shown in **FIG 5**. The belts are checked for tension by applying a pressure of 6 kg (13 lb) and noting the amount of deflection from

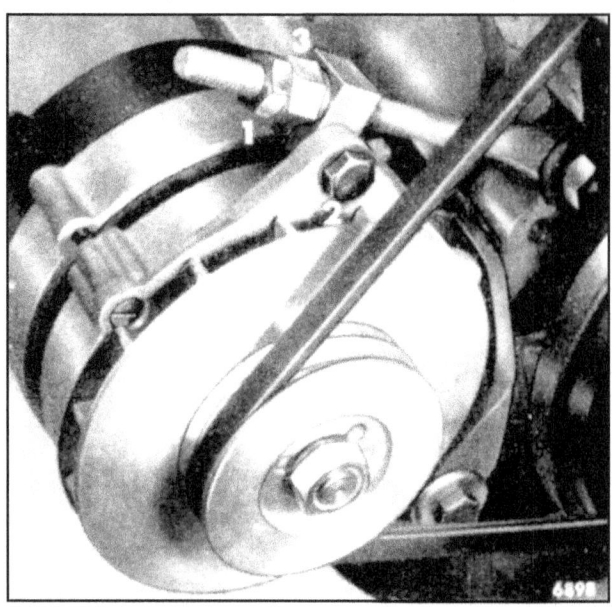

FIG 7 The adjustment point for a standard alternator

the straight line. Moderate thumb pressure will be approximately correct. If the belts are too tight, they will cause damage to bearings and rapid wear in the belts, while if they are too slack they will slip and not transmit drive. The correct deflections for the belts shown in the figure are as follows:

Steering pump **A**	7 mm (.3 inch)
Air-conditioning **B**	13 mm (.5 inch)
Alternator and water pump **C**	10 mm (.4 inch)

and the deflection is taken at the centre of the longest run.

Adjusting steering pump:

The attachments of the pump are shown in **FIG 6**. Slacken the two front bolts, the bolt 18, and the counter nut 15. Adjust to the correct tension using the nut 16 and then tighten all the attachments again.

Adjusting air-conditioning:

The correct tension is set by moving the idler pulley 1 (see **FIG 5**).

Adjusting alternator:

On the standard alternator the adjustment point is shown in **FIG 7**. Slacken the nut 1 and bolt 2 then use the nut 3 to set the correct belt tension. Firmly tighten the nut 1 and bolt 2 when the adjustment is correct.

If a 55 amp alternator is fitted the drive belts are shown in **FIG 8. The two belts 13, though of differing lengths, must be renewed as a set.** The two belts are tensioned at the alternator after slackening the bolts 8 and 11. Use a wooden lever behind the drive end bracket of the alternator 1 to pull the alternator out until the tension is correct and the belts can be tightened again. The long belt should be set to a deflection of 10 mm (.4 inch) under a load of 6 kg (13 lb). On the initial adjustment after fitting new belts it will be found that the short belt is slack. Do not tighten the long belt further in an attempt to take up this slack. After a little use the long belt will stretch and when it is again adjusted to its correct tension the shorter belt will also come under tension.

7 The cooling fan

The cooling fan is fitted with a viscosity coupling operated by a thermostat so that the fan does not take full power when it is not required.

A sectioned view of the coupling is shown in **FIG 9**. The unit is sealed and cannot be repaired if it is defective. **The unit should always be stored and transported in an upright condition.**

The input shaft 4 is bolted to the water pump and revolves with it at a speed proportional to the engine. The drive plate 2 is driven by the input shaft. The clutch body 3 fits closely to the driven plate with only a small air gap separating them. The reservoir 13 is filled with a silicone fluid of constant viscosity. When the parts are moving, the centrifugal force and relative movement pushes the silicone fluid out through the outlet bore 6 so that the fluid all returns to the reservoir. The body 3 is then practically free from the drive plate 2 and the fan blades are not driven. This can be checked by starting the engine from cold and allowing it to run for a few minutes. When the engine is stopped the fan blades should revolve freely. As the temperature of the air from the radiator rises, it heats the bimetallic strip 8 causing it to bend and press in on the thrust pin 7. This allows the valve lever 12 to progressively open the port 11 and allow the fluid to pass into the air space between the clutch body and drive plate. Drive is then transmitted through the silicone fluid to the fan blades. Check this

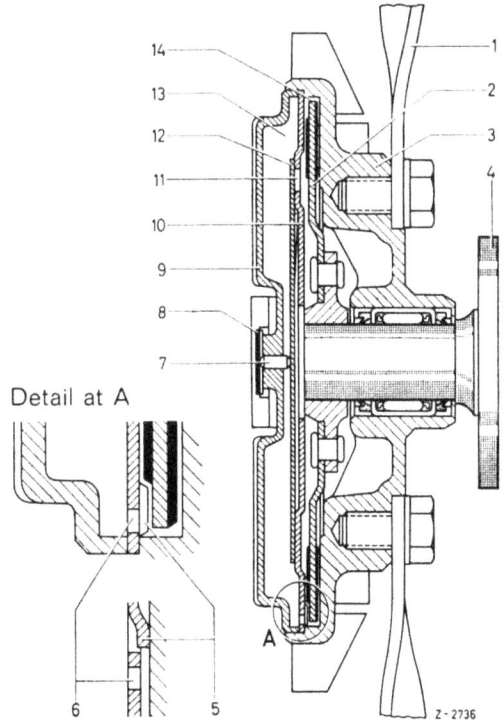

FIG 9 Sectioned view of the visco fan coupling

1 Fan
2 Drive pulley (primary member)
3 Coupling body (secondary member)
4 Drive shaft with flange
5 Oil scraper lug
6 Return flow hole
7 Thrust pin
8 Bimetallic strip
9 Cover (secondary member)
10 Intermediate plate
11 Flow-in hole
12 Valve lever
13 Supply chamber
14 Working chamber

FIG 8 The adjustment point for a 55 amp alternator

by running the engine until it is overheated and after stopping the engine the fan blades should only be able to turn with heavy pressure. If the radiator was blanked off to ensure that the engine was hot, the engine should be run for a few minutes with the blanking removed so that air from the radiator can heat the bimetallic strip.

The cooling fan runs at approximately 25 per cent of engine speed to ensure that accessories receive a flow of cooling air at all times. When the engine is hot to the maximum speed of the fan is limited to 3400 rev/min by the slip of the silicone fluid. Full engagement is not obtained until the air temperature from the radiator exceeds 62°C.

If the coolant temperature rises to a dangerous level, stop the car and allow it to cool. Check that the drive belt has not broken or the tension slipped. **Wait until the engine temperature has dropped below 90°C before removing the radiator filler cap and checking that the coolant level is correct.** If these are satisfactory and no other cause of the overheating can be found it is likely that the viscosity coupling is defective. Check if the fan blades spin freely with the bimetallic strip hot. Inter-city driving with a defective viscosity coupling will present no problems as the water pump will circulate the coolant and the passage of air will keep the engine cool. If there is still some drive in the coupling, keep the engine speed high in cities to obtain the benefit of the drive, but if the coupling has totally failed, keep the engine speed low and allow frequent stops for cooling down.

8 Frost precautions

Antifreeze should always be used in freezing weather. The thermostat limits the flow of coolant through the radiator and in extreme conditions the water in the bottom of the radiator may freeze even with the engine running. Draining overnight is not always an adequate precaution as some water will remain in the heater.

Provided that the engine is in good condition, serviced correctly and adequate antifreeze is used, the engine should start satisfactorily down to temperatures of —25 to —30°C (—13 to —22°F) without taking any special precautions. In extreme cold, drain out the coolant and preheat it before pouring it back into the system will assist in starting. In such cases, removal of the battery and storing it overnight in a warm room will increase its efficiency and therefore make starting easier. Platinum-tipped sparking plugs may also be used but it must be noted that the maximum engine speed must be severely reduced when these plugs are fitted.

If the car is kept regularly in very cold climates, consideration should be given to fitting a reputable make of immersion heater into a water hose so that the coolant can be kept warm overnight. This will not only give easier starting but will reduce the engine wear as well.

The capacities of the cooling system and the percentages of antifreeze required are all given in Technical Data.

9 Fault diagnosis
(a) Internal water leakage
1 Loose cylinder head bolts
2 Defective cylinder head gaskets
3 Cracked cylinder head or cylinder block
4 Warped or damaged block or head faces
5 Defective oil cooler

(b) Poor circulation
1 Perished or collapsed coolant hoses
2 Defective thermostat
3 Low coolant level
4 Loose or broken drive belt
5 Engine water passages restricted
6 Radiator tubes blocked

(c) Corrosion
1 Impurities in the water
2 Lack of inhibitor or antifreeze
3 Inhibitor or antifreeze exhausted
4 Lack of regular draining and flushing

(d) Overheating
1 Check (a) and (b)
2 Incorrect ignition timing
3 Mixture too weak
4 Low oil level in sump
5 Sludge in crankcase
6 Binding brakes
7 Slipping clutch or defective automatic transmission
8 Choked exhaust
9 Tight engine
10 Defective viscosity coupling for cooling fan

CHAPTER 5 – CLUTCH

1 Description
2 Maintenance
3 Servicing hydraulic components
4 The slave cylinder
5 The master cylinder
6 Bleeding the clutch hydraulic system
7 The clutch release bearing
8 Servicing the clutch
9 The earlier type of clutch
10 Fault diagnosis

1 Description

A sectioned view of the assembled clutch is shown in **FIG 1** and the components are shown in **FIG 2**. All 280 SL/8 models and earlier versions of other models (up to May 1969) are fitted with a slightly differing clutch slave cylinder and release mechanism. The differences of this type will be dealt with in **Section 9**.

The clutch cover assembly 1 is bolted to the engine flywheel so that the cover assembly rotates with the engine. The driven plate assembly 2 has a splined hub which fits onto the splines of the transmission input shaft. The clutch cover assembly contains a diaphragm spring which presses the pressure plate firmly forwards. When the parts are assembled, the pressure plate grips the driven plate 2, by its friction linings, between the face of the flywheel and the face of the pressure plate so that the driven plate is forced to revolve and drive is therefore transmitted from the engine to the transmission.

A hydraulic master cylinder is connected to the clutch pedal so that when the pedal is pressed hydraulic pressure is generated in the master cylinder. This pressure is led to the slave cylinder 8 through a system of flexible and metal pipes. When pressure is applied the piston of the slave cylinder extends, pivots the release lever 6 in such a way that the release bearing 4 presses the fingers of the diaphragm spring forwards. This action pivots the diaphragm spring so that its outer edge draws back the pressure plate, releasing the pressure on the driven plate. The driven plate and transmission are then free to revolve independently or even come to a stop with the engine still running.

When the clutch pedal is released, the pressure on the driven plate is gradually taken up and at first it slips to give a smooth take-up of drive.

The clutch slave cylinder is of the self-adjusting type.

2 Maintenance

Master cylinder:

At regular intervals check the fluid level in the master cylinder reservoir. The reservoir is fitted to the rear bulkhead of the engine compartment. If the level is low, wipe the top of the reservoir and filler cap before removing the cap, to prevent dirt from falling into the reservoir. Top up only with an approved fluid, such as ATE Blue or one that meets the SAE 70 R 3 specification. **The use of an incorrect fluid can cause the seals in the system to fail.**

If constant topping-up is required it is likely that there is a leak in the pipelines. A leak in the system may mean that the clutch cannot be fully disengaged and eventually if all the fluid escapes the clutch cannot be operated at all.

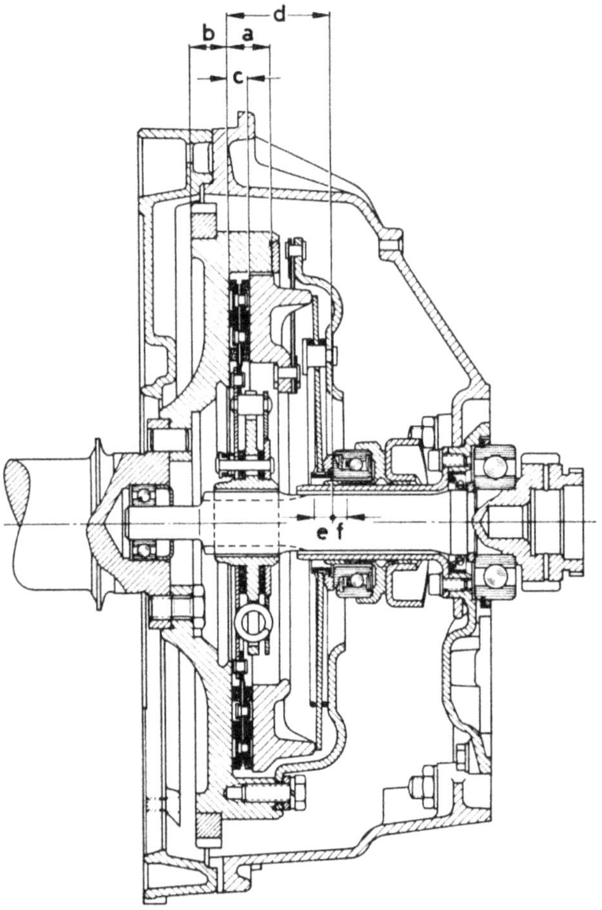

FIG 1 A sectioned view of the later clutch assembled

a. Indicates the distance between the clutch face and the contact face at the flywheel;
b. Indicates the distance between the clutch face and the flywheel attaching flange;
c. Indicates the thickness of the new driven plate in compressed condition (clutch contact pressure);
d. Indicates a control dimension between the clutch face at the flywheel and the external thrust ring face at the clutch with new driven plate.
e. Indicates the throwout travel
f. Indicates the thrust ring travel due to permissible wear of the driven plate.

Slave cylinder:

The slave cylinder is fitted with a spring behind the piston so that all clearance in the system is taken up. As a result no adjustments are required. However, the clutch plate should be periodically checked for wear. The method of checking the earlier clutches is dealt with in **Section 9**. Parts do not require to be removed or dismantled in order to check for wear. A measuring gauge 115 589 07 23 00 is used as shown in **FIG 3**. The piston rod has a narrow portion on it, as shown in **FIG 4**, and when there is no significant wear the fork of the gauge slides onto the narrow portion so that the notches on the gauge are hidden. When the wear is excessive, the fork cannot slide onto the thrust rod and the notches are left, showing when the gauge is pushed in as far as it will go. Renew the driven plate assembly when the notches are no longer covered.

Pedal clearance:

This is not strictly maintenance and normally only needs to be carried out after the master cylinder or pedal parts have been disturbed.

It is essential that there is a small clearance between the pushrod on the pedal and the master cylinder piston. If the clearance is not present, the master cylinder piston will not return fully and pressure will build up in the system, making the clutch slip and spin. The actual clearance cannot be measured, as it is hidden inside the master cylinder, and it must be set by feel using the pedal. Operate the pedal by hand as the foot is not sensitive enough to detect the change in pressure when the pushrod contacts the master cylinder. The adjustment is made by altering the eccentric bolt that secures the pushrod to the pedal.

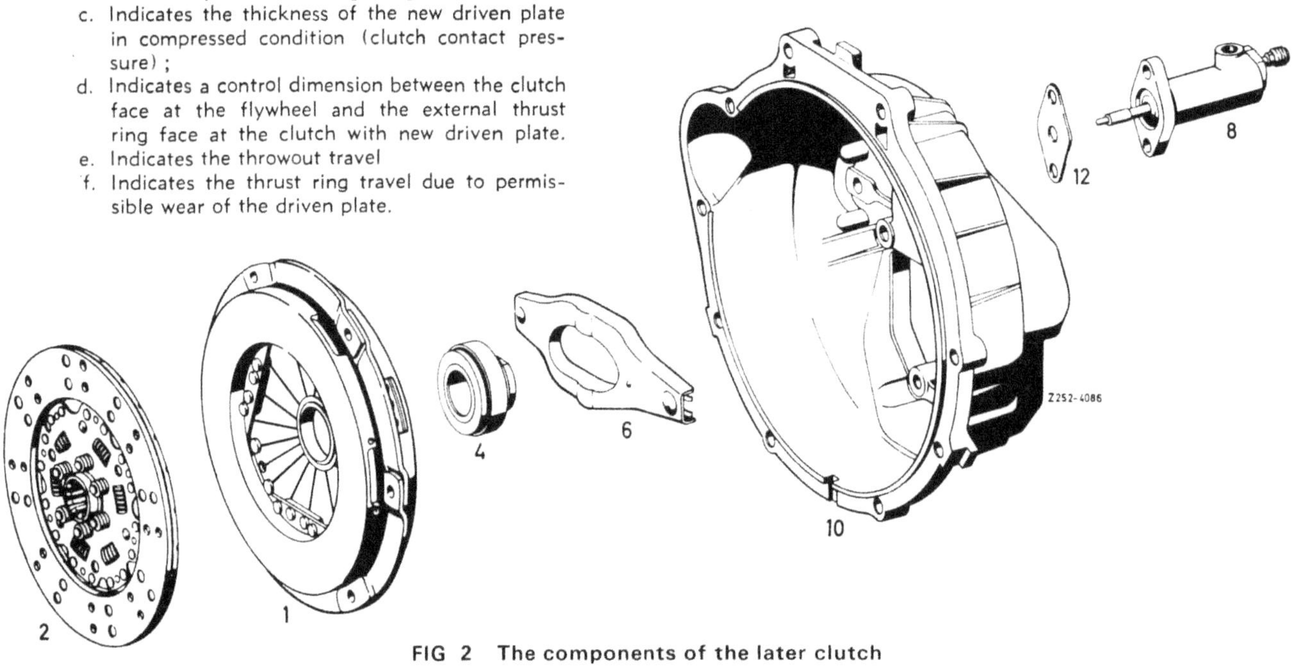

FIG 2 The components of the later clutch

1 Diaphragm or spring plate clutch
2 Driven plate
4 Throwout (from May 69)
6 Throwout rocker (from May 69)
8 Slave cylinder (from May 69)
10 Clutch housing (as from May 69)
12 Shim

3 Servicing hydraulic components

To save repetition for individual components, general notes on servicing all hydraulic components are given in this section. This section also applies to the components of the brake system (see **Chapter 11**).

It is essential that strict cleanliness is observed when dealing with any parts of the hydraulic system. This includes washing the outside of a component before dismantling it, washing the internal parts in the correct type of solvent as they are dismantled and then washing them again before reassembling them. Benches should be covered with clean paper and the hands should be washed with soap and water before starting reassembly operations.

The method of dismantling the component will be given in the relevant section. In some cases the internal parts are held in place by circlips and circlip pliers should be used to remove these, taking great care not to damage or score the bore. Tap the open end of the cylinder onto the palm of the hand or use gentle air pressure through the inlet to dislodge the internal parts.

Seals:

All the old seals should be discarded as they are removed and new seals installed on reassembly. Sets of new seals for individual components are available in service kits and these kits usually contain new parts, such as circlips and dust excluders, which should also be used on reassembly. Take great care when ordering parts as the diameter of cylinders may not only vary between models but with year of manufacture.

If the old seals are to be used again they must be closely examined. Do not refit seals which are in the slightest way defective or suspect. **Do not turn seals inside out to check them as this will cause damage.** Check the lips for wearing or scoring, and check the material for softening, swelling, or any other form of failure. If the incorrect type of fluid has been used, all the seals in the system will swell and fail, so all seals in the system must be renewed and the pipelines and parts flushed through liberally with methylated spirits (denatured alcohol).

No tools other than the fingers should be used to refit the seals. Dip the seal into clean hydraulic fluid and refit it wet, working it around until it is fully and squarely seated. Make sure that the seals are installed so that their lips face in the correct direction, into the high pressure side.

Cleaning:

Only methylated spirits or hydraulic fluid of the correct grade may be allowed to come into contact with the seals. Once the unit has been dismantled, the metal parts only may be cleaned with any suitable solvent, provided that it evaporates completely and rapidly. **It is essential that no traces of other solvents remain when the unit is being reassembled, and the parts should be swilled in methylated spirits as a safety precaution.**

Small bores and ports can be cleaned out by blowing through them or else using a blunt-ended piece of soft wire.

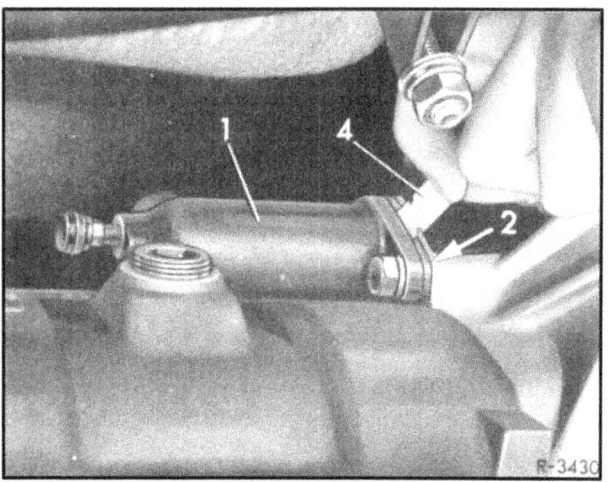

FIG 3 Checking the later clutch driven plate for wear, using the special gauge at the slave cylinder

1 Slave cylinder   2 Shim (plastics)   3 Measuring template

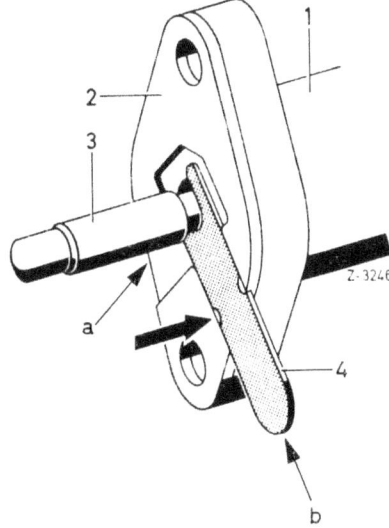

FIG 4 The gauge fitting to the pushrod when wear is within limits

1 Clutch slave cylinder
2 Shim (plastics)
3 Thrust rod
4 Measuring template
115 589 07 23 00

a Direction of measuring on lefthand steering vehicle with steering wheel and center shift, as well as on righthand steering vehicles with center shift
b Direction of measuring on righthand steering vehicles with steering wheel shift

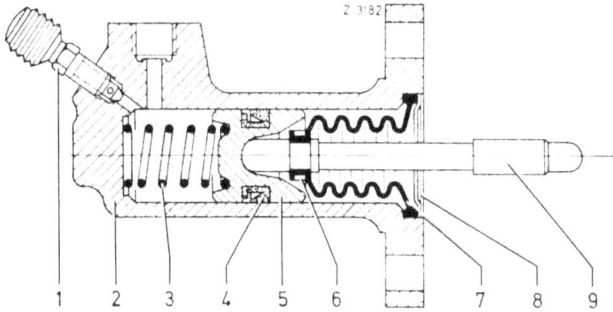

FIG 5 A sectioned view of the later slave cylinder

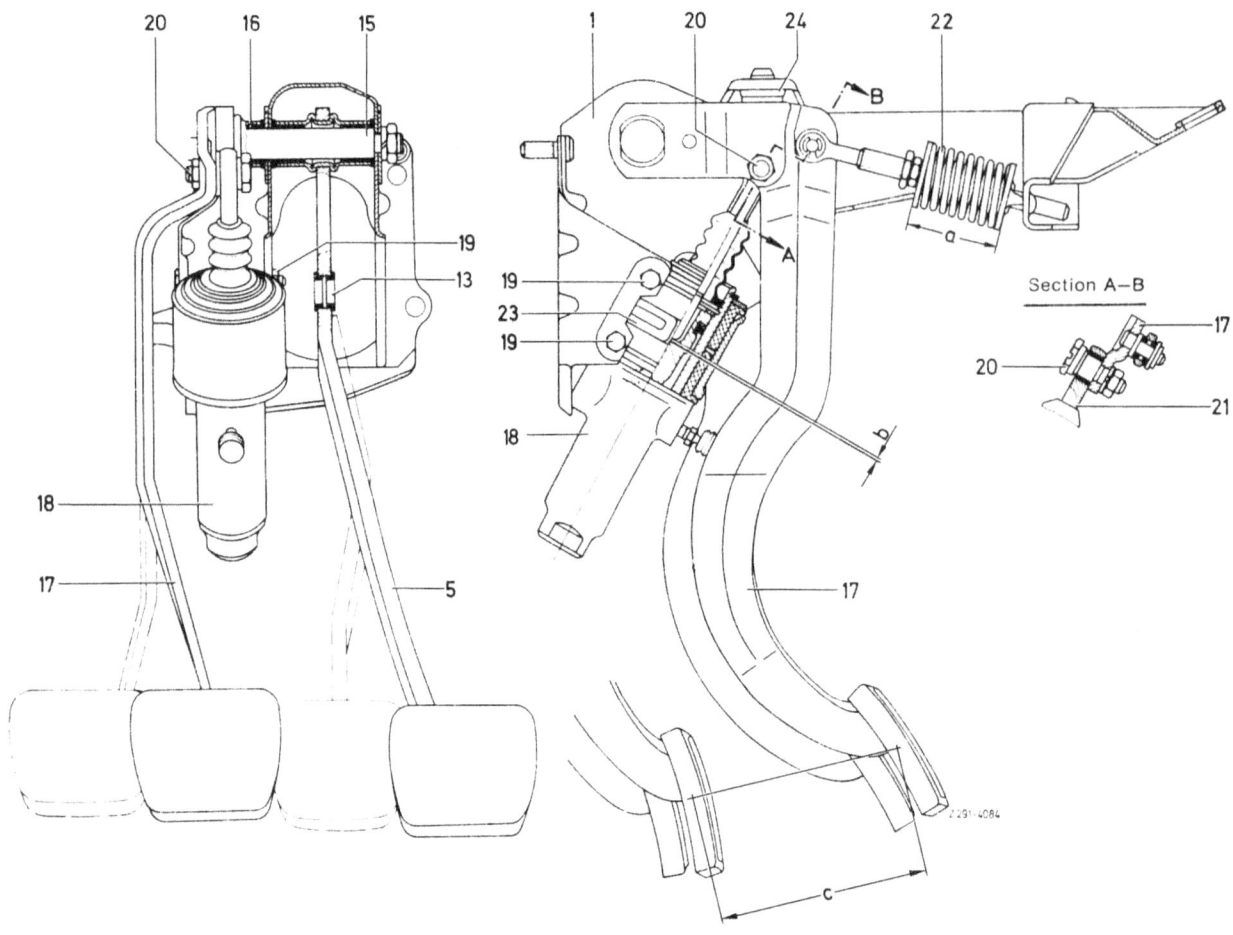

FIG 6 The master cylinder attachments

a Adjusting dimension of beyond-dead-center spring   b Clearance between piston in master cylinder and thrust rod   c Pedal travel

1 Pedal assembly mounting bracket	15 Bearing bolt	18 Master cylinder	21 Thrust rod	24 Rubber stop
5 Brake pedal	16 Bearing bushing	19 Fastening bolt	22 Beyond-dead-center spring	
13 Flange washers	17 Clutch pedal	20 Adjusting screw	23 Restriction of pedal travel	

Examination:

The parts should be cleaned and then checked for wear or damage. If new springs and clips are supplied in the service kit they should be fitted on reassembly and the old parts discarded. Pay particular attention to the bores of cylinders and renew the complete component if the bore is worn, damaged or scored. The bore must be smooth and highly-polished. **Do not attempt to clean defective or corroded bores with abrasive.**

Reassembly:

All the internal parts must be dipped into clean hydraulic fluid and installed while wet. On most components it will be found that the piston complete with seals must be inserted into the open end of the bore of the cylinder and that the lips of the seal will face into the cylinder. Enter the piston partially into the bore, taking great care not to cock it if the bore is large compared with the length, and press it in until the seal is just about to enter. Use either the fingers or a very blunt tool to press down the lips of the seal while gently pressing the piston down the bore. **Make sure that the lips of the seal are fully entered all the way around and that they are not bent back or damaged.**

4 The slave cylinder

A sectioned view of the later slave cylinder is shown in **FIG 5**.

Removal:

Attach a length of plastic or rubber tube to the bleed nipple 1, after removing the rubber protective cover, and open the bleed nipple by a turn. Insert the free end of the tube into a suitable container and pump the clutch pedal until the hydraulic fluid has been drained out. Discard the old fluid, using fresh fluid after reassembly.

Disconnect the flexible hose from its bracket on the chassis, taking great care not to twist the flexible portion of the hose when undoing the unions. Remove the two bolts that secure the slave cylinder and remove it from the car.

The unit is refitted in the reverse order of removal, again taking great care not to twist or strain the flexible portion of the hose. Once the unit is installed, fill and bleed the hydraulic system as described in **Section 6**.

Dismantling:

The internal parts can be removed after the circlip 8 and dust seal 7 with pushrod 9 have been removed.

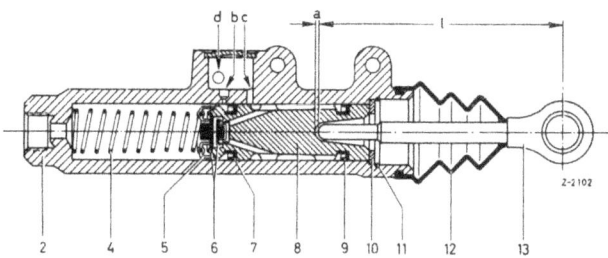

FIG 7 Sectioned view of typical master cylinder

2 Housing
4 Pressure spring
5 Cap
6 Valve
7 Primary cup
8 Piston
9 Secondary cup
10 Stop washer
11 Snap ring
12 Protective cap
13 Piston rod

c = Connecting port
d = Intake port from reservoir
l = Length of piston rod
a = Clearance between rod and piston
b = Compensating port

5 The master cylinder

The master cylinder attachments are shown in **FIG 6** and a sectioned view of a typical master cylinder is shown in **FIG 7**.

Removal:

Drain the fluid from the reservoir by attaching a bleed tube to the bleed nipple on the master cylinder, opening the bleed nipple and pumping the pedal. Disconnect the supply line from the reservoir at the master cylinder and similarly disconnect the outlet pipe from the master cylinder. **It is advisable to lay old rags or blankets on the carpets to catch any spillage or drips of hydraulic fluid.** Free the eccentric adjusting bolt from the clutch pedal and remove the two bolts that secure the unit so that it can be withdrawn from the car.

Install the master cylinder in the reverse order of removal. Fill and bleed the system as described in **Section 6**, and then set the pedal free travel.

Dismantling:

The internal parts can be extracted after the dust cover 12 and circlip 11 have been removed.

Pedal free travel:

The importance of the correct pedal free travel has already been stressed in **Section 2**. A typical adjustment is shown in **FIG 8**. Before making any adjustment, make sure that the mark for maximum eccentricity **b** on the head of the eccentric bolt is pointing to the rear of the car. The gap **a** is adjusted by feel to approximately .2 mm (.008 inch). When the gap is correct there will be approximately 1 mm (.04 inch) of free travel at the pedal plate. The correct movement is set by turning the eccentric bolt 31 with its locknut slack. Tighten the locknut when the adjustment is correct.

6 Bleeding the clutch hydraulic system

This is not routine maintenance and need only be carried out when air has entered the system, either by allowing the level in the reservoir to fall too low, or after the system has been dismantled.

Mercedes-Benz strongly recommend that the system is bled from the slave cylinder to the master cylinder and reservoir. This leads to a rather unconventional method if the owner carries out the work. A service agent will have pressure equipment for bleeding the system but the owner should use the braking system in place of the pressure bleeder.

1 Drain or syphon out any remaining fluid from the clutch master cylinder reservoir. Top up the reservoir of the brake master cylinder with ATE blue fluid to the upper mark. An eye should be kept on the level in the brake master cylinder reservoir during the bleeding operation and the level should not be allowed to fall too low, otherwise air may be drawn into the brakes.

2 Attach a sufficiently long piece of plastic or rubber tube to the bleed nipple on the righthand front brake caliper, making sure that the tube fits tightly with no leaks. Partially open the bleed screw and have an assistant gently pump the brake pedal until fluid free from air bubbles comes out the end of the tube. Discard fluid that comes out first and pinch the end of the tube to prevent air from being drawn back into it.

3 Fit the free end of the bleed tube onto the bleed nipple on the clutch slave cylinder and partially open this bleed nipple.

4 Have the assistant press the brake pedal right down, close the bleed screw on the brake caliper and have the assistant release the brake caliper. Open the bleed screw again and carry on in sequence until the reservoir of the clutch master cylinder is filled to the correct level. Close both bleed screws and remove the bleed tube. Top up the reservoir for the brakes to the maximum level.

5 Start the engine and check the time required before reverse gear will engage without noise after de-clutching. When the transmission fluid is at the normal temperature and the clutch in good condition and correctly bled, it will take 3 to 5 seconds before the driven plate stops rotating.

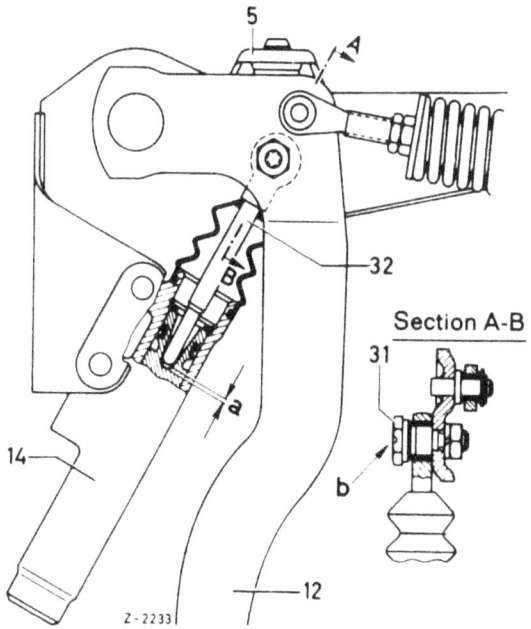

FIG 8 Typical pushrod adjustment

5. Rubber stop for clutch pedal
12. Clutch pedal
14. Supply cylinder
31. Adjusting bolt with hexagon nut and lockwasher
32. Pushrod

a = Clearance between pushrod and piston
b = Line marking

FIG 9 Removing the later clutch throwout arm
2 Throwout rocker   3 Ball pin

7 The clutch release bearing

The later clutch release mechanism parts are shown in **FIG 2**. Once the transmission has been removed from the engine, the release bearing 4 is slid directly off the input shaft, there being no attachments to hold it. The method of removing the throwout rocker 2 from its ball pin 3 is shown in **FIG 9**. Move the rocker in the direction **A** to clear it from the thrust pin and then pull it off in the direction **B**.

Check the bearing for wear, chipping or noisy operation and check the throwout for cracks or distortion. Renew defective parts.

Lubricate all pivot and bearing points with a suitable lubricant (not pure molybdenum disulphide) including the rocker. Engage the throwout rocker in the reverse order of removal and push back the bearing into place, turning it until it engages with the lateral cut-out in the rocker.

8 Servicing the clutch

The method of removal and installation is dealt with in **Chapter 1**. Note that it is essential that a centralizing arbor is used when installing the clutch. The side of the driven plate marked 'Kupplungseite' must face towards the transmission.

Driven plate condition:

Examine the driven plate for signs of mechanical damage or wear. Check that all rivets are tight and secure and examine the hub for security or worn and damaged splines. Renew the driven plate if it has mechanical damage or the linings are worn down nearly to the rivet heads.

Fit the driven plate back onto the splines of the transmission input shaft and check that it slides freely without excessive rotational play or movement of the damper springs.

The friction linings are operating at their maximum efficiency when they have a smooth polished glaze through which the grain of the friction material is clearly visible. Any oil on the linings will reduce efficiency and cause operating faults.

Small quantities of oil on the driven plate linings will leave dark coloured smears on the surface while larger amounts will leave a dark coloured deposit. Excessive amounts of oil will be obvious from the oil-soaked

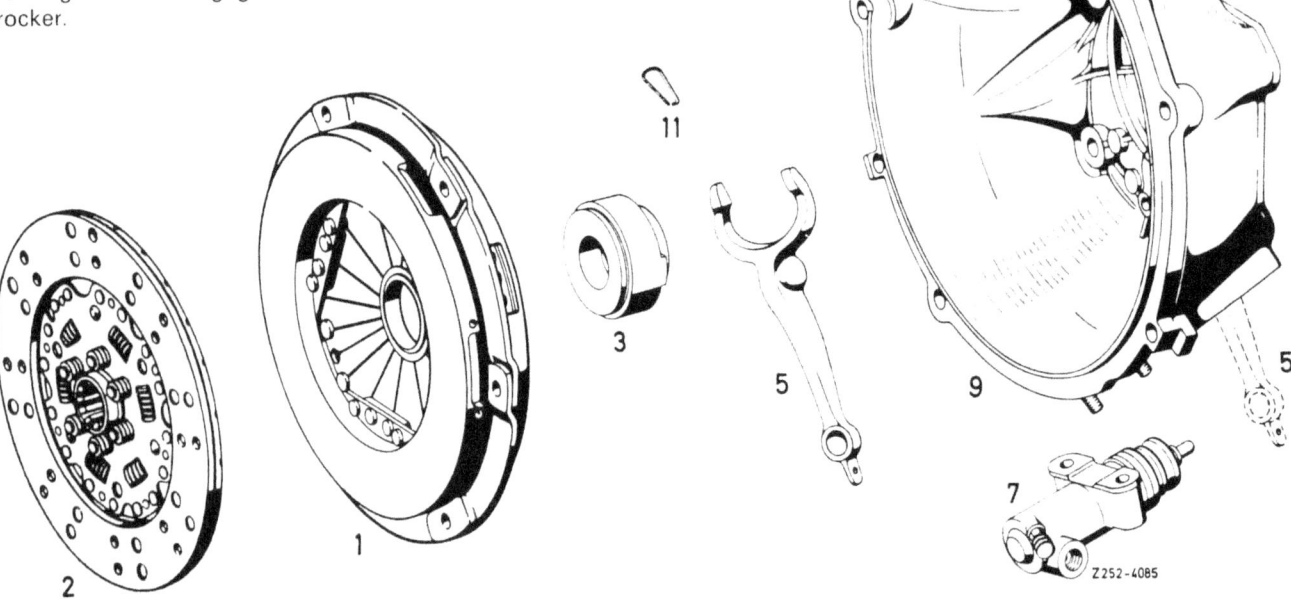

FIG 10 The early clutch components

1 Diaphragm or spring plate clutch
2 Driven plate
3 Throwout (up to May 69)
5 Throwout fork (up to May 69)
7 Slave cylinder (up to May 69)
9 Clutch housing (up to May 69)
11 Spring clip

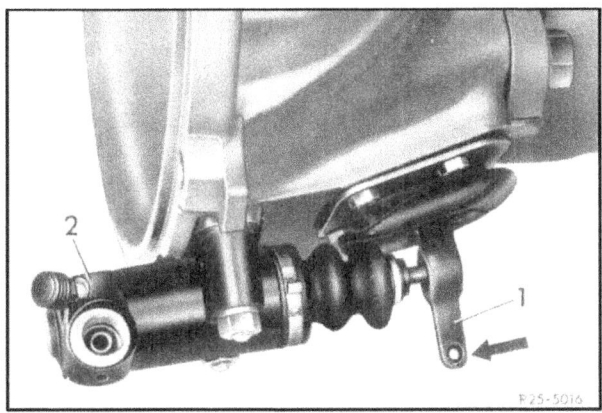

FIG 11 The early slave cylinder attachments

1 Throwout fork   2 Slave cylinder

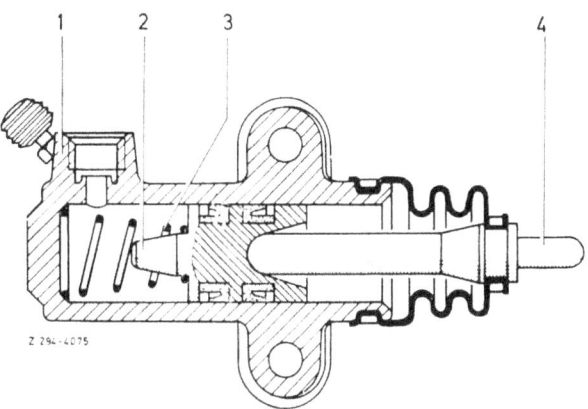

FIG 12 Sectioned view of the early slave cylinder

appearance of the linings and the quantities of free oil in the housing. **Oil must not be removed from the linings by washing with solvent or baking as any treatment effective enough to take out the oil will ruin the linings.**

If there is oil on the clutch but the grain of the friction material is still visible then the driven plate may be used again. If the grain is hidden a new driven plate must be fitted.

Cover assembly:

This cannot be dismantled and must therefore be renewed if defective. Clean the assembly by careful brushing and blowing away loose dirt with an airline. Only if the parts are oily should they be wiped externally with a cloth moistened in fuel or suitable solvent.

Examine the cover for cracks or distortion, paying particular attention to the areas around mounting holes and rivets. The operating face of the pressure plate should be checked for scores or burn marks.

If possible, lightly lubricate the pivot points with white zinc-based grease. Note that the assembly must not be washed in solvent as this will remove lubricant which cannot be put back.

9 The earlier type of clutch

This is the type of clutch fitted to all models before May 1969 as well as all later 280 SL/8 models.

The general instructions for the later type of clutch apply equally well to this earlier clutch and only differences are given in this section. The components of the clutch are shown in **FIG 10**.

Checking wear:

The attachment of the slave cylinder is shown in **FIG 11**. Press the throwout lever in the direction indicated by the arrow. If the resistance is elastic and yielding then the driven plate is fit for further service. If the lever can only be moved a maximum of 2 mm (.08 inch) then the driven plate is excessively worn and must be renewed.

Slave cylinder:

A sectioned view of the slave cylinder is shown in **FIG 12**. Removal is the same as for removal of the later slave cylinder and the unit is dismantled after removing the dust cover and thrust pin.

Release mechanism:

The bearing 3 is secured to the fork 5 by the clips 11 which must be freed before the bearing can be removed. The fork is pulled forwards off its ball pin and then turned through 90 deg. so that it can be drawn out. Checking of the parts is the same as for the later type.

10 Fault diagnosis

(a) Drag or spin

1 Oil or grease on friction linings
2 Incorrectly adjusted pedal clearance
3 Misalignment between engine and gearbox
4 Leaking master cylinder, slave cylinder or pipeline
5 Defective clutch spigot bearing in crankshaft
6 Distorted driven plate
7 Warped or damaged pressure plate
8 Broken drive plate linings
9 Dirt or foreign matter in clutch
10 Air in the hydraulic system

(b) Fierceness or snatch

1 Check 1, 2 and 3 in (a)
2 Worn friction linings

(c) Slip

1 Check 1, 2 and 3 in (a) and 2 in (b)
2 Weak diaphragm spring
3 Seized piston in slave cylinder

(d) Judder

1 Check 1, 6, 7 and 8 in (a)
2 Contact area of linings not evenly distributed
3 Faulty engine mountings
4 Defective rear suspension or propeller shaft

(e) Tick or knock

1 Check 5 in (a)
2 Badly worn splines on driven plate hub or input shaft
3 Worn release bearing
4 Loose flywheel

NOTES

CHAPTER 6 – GEARBOX

1 Description
2 Removing the later gearbox
3 Removing the earlier gearbox
4 The steering column mounted shift
5 The floor mounted shift
6 Dismantling the later type of gearbox
7 Dismantling the earlier type of gearbox
8 Reassembling the earlier type of gearbox
9 Fault diagnosis

1 Description

Various transmissions are or can be fitted to the models covered by this manual. On all models the standard transmission has four forward speeds, all with synchromesh engagement, and one reverse gear engaged by sliding an idler into mesh. As an optional extra a five-speed transmission can be fitted in place of the standard four-speed unit. The fifth speed is an overdrive ratio and therefore used to reduce the engine speed when cruising.

All models were fitted with a G 72 gearbox from the start of the series but, on all models except the 280 SL/8, after May 1969 the gearbox was changed for the G76/27. The 280 SL/8 continues with the earlier type G 72 gearbox. A ZF S 5-20 five speed gearbox can be fitted as an optional extra to all models of the 280 SL/8. From May 1969 the remainder of the 280 series can be fitted with an optional five-speed G 76/27-5 gearbox. The optional five-speed gearbox for the later models is a modified version of the standard four-speed gearbox with an attached housing section for the fifth speed and reverse.

On all types of gearbox, lubrication is by the gears dipping into an oil bath and the splash from the gears lubricating the remainder of the parts. **Automatic Transmission Fluid (ATF Type A) is used as the** lubricant. On most makes of car some form of Hypoid or engine oil is used in the transmission, so it is important to note that ATF is used on Mercedes gearboxes. A drain plug is fitted under the gearbox casing but seasonal or routine fluid changes are not required. A combined level and filler plug is fitted to the side of the casing and the level should be periodically checked and topped up to the bottom of the filler aperture if it is low.

2 Removing the later gearbox

This section refers to the removal of the G 76/27 and optional five-speed G 76/27-5 gearboxes fitted after May 1969. The instructions apply to both types of gearbox but it is advisable to support the five-speed unit on a stand at the rear of it because of the increased weight.

The gearbox is removed from under the car, leaving the engine in position. It is best and safest to work from a pit or under a garage hoist but if neither is available, **make sure that any stands and ramps are strong enough to take the weight of the car and that they are firmly based.**

1 Disconnect the battery. Though not necessary, it is also advisable to drain the lubricant from the gearbox.
2 Disconnect the shift rods. The method of removing

the SL clips are shown in **FIG 1** and the clips are refitted in the reverse order of removal. On models fitted with a steering column shift, the rods 1 and 2 should be disconnected at the bearing bracket end, shown in **FIG 2,** and the reverse shift rod 3 at the shift lever 4, shown in **FIG 3**. On models fitted with a central shift, disconnect all three rods from their levers at the transmission itself.

3 A view from the rear of the gearbox is shown in **FIG 4**. Slacken the clamping screw 6 and remove the speedometer drive cable 5 from the gearbox. Disconnect the clutch flexible hose 7 from the metal pipe 8 at the point **A, taking great care not to twist or strain the flexible portion of the hose.** When the hose has been disconnected, plug it with a dummy plug to prevent fluid from leaking out or dirt from entering.

4 Slacken the clamp nuts on the propeller shaft, free the centre main bearing and remove the bolts 9 and their Polystop nuts that secure the propeller shaft to the three-way drive flange of the gearbox. Details of the propeller shaft are given in **Chapter 8**. The universal plate is left on the transmission flange. Remove the nuts 12 for the exhaust pipe clamp and slacken the nuts 13 so that the exhaust pipe support can be hung vertically downwards. Support the propeller shaft up out of the way using a block of wood on the cross strut 17 and use another block of wood (80 mm—3 inch high) to move the exhaust pipes slightly downwards, as shown in **FIG 5**.

5 Support the power unit with a jack and pad of wood under the engine sump and take the weight so that the transmission end is raised slightly. Remove the bolts 10 that secure the rear mounting crossmember to the frame. Take out the bolt 11 and remove the crossmember complete with the rear engine mounting.

6 Remove the two bolts that secure the starter motor as well as the ring of bolts that secure the clutch housing to the engine intermediate flange. **Support the weight of the transmission by hand and draw it rearwards until the input shaft is well clear of the clutch.** Rotate the gearbox through 90 deg. in a clockwise direction so that the starter motor dome clears the leading edge of the propeller shaft funnel and lower the gearbox down out of the car.

Installation:

The gearbox is refitted in the reverse order of removal. Lightly lubricate the splines of the input shaft with a high-viscosity oil. Hoist the gearbox back into position and align it with the engine so that the input shaft will pass through the clutch. Still supporting the weight, slide the gearbox forwards into place until it is snug against the intermediate flange. If necessary, select a gear and rotate the drive flange until the splines of the input shaft align with those of the clutch driven plate hub. Secure the gearbox with its attachment bolts and the two bolts for the starter motor.

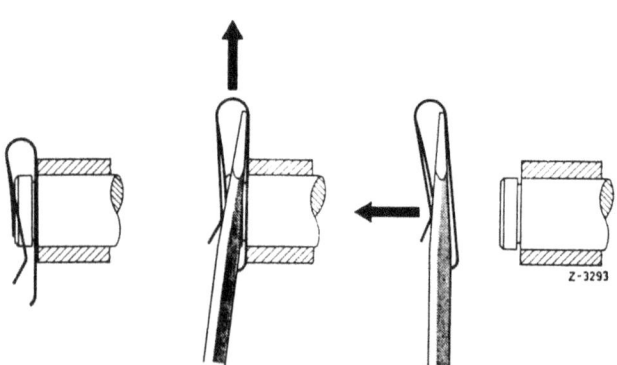

FIG 1   Removing shift rod clips

FIG 2   The shift rods at the bearing bracket for later models fitted with steering column shift

1 Shift rod for 1st and 2nd speed   3 Shift rod for reverse speed
2 Shift rod for 3rd and 4th speed

FIG 3   The shift rods at the levers on the transmission

1 Shift rod for 1st and 2nd speed   7 Pressure hose for clutch
2 Shift rod for 3rd and 4th speed   actuation
3 Shift rod for reverse speed   8 Pressure line for clutch
4 Shift lever for reverse speed   actuation
5 Drive shaft for speedometer   13 Bolts for exhaust bracket

   A Connection point pressure hose to pressure line

Install the rear mounting and secure the exhaust pipe in place, after removing the block of wood. Refit the propeller shaft, noting that the clamp nuts should not be tightened until after the car has been lowered back onto its wheels and rolled backwards and forwards several times.

Reconnect all the other parts that were freed or dismantled. The clutch hydraulic system must be bled as described in **Chapter 5 Section 6**. Check the fluid level in the gearbox, filling or topping up to the level of the filler plug as required.

It is advisable to check the adjustments of the selectors and then road-test the car to check that the selections are made smoothly and easily.

3 Removing the earlier gearbox

This section refers to the removal of the G 72 gearbox and optional five-speed ZF S 5-20 fitted to earlier models and all 280 SL/8 models. The instructions apply equally to both types of gearbox but because of the extra weight the five-speed gearbox should be supported on a stand. **Observe all safety precautions for raising the car.**

1 Disconnect the battery. It is advisable, though not absolutely necessary, to drain the fluid from the gearbox.
2 Disconnect the selector shift rods. On models with steering column shift, force off the selector rod 1 and shift rod 2 from the ball pins of the selector lever 6 and intermediate lever 4, shown in **FIG 6**. On models fitted with a central shift, disconnect both pushrods 8 from the top cover of the gearbox and loosen the clamping screw 3 so that the shift tube 4 can be pulled rearwards out of the fork head 2, shown in **FIG 7**. In all cases lay the shift and selector rods, or pushrods, out of the way so that they will not be trapped on removal or installation of the gearbox.
3 Remove the two nuts that secure the slave cylinder to the clutch housing and take off the slave cylinder. Hang the slave cylinder safely out of the way, without disconnecting the flexible hose, **taking care not to strain the flexible portion of the hose**. Remove the clamp screw that secures the speedometer drive cable and free the cable from the gearbox. Disconnect the leads for the reverse light switch at the plug connection on the splash wall.

FIG 5 Supporting the propeller shaft and clearing the exhaust pipes

17 Cross strut

FIG 4 View of the rear mounting and attachments

- 5 Drive shaft for speedometer
- 6 Clamping screw
- 7 Pressure hose for clutch actuation
- 8 Pressure line for clutch actuation
- 9 Universal shaft screw
- 10 Fastening screw for cross member on frame floor
- 11 Fastening screw for cross member with rubber mount on transmission
- 12 Fastening nuts (covered) for exhaust support on transmission
- 13 Screws for exhaust bracket
- 14 Clamp
- A Pressure hose connecting point

FIG 6 The shift rods attached to the bearing bracket on earlier model

- 1 Selector rod
- 2 Shift rod
- 3 Cover
- 4 Intermediate lever
- 5 Fastening clip
- 6 Selector lever
- 7 Flexible drive shaft
- 8 Elastic intermediate piece

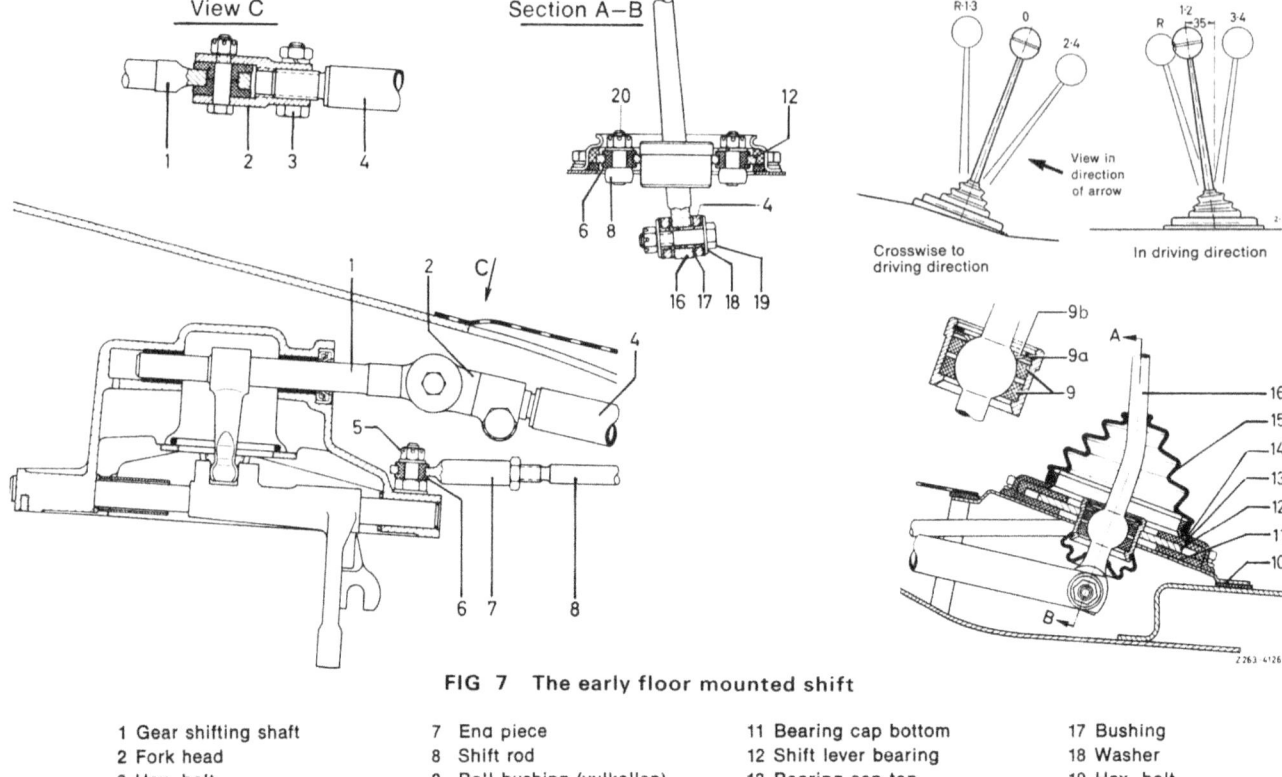

FIG 7 The early floor mounted shift

1 Gear shifting shaft	7 End piece	11 Bearing cap bottom	17 Bushing
2 Fork head	8 Shift rod	12 Shift lever bearing	18 Washer
3 Hex. bolt	9 Ball bushing (vulkollan)	13 Bearing cap top	19 Hex. bolt
4 Shift tube	9a Inner locking ring	14 Cover plate	20 Castle nut
5 Castle nut	9b Undulated washer	15 Sleeve	
6 Bushing	10 Transmission tunnel	16 Shift lever	

4 The rear attachments are shown in **FIG 8**. Take out the two bolts 21 and slacken the nut 23 so that the exhaust pipe support can be hung vertically downwards. Mark the position of the rear support 12 with relation to the frame, marks 20. Support the engine with a jack and pad of wood under the sump and just take the weight. Unscrew the nut 16 and remove the four bolts 18 so that the rear support member 12 can be removed. On 280 SL/8 models, take out the sixteen screws which secure the tunnel plate instead of removing the support member.

5 Take off the nuts 1 and remove the rear engine carrier complete with the fastening plate 9, shown in **FIG 9**. Disconnect the propeller shaft from both the gearbox and rear axle and move the shaft as far rearwards as possible (see **Chapter 8**) and collect the sealing ring from the drive flange.

6 Remove the bolts that secure the clutch housing to the engine intermediate flange. Support the weight of the gearbox and draw it rearwards until the input shaft is well clear of the clutch, then lower the gearbox down and out of the car. **The weight of the gearbox must not be allowed to hang by the input shaft in the clutch otherwise the clutch will be damaged.**

Installation:

The gearbox is refitted in the reverse order of removal. Take care to install the propeller shaft correctly with the universal plate correctly attached (see **Chapter 8**). When installing the rear support, make sure that the marks 20 are again in alignment and do not fully tighten the attachment bolts 18 until the weight of the car is back on the road wheels. On the 280 SL/8 the sixteen bolts for the tunnel closing plate can be tightened immediately without having to lower the car to the ground.

4 The steering column mounted shift

Adjusting the later linkage:

This covers all the models (after May 1969) fitted with the G 76/27 gearbox.

Free all the rods from the bearing bracket end by forcing them off the ball pins. Set the selector levers on the gearbox to their neutral positions and check that they are at the correct dimensions shown in **FIG 10**. If the settings are incorrect, remove the clamp nut and bolt so that the lever can be removed and refitted onto the correct splines. Do not move the levers from their neutral positions. Move the gearlever so that a pin can be inserted through the three levers on the bearing bracket, shown in **FIG 11**. The gearbox and gearlever are now correctly set. Slacken the nuts 6 on the stepless linkages, shown in **FIG 12**, and adjust the lengths of the shift rods until the ball joints can be fitted back without any tension or pressure in the rods. Lubricate the ball joints lightly with grease before finally pressing them back into place. Remove the lockpin and check the gearlever for smooth and correct operation.

Adjusting early linkage:

Check that the linkage moves freely and that the lever returns freely after being pulled against the reverse gear stop. Sectioned views of the bearing bracket at the base of the steering column are shown in **FIG 13**. Move the gearlever into the neutral position and slacken the clamp screw 5 on the lever 6 and pull the selector lever forwards. At the same time pull the intermediate lever 4 forwards at the bottom to engage fourth speed. Remove the rubber sleeve on the gearlever from its recess in the steering tube and have an assistant pull the gearlever upwards until there is only 2 mm (.08 inch) clearance between the flange on the shift tube and the recess in the jacket tube. Tighten the clamp bolt 5 while pushing the lever 6 towards the bearing body so that the spring plate 33 is preloaded.

The linkage should now be correctly set so check that all speeds engage smoothly and freely, with the clutch pedal pressed down. Check that the reverse detent is clearly felt when selecting reverse. If there is no detent felt, the parts in the gearbox cover must be renewed.

Move the gearlever into either second or fourth speed and check that the end of the knob is 15 mm (.6 inch) below a horizontal line through the centre of the steering wheel, when viewed from the driver's seat. Small adjustments to the position of the gearlever can be made by altering the length of the shift rod.

5 The floor mounted shift

Adjusting the later shift for four-speed models:

The positions of the levers on the gearbox case should be set to the dimensions shown in **FIG 14**, when the rods are disconnected and all gears in neutral. Set the gearlever so that the levers 1, 2 and 3, shown in **FIG 15** are aligned and a pin passed through the holes in them to lock them. Adjust the lengths of the rods until they can be fitted back without tension or pressure.

FIG 8 The attachments of the early gearbox

9 Fastening plate	16 Hex. nut	21 Hex. bolt
11 Rubber mount	18 Hex. bolt	23 Hex. bolt
12 Rear support	20 Marking lines	24 Slave cylinder

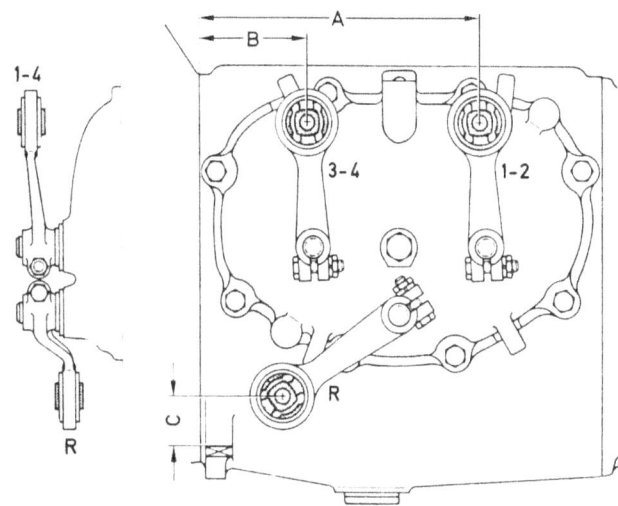

FIG 10 The setting of the levers on the later four-speed gearbox on cars fitted with steering column shift

A = 158 mm **B** = 58 mm **C** = 26 mm

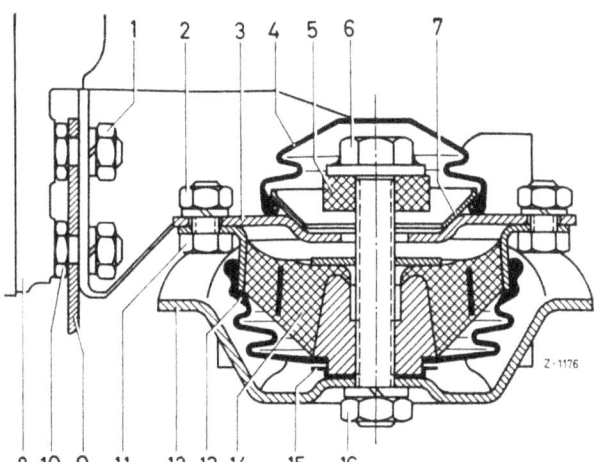

FIG 9 Sectioned view of the rear mounting for early gearboxes

1 Hex. nut	9 Fastening plate
2 Hex. nut	10 Collar screw
3 Engine mount	11 Hex. bolt
4 Bellows	12 Carrier
5 Rubber shim	13 Bellows
6 Hex. bolt	14 Rubber mount
7 Holder for bellows	15 Plate
8 Rear transmission housing cover	16 Hex. nut

FIG 11 The setting of the levers on a later steering column shift bearing bracket

51 Lever for reverse speed 53 Lever for 3rd and 4th speed
52 Lever for 1st and 2nd speed

The reverse light switch 5 should be adjusted so that the dimension **a** is correct at 4±1 mm (.16±.04 inch) when the gearlever is in the first or second speed positions.

Adjusting later five-speed linkage:

This is fitted with a floor mounted gearlever and the adjustment is very similar to that of the four-speed floor mounted shift. The levers on the gearbox must be set to the dimensions shown in **FIG 16** and the shift rods are then adjusted to fit to the levers of the bearing bracket after they have been set with a pin through them.

The bottom of the parcel box should be removed and the bolts 3 slackened, as shown in **FIG 17**. With the gearlever moved to the right against the stop and pushed in the direction of fifth speed, and with the levers held by the pin, adjust the stop plate 1 in relation to the stop finger 2 until both lines are in alignment as shown at **A**, so that there is no clearance between the inclined surfaces and they rest on one another. Tighten the fastening bolts 3 with the stop plate 1 in this position. With the parts held in this position, adjust the reverse light switch until the dimension **a** is correct at 1.5 mm (.06 inch). When all adjustments are set, remove the pin and install the bottom of the parcel box.

Adjusting the earlier floor-mounted linkage:

The parts of the linkage are shown in **FIG 7**. When installing the parts, such as after gearbox removal, position the gear shifting shaft 1 against the stop for reverse and then engage second speed by pushing the shaft in. Move the gearlever 16 into the plane of first and second speed

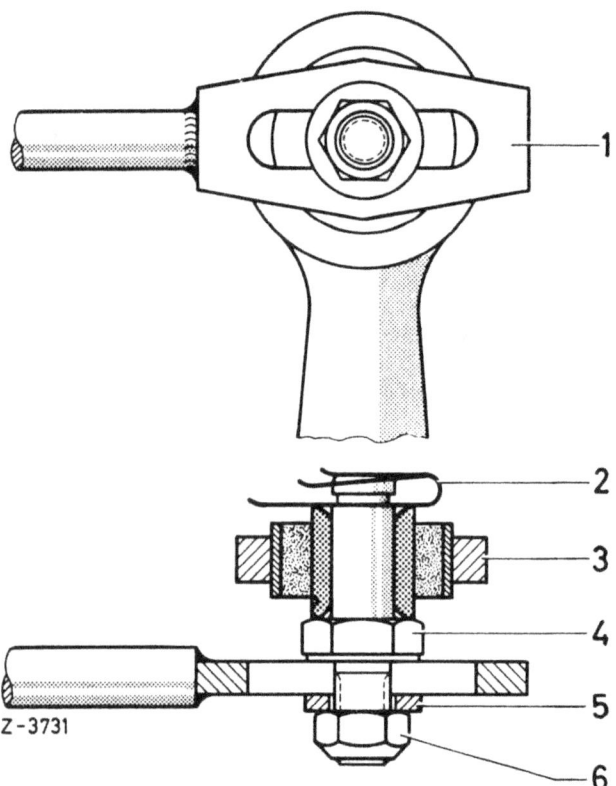

FIG 12 The stepless adjustment for shift rods

1 Shift hole with oblong hole
2 SL lock
3 Shift lever on transmission
4 Adjusting pin
5 Shim
6 Adjusting nut

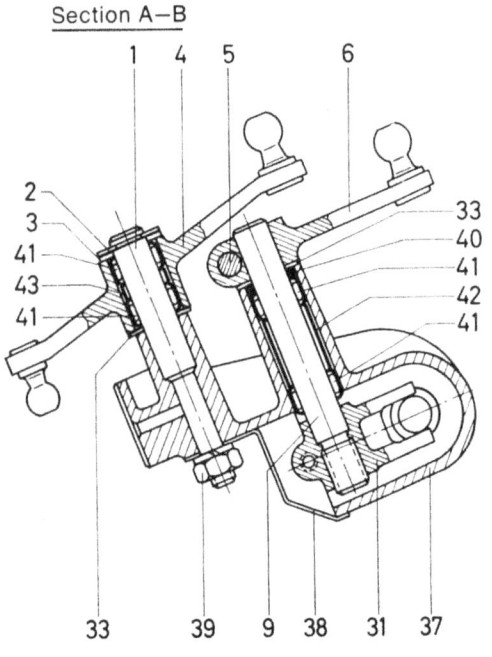

FIG 13 Sectioned view of the bearing bracket for early models

1 Shaft for intermediate lever
2 Locking ring
3 Washer
4 Intermediate lever
5 Hex. bolt (clamping screw)
6 Selector lever
7 Lever on shift tube
9 Selector shaft
16 Selector tube
17 Vulkollan bushing
17a Spacer ring
18 Cage nut
19 Front wall
20 Hex. bolt with washer
21 Washer
22 Hex. nut with lockwasher
23 Clamping bolt
31 Selector lever on shift tube
32 Hex. bolt (clamping bolt)
33 Spring plate
37 Bearing body
37a Water drain hole
38 Cover
39 Hex. nut with lockwasher
40 Sealing ring
41 Needle bearing
42 Spacing sleeve
43 Spacing sleeve

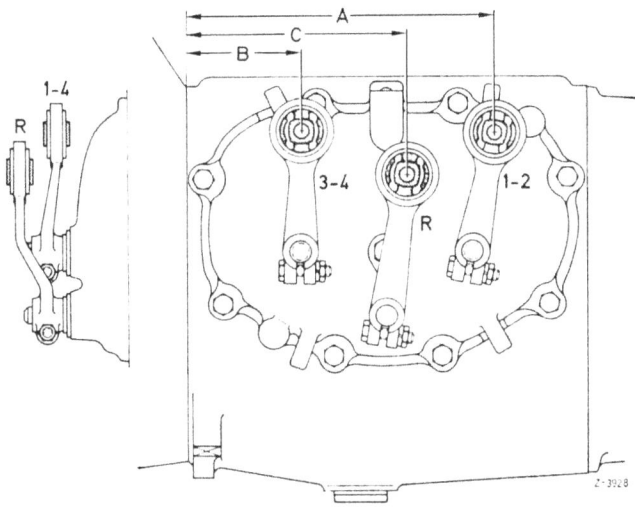

FIG 14 The setting of the levers on the later four-speed gearbox on cars fitted with floor shift

$A = 168$ mm $B = 62$ mm $C = 120$ mm

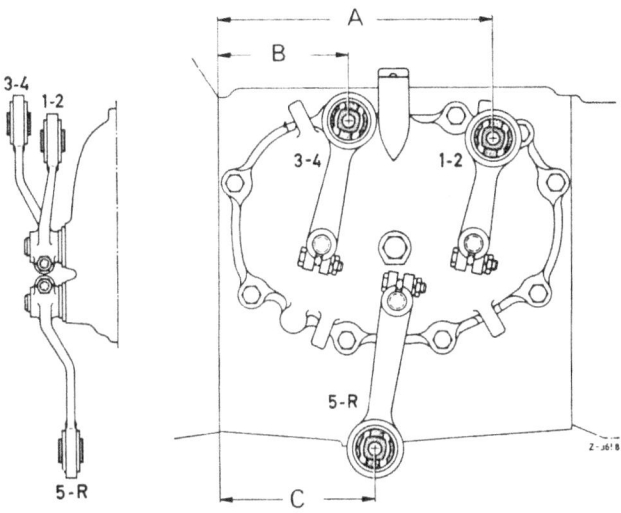

FIG 16 The settings of the levers on a five-speed gearbox

$A = 168$ mm $B = 81$ mm $C = 95$ mm

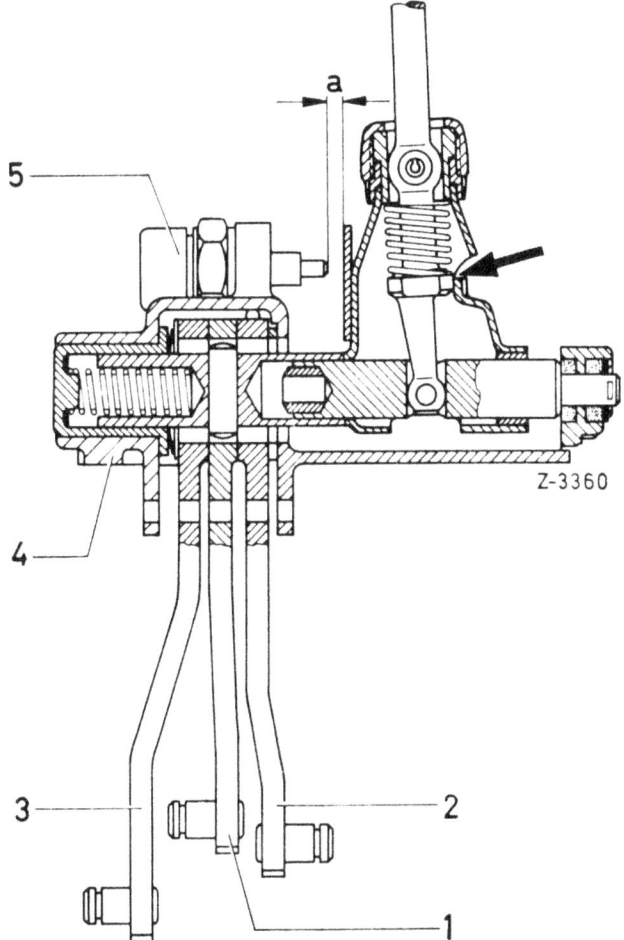

FIG 15 Sectioned view of the later four-speed floor mounted shift

1 Shift lever for 1st and 2nd speed
2 Shift lever for 3rd and 4th speed
3 Shift lever for reverse speed
4 Bearing body
5 Backup light switch

a = Adjusting dimension for backup light switch 4 ± 1 mm with shift lever in 1st or 2nd speed position

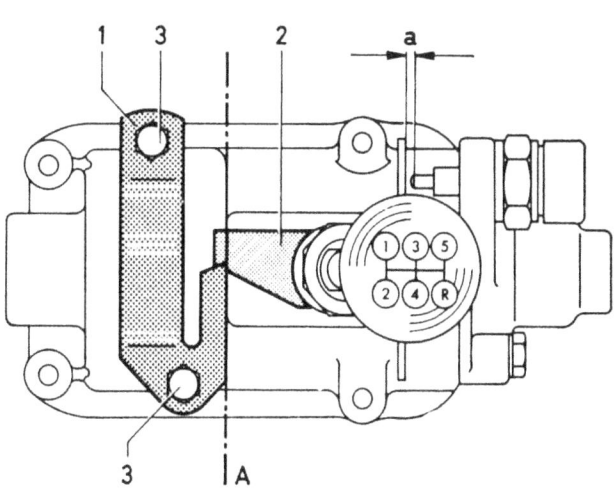

FIG 17 The adjustments of the five-speed shift

1 Stop plate
2 Stop finger
3 Fastening bolt
"A" Straight line between stop plate and stop finger

"a" = 1.5 mm adjusting dimension for contact pin of backup light switch when stop plate (1) and stop finger (2) are aligned according to "A"

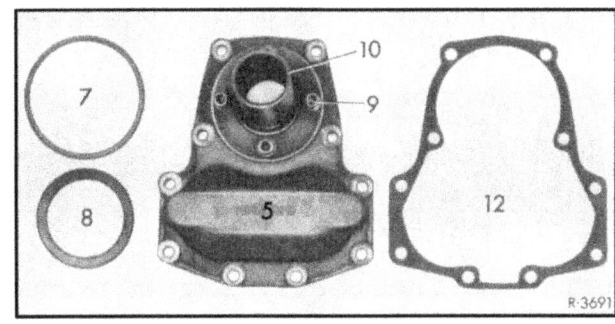

FIG 18 The components of the later front cover

5 Front transmission cover
7 Spacing washer for drive shaft
8 Spacing washer for countershaft
9 Fastening bolts
10 Bearing tube
12 Paper gasket

and insert the shift tube 4 into the splines of the fork head 2. The shift tube must be inserted to a minimum depth of 15 mm (.6 inch) before securing it in place with the clamp bolt 3.

When the installation has been completed, check that all gears engage smoothly and freely and that the gearlever does not hit on the bearing. If the adjustments are correct, the gearlever will be in the positions shown in **FIG 7** in the various selections.

Very small adjustments can be made by altering the depth of insertion of the shift tube 4 in the fork head 2, provided that the minimum depth is not less than 15 mm.

If the lever is not in the correct positions, or the lever hits the bearing 12 in any selection, adjust the lengths of the rods 8. Disconnect both pushrods from the top cover of the gearbox and adjust the end pieces 7 so that both bolts which secure the rods 8 to the bearing 12 are at the centre of the coverplate when the rods are reconnected. It is important to adjust both rods to equal settings.

6 Dismantling the later type of gearbox
Clutch housing and front cover:

The clutch housing can be removed separately after taking off the nuts that secure it to the casing. The clutch throwout rocker and bearing must be removed first. Once the nuts and washers are off, tap the housing free using rubber hammers, and remove it with the slave cylinder still attached. Install the cover in the reverse order of removal, tapping it gently into place until it is snug.

The front cover can be removed after the clutch housing has been taken off. Remove the bolts that secure the front cover and pull it off the casing. The components of the front cover are shown in **FIG 18**. Carefully collect the spacer washers 7 and 8 fitted between the cover and case, as these control the end play of the gearbox shafts.

The mounting tube 10 can be removed after taking out the bolts 9. A sealing ring is fitted between the cover and mounting tube. If the sealing ring is defective, prise it out with an arbor of 45 mm (1.8 inch) and press a new sealing ring back into place so that it is flush with the separating face. Install the mounting tube 10 but **do not fully tighten the attachment bolts 9 at this stage.**

Secure the spacer washers 7 and 8 as well as a new paper gasket 12 to the cover using a thin smear of grease. Lightly grease the lips of the sealing ring and slide the cover assembly back into place so that it is flush with the face of the case. Wash the bolts that secure the cover in clean fuel to degrease them. Dip the threads into non-setting jointing compound before fitting and tightening the bolts. Tighten the bolts in a diagonal sequence. Install the clutch housing and tap it fully back into place. Evenly tighten the nuts that secure the clutch housing and only then fully tighten the bolts 9 that secure the mounting tube.

FIG 19 Installing the later rear cover

1 Transmission cover rear 11 Reversing shaft
8 Fitted sleeve

FIG 20 Freeing the later side cover

1 Shift cover 9 Pin
8 Gear shifting shaft reverse speed

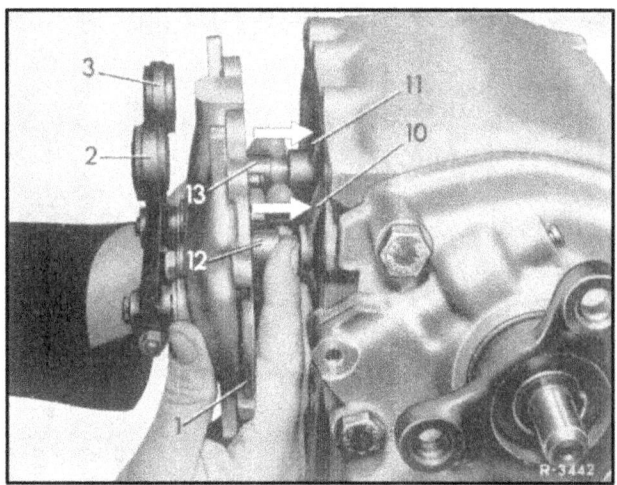

FIG 21 Freeing the shift yokes

1 Shift cover 12 Shift rocker 1st and
2 Shift lever 1st and 2nd speed   2nd speed
3 Shift lever 3rd and 4th speed 13 Shift rocker 3rd and
10 Shift fork 1st and 2nd speed   4th speed
11 Shift fork 3rd and 4th speed

Rear cover:

Provided that the correct tools are used it is possible to remove the rear cover from the gearbox with the gearbox installed in the car. The propeller shaft must be disconnected before removing the cover.

Free the locking on the grooved nut securing the three-way flange to the gearbox mainshaft. Hold the flange with the retaining wrench 115 589 00 70 00 and unscrew the grooved nut with the wrench 115 589 01 07 00. When the nut has been removed, pull off the drive flange by hand. Take out all the attachment bolts and pull the rear cover off from the case.

A sealing ring is fitted to the rear cover and if it is defective it can be prised out using a 52 mm (2 inch) diameter arbor. The new ring should be pressed in so that it is flush with the external edge of the cover.

Secure a new paper gasket in place with a thin smear of grease. Fit the cover back in to place, making sure that the milled portion arrowed on the reverse shaft 11 is upwards (shown in **FIG 19**), so that it mates with the flat in the cover. Also make sure that fitting sleeve 8 fits correctly into its bore.

Before installing the drive flange, grease it lightly at the running surface of the sealing ring. If the drive flange running surface is scored or damaged than a new drive flange should be fitted. Light burrs or nicks can be smoothed down with an oilstone.

Removing the side cover:

Take out the clamp nut and bolt that secure the reverse shift lever to its shaft and remove the lever. Push off the locking plate fitted to the reverse gear shifting shaft. Take out the eight bolts that secure the cover to the case, noting that it may be necessary to move the remaining two shift levers in order to gain access to all the bolts. Carefully tap the cover off from its dowels 9 and at the same time use another soft-faced hammer to drive the reverse gear shifting shaft inwards, as shown in **FIG 20**.

FIG 23 Setting the follower for reverse gear

9 Pin
10 Shift fork 1st and 2nd speed
11 Shift rod 3rd and 4th speed
14 Shifter for reverse speed
15 Shift rod for reverse speed

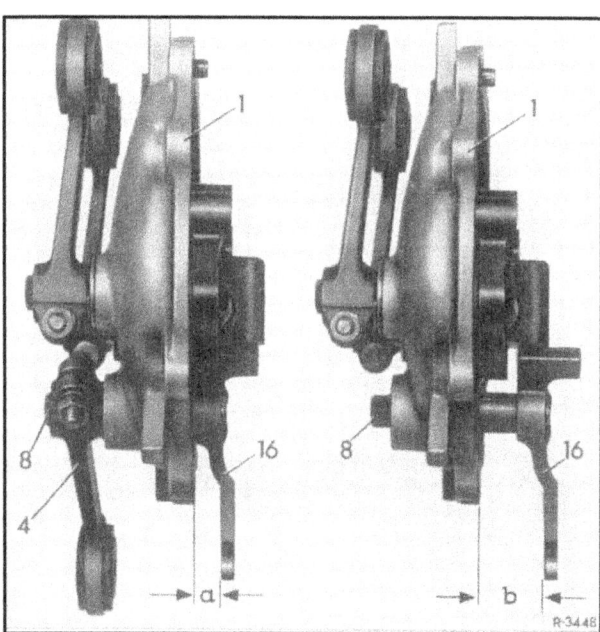

FIG 24 Set the shift lever finger to dimension 'b' before installation

1 Shift cover
4 Shift lever for reverse speed
8 Gear shifting shaft for reverse speed
16 Shift finger for reverse speed

a Distance between parting surface and shift finger of cover ready for operation = approx. 10 mm
b Distance between shift finger and cover prior to assembly = approx. 25 mm

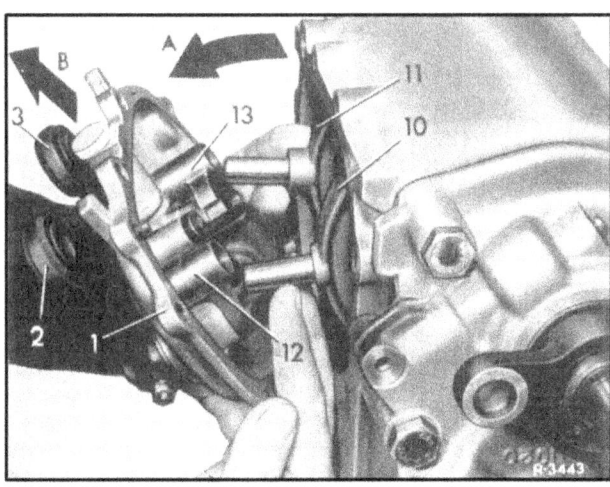

FIG 22 Removing the cover

1 Shift cover
2 Shift lever 1st and 2nd speed
3 Shift lever 3rd and 4th speed
10 Shift fork 1st and 2nd speed
11 Shift fork 3rd and 4th speed
12 Shift rocker 1st and 2nd speed
13 Shift rocker 3rd and 4th speed

Drive the cover off far enough to allow a hand to be inserted between it and the case. Slide the shift forks 10 and 11 out of the yokes 12 and 13, as shown in **FIG 21**. The cover can then be removed by first tilting it in the direction of the arrow **A** and then lifting it off in the direction of the arrow **B**, shown in **FIG 22**.

The cover assembly is refitted in the reverse order of removal. The old paper gasket will most likely have been damaged on removal, so install a new one, using a thin smear of grease to hold it in place. Move the follower for the reverse speed 14 into the exact centre, as shown in **FIG 23**. Set the shift lever finger 16 so that the distance between it and the cover b, shown in **FIG 24**, is approximately 25 mm (1 inch). The dimension **a** shown in the figure is only for when the shaft has been pressed fully back into place, approximately 10 mm (.4 inch).

The cover is lowered down in the opposite direction to the arrow **B**, shown in **FIG 22**, making sure the finger 16 fits into the groove of the follower 14 (**FIG 23**). Once the cover is down in place, pivot it in the opposite direction to the arrow **A** and at the same time insert the shift forks 10 and 11 back into the yokes 12 and 13. Gently tap the cover back into place on its dowels, allowing shaft 8 (**FIG 20**) to slide through the cover. Tighten the attachment bolts in a diagonal sequence to avoid straining the cover. Refit the locking plate to the reverse shifting shaft and then install the lever. The lever should be set in neutral as described in **Section 4** or **Section 5**, depending on the position of the gearlever.

Dismantling the side cover:

An external view of the cover is shown in **FIG 25** and an internal view in **FIG 26** while the components are shown in **FIG 27**. If the detent cage 7 is defective, it can be renewed without fully dismantling the cover assembly.

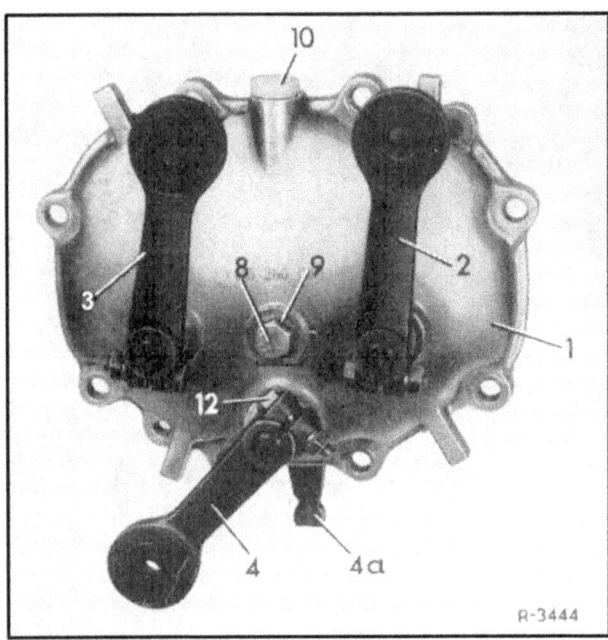

FIG 25 External view of the later side cover

1 Shift cover
2 Shift lever for 1st and 2nd speed
3 Shift lever for 3rd and 4th speed
4 Shift lever for reverse speed
4a Shift finger for reverse speed
8 Fastening bolt
9 Lock washer
10 Transmission breather
12 Clamping bolt

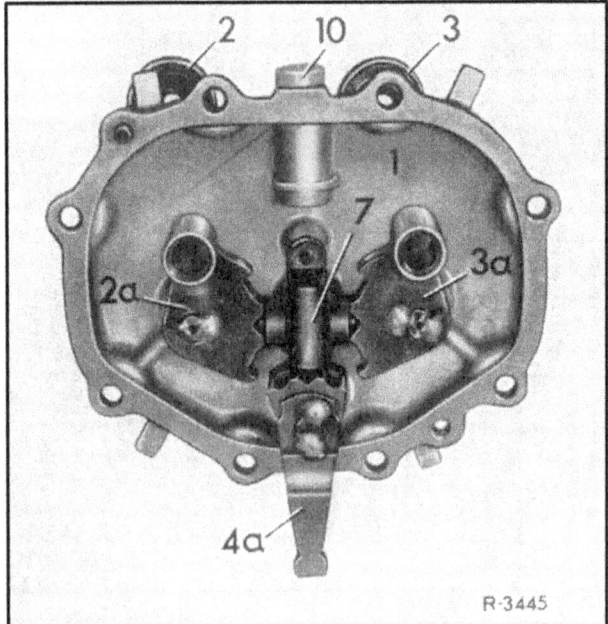

FIG 26 Internal view of the later side cover

1 Shift cover
2 Shift lever for 1st and 2nd speed
2a Shift rocker for 1st and 2nd speed
3 Shift lever for 3rd and 4th speed
3a Shift rocker for 3rd and 4th speed
4a Shift finger for reverse speed
7 Notch cage
10 Transmission breather

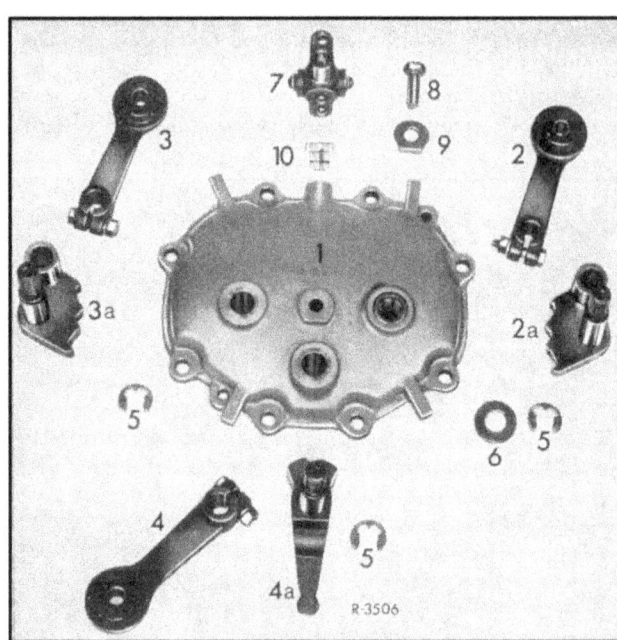

FIG 27 The components of the later side cover

1 Shift cover
2 Shift lever for 1st and 2nd speed
2a Shift rocker for 1st and 2nd speed
3 Shift lever for 3rd and 4th speed
3a Shift rocker for 3rd and 4th speed
4 Shift lever for reverse
4a Shift finger for reverse
5 Shaft lock
6 Washer
7 Notch cage
8 Fastening bolt
9 Lock washer
10 Transmission breather

Remove the clamping bolts 12 and take off the levers 2 and 3, noting that the lever 4 will already have been taken off when removing the cover. Prise off the circlips 5 and remove the washer 6 fitted to the first/second selector only. From inside the cover, pull off the shift yokes 2a and 3a as well as the shift lever finger 4a. Free the locking plate 9 so that the bolt 8 can be unscrewed and the detent cage 7 can be removed.

O-rings seal the shift yoke shafts 3a and 4a and the O-rings should be renewed if fluid leaks are found around the shafts. A self-sealing needle roller bearing is fitted to the yoke shaft 2a and the bearing should be renewed complete if leaks are found.

The parts are installed in the reverse order of removal. The shafts should be lightly lubricated with anti-friction grease and care must be taken not to damage the O-rings or sealing bearing when inserting the shafts. The three levers 2, 3 and 4 should be left off until after the cover is fully in place so that they can then be set as described in **Section 4** or **Section 5**, depending on where the gearshift is fitted.

7 Dismantling the earlier type of gearbox

This is the type of gearbox fitted to all pre-May 1969 models as well as all 280 SL/8 models.

Typical gearbox components are shown in **FIG 28** and typical top covers are shown in **FIG 29** for models with steering shift and **FIG 30** for models with floor shift.

1 Remove the bolts that secure the top cover to the case and lever off the cover, using a screwdriver in the notches provided. If not already done, remove the clutch release bearing and release lever from the clutch housing.

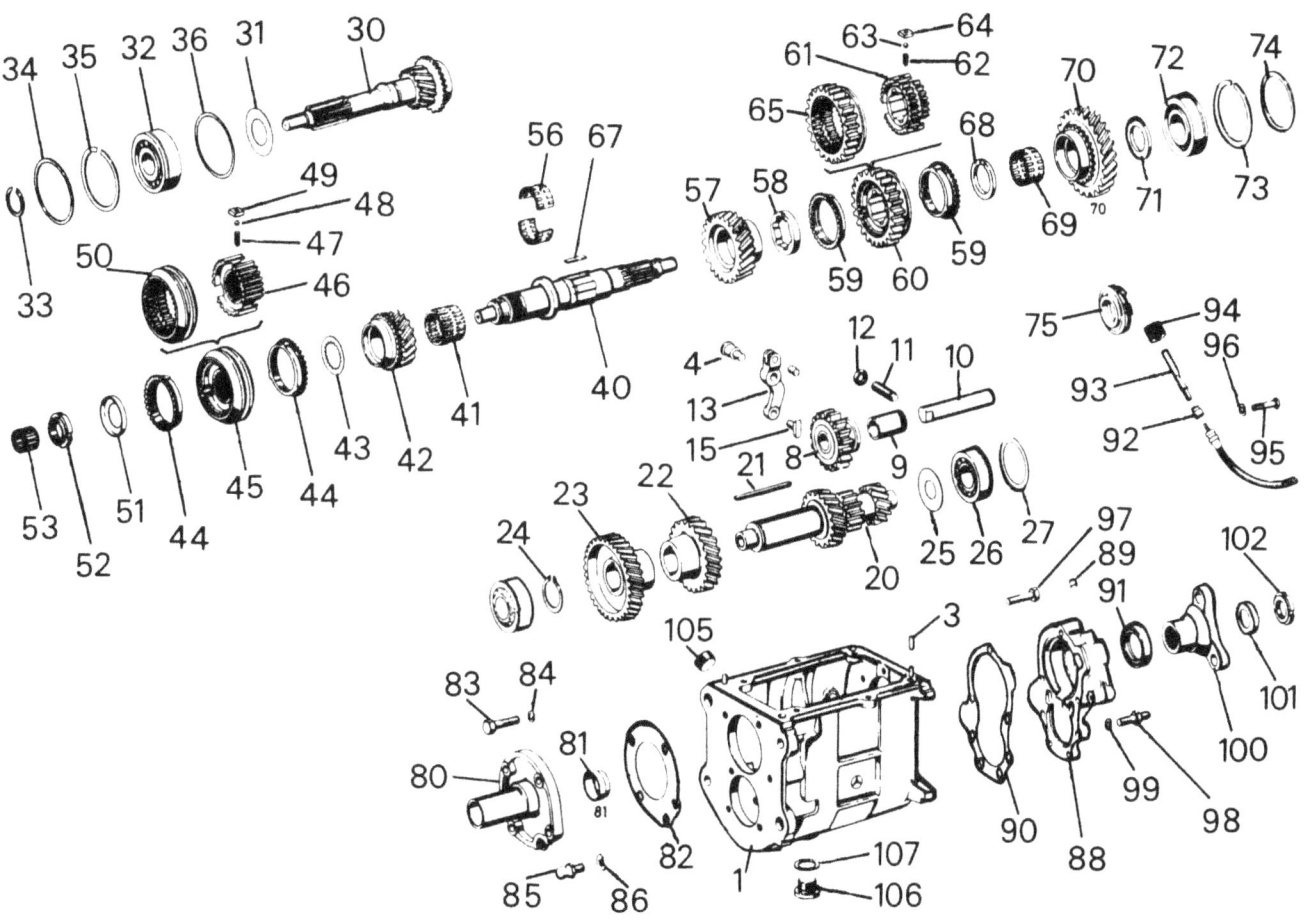

FIG 28 Typical earlier gearbox components

1. Gearbox case	27. Shim	49. Key
3. Dowel pin	30. Main drive shaft (clutch shaft)	50. Operating sleeve
4. Pivot pin	31. Shim	51. Cup washer
8. Reverse idler gear	32. Ball bearing	52. Grooved nut
9. Reverse idler gear bush	33. Snap ring	53. Needle roller bearing
10. Reverse idler shaft	34. Spacer ring	56. Needle roller halves
11. Locking stud	35. Bearing retaining ring	57. 2nd speed gearwheel
12. Lock nut	36. Shim	58. Splined spacer ring
13. Reverse selector lever	40. Mainshaft	59. Baulk ring, 2nd speed
15. Engagement shoe	41. Needle roller bearing	60. Synchronizer 1st and 2nd speed
20. Countershaft	42. Mainshaft 3rd speed gearwheel	61. Synchronizer hub
21. Key	43. Locking washer	62. Detent spring
22. Countershaft 3rd speed gear	44. Baulk ring 3rd speed	63. Detent ball
23. Countershaft constant drive gear	45. Synchronizer 3rd and 4th speed	64. Key
24. Retaining ring	46. Synchronizer hub	65. Operating sleeve
25. Thrust washer	47. Detent spring	67. Locking key
26. Ball bearing	48. Detent ball	68. Spacer ring
69. Needle roller bearing	91. Rear oil seal	
70. 1st speed gearwheel	92. Coupling	
71. Thrust washer	93. Spindle	
72. Mainshaft bearing	94. Spedometer gear	
73. Outer retaining ring	95. Bolt	
74. Shim	96. Wave washer	
75. Speedometer drive gear	97. Bolt	
80. Gearbox front cover	98. Stud	
81. Insert	99. Wave washer	
82. Gasket	100. Gearbox drive flange	
83. Cover bolt	101. Lock washer	
84. Wave washer	102. Grooved nut	
85. Bolt	105. Oil filler plug	
86. Wave washer	106. Oil drain plug	
88. Gearbox rear cover	107. Sealing washer	
89. Plug		
90. Gasket		

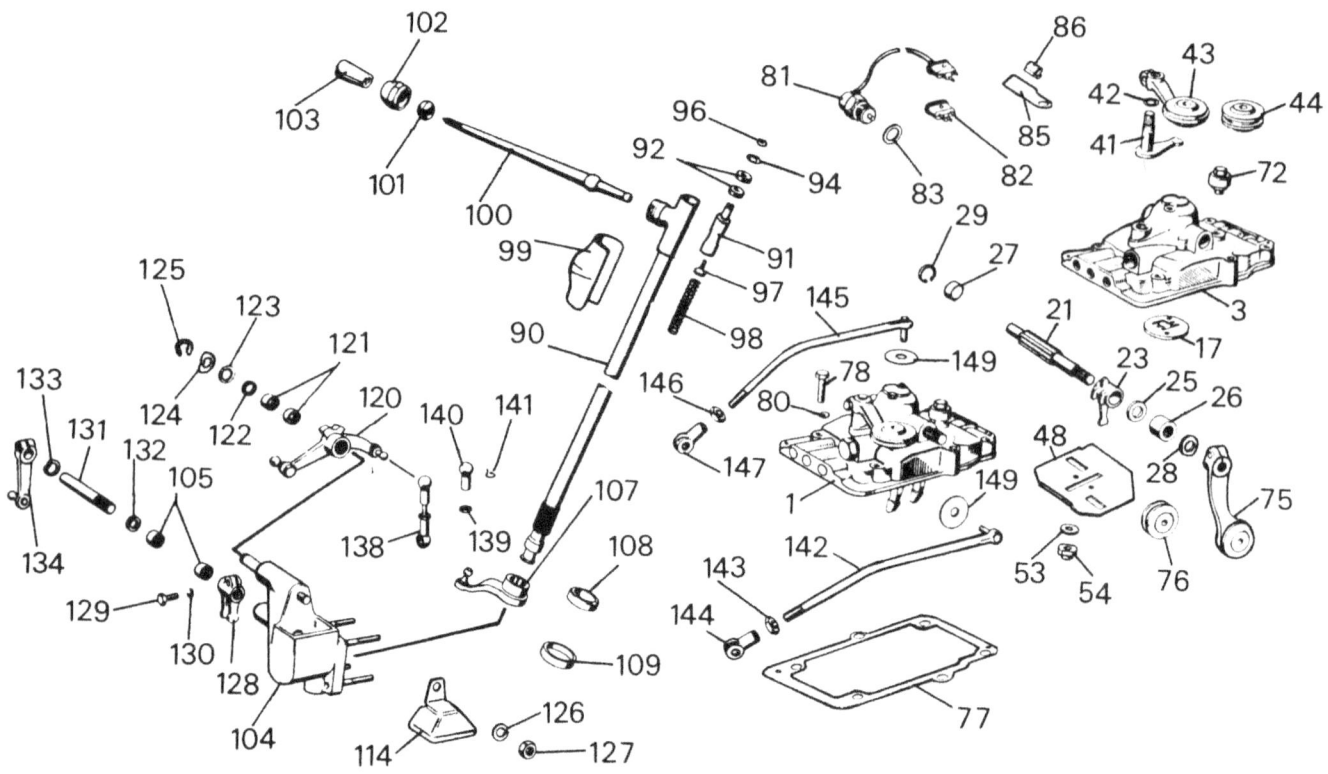

FIG 29 Typical top cover assembly for earlier models fitted with steering column shift

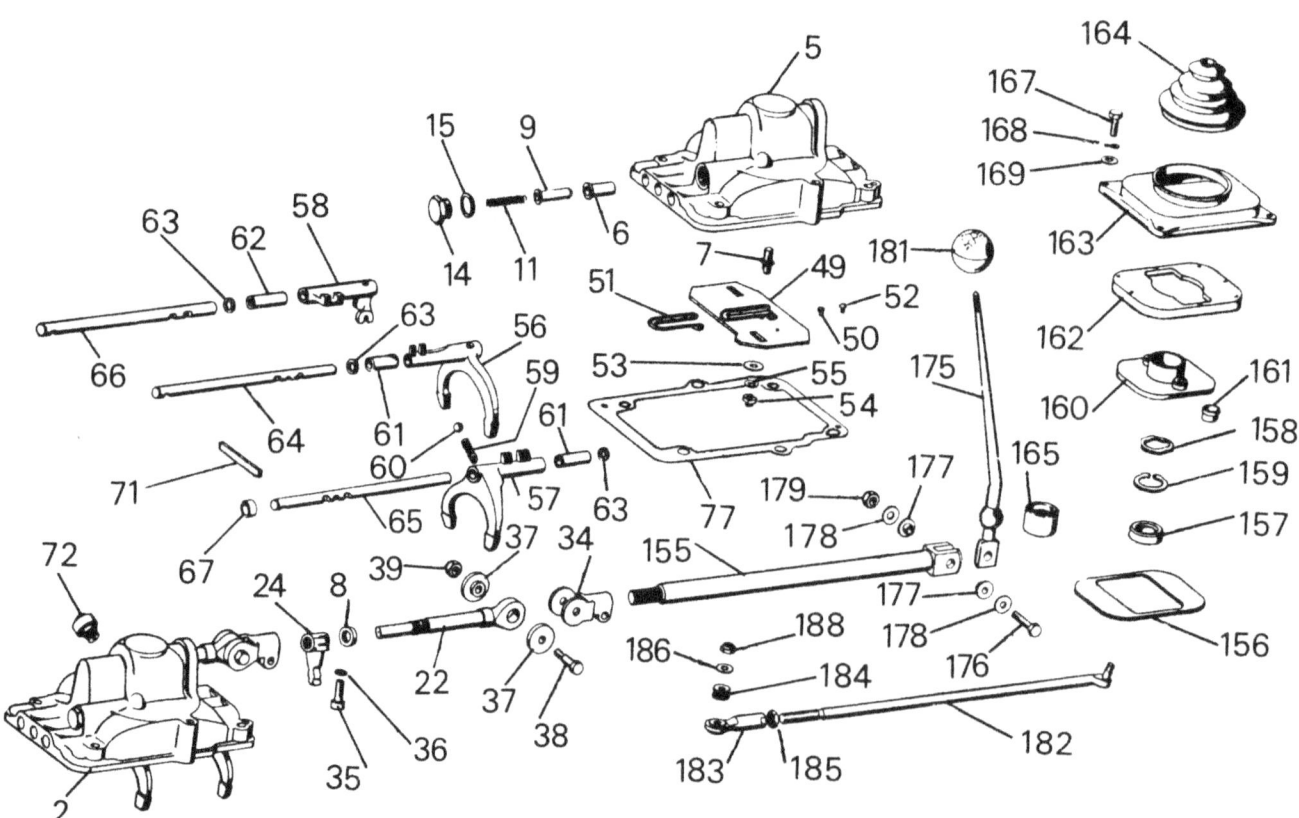

FIG 30 Typical top cover assembly for earlier models fitted with floor shift

2 Remove the bolts that secure the front housing and clutch cover. Remove the housing and cover, carefully collecting shims fitted under the front cover. **These shims set the end plays of the shafts and must therefore be installed back into their original positions. It is advisable to tie all the shims in a set together and label them so that there will be no confusion on reassembly.**

3 Fit the special clamp No. 136 589 38 61 to the first/second speed synchromesh unit, as shown in **FIG 31**, to keep the parts together, then refer to **FIG 28**.

4 Select top and reverse gears simultaneously so that the mainshaft is locked. Free the lockwasher 101 from its groove in the nut 102 and remove the nut with a suitable special wrench. Pull off the drive flange 100 by hand.

5 Take out the bolts 97 and studs 98 that secure the rear cover in place and withdraw the cover assembly. Pull the speedometer drive gear 75 off the mainshaft 40. The parts of the rear cover can be removed after taking out the bolt 95. Use a drift to drive out the speedometer drive parts 92, 93 and 94. If the oil seal 91 is damaged it should be driven out and a new one installed on reassembly.

6 Remove the snap ring 33 that secures the front bearing 32 and also remove the two snap rings 35 and 73 from the annular grooves in the bearings 32 and 72. Use a plastic-faced hammer and drive the mainshaft assembly forwards so that it in turn drives the input shaft assembly out of the front casing. Carry on driving out until sufficient of the bearing 32 is out of its bore for two screwdrivers to be used to lever it right out, as shown in **FIG 31**.

7 Drive the input shaft rearwards until the bearing 72 can be levered out with two screwdrivers. Fit a suitable length of tube or pipe over the mainshaft and use the nut 102 to tighten it down so that it keeps the mainshaft parts in place. The special clamp fitted earlier can now be removed.

8 Either tie or hold up the mainshaft and input shaft assemblies so that their gears are held out of mesh with the countershaft gears. Drive the countershaft assembly rearwards until the rear countershaft bearing can be removed, using a soft metal drift to drive the parts. Allow the countershaft parts to fall to the bottom of the case and withdraw the front countershaft bearing using a suitable puller.

9 Pull the input shaft 30 out through the front of the casing and collect the needle roller bearing 53. Lift up the front end of the mainshaft assembly and remove the assembly through the top aperture in the case.

10 Lift out the countershaft assembly through the top aperture in the case. If required, remove the circlip 24 and use a suitable puller to remove the gears 22 and 23. The key 21 should be carefully tapped out of its slot.

11 The reverse idler 8 and its parts can now be removed from the case.

Mainshaft:

Free the lockwasher 51 from its groove in the nut 52 and unscrew the nut. Fit a 'Bulldog' type clip over the baulk rings and synchromesh unit to keep the parts together and withdraw the parts from the front end of the mainshaft.

FIG 31 Removing the bearing. Note the special clamp fitted to synchromesh unit

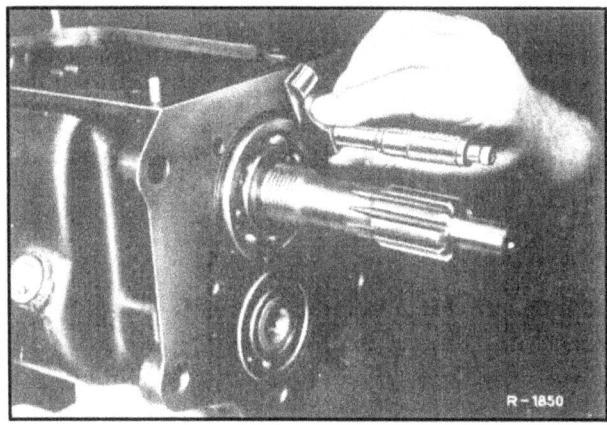

FIG 32 Measuring the bearing protrusion

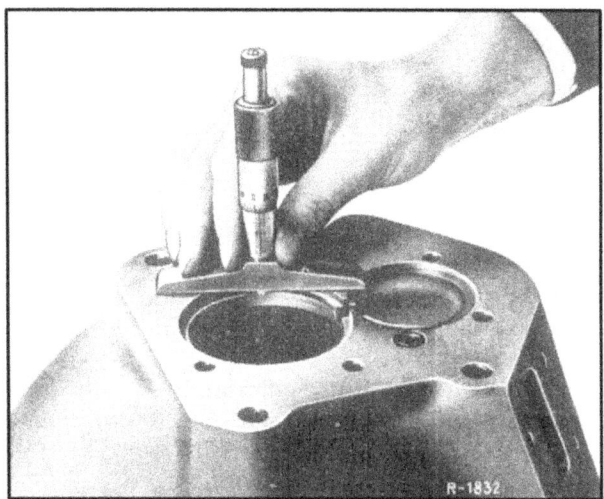

FIG 33 Measuring the housing recess

Take off the nut 102 and remove the temporary sleeve fitted earlier. Secure the parts of the synchromesh unit 60 and baulk rings 59 with another Bulldog clip and remove the parts from the rear of the mainshaft. Remove the key 67 before turning and removing the splined ring 58. The remainder of the parts can then be removed and laid out in order.

Synchromesh units:

Service one unit at a time to avoid any danger of intermixing parts and make sure that the baulk rings, sleeve, and hub are all indelibly marked so that they will be reassembled back into the same positions.

Wrap the unit in a piece of cloth to catch all the parts, after removing the Bulldog clip, and press the hub out of the sleeve. If the parts are not wrapped in cloth on dismantling there is a great danger that the balls and springs will be lost.

Clean all the parts and check for wear, damage or broken teeth.

Fit the springs 47 or 62 and keys 49 or 64 back into the hub 46 or 61, omitting the balls at this stage, and holding the parts in place with a little grease. Slide the inner hub, so that it faces in the correct direction, back into the operating sleeve 50 or 65. Adjust the position of the hub in the sleeve so that the bores in the hubs are just accessible. Press each key into the sleeve so that the bore is fully exposed and fit a ball 48 or 63 into the bore. Hold the ball in place by pulling the key slightly out again. When all the balls are in place, slide the hub back into the sleeve so that the balls click into place in the annular detent inside the sleeve.

Use a spring balance to pull the hub partially out of the sleeve, taking great care not to pull it so far that the parts fly out, and check the load required to move the hub out of the detent groove. If the axial load required is not within the limits of 7 to 11 kg renew parts as required.

Fit the baulk rings 44 or 59 back onto their correct sides and hold the assembly together with a Bulldog clip.

8 Reassembling the earlier type of gearbox

The dismantling of this gearbox is described in the previous section.

Before reassembling the gearbox, clean all the parts and check them for wear or damage. Check all the gears for worn or broken teeth, paying particular attention to the mating gear if teeth are damaged. Check all the shafts for scores, fret marks, or other damage. Wash the bearings separately in clean solvent and check them for damage or rough running. If the bearings have been in use for more than 100,000 kilometres (60,000 miles) it is advisable to fit new bearings on reassembly. Renew all defective parts.

Mainshaft:

Lightly lubricate all parts with ATF as they are being reassembled.

1 Mount the mainshaft 40, front end upwards, vertically in the padded jaws of a vice. Refit the needle roller bearing 41 and slide on the third speed gear 42 with its cone facing upwards. Fit the serrated washer 43 followed by the synchromesh assembly 45 and its baulk rings 44. Secure the parts in place using the nut 52.

2 Check that the third-speed gear 42 rotates freely about its bush and use feeler gauges to check the end float. The end float should be .10 to .18 mm (.004 to .007 inch) and if it is incorrect fit a new serrated washer 43 to bring it within limits. Serrated washers are available in thicknesses of 7.9 to 8.1 mm. When the end float is correct, fit a new lockwasher 51 and tighten the nut 52 to a torque load of 20 kgm (145 lbft). Lock the nut by staking the lockwasher into a groove on the nut.

3 Remove the assembly from the vice, turn it over and mount it vertically again.

4 Slide the second-speed gear 57 down onto the shaft with its cone upwards. Slide the splined ring 58 down the splines of the mainshaft and then rotate it so that it locks the gear into place. Check that the gear rotates freely and use feeler gauges to check the end float. Splined rings 58 are available in increments of .05 mm (.002 inch) and should be selectively fitted until the end float of the gear is within the limits of .10 to .18 mm (.004 to .007 inch).

5 When the correct splined ring has been selected, remove it and the gear from the mainshaft and install them again after having fitted the halves of the needle roller bearing 56. The splined ring must be set so that the key slot faces upwards and is in line with the keyway in the shaft.

6 Fit the key 67 back into place in the keyway and slot in the splined ring. Slide on the assembled synchromesh unit 60 complete with its baulk rings 59. Fit the spacer ring 68 back into place with the slot for the key downwards and over the key 67. Check that there is a clearance of .1 mm (.004 inch) between the end of the key and the bottom of the slot. If necessary either fit a new key or carefully file down the end of the key to set the correct clearance.

7 Install the first-speed gear 70 with its cone facing downwards, followed by the thrust washer 71 with its shoulder upwards. Secure the parts in place with the piece of tubing and nut 102. Check that the gear 70 rotates freely. Adjust its end float to .10 to .18 mm (.004 to .007 inch) by selectively fitting of the thrust washer 71 (available in increments of .05 mm—.002 inch).

8 Remove the parts installed in operation 7, fit the needle roller bearing 69 and again install the parts as described. Use the tube and nut to prevent them from coming off the mainshaft.

Reassembly:

Reassemble the input and countershaft parts in the reverse order of dismantling. The three main sub-assemblies are then installed in the reverse order of removal. The bearings 32 and 72 are fitted with their annular grooves outwards and once the snap rings have been fitted they are driven in until the snap rings firmly contact the case.

1 Use a depth gauge to measure the protrusion of the front bearing from the casing, as shown in **FIG 32**. Similarly measure the depth of the recess in the clutch housing, as shown in **FIG 33**. Make up a shim pack so that the clearance between the snap ring on

the bearing and the end of the recess in the clutch housing will be .00 to .05 mm (.000 to .002 inch) when the parts have been installed. Refit the clutch housing with the shim pack in place.
2 Similarly make up a shim pack for the rear bearing and rear housing, but once the shims have been selected keep them safely and do not yet install the rear housing. Make due allowance for the thickness of the gasket 90 when making up the shim pack.
3 Use a soft-faced hammer to drive the rear bearing 26 off the countershaft assembly until its front bearing is in firm contact with the clutch housing. Make up a shim pack, with due allowance for the thickness of the gasket 90, so that there will be a clearance of .15 to .20 mm (.006 to .008 inch) between the end of the bearing 26 and the recess in the housing 88 after the parts have been installed.
4 Reassemble the speedometer drive parts and oil seal to the rear housing. Remove the nut and temporary sleeve and press the speedometer drive gear 75 back into position on the mainshaft. Refit the rear housing with a new gasket 90 and the correct shim packs in place.
5 Refit the drive flange 100 and a new lockwasher 101. Tighten the nut 102 to a torque of 20 kg m (145 lb ft) and lock it by staking in the lockwasher into a groove.
6 Set the outer sleeves of the synchromesh units to their neutral positions and refit the top cover assembly, making sure that the selector forks engage correctly with the outer sleeves and the selector for the reverse idler.

9 Fault diagnosis

(a) Jumping out of gear

1 Gearshift mechanism incorrectly adjusted
2 Defective detent cage or detent springs and balls
3 Worn detent grooves in shift yokes or striker rods
4 Worn coupling dogs
5 Selector fork loose on striker rod

(b) Noisy gearbox

1 Insufficient or incorrect lubricant
2 Excessive end floats
3 Worn or damaged bearings
4 Worn or damaged gear teeth

(c) Difficulty in engaging gear

1 Check 1 in (a)
2 Stiff gearchange linkage
3 Defective clutch or leaks in clutch hydraulics
4 Insufficient clutch pedal free play
5 Worn synchromesh units

(d) Oil leaks

1 Defective gaskets
2 Worn or damaged oil seals
3 Damaged cover or case faces
4 Blocked vent

NOTES

CHAPTER 7 – AUTOMATIC TRANSMISSION

1 Description
2 Operation
3 Maintenance
4 Linkage adjustments
5 Removing and installing the transmission
6 Fault diagnosis

1 Description

A fully automatic four-speed transmission can be fitted in place of the manually-operated transmission described in the previous chapter. Up to May 1969 a K4A.025 transmission was fitted but after May 1969 it was changed to a K4C.025 transmission. The differences will be called out as required.

A fluid flywheel is fitted in place of the conventional clutch and as the unit is fully automatic in operation the clutch pedal is no longer necessary. The gearbox is of totally different construction from the conventional gearbox and uses epicyclic drives instead of the meshed gears used in the standard gearbox. The selection of the speeds is carried out by brake bands and clutches instead of synchromesh units. Control of the brake bands and clutches is by a very complex hydraulic system built into the unit and pressurized by internal pumps.

The unit is fitted with an oil cooler mounted integrally in the bottom tank of the cooling system radiator. Flexible hoses and metal pipes connect the transmission to the oil cooler. The radiator and oil cooler are dealt with in **Chapter 4, Section 3**.

The unit is a very complicated piece of mechanism and should only be stripped and repaired by experts. The owner should not be tempted to carry out more work than is described in this chapter. If the unit suffers from faults beyond the power of the owner to cure, the car should be taken to a service agent specializing in automatic transmissions. Few small garages have the skill, equipment or knowledge to deal satisfactorily with automatic transmissions.

Fluid flywheel:

A schematic sectioned view of a typical transmission is shown in **FIG 1**. The fluid flywheel at the front of the unit is filled with fluid and also has a constant flow of fluid through it. The force through it is used for cooling purposes, as large amounts of heat can be generated in the fluid flywheel when it is slipping. The flywheel case is bolted to the engine flywheel and revolves with it. The vanes of the pumping rotor also rotate with the cover and flywheel. The vanes of the pumping rotor drag the fluid around with them and the vanes of the impeller turn this fluid flow back into torque. There is a speed difference between the two rotors under all conditions because of friction losses (though the difference is only in the order of 2 per cent in normal drive), and there is a greater centrifugal force acting on the fluid at the tips of the pumping rotor vanes than there is at the inner edges. This pressure difference causes a rotational flow of the fluid to

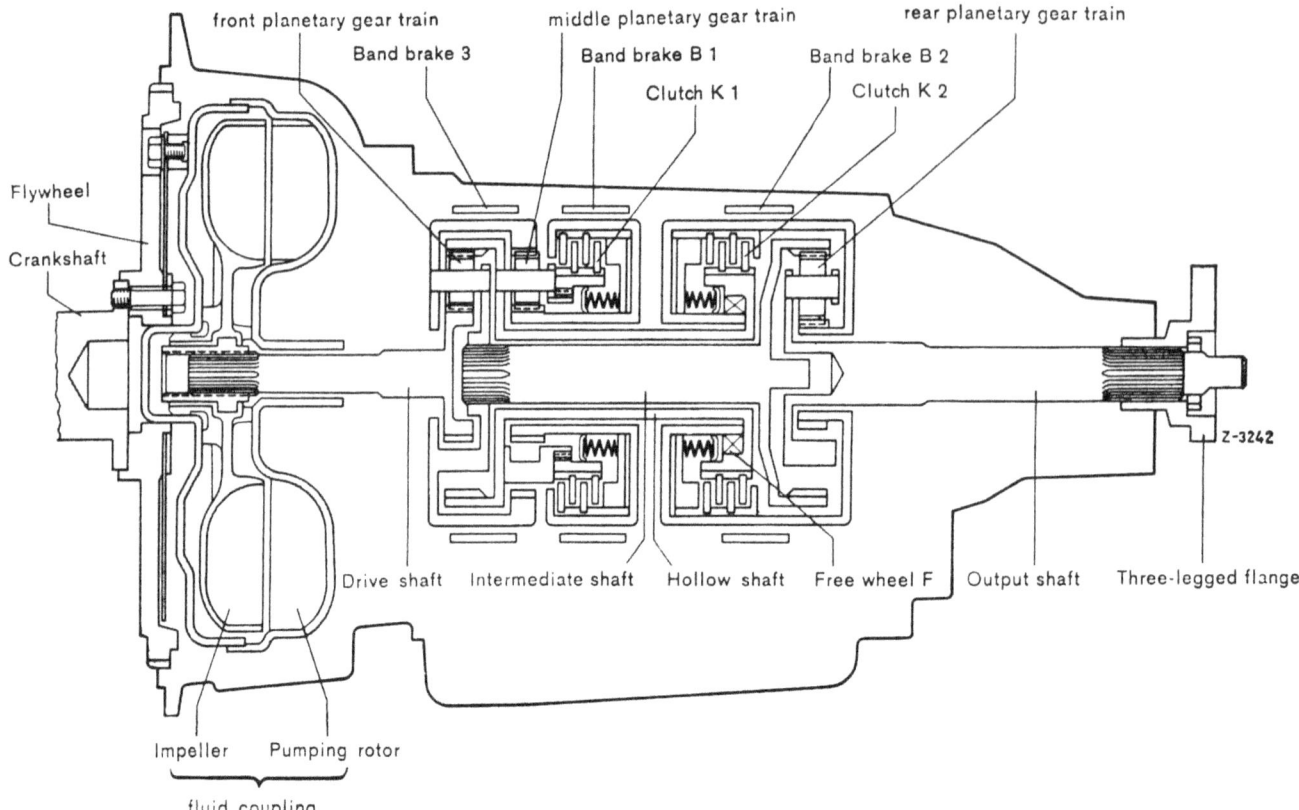

FIG 1 A schematic sectioned view of the transmission

be set up in the plane of the section shown and the resultant flow of oil around the unit follows the path of an imaginary spring coil wound between the two rotors. The combined fluid flow drives the impeller when the pumping rotor is turning.

The fractional losses will be dissipated as heat in the fluid. Under normal conditions the gearbox automatically selects the correct speed to ensure that slip is kept to a minimum and large amounts of slip only occur when starting off from rest. **The engine should only be run with large amounts of slip in the fluid flywheel (by holding the car stationary with drive selected), for testing purposes, and even then the time taken for test must be strictly limited.**

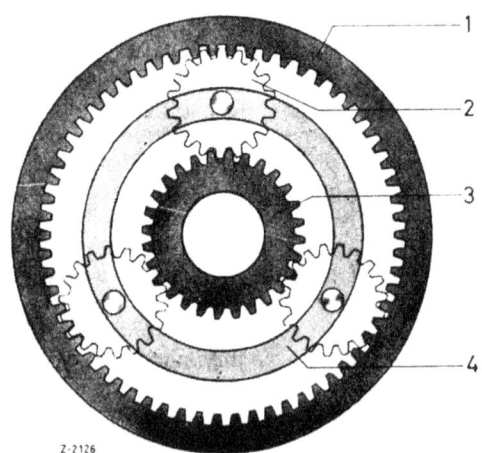

FIG 7:2 An epicyclic gear train

Gearbox:

An epicyclic gear train is shown in **FIG 2**. A combination of two such trains is used in the transmission to give the four forward speeds and one reverse. The ratio of the input to the drive can be varied, or even reversed in direction, by driving one member, holding the second, and taking the drive from the third. As examples, if the drive is put in at the sun gear 3 and the outer gear 1 is held stationary, then a slower speed but higher torque can be taken from the planet carrier 4. Drive the sun gear as before but this time hold the planet carrier 4 stationary, and a slower but reversed drive can be taken from the outer gear 1.

Control and lubrication:

A selector lever is fitted, either on the steering column or the floor, for selecting the direction of drive and overriding the controls and selections in the transmission. On models fitted with a steering-column-mounted selector an indicator is fitted to the instrument panel to show the selection made. On floor-mounted selectors, the lever moves through a marked gate so that the selection is readily seen.

Two pumps are fitted to the unit to supply oil pressure for lubrication and actuation of the components. The valve system is controlled by step pressures generated by the governor on the output shaft. A control pressure dependent on the throttle position modulates the shift points and a kick-down linkage is also fitted to downshift the transmission, provided that it is within the speed range, when the accelerator pedal is pressed right down to the floor.

Road test:

The owner is not the best person to carry out a road test, unless he has had recent experience of a similar car fitted with an automatic transmission that is known to be in good condition. The owner will have become used to the vagaries of his own car and therefore may not recognize them as faults.

The road test consists of checking that the up and down shifts occur at the correct speeds for the different throttle openings. Shift speeds are given in **Technical Data**. Safety devices such as the starter lock switch, hydraulic safety interlock, and parking lock should also be checked. Investigate undue noises or slip if they are present.

2 Operation

This section gives the uses of the various selections and the limits that apply and covers the operation of the transmission from the driver's point of view.

Position P:

When the selector is moved into this position a pawl locks into a square-toothed gear on the mainshaft. This prevents the car from rolling or moving unintentionally. This selection should be made when parking or stationary for long periods with the engine running. The engine can be started in this selection. Always use this selection when working on the car with the engine running.

The selection will hold the car on gradients but it should be used in conjunction with the handbrake as it may be difficult to release otherwise.

The selection can be made with the engine running or off and it should only be made with the car stationary. A hydraulic safety interlock is fitted to prevent the selection occuring if the lever is accidentally moved at road speeds faster than 10 kilometre/hr (6 mile/hr).

Moving off:

The footbrake should be applied when moving the selector lever to a drive selection as this prevents the slight jerk that would otherwise be felt as a gear is selected. Release the footbrake and apply pressure to the accelerator pedal and the car will move off with no further action. To stop, release the accelerator pedal and apply the brake, without moving the selector lever.

Position R:

This is equivalent to a normal reverse and should be used as such. The hydraulic interlock prevents inadvertent selection if the car is moving forwards faster than 10 kilometre/hr though obviously the selection should normally only be made with the car stationary.

Position O or N:

This is equivalent to the normal neutral position where there is no drive between the engine and rear wheels. With the brakes released the car can be moved freely for towing or pushing.

The starter motor will only operate in **N** or **P** because of the starter switch, which acts as a safeguard against the car moving off immediately the engine is started.

The selector lever should not be moved into this position above road speeds of 50 kilometre/hr (30 mile/hr).

FIG 3 The dipstick and filler tube

1 Oil filler pipe   2 Oil dipstick

FIG 4 The later flywheel drain plug

1 Oil filler tube   2 Oil drain plug   3 Oil pan

FIG 5 The later filter attachments

4 Oil filter   5 Fastening bolts

FIG 6 The early sump attachments and drain plug

1 Oil filler pipe
3 Transmission oil pan
7 Drain plug
8 Cover plate

Position 4:

This is the normal selection for driving forwards. All four speeds are automatically shifted in sequence and the car can be started, stopped, and driven at all speeds without the driver having to make any further selections.

The shift points will take place depending on the position of the throttle as the wider the throttle opening the higher the shift points.

When the accelerator pedal is pressed down there will be a slight resistance at full throttle. If the accelerator pedal is pressed past this point the kick-down will operate and, provided that the road speed is within limits, the transmission will downshift into a lower gear for rapid acceleration.

Position 3:

This is similar to position 4 but fourth-speed is cut out so that the transmission will not change up into it. Engine braking will be available and the selection should be used for climbing or descending average gradients. This selection may also be made when negotiating winding roads where constant shifts to and from top speed will be avoided.

As top speed is not available, care must be taken not to overspeed the engine in this selection.

Position 2:

This selection isolates both third and top speeds so that the transmission will not upshift into them. The selection should be used when negotiating steep mountain roads, driving for long periods at very slow speeds (such as in convoy) or for maximum engine braking. **Great care must be taken not to overspeed the engine in this selection.**

Starting the engine:

Normally the engine can only be started with either selection **P** or **N** made.

If the battery is flat, or there is some other cause which prevents the engine from starting normally, the car may be tow-started. **Use a sufficiently long tow rope to avoid any danger of an end-to-end collision when the engine starts.** Start towing with the selector in **N** and when the road speed reaches 40 to 50 kilometre/hr (25 to 30 mile/hr) move the selector to position **2** and do not touch the accelerator until the engine is running. As soon as the engine is running, return to **N** to prevent overrunning the tow rope. If the engine is not driven when drive is selected it indicates that the secondary pump cannot yet cope with the flow required. Select **N** again and wait a minute before attempting to start again. On the later models the operation of the secondary pump is noticed by a ticking or knocking noise.

The technique for the models with the earlier transmission (pre May 1969) is similar but the speed should only build up to 30 kilometre/hr and either position **3** or **4** should be used for starting.

Towing:

Provided that the transmission is in good condition and correctly filled with fluid the car may be towed between the speed range of 20 to 50 kilometre/hr (12 to 30 mile/hr) without causing damage to the transmission. **N** position must of course be selected while towing.

If the speed range cannot be kept to or the transmission is damaged, the car should be towed after the propeller shaft has been disconnected from the rear axle and hung safely out of the way.

Note that a higher pedal pressure will be required on the brakes as there will be no vacuum to the brake servo. The rope should be attached to the built-in eyes on the body, one at the rear and the other at the front.

Slow-speed manoeuvring:

When moving in confined spaces, such as when parking, select drive normally but hold the car on the footbrake. Increase the throttle opening slightly to give a fairly fast idle and then control the speed of the car on the footbrake. The action is similar to slipping the clutch on a conventional transmission and will therefore be fairly instinctive once it has been initiated.

Rocking:

If the car is stuck in mud or snow a rocking action will often help to free it. **Avoid spinning the wheels as this only digs the car in deeper.** Set a fast idle speed

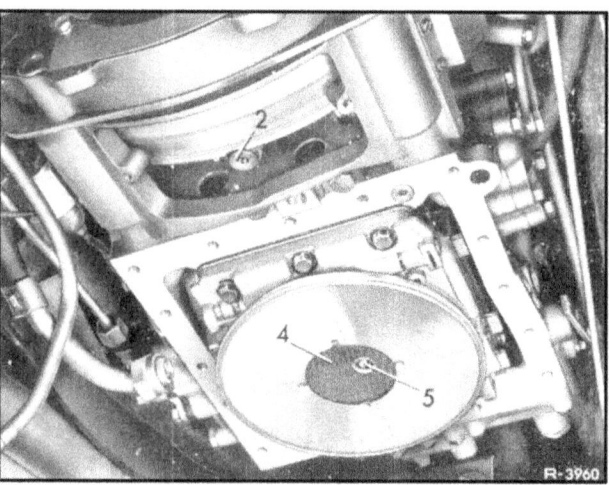

FIG 7:7 The early oil filter and flywheel drain plug

4 Oil filter 5 Fastening bolt

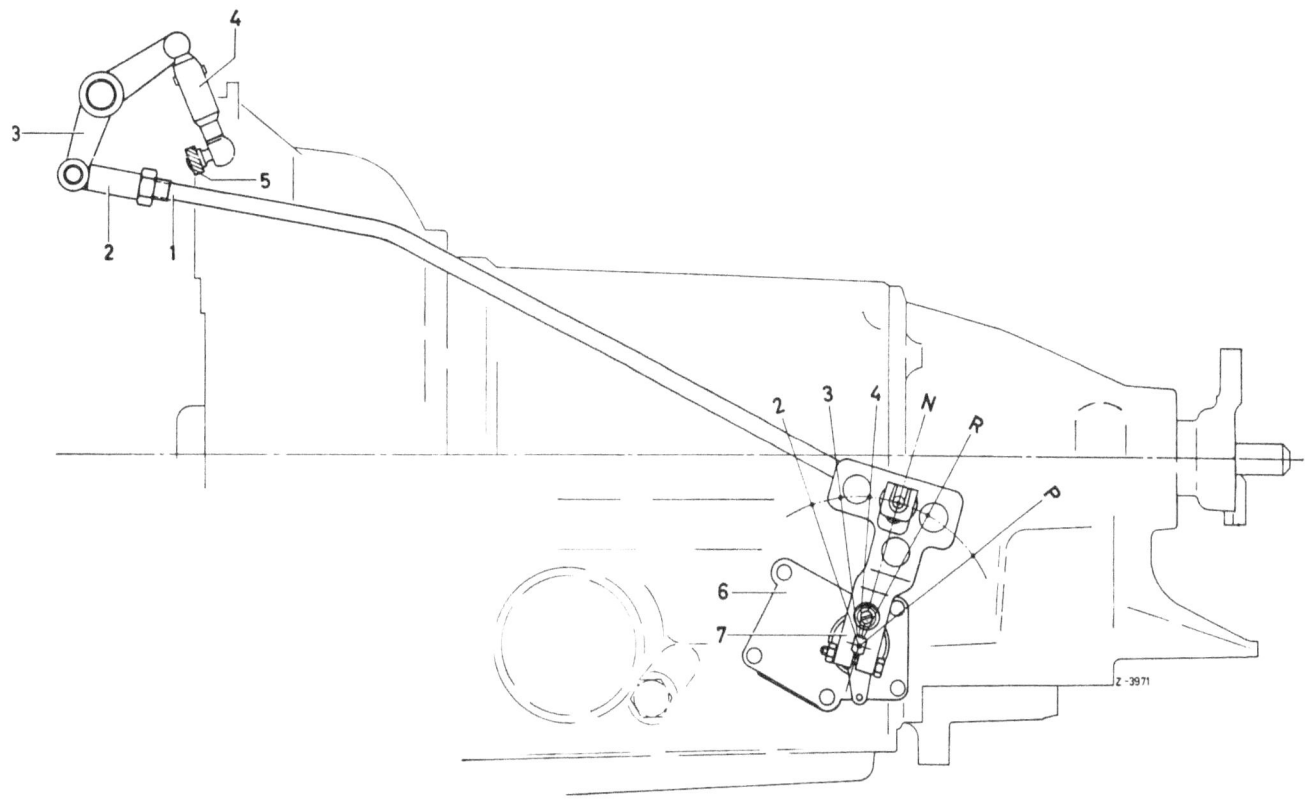

FIG 8 The linkage fitted with later transmissions using a steering mounted shift

1 Selector rod
2 Ball socket
3 Intermediate lever
4 Resilient intermediate piece
5 Shift lever
6 Starting locking and backup light switch
7 Range selector lever

using the accelerator pedal and move the selector backwards and forwards between **R** and a forward selection. Try to synchronize the movement of the selector with the movement of the car so that the direction of drive is changed as the car comes to a stop, and before the wheels spin, so that the car gradually increases the distance it moves each time and eventually drives out in one direction or the other.

3 Maintenance

Fluid level:

The fluid level should be checked at intervals not exceeding 5000 kilometres (3000 miles) and it should also be checked before any long run.

The level must be checked with the engine running at idle, the selector at P and the transmission at its normal operating temperature. The car must be standing on level ground. If any of these conditions are not met, a false reading may easily result.

Wipe the top of the dipstick 2 and filler tube 1, shown in **FIG 3**, clean and withdraw the dipstick. Wipe the dipstick clean with a piece of leather or lint-free cloth, insert it fully back into place and withdraw it again immediately. The lower mark will be the correct level if the engine is idling but cold and the upper mark correct when the engine is idling and the transmission hot. Add fresh clean fluid to bring the level up to the mark.

If the fluid level is very low, froth will form in it and will give a false reading. Stop the engine and allow two minutes at least for the froth to subside. Froth is also an indication of water (possibly through a defective oil cooler) being in the fluid.

If the unit has been refilled from empty, it is advisable to recheck the fluid level after 200 kilometres (125 miles).

Do not overfill the unit as this is nearly as harmful as underfilling. If the unit is accidentally overfilled, drain or syphon out the surplus.

When filling the unit from empty approximately 5.3 litres (9.3 Imp pints) of fluid will be required. If the unit is being filled after an oil change and filter clean, only 4.6 litres (8.1 Imp pints) will be required, as some fluid will remain in the oil cooler. With the engine stopped, pour in 3 litres (5.25 Imp pints) and then start the engine, leaving it at idle. Pour in the remainder of the fluid to the mark with the engine running at idle.

Oil change:

The oil should be changed at intervals of 25,000 kilometres (20,000 miles). The oil cooler should be drained out of the unit when it is at operating temperature as all dirt will be held in suspension. **Great care must be taken as the oil will be hot enough to cause serious scalding.**

Turn the engine until the drain plug 2, shown in **FIG 4**, is accessible through the stone guard in the converter

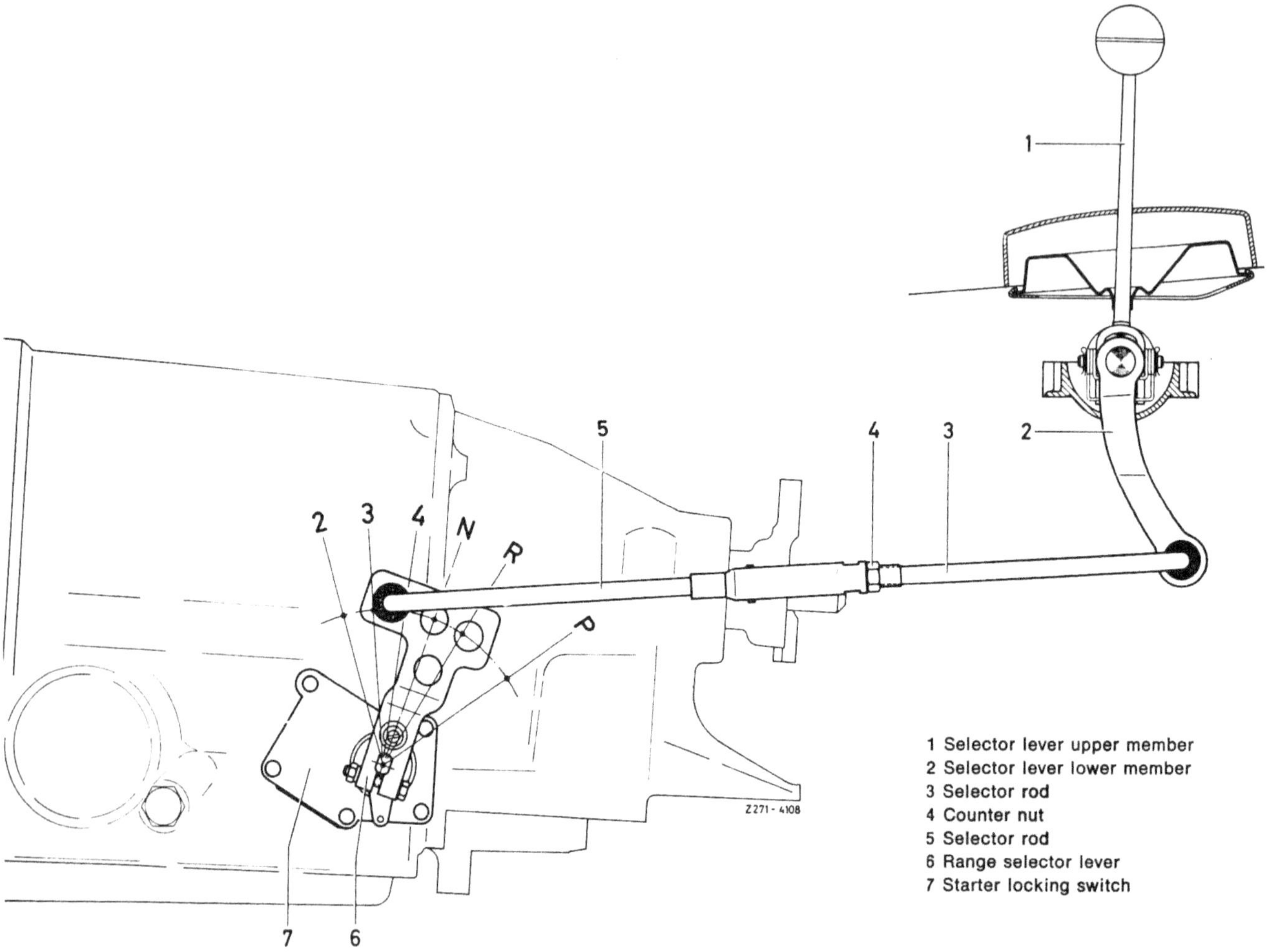

FIG 9 The linkage fitted with later transmissions using a floor mounted shift

1 Selector lever upper member
2 Selector lever lower member
3 Selector rod
4 Counter nut
5 Selector rod
6 Range selector lever
7 Starter locking switch

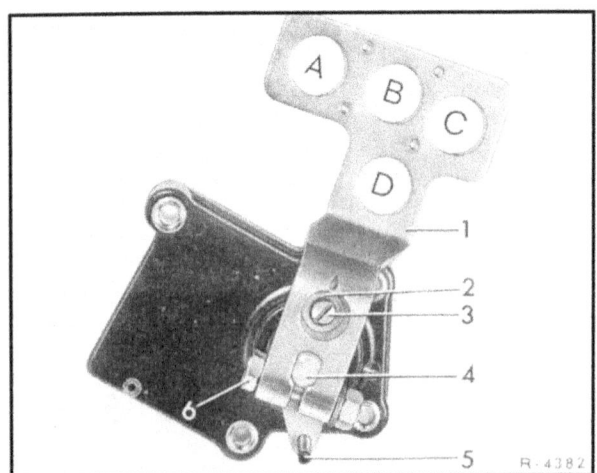

FIG 10 The later starter lock switch

1 Selector range lever
2 Washer
3 Adjusting screw
4 Shaft
5 Locating pin
6 Clamping screw

A Left and righthand drive for 280 S/8 and 280 SE/8 with floor shift
D Lefthand drive for 280 S/8 and 280 SE/8 with steering shift

housing. Remove the drain plug and allow all the oil to drain out into a suitable container. Carefully remove the bolts that secure the sump 3 after freeing the filler tube 1 and tilt the sump so that the remaining fluid can be poured out.

If the oil is black and evil smelling, the car should be taken to a service agent as it is likely that clutches or drive bands are burning in use.

Install the sump and drain plug. Fill the unit to the correct level with fresh automatic transmission fluid.

Oil filter:

This should be renewed at intervals of 50,000 kilometres (40,000 miles). The fastening bolts of the oil filter 4 are shown at 5 in **FIG 5** and they are accessible after the sump has been removed.

It should be noted that cars used in difficult conditions, such as for mainly city work, should have the transmission fluid changed an extra time between filter changes.

Cleanliness:

All operations involving the automatic transmission must be carried out with utmost care and cleanliness. Dirt inside the unit can easily jam a valve or cause faulty operation.

The outside of the unit and the stone guards should also be cleaned at intervals. This is particularly important if the car is used in very dirty or muddy conditions. The unit produces large amounts of heat, and a layer of dirt on the outside, or stones blocking the stone guards, can prevent heat from being carried away by the air stream and cause overheating, particularly in areas of high ambient temperatures.

Early transmission:

Maintenance on the earlier K4A.025 transmission is generally the same as on the later transmission. The main differences are in the attachments of the sump and oil filter and in the quantities of fluid required. The sump attachments are shown in **FIG 6** and the filter attachments in **FIG 7**. Note that the sump has a drain plug 7 and therefore need not be removed for oil change only. The unit will require 4.75 litres (8.25 Imp pints) for refilling from completely empty and 3.75 litres (6.5 Imp pints) for refilling after an oil and filter change.

4 Linkage adjustments

The adjustments to any linkage on the automatic transmission should only be carried out with the weight of the car resting on its wheels.

Steering wheel shift with later transmission:

The linkage is shown in **FIG 8**. Slacken the locknut on the ball socket 2 and disconnect the ball socket from the intermediate lever 3. Move the selector lever on the steering column to the Neutral position. Move the range selector lever 7 to the neutral position and adjust the ball socket 2 on the rod 1 until it can be fitted back to the intermediate lever 3 without any tension or pressure in the rod 1. Tighten the locknut on the ball socket at this position.

Floor shift with later transmission:

The linkage is shown in **FIG 9**. Disconnect the selector rod 5 from the range selector lever 6 and move the range selector lever to the neutral position. Move the selector lever 1 in the car to the neutral position, making sure that there is approximately 1 mm (.04 inch) clearance between the lever and the stop on the gate plate. Adjust the length of the selector rod 5 until it fits easily back into place in the range selector lever 6.

Adjustment of later starter lock switch:

The installation of the switch is shown in **FIG 10**. Set the range selector lever 1 into the neutral position, preferably after disconnecting the selector rod from it. Make sure that the clamp nut 6 is tight. Slacken the

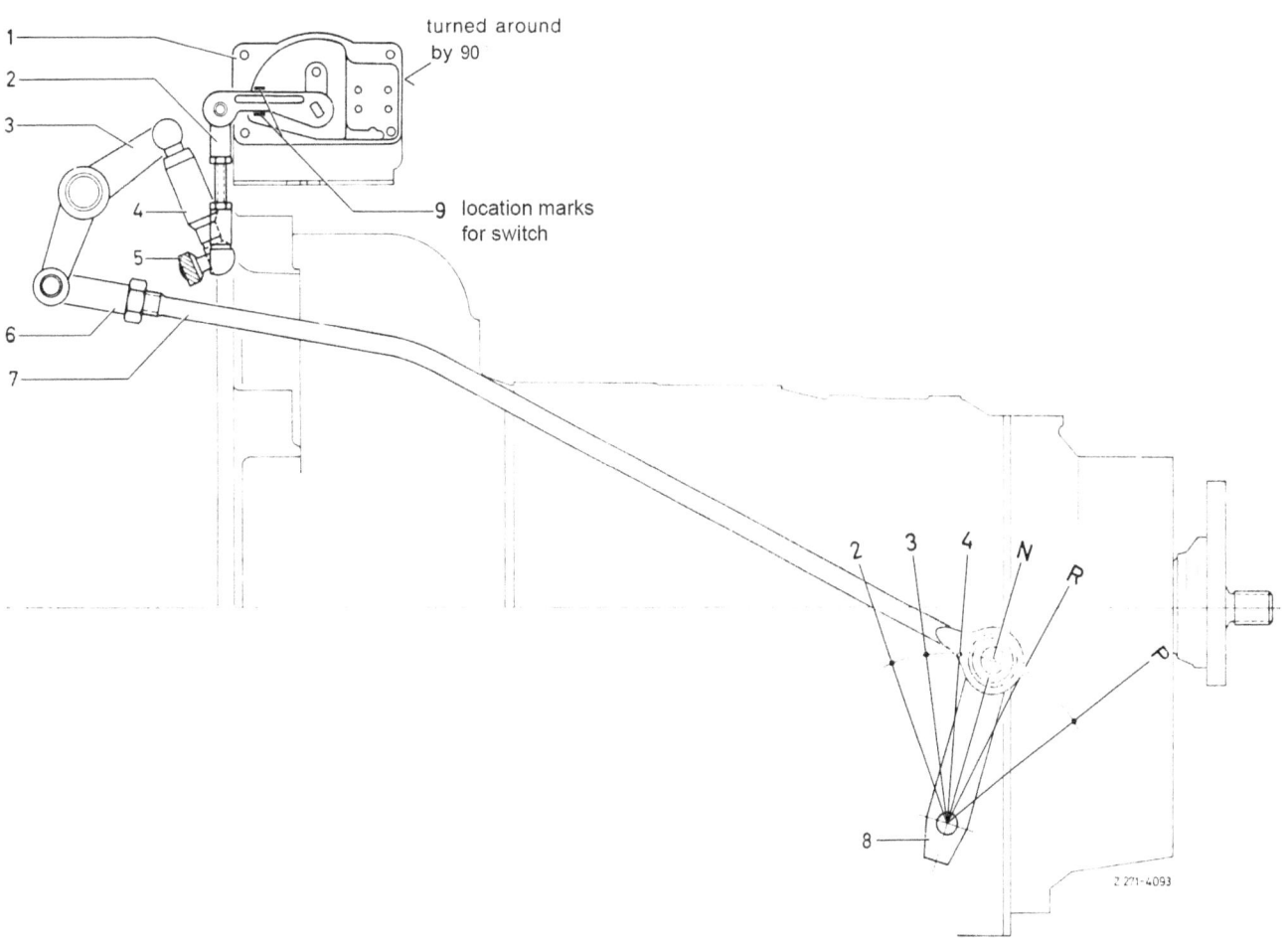

FIG 11 The linkage fitted with earlier transmission using a steering mounted shift

1 Starter locking switch
2 Connecting rod
3 Intermediate lever
4 Resilient intermediate piece
5 Shift lever
6 Ball socket
7 Shift rod
8 Range selector lever

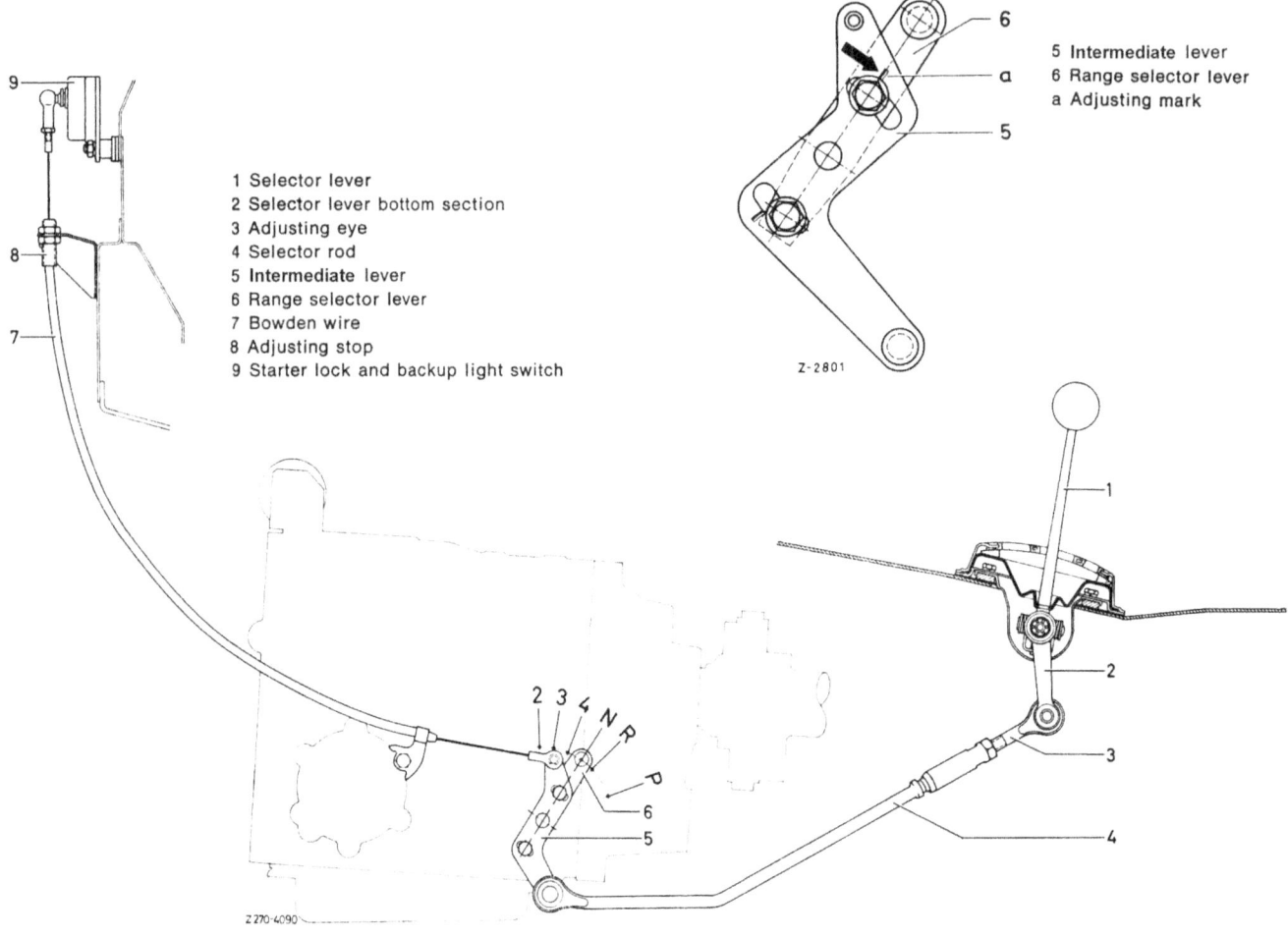

FIG 12 The linkage fitted with an earlier transmission using a floor mounted shift

adjusting screw 3 and fit a locating pin 5 through to the locating hole in the shift housing. Tighten the adjusting screw 3 and remove the pin 5. Check that the engine will only start in **N** or **P** selections and that the reverse lights come on in **R** selection.

Steering wheel shift with earlier transmission:

The linkage is shown in **FIG 11**. Disconnect the shift rod 7 at the intermediate lever 3 and also disconnect the starter switch connecting rod 2. Slacken the locknut on the ball socket 6. Set the range selector lever 8 to its neutral position and similarly set the selector lever on the steering to its Neutral position. Adjust the length of the shift rod 7, using the ball socket 6, until the ball socket can easily be fitted back to an intermediate lever without any strain. Tighten the locknut on the ball socket when the adjustment is completed. Adjust the length of the connecting rod 2 until the actuating lever on the starter switch 1 is between the white lines 9. Check that the engine will only start in **N** and **P** selections.

Floor shift with earlier transmission:

The linkage is shown in **FIG 12**. Remove the selector rod 4. Move both the range selector lever 6 and selector lever 1 to their neutral positions. The selector lever 1 should have approximately 1 mm (.04 inch) clearance between it and the stop in the gate. Slacken the bolts on the intermediate lever 5 and set the intermediate lever so that the adjusting mark 'a' is in line with the centre of the range lever, then tighten the bolts again. On the 280 SL/8 the levers are set so that both their centre lines are in line. Fit the selector rod 4 back onto the bearing of the intermediate lever 5. Set the adjusting eye 3 until it can easily be fitted back onto the bottom section of the selector lever 2, without strain. If necessary, fine adjustments can then be made by slightly altering the position of the intermediate lever 5 on the range lever 6.

Adjust the length of the Bowden cable 7, at the adjuster 8, so that the engine will only start in **N** and **P** selections and the reverse lights come on in **R** selection.

Adjusting indicator:

This is only fitted to models which have a steering column mounted selector and the method of adjustment is the same on both types of transmission. The indicator 6 is secured to the panel 7 by the bridge 1 and nut 2, shown in **FIG 13**. To adjust the indicator, slacken the locknut 5 and adjust the length of the cable 3 at 4 until the indicator corresponds with the selector lever position.

Control pressure linkage on later models with carburetters:

The linkage is shown in **FIG 14**. Make sure that the cold start system is not holding the throttle valves open. Disconnect the pullrod 7 on the ball head 11 and push the lever 8 to the idling throttle stop. Slacken the clamping screw 4 on the intermediate lever 2 and turn the adjusting lever 3 in relation to the intermediate lever 2 until the pullrod 7 can be fitted back on the ball head 11 without strain.

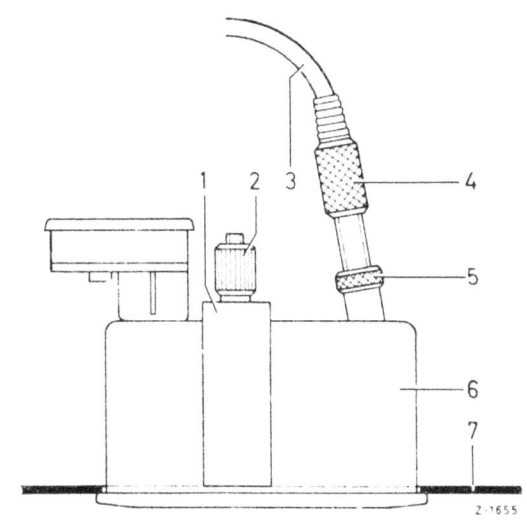

FIG 13 The instrument panel mounted indicator

1 Clamping bracket
2 Clamping nut
3 Bowden wire
4 Knurled nut
5 Counter nut
6 Housing
7 Instrument panel

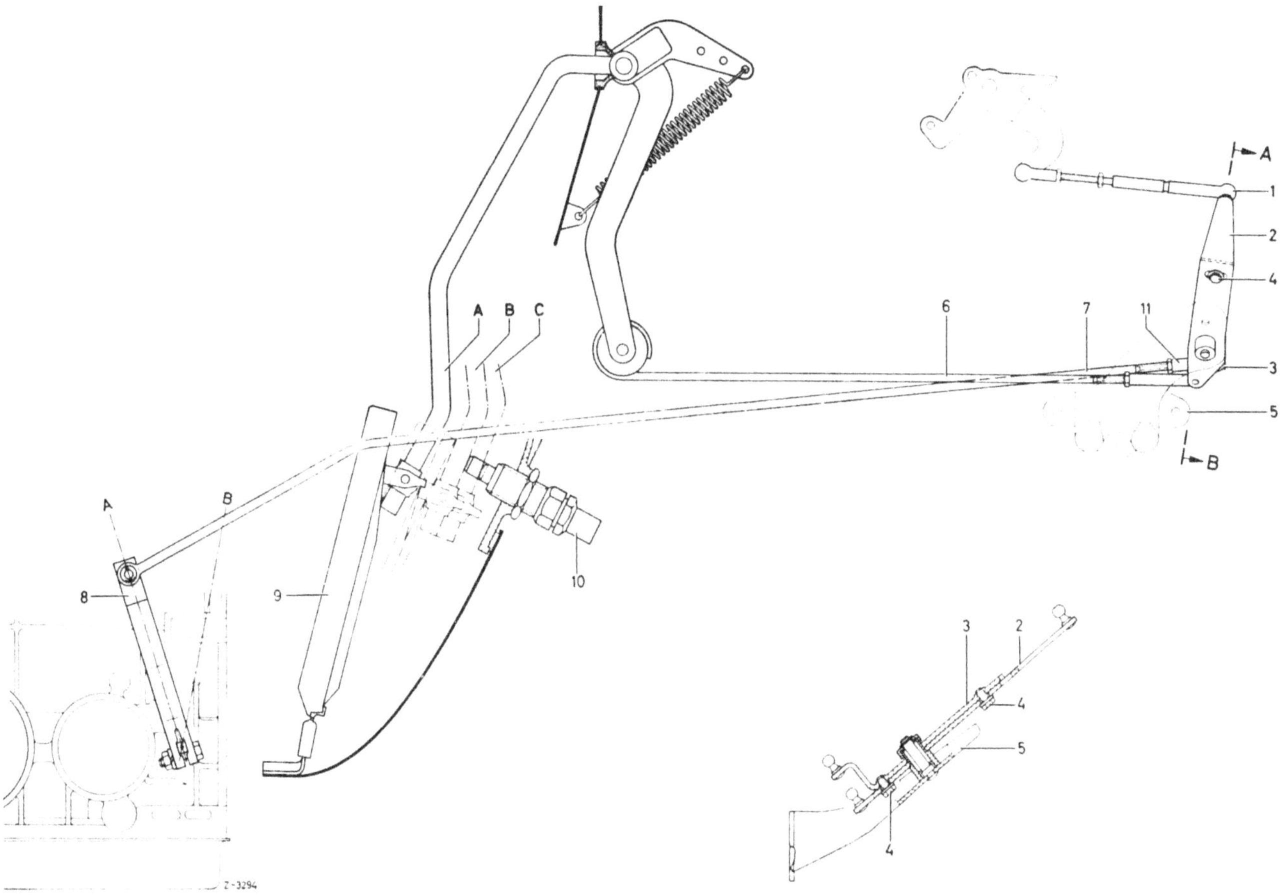

FIG 14 The control pressure linkage for later 280 S/8 models

1 Push rod
2 Intermediate lever
3 Adjusting lever
4 Clamping screw
5 Bearing bracket
6 Intermediate rod
7 Pull rod
8 Lever
9 Accelerator pedal
10 Kickdown switch
11 Ball head
A Idling throttle position
B Full throttle position
C Kickdown position

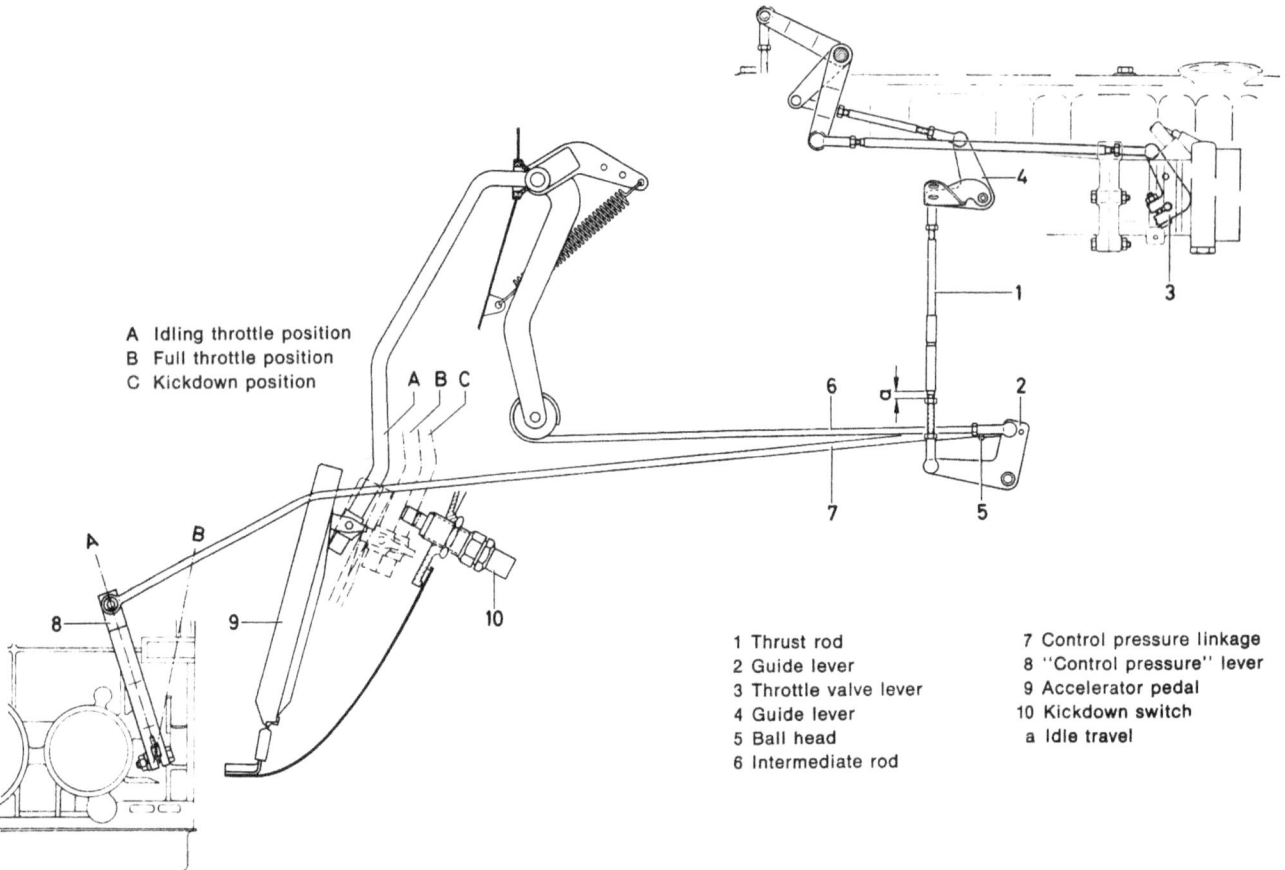

FIG 15 The control pressure linkage fitted to later models

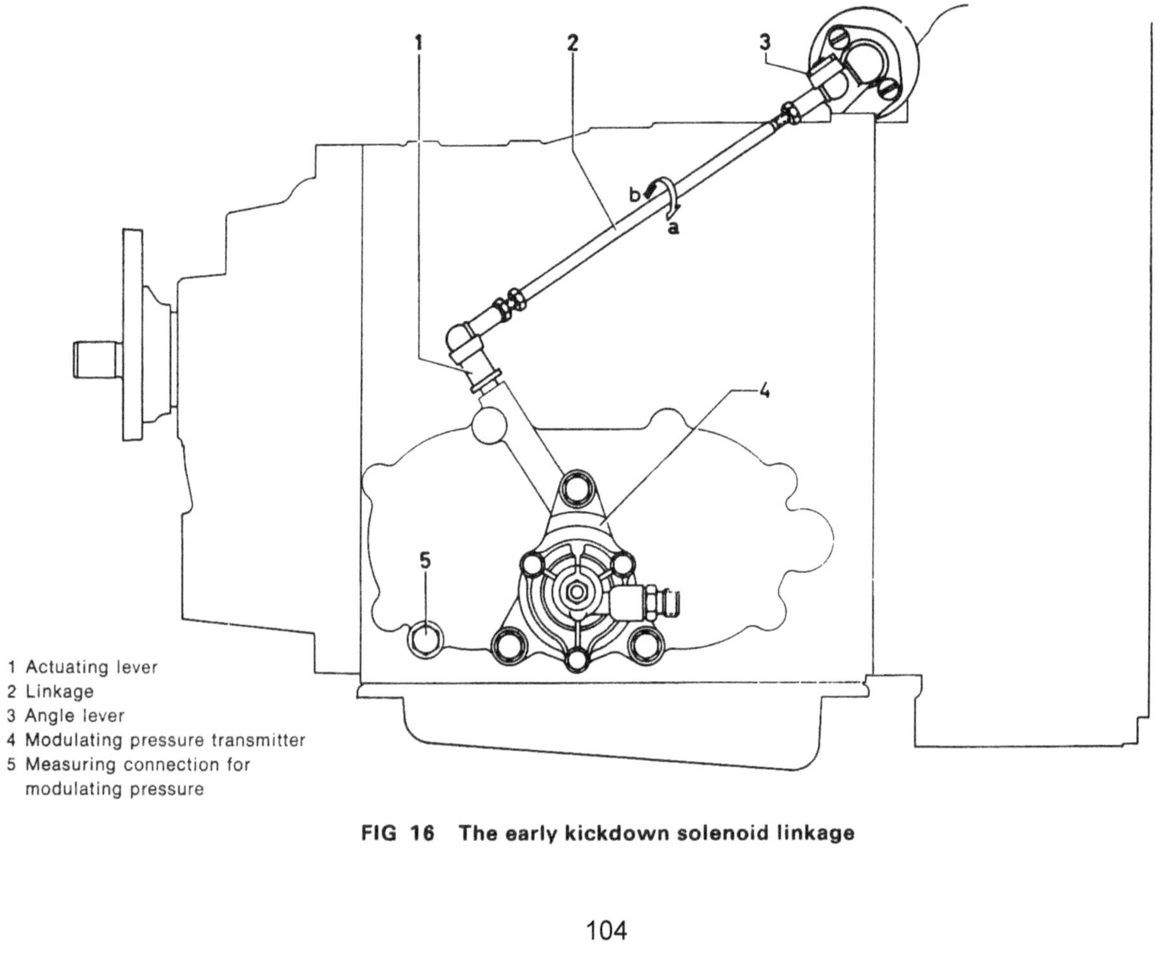

A Idling throttle position
B Full throttle position
C Kickdown position

1 Thrust rod
2 Guide lever
3 Throttle valve lever
4 Guide lever
5 Ball head
6 Intermediate rod
7 Control pressure linkage
8 "Control pressure" lever
9 Accelerator pedal
10 Kickdown switch
a Idle travel

1 Actuating lever
2 Linkage
3 Angle lever
4 Modulating pressure transmitter
5 Measuring connection for modulating pressure

FIG 16 The early kickdown solenoid linkage

Control pressure linkage on later models with fuel injection:

The linkage is shown in **FIG 15**. Disconnect the control pressure linkage on the ball head and push the lever 'control pressure' against the idling throttle stop. The throttle valve lever 3 should rest against the idling speed stop and the idle travel 'a' must be extended on the linkage. Push the control pressure lever 8 back against the stop. Adjust the length of the linkage 7 so that it can be refitted without tension or pressure.

Kick-down switch:

The kick-down switch should be adjusted so that when the accelerator pedal is down to the full throttle position there is a clearance of 3 to 4 mm on later models and 5 mm on earlier models between the throttle valve lever and the full load stop. When the adjustment is correct the throttle lever will be against the stop on later models and approximately 1 mm from it on earlier models when the accelerator pedal is pressed right down to the kick-down position.

Kick-down on earlier models:

The operating solenoid and its linkage are shown in **FIG 16**. The parts can be seen and adjusted through the aperture in the transmission tunnel. Switch on but do not start the engine. The linkage should move rearwards with the throttle closed. Lightly depress the accelerator and check that the linkage moves to the central position. Fully depress the accelerator pedal and check that the linkage moves forwards. Failure to operate correctly indicates a failure in the electrical supply, or jammed parts. The linkage should only be set by a service agent using test equipment to measure the kick-down modulating pressure.

5 Removing and installing the transmission

Because of the extra weight of the transmission it cannot be hand-held as on manual-shift models and a jack must be used to raise and lower it. A special attachment, shown in **FIG 17**, should be used to hold the transmission on the jack where possible, as it will allow slight movement for aligning the parts. The car itself must be raised off the ground by some means, so make sure all supports are strong enough and firmly based.

If the automatic transmission has been damaged, the radiator should be removed (see **Chapter 4**) and the transmission oil cooler thoroughly flushed through to remove any particles from inside it. The fluid flywheel should also be flushed out and the oil cooler lines blown through to clear them.

This section deals with the removal of both types of automatic transmission and differences will be called out as they occur.

1. Disconnect the battery. Drain the fluid from the transmission and fluid flywheel. If the sump has to be removed to drain the fluid, install the sump again after the fluid has been poured out. Disconnect the oil cooler lines from the transmission.
2. On the later models, disconnect the wire from the kick-down switch (shown in **FIG 18**), the vacuum line 30 from vacuum unit 10 (shown in **FIG 19**) and the connector from the starter switch (shown in **FIG 20**).

FIG 17 The BE.11.857 transmission support adaptor
1 Support plate   2 Base plate   3 Compression springs

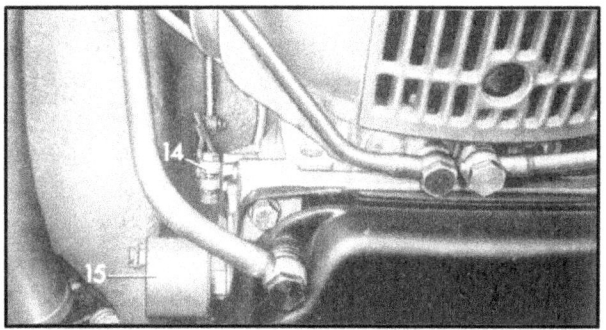

FIG 18 The later kickdown solenoid
14 Lever control pressure   15 Kickdown solenoid valve

FIG 19 The later vacuum unit connection
1 Oil filler pipe   3 Oil pan   10 Vacuum unit
2 Oil drain plug   30 Vacuum line

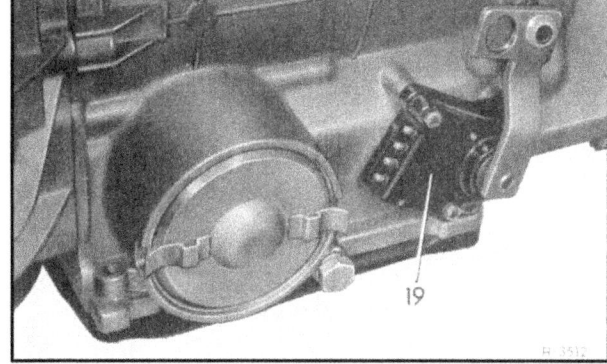

FIG 20 Later starter lock and back-up light switch connector (19)

FIG 21 Early transmission vacuum line and fluid filler tube

1 Vacuum line   2 Oil filler pipe

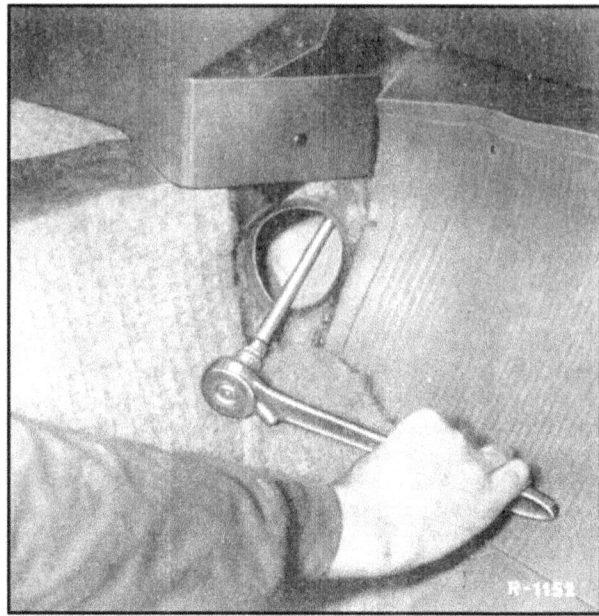

FIG 24 Removing starter motor bolt on earlier models

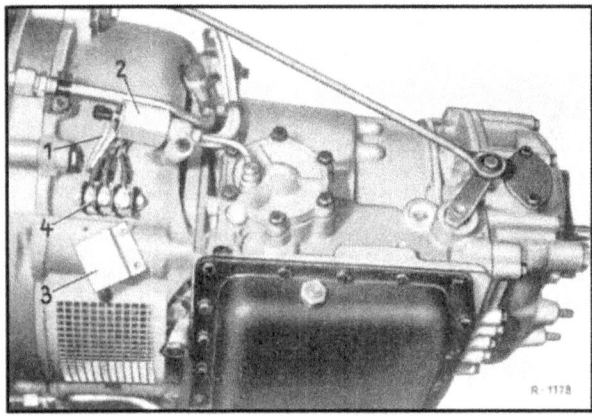

FIG 22 Early transmission electrical connections

1 Electric line   3 Protective plate
2 Oil pressure switch   4 Cable connector

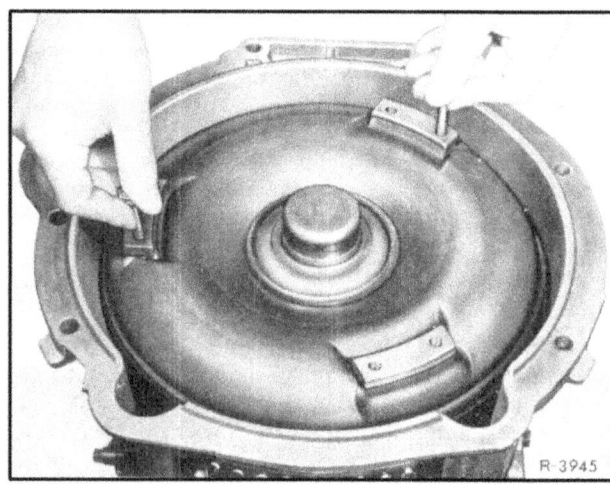

FIG 25 Lifting out the fluid flywheel

FIG 23 The pairs of bolts that secure the fluid flywheel   21 Fastening bolts

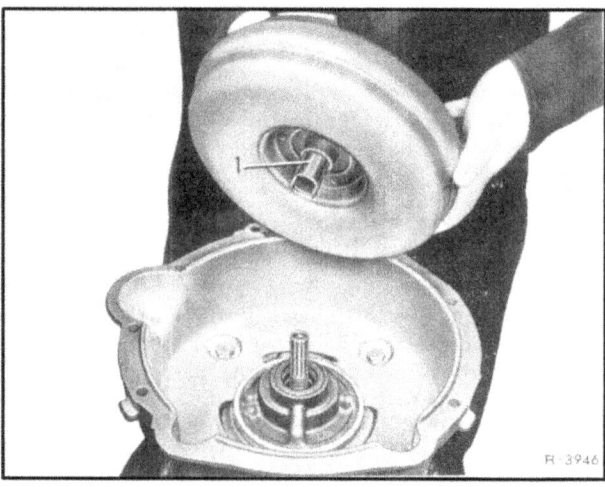

FIG 26 Installing the fluid flywheel
1 Hollow shaft

3 On the earlier models, remove the splash guard and disconnect the vacuum line 1 and filler tube 2 (shown in **FIG 21**), remove the plate 3 and disconnect the leads to the cable connector 4 and oil pressure switch 2 (shown in **FIG 22**).

4 On all models disconnect the speedometer drive cable and the selector linkage. Disconnect the exhaust support from the transmission and free the clamp nuts so that the support can be swivelled out of the way.

5 On the earlier models, use a jack and pad or wood to raise the transmission slightly and insert a block of wood between the engine and the front axle carrier to support the weight of the engine. On all models remove the rear mount with the jack supporting the transmission under its oil pan. Disconnect the propeller shaft (see **Chapter 8**).

6 Remove the cover from in front of the flywheel housing and take out the three pairs of bolts that secure the fluid flywheel to the engine drive plate, shown in **FIG 23**. Remove the two bolts for the starter motor. On the earlier models the upper bolt is best removed from inside the car, as shown in **FIG 24**, but the other bolt will require a socket with extensions and a universal joint. Remove the bolts that secure the flywheel housing to the engine intermediate flange.

7 Check that there are no connections left between transmission and car or engine. Force the transmission rearwards until the boss on the fluid flywheel is well clear of the intermediate flange and then lower the transmission down and out of the car, on the jack.

Install the transmission in the reverse order of removal. Check all adjustments and fill the unit to the correct level with automatic transmission fluid.

Fluid flywheel:

The unit is sealed on manufacture and therefore cannot be repaired if it is defective.

To remove the fluid flywheel, first take out the transmission and stand it upright. Screw two M8 bolts into the threaded plates of the flywheel, as shown in **FIG 25**, and use them to lift out the fluid flywheel.

Install the fluid flywheel in the reverse order of removal. Make sure that the claws on the hollow shaft, shown in **FIG 26**, align with the mesh of the gear pump and move the unit slightly to align the splines. Take great care not to damage the lips of the primary seal when installing the flywheel.

6 Fault diagnosis

Only a limited list of faults is given in this section as they are the ones that can be cured by the owner. Other faults necessitate taking the car to an agent specializing in automatic transmissions.

(a) Overheating
1 Stone guards blocked
2 Transmission covered with dirt
3 Oil cooler defective
4 Incorrect fluid level (either too low or too high)

(b) Engine will not start or starts in gear
1 Linkage incorrectly adjusted
2 Starter lock switch defective or incorrectly adjusted

(c) Noisy operation
1 Oil oil level
2 Oil filter dirty or choked

NOTES

CHAPTER 8 – PROPELLER SHAFT, REAR AXLE AND REAR SUSPENSION

1 The propeller shaft
2 The rear suspension
3 The dampers
4 The road springs
5 The steel compensating spring
6 The hydropneumatic compensator
7 The radius arms
8 The drive shafts and hub bearings
9 The rear axle
10 Removing the rear axle
11 Suspension geometry
12 Fault diagnosis

1 The propeller shaft

A two-part propeller shaft, shown in **FIG 1**, is fitted to the series covered by this manual. The attachment to the transmission was changed, with the transmission, in May 1969 and the earlier attachment is shown in **FIG 2** while the later attachment is shown in **FIG 3**. The intermediate bearing is attached to the frame of the car as shown in **FIG 4**.

Propeller shaft removal:

On all models, support the weight of the transmission on a jack and pad of wood so that the engine rear mounting can be removed. On the earlier models, make alignment marks on the support member and frame so that the member will be installed back into its original position. On the 280 SL/8 models remove the tunnel closing plate which is secured by sixteen bolts.

Slacken the clamping nuts, which are situated in front of the intermediate bearing, by approximately two turns. Do not slide the rubber sleeve back as it will move on its own.

Remove the three sets of nuts and bolts which secure the propeller shaft to the universal plate on the front mounting. If the nuts can be run along the threads by hand they are worn and new self-locking nuts should be fitted on reassembly.

Disconnect the rear end of the propeller shaft from the rear axle by removing the nuts and bolts that secure it. Remove the bolts that secure the intermediate bearing to the frame. Press the propeller shaft slightly together, lower the rear end and withdraw the shaft from the rear. Take care not to lose or drop the centering sleeve as the front end frees from the transmission.

Installation:

The propeller shaft is refitted in the reverse order of removal. On the earlier models check the sealing rings 3 and 7, **FIG 2**, renew them if they are defective. If the universal plate has been removed on earlier models, it must be installed so that the double links are under tension, as shown in **FIG 5**. **The engine mounting member attachment bolts on earlier models should not be fully tightened until after the car is back on its road wheels.**

On all models, lower the car back onto its wheels and roll it backwards and forwards several times, to settle the length of the propeller shaft, before tightening the clamp nuts on the shaft. The clamping nut should be tightened to $3 + 1$ kg m ($21\frac{1}{2} + 7$ lb ft).

On the earlier models, inject grease through the grease fitting 8, noting that relief valve 5 should allow air to escape as grease is pumped in. The later models should have 6 gramme of Mobil-Grease MP or Mobil Oil Ag packed into the centering sleeve on the front attachment.

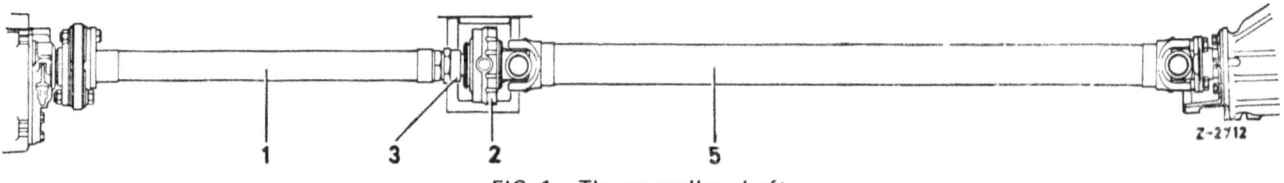

FIG 1 The propeller shaft

1 Front universal shaft   2 Intermediate bearing   3 Clamping nut   5 Rear universal shaft

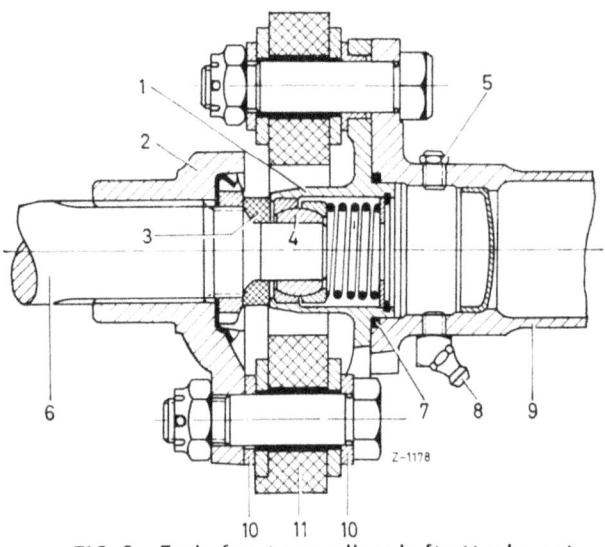

FIG 2 Early front propeller shaft attachment

1 Center cross
2 Three-way flange on the transmission main shaft
3 Rubber sealing ring
4 Locating ball
5 Relief valve
6 Transmission main shaft
7 Rubber sealing ring
8 Piston rim grease fitting
9 Front propeller shaft
10 Washer
11 Shaft plate

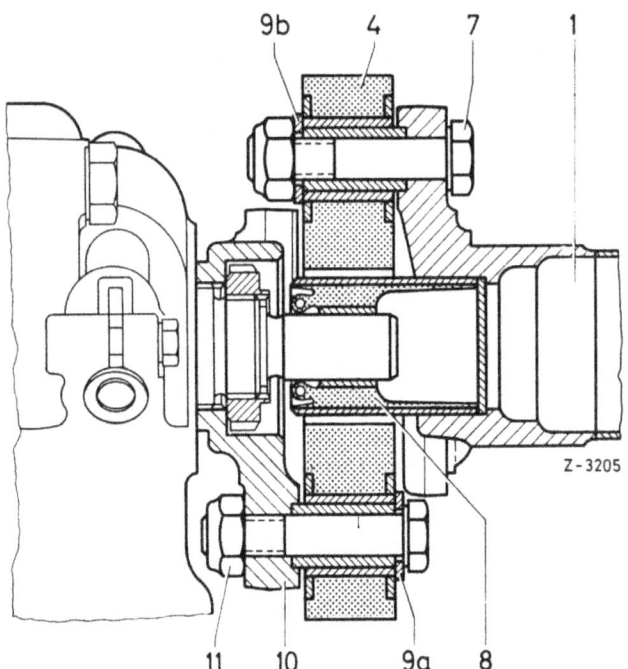

FIG 3 Later front propeller shaft attachment

1 Front universal shaft
4 Universal plate
7 Hex. bolt
8 Centering sleeve
9a Washer
9b Washer
10 Universal flange
11 Selflocking nut

Universal joints:

Kits of parts are available to service worn or defective universal joints but a press is required to remove the old parts and install the new ones. A sectioned view of a typical universal joint is shown in **FIG 6**. Worn bores for the bearing cups will necessitate installing a new propeller shaft.

Intermediate bearing:

A new bearing can be fitted if the old one is worn or defective. A sectioned view of the complete bearing is shown in **FIG 7**.

Remove the propeller shaft and mark the front universal shaft in relation to the rear shaft. Slacken the clamp nut 9 and pull off the front universal shaft 10. Remove the bearing bracket 3, rubber mount 4, rubber sleeve 5, locking ring 11 and protective cap 8.

Use a suitable puller to remove the bearing housing 12 with the locking ring 13 and grooved ballbearing 7 from the yoke 14 of the rear shaft. Remove the locking ring 13 and press the ballbearing 7 out from the housing 12.

The correct type of sealed-for-life ballbearing must be used. Do not wash the bearing in solvent otherwise the lubricant will be washed out.

Check the rubber mount 4 and protective sleeve 5 for damage, perishing, or failure, and renew them if they are defective.

Assemble the parts in the reverse order of dismantling, coating the splines with a suitable long-lasting grease.

Centering sleeve:

If the sealing lip is worn or damaged a new centering sleeve can be fitted without having to renew the complete shaft. Drill a 10 mm (.4 inch) hole diametrically through the sleeve. Insert a suitable rod through the hole and use two bars to pull the old sleeve out, as shown in **FIG 8**. Press a new sleeve back into place and fill the cavity with 6 grammes of grease before installing the shaft.

2 The rear suspension

A typical 280 SL/8 rear suspension is shown in **FIG 9**. Other models are very similar except that a hydropneumatic compensating spring is fitted in place of the coil compensating spring 13 shown in the figure. The compensating spring stiffens the suspension for roll but not for bumps. The hydropneumatic unit also acts as a self-levelling device.

A wide variety of springs and dampers is made to suit varying road conditions or use of the car. If the car is used regularly on bad roads or for special cases where a harder suspension is required, a local agent should be consulted about the best combination of dampers and springs.

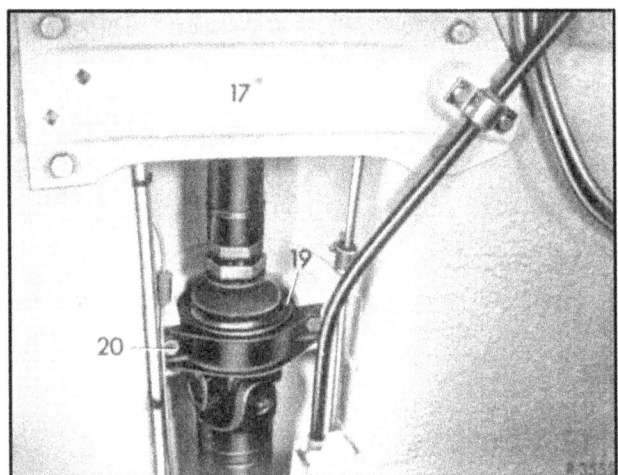

FIG 4 Intermediate bearing attachment
17 Cross strut 20 Fastening bolts
19 Universal shaft center bearing

3 The dampers
Removal:

The upper attachment is shown in **FIG 10** and the lower in **FIG 11**. The lower attachment is accessible from under the car at the rear axle. On all models except the 280 SL/8 the upper attachment is accessible in the luggage compartment beside the wheel arch after removing the protective cap. On the 280 SL/8 the attachment is accessible, after removing the coverplate, from the top box when the roadster top is closed. If a coupé top is fitted then this must be removed in order to gain access to the upper attachment.

The rear dampers serve as the deflection stops for the rear wheels and therefore the axle tube must be supported when removing a damper.

Remove the nuts 5a from the top of the damper and

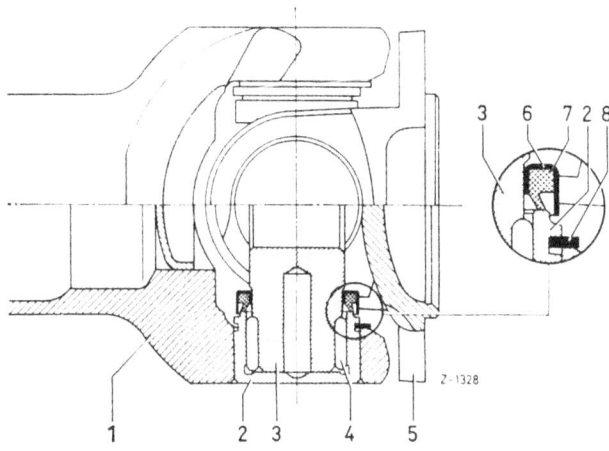

FIG 6 A sectioned view of a typical universal joint
1 Yoke   4 Needle   7 Sealing ring
2 Needle bearing cup   5 Joint flange   8 Snap ring
3 Universal joint spider 6 Sealing ring retainer

take off the washer 5b and rubber ring 5c, noting the directions in which the washer and ring face. Remove the bolt that secures the lower attachment and take off the damper in a downward direction.

Testing:

Examine the damper for signs of physical damage such as a bent ram or dented body. Physically damaged dampers should be rejected and new ones fitted in their place. Note that it is always advisable to renew the dampers in axle pairs.

The method of mounting a damper vertically in a vice and then pumping it by hand will only detect a faulty damper but will not ensure that it is working efficiently. If the damper makes odd noises (dirt on the ram can cause a groaning noise so wipe the ram) or the resistance varies through the stroke then it is likely that the damper

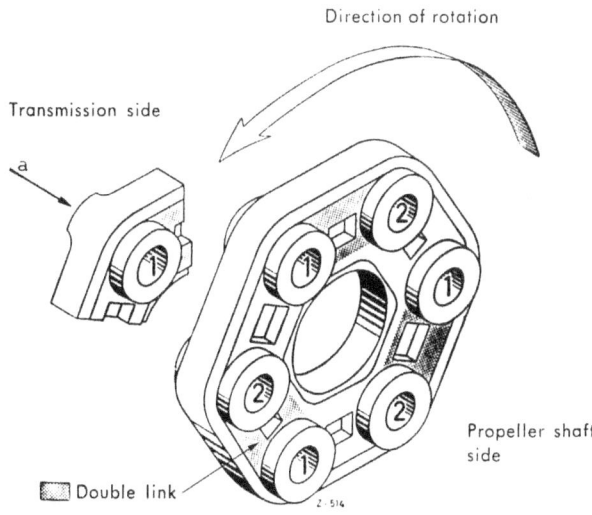

FIG 5 Correct fitting of the early universal plate
1 Connect to three-way flange of the transmission
2 Connect to three-way flange of the propeller shaft

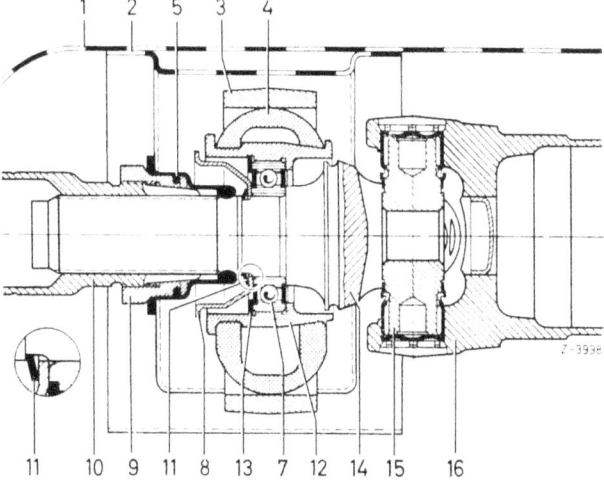

FIG 7 Sectioned view of the intermediate bearing

1 Body/frame   10 Front universal shaft
2 Universal shaft tunnel   11 Locking ring
3 Bearing bracket   12 Bearing housing
4 Rubber mount   13 Locking ring
5 Rubber sleeve   14 Yoke
7 Grooved ball bearing   15 Universal joint spider
8 Protective cap   with needle bearing bushings
9 Clamping nut   16 Rear universal shaft

FIG 8 Removing the old centering sleeve (8)

is defective. The only effective way of testing the dampers is to have them checked on a special test machine at a service agent so equipped. Dampers wear with use and usually they no longer perform efficiently after 50,000 kilometres (30,000 miles).

Slight oil leaks are acceptable provided that there is still sufficient oil in the unit. Check the oil level by compressing the damper and measuring the dimension **a** shown in **FIG 12**. As oil is lost the extension will increase. When new the extension will only be 5 ± 2 mm ($.2 \pm .04$ inch) and the damper should be renewed when the extension exceeds 30 mm (1.2 inch). The front dampers are checked in the same way and their initial extension is the same but they should be renewed when the extension exceeds 36 mm (1.4 inch).

Installation:

The damper is installed in the reverse order of removal. Before installing the damper, check all the rubber rings and bushes for wear or perishing and renew them if they are defective. The lower nut 5a should be tightened down to the end of the threads and then locked with the upper nut.

4 The road springs

The dampers act as the deflection stops for the rear axle and therefore they should be left in place when removing or refitting the road spring.

Removal:

Jack up the rear of the car and place it securely onto stands. Support the radius arm 2 with a jack and the special adaptor 111 589 22 63 00 as shown in **FIG 13**. **Make sure that the radius arm is free from grease or dirt in the area of support and take great care to prevent the adaptor slipping off or along the radius arm.** Loosen the fastening plate 12 and swing it to one side, collecting any shims fitted under it. Very carefully lower the jack so that the radius arm pivots about the rear end and as the front end comes down the spring pressure is relieved. When the spring is free, lift it out together with its upper and lower rubber mounts.

A sectioned view of the spring mounting is shown in **FIG 14**. Note that the position of the spring disc 5 and the thickness of the rubber mounting is used to compensate for the different lengths of the differing springs, so be sure to set the disc correctly and obtain the correct rubber mounting.

FIG 9 Typical rear suspension

1 Rear shock-absorber
2 Rubber buffer for axle tube
3 Rear spring
4 Brake line
5 Brake hose
6 Distributor fitting
7 Rear brake cable
8 Torque arm
9 Brake line (connection to left brake hose)
10 Main muffler
11 Rear exhaust pipe
12 Intermediate muffler
13 Compensating spring

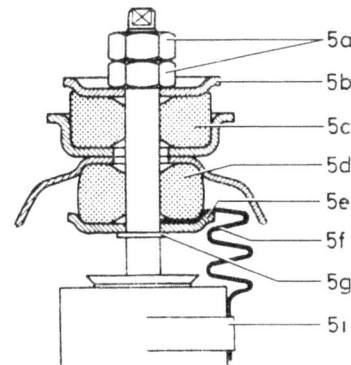

FIG 10 Damper upper attachment

5a Hex. nut	5e Disc washer
5b Disc washer	5f Dust protection
5c Rubber ring top	5g Locking ring
5d Rubber ring bottom	5i Clamping strap

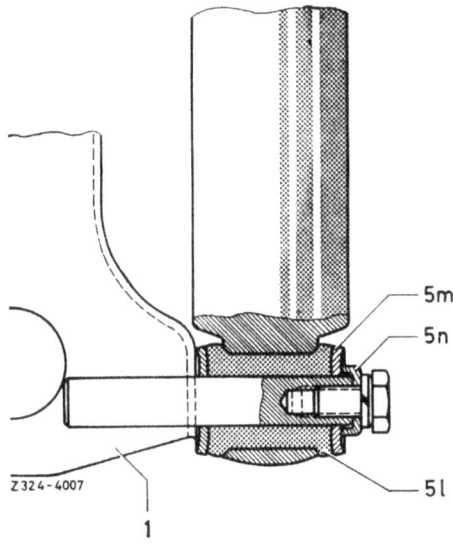

FIG 11 Damper lower attachment

1 Supporting tube	5m Washer
5l Rubber mount	5n Disc

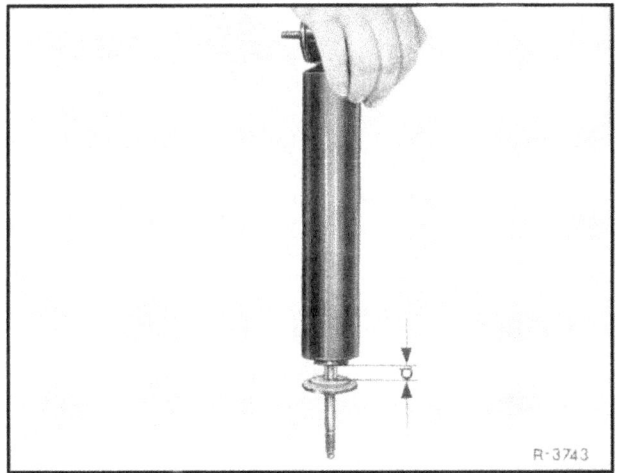

FIG 12 Checking the damper oil level
a = Piston rod extension

FIG 13 Removing the road spring

1 Support tube	8 Rubber mount bottom
2 Thrust rod	9 Spring disc
3 Rear spring	10 Rubber mount front
5 Shock absorber	12 Fastening plate
6 Spring disc	62 Adaptor 111 589 22 63 00
7 Rubber mount top	63 Bracket 115 589 02 63 00

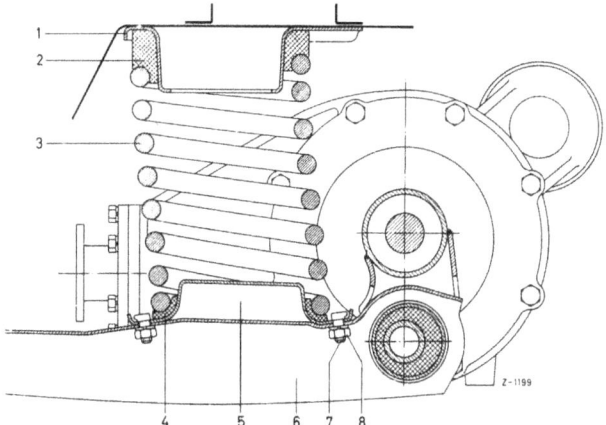

FIG 14 Sectioned view of the spring mounting

1 Upper spring disc on chassis	5 Lower spring disc
2 Upper rubber mounting	6 Torque arm
3 Rear spring	7 Spring disc to torque arm bolts
4 Lower rubber mounting	8 Hexagon nuts and lock washers

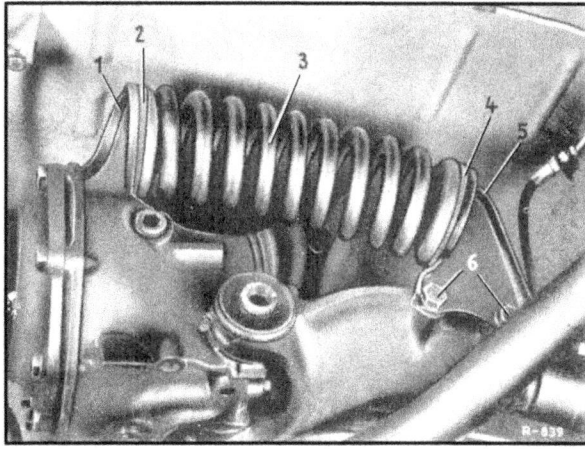

FIG 15 The compensating spring attachments

1 Rear axle carrier	3 Spring	5 Righthand carrier
2 Rubber ring left	4 Rubber ring right	6 Carrier bolts

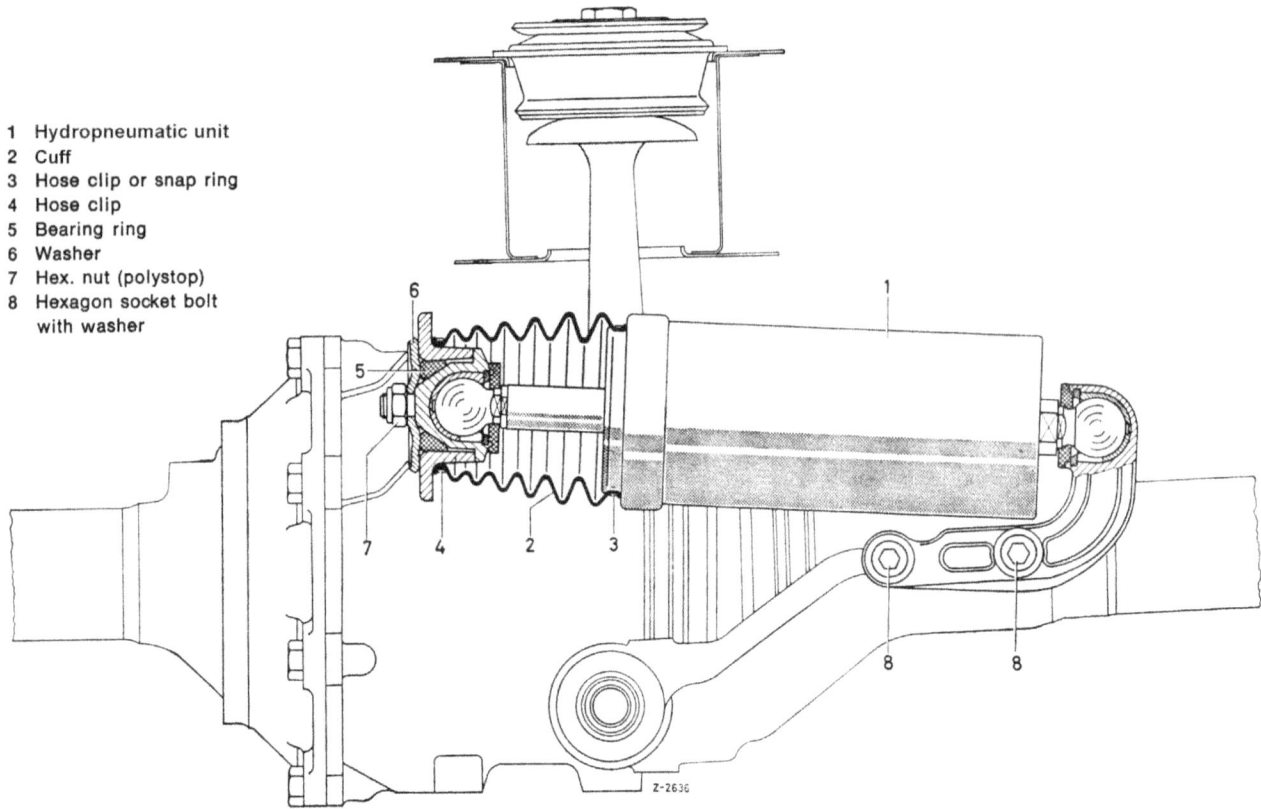

1 Hydropneumatic unit
2 Cuff
3 Hose clip or snap ring
4 Hose clip
5 Bearing ring
6 Washer
7 Hex. nut (polystop)
8 Hexagon socket bolt with washer

FIG 16 The hydropneumatic unit attachments

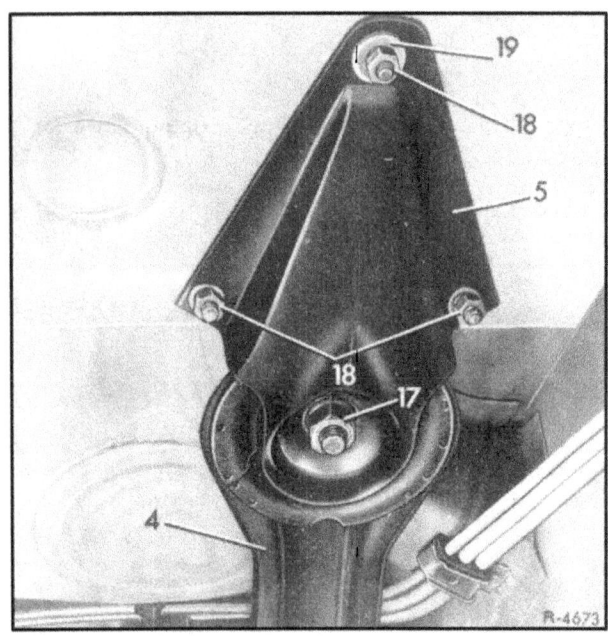

FIG 17 The radius arm front attachment

4 Radius arm
5 Fastening plate
17 Hex. nut with lockwasher
18 Hex. nut with lockwasher
19 Washer

Checking:

Examine the rubber mountings for wear or splitting and renew them if they are defective, taking care to obtain the correct replacement parts.

If the spring is cracked or obviously weakened it should be renewed, again with the correct type, but if it is only suspected of being weak it is advisable to have it checked at an agent.

Installation:

The spring is refitted in the reverse order of removal. Make sure that both the spring and its rubber mountings are correctly located. An installation mandrel No. 120 589 07 61 00 fitted to the receiving cup for the front of the radius arm will make it easier to guide the radius arm back into place when raising it on the jack and adaptor.

It is advisable to have the rear wheel camber checked after the spring has been installed.

5 The steel compensating spring

The attachments of the spring are shown in **FIG 15**. Different lengths of compensating spring are available and they are compensated for by the use of different mounting rubbers 2 and 4. Selective fitting of the spring and mounting rubbers can also be used to adjust the camber of the rear wheels if there is not sufficient normal adjustment.

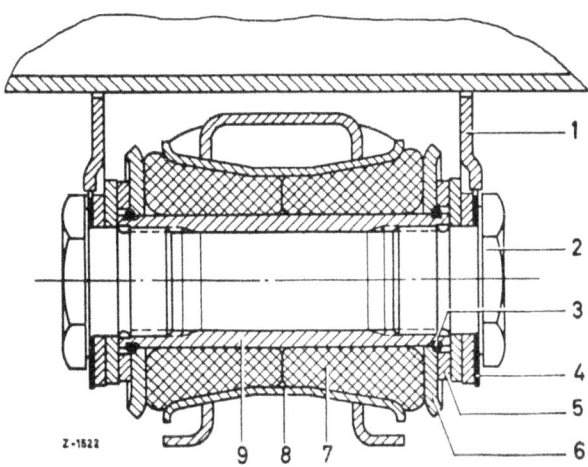

FIG 18 Sectioned view of rear axle radius arm pivot

1 Bearing bracket on supporting tube
2 Hex. bolt
3 Lock ring
4 Lock washer
5 Spacer ring
6 Clamping plate
7 Rubber mount
8 Radius arm
9 Bearing bolt

FIG 19 Dismantling the radius arm pivot
Assembly fixture 111 589 09 61 00

1a Base plate with guide bushing
1c Punch
3 Circlip
6 Clamping plate
7 Rubber mount
8 Radius arm

Jack up the rear of the car until the load is taken off the two axle tubes. Fit a tensioner No. 111 589 00 31 between as many coils of the spring as possible. Tighten the tensioner until the pressure is removed from the bracket 5. Remove the bolts 6 that secure the bracket 5 and take off the bracket with the spring and two mounting rubbers.

The spring is installed in the reverse order of removal but the bracket 5 should be attached by the inner bolt 6 only at first. Install the spring, held compressed by the tensioner, together with mounting rubber rings, and pivot the bracket so that they are held in place. Fit the remaining bolt 6.

6 The hydropneumatic compensator

The attachments of the unit are shown in **FIG 16**. The unit automatically adjusts the height of the car at the rear to compensate for varying loads. As the suspension moves the compensator is pumped up and sets the level of the axle tubes. The compensator requires no maintenance or service and should be renewed if it becomes defective. Slow leaks in the unit are checked by measuring the camber of the rear wheels and then leaving the car standing on special sliding plates that will allow the rear wheels to slide outwards. An excessive camber change indicates a leak. A new unit is supplied complete with all installation parts required.

To level the car, as for setting the headlamp beams, load to the correct weight and then rock the rear end of the car strongly 20 to 30 times.

To remove the unit, raise the rear of the car on jacks until the axle tubes have no load on them. Free the clip 4 that secures the cuff 2 and pull back the cuff. Take out the two bolts 8 to free the righthand bracket. Unscrew the nut 7 and remove the special washer 6. Pull the unit out of the car and remove the bearing ring 5.

Refit the unit in the reverse order of removal, partially raising or lowering the axle tubes as required to insert the bolts. Turn the unit so that its charging screws, on the side of the body, face towards the rear before fitting the cuff.

1 Washer
2 Fastening plate
3 Hex. nut with lockwasher
4 Rubber mount
5 Radius arm
6 Supporting bearing

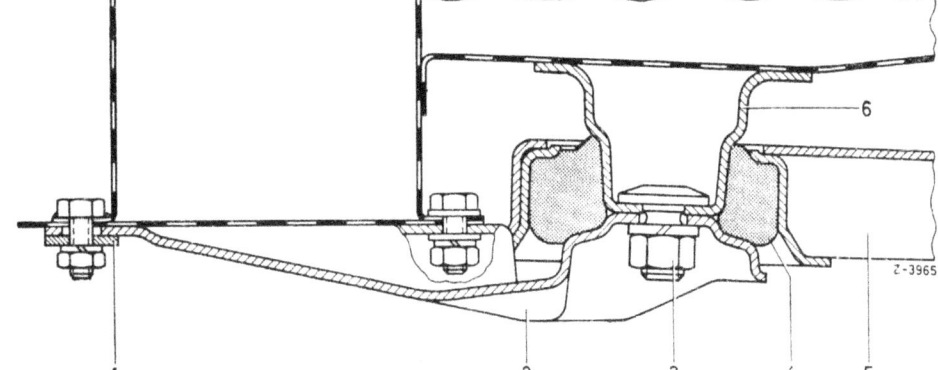

FIG 20 Sectioned view of front radius arm attachment

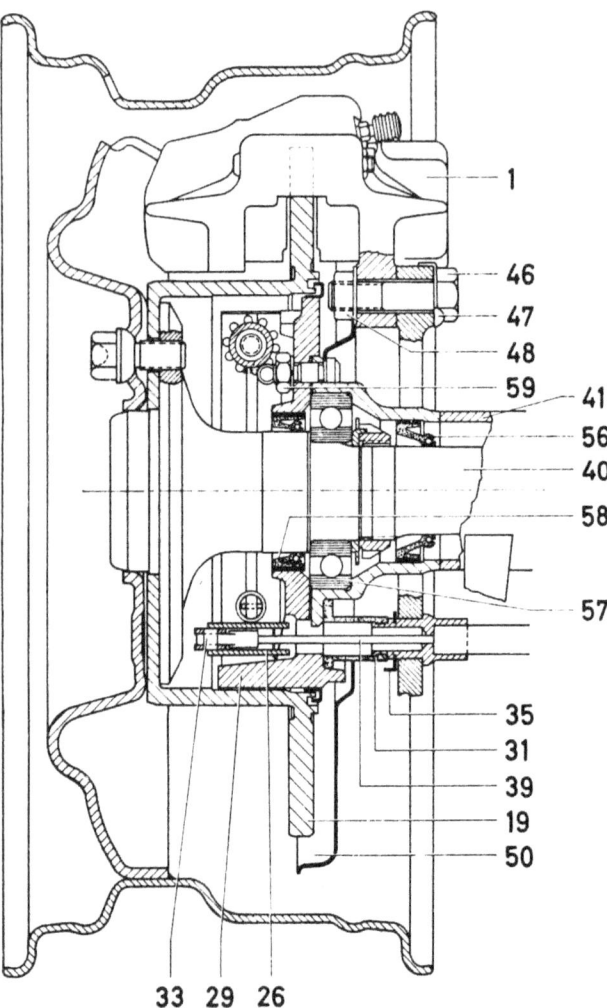

FIG 21 Sectioned view of the rear hub

1 Brake caliper
19 Brake disc
26 Expanding lock
29 Brake carrier plate
31 Rubber sleeve
33 Pin for brake cable control
35 KL-lock for brake cable control
39 Brake cable control
40 Drive shaft
41 Supporting tube
46 Hex. bolt
47 Lock washer
48 Holder with weld nut
50 Cover plate
56 Oil seal
57 Grooved ball bearing
58 Sealing ring
59 Set screw with lockwasher and hex. nut

It may be necessary to disconnect the lower damper attachments in order to obtain sufficient movement on the axle tubes when removing or installing the compensator unit. If the dampers are disconnected, support the axle tubes on stands as the dampers provide the deflection stops.

7 The radius arms

The front attachment is shown in **FIG 17** and the rear attachment sectioned in **FIG 18**.

To remove the radius arm, first remove the road spring as described in **Section 4**. Unscrew the two bolts 2 from either side of the rear mounting and withdraw the arm, collecting the spacer rings 5.

The arms are handed and must not be interchanged. A holder plate is welded to the front end and it must always face towards the centre of the car. Check the arms for cracks or distortion.

The method of dismantling the rear pivot bearing, using the tools 111 589 09 61 00 and a press, is shown in **FIG 19**. Compress the rubber mount as shown and use a screwdriver to remove the circlip 3. Remove the rubber mount 7 and bearing bolt 9. Assemble the rear pivot in the reverse order of dismantling, using the other end of the punch to compress the rubber mounts so that the lock ring can be installed.

The rubber mount for the front end can be pulled out of the radius arm. Renew the mount if it is defective or has seen long service. Lubricate the mount with talc and fit it back to the radius arm so that word UNTEN is at the bottom.

Before installing the radius arm it is worthwhile screwing the installation arbor 120 589 07 61 00 onto the thread on the car for the front mounting to guide the radius arm back into place.

Install the radius arm in the reverse order of removal. A sectioned view of the front attachment correctly installed is shown in **FIG 20**.

FIG 22 Undoing the drive shaft slotted nut

1 Slot nut spanner 136 589 09 07 00

FIG 23 The rear axle filler and drain plugs

8 The drive shafts and hub bearings

FIG 21 shows a sectioned view of the hub assembly.

Removal:

Remove the brake caliper and brake disc, shoes for parking brake and free the brake carrier plate (see **Chapter 11**).

Attach the fixture 100 589 02 33 00 to the flange of the drive shaft and use the fixture to draw the assembly out of the axle tube.

Dismantling:

Support the drive shaft in the assembly plate 136 589 05 31 00. Free the lockwasher that secures the slotted nut and undo the nut using the special wrench 136 589 09 07 00, as shown in **FIG 22**.

Use a suitable puller to withdraw the ballbearing 57 from the drive shaft 40. Remove the brake carrier plate 29 and press out the sealing ring 58 from it.

Examination:

The drive shaft should be checked for vertical or lateral run-out and concentricity of the bearing seat. **Excessive vertical run-out will induce vibration at speed.** Renew the drive shaft if the run-out is excessive or the contact surfaces are scored or have worn splines.

Wash the bearing in clean fuel and dry it with air. Oil the bearing with a thin oil and check that it rotates freely without grating. Any defects require renewal of the bearing and it is advisable to renew the bearing automatically if it has done 100,000 kilometres (60,000 miles). Make sure that the correct type of bearing is fitted as on some models they vary from side to side.

Assembly and installation:

Coat a new seal on the outside circumference with jointing compound and press it back into the brake carrier plate so that lips will face towards the bearing and it is flush outside.

FIG 24   The rear axle pivot grease fittings

FIG 25   The axle cross strut

1	Nut with lock nut	6	Rear link
2	Pot	7	Bolt with washer
3	Rubber buffer	8	Front link
4	Cross strut	9	Bolt with washer
5	Hex. nut	10	Rubber mount

Coat the contact surface for the sealing ring on the drive shaft with molybdenum disulphide paste and carefully slide the brake carrier plate back into position.

Press the bearing back into place on the shaft. Install a new lockwasher, making sure that it is fully seated against the inside face of the bearing. Tighten down the slotted nut using the special wrench to a torque of 20 kg m (145 lb ft) and lock it by staking the lockwasher into a groove.

If the old oil seal 56 is damaged, pull it out and press a new seal back into place after coating the outer surface with jointing compound.

Pack the cavity between the inner and outer seals, as well as the bearing, with a suitable anti-friction grease.

Carefully insert the assembly back into the axle tube, taking great care not to damage the oil seal in the tube. Secure the brake carrier plate to the axle tube, tightening the nuts to a torque of 2.5 kg m (18 lb ft).

Install the brake parts and with the axle tubes level, check the oil level in the rear axle.

9 The rear axle

The rear axle should not be dismantled by the average owner. When reassembling the rear axle the parts must be fitted to the correct preloads and settings and the crownwheel and pinion must be set so that they mesh correctly. Skill and experience are required as well as special tools and jigs and it is for these reasons that the owner should not attempt to dismantle the rear axle.

There are still tasks that can be carried out without dismantling the axle.

Lubrication:

At regular intervals check the oil level in the rear axle. With the car on level ground the oil should just come up to the bottom of the filler orifice. The drain and filler plugs are shown in **FIG 23**. At the same time as checking the oil level, check that the breather on top of the axle tube is clear, as a blocked breather will not vent internal pressure and therefore can cause oil leaks.

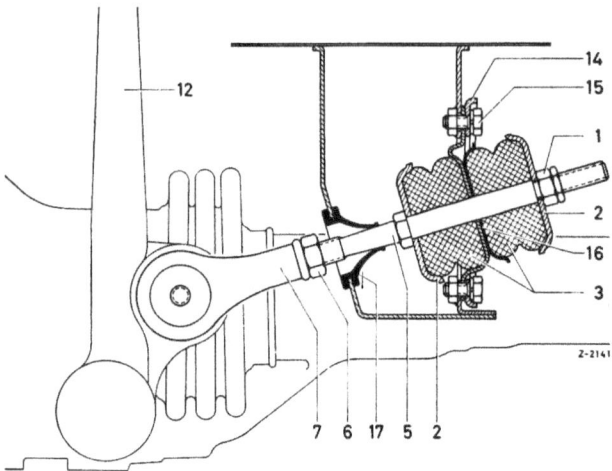

FIG 26 The cross strut fitted to 280 SL/8 models

1 Hex. nut with lock nut
2 Cup
3 Rubber buffer
5 Cross strut
6 Hex. nut (lock nut)
7 Link
12 Rear axle suspension carrier
14 Retainer for rubber buffers
15 Hex. bolt
16 Intermediate cup
17 Sleeve

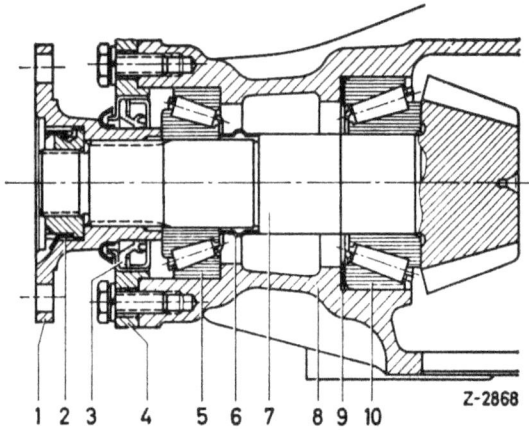

FIG 27 Sectioned view of the drive pinion

1 Universal flange
2 Slot nut with lock washer
3 Sealing ring
4 Cover
5 Tapered roller bearing
6 Spacing sleeve
7 Drive pinion
8 Rear axle housing
9 Compensating washer
10 Tapered roller bearing

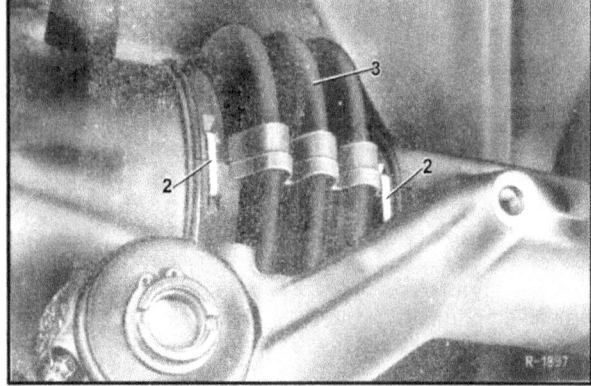

FIG 28 Fitting the axle cuff in place

2 Auxiliary clip
3 Split rear axle sleeve

Seasonal oil changes are not required, but it is advisable to stick to one brand of oil. If the oil in the axle is unknown, drain it out and refill with fresh oil rather than mix brands on topping up. The axle must not be flushed through with any solvent as some will remain to dilute the fresh oil.

At regular intervals grease the pivot point of the axle through the grease fittings shown in **FIG 24**. Also grease the bearings of the brake hold downs.

Cross strut:

A cross strut locates the rear axle laterally. The installation of the strut is shown in **FIG 25**. If the rubber buffers are damaged or perished or the pots 2 are distorted then new parts must be installed.

To remove the strut, take out the bolts 7 and 9 and remove the front link 8. Remove the nut 1, push the strut and rear link 6 towards the rear and free it after removing the outer rubber buffer 3 and pot 2. Install the strut in the reverse order of removal. It is advisable to have the axle lateral location checked by a service agent.

The cross strut for the 280 SL/8 models is shown in **FIG 26** and to remove the inner buffer and pot it will be necessary to remove the holder 14.

Drive pinion seal:

This seal can be renewed without having to remove the axle from the car. A sectioned view of the assembly is shown in **FIG 27**. **Great care must be taken in this operation otherwise there may be damage to the bearings or rough running of the gears later on.**

1 Jack up the rear of the car and place it securely on stands. Raise and support the two axle tubes into a level position. Drain the oil from the rear axle.

2 Disconnect the propeller shaft from the rear axle and hang it out of the way. Mark the drive flange on the rear axle and the pinion shaft with aligning dot marks so that the flange will be installed back into the same relative position.

3 Unlock the slotted nut that secures the drive flange and unscrew the nut while holding the drive flange. Special wrenches are made for undoing the nut and holding the drive flange. When the nut has been removed, pull the drive flange off from the shaft. Check the running surface of the drive flange and renew the flange if the surface is cored or damaged. On some models there will be a portion which is cut with a light thread pattern and this is not a defect.

4 Prise out the old sealing ring 3 from the cover 4. Coat the circumference of the new seal lightly with sealing compound and press the seal back into place so that the lips of the seal face inwards. Coat the running surface of the drive flange with molybdenum disulphide paste and press it back into place so that the punch marks again align.

5 Fit a new lockwasher and screw back the slotted nut. Tighten the slotted nut carefully. Check that the brakes are not binding and use a torque spanner to check the force required to turn the whole axle after each tightening of the nut. The nut should only be tightened until the torque required to turn the complete axle is 20 to 25 kg cm. If the torque required to turn the axle goes above the upper limit then the pinion parts must be dismantled and a new spacer 6 installed. Do not

slacken back the nut to reduce the torque as the spacer will already have been compressed and excess play will be the only result. When the correct torque to turn the axle is reached, lock the slotted nut by staking the lockwasher.

6 Install the propeller shaft. Fill the axle to the correct level with fresh oil. Note that if a limited slip differential is fitted, special lubricant must be used.

Axle cuff:

A seamless type of axle cuff is fitted between the two axle tubes to prevent the entry of dirt or leakage of oil. The cuff must be renewed if it is damaged or split. A new cuff of the split type can be installed without dismantling the rear axle.

1 Remove the hydropneumatic unit, or compensating spring. **Thoroughly clean the area all around the cuff to prevent dirt from falling into the axle or entering it when the cuff is off.** Drain the oil from the axle. Remove the two clips that secure the cuff and split the cuff with a sharp knife so that it can be taken off.

2 Take two clips and use the special pliers to compress them lightly so that the ends are at 45 deg. Fit the new split cuff around the axle so that the seam is horizontal at the rear. **Do not use any sealing compound.** Secure the cuff with the two preshaped clips, as shown in **FIG 28,** and then fit the two original screw-tightened clips over the ends.

3 Fit the five remaining clips to the folds, as shown in **FIG 29,** using the special pliers 111 589 06 37 00.

4 Fill the axle with oil after installing the compensating spring. Test drive the car and check for leaks. Small amounts of oil may weep at joints of the cuff but these may be ignored. If large oil losses are found the sleeve has been incorrectly installed.

Brake hold down bearing:

The bearing fitted is shown in **FIG 30** and the components in **FIG 31**.

To remove the parts, take off the brake parts and remove the lever from the bearing. Remove the rubber rings 5 as shown and then take out the bolts 2 so that the bearing parts can be removed.

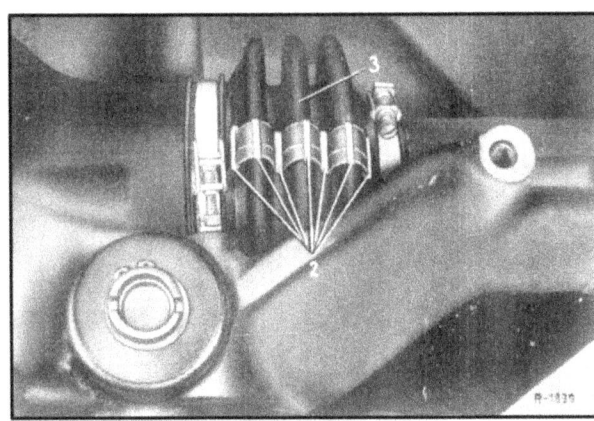

FIG 29   Fully securing the axle cuff in place

2 Clips   3 Split rear axle sleeve

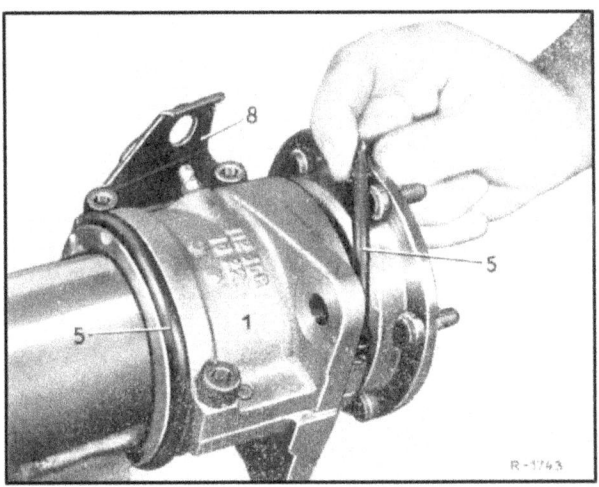

FIG 30   The brake hold-down bearing

1 Bearing housing   8 Brake hose holder
5 Rubber ring

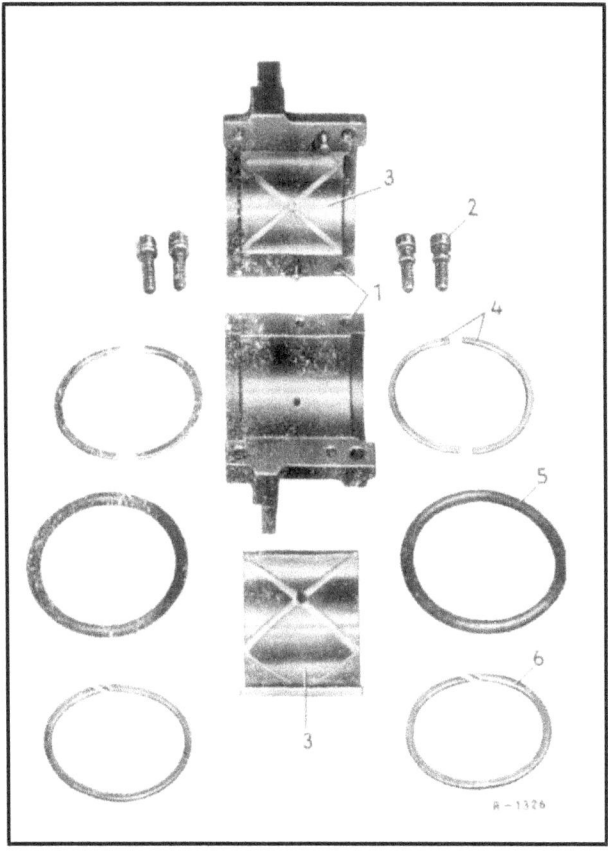

FIG 31   Components of the brake holddown bearing

1 Bearing housing   4 Compensating washer
2 Hexagon socket screw   (ring half)
   with washer   5 Rubber ring
3 Bearing shells   6 Felt ring

FIG 32 Installing the felt rings and inner rubber ring
5 Rubber ring
6 Felt ring

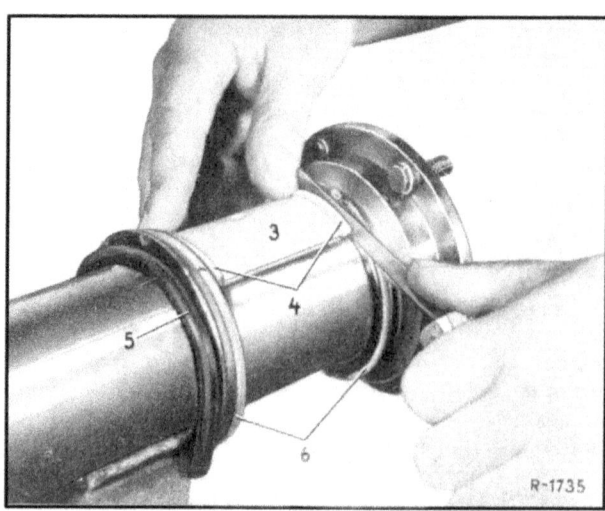

FIG 33 Checking the end play on the bearing shells
3 Bearing shells
4 Compensating washer (ring half)
5 Rubber ring
6 Felt ring

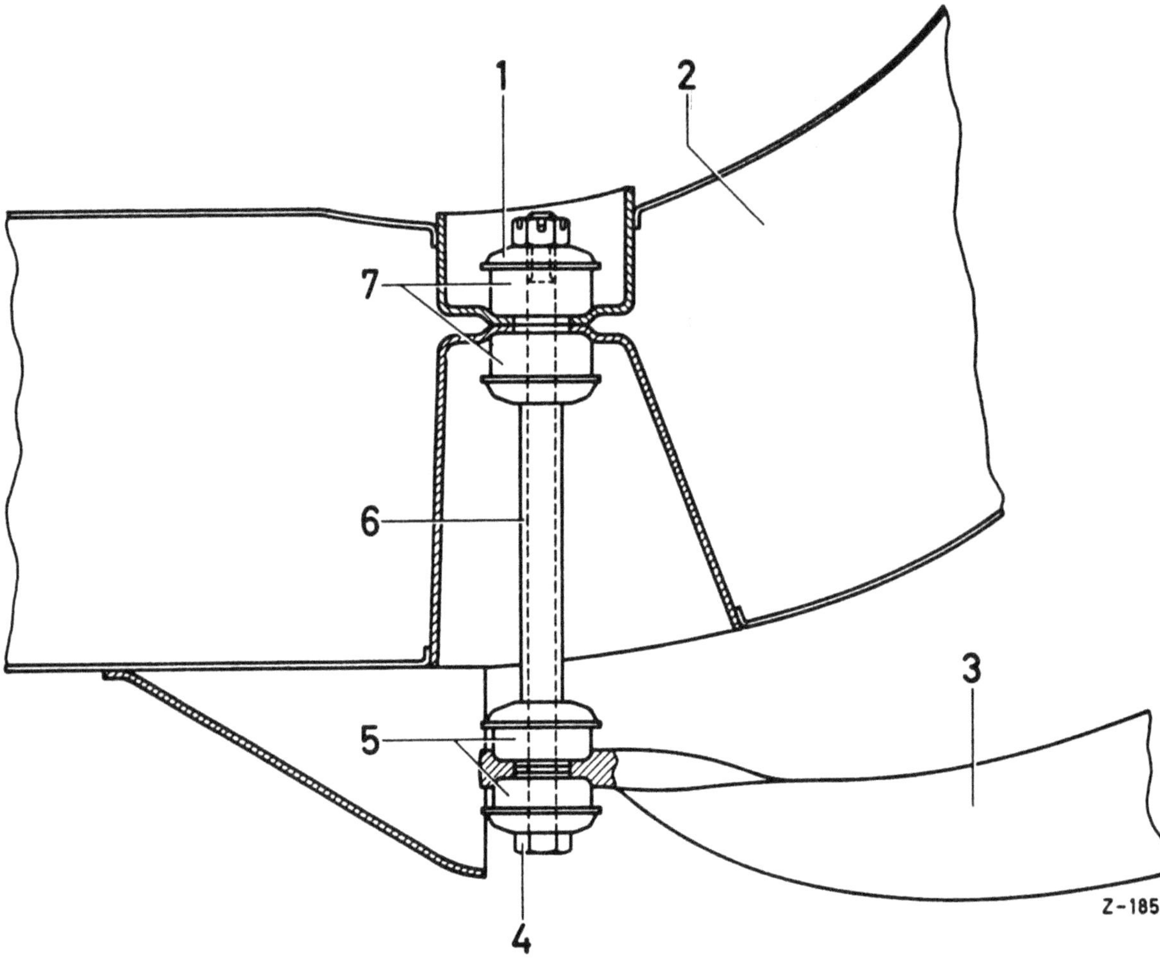

FIG 34 The attachment of the brake holddown lever to the frame

1 Disc
2 Frame side member
3 Lever for brake holddown
4 Hex. bolt
5 Rubber buffer bottom
6 Spacing tube
7 Rubber buffer top

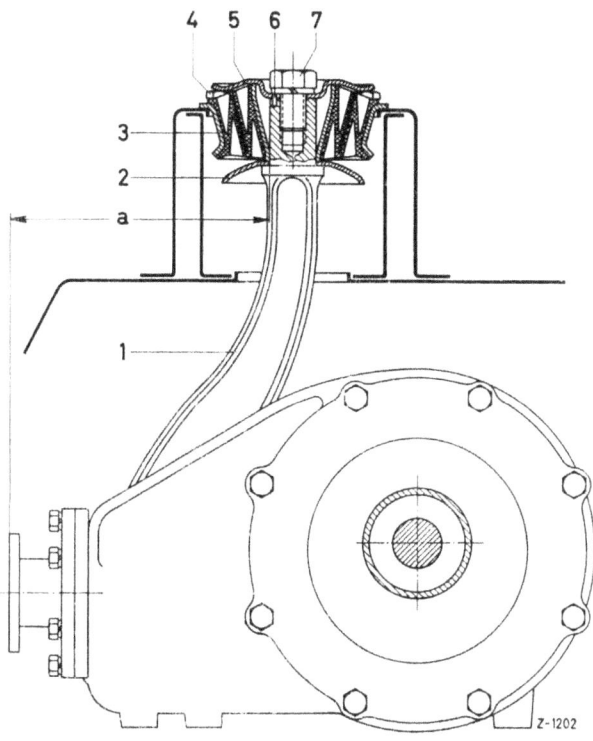

FIG 35 The rear axle carrier

a 158 ± 1 mm (5.22 ± 0.04 inch)
1 Rear axle carrier
2 Lower clamping disc
3 Rubber mount
4 Bolts for attaching mount to chassis
5 Upper clamping disc
6 Notched cylindrical pin
7 Hex. bolt with washer

Renew parts as required. New felt seals 6 and rubber rings 5 must be fitted if the old ones are defective. If new bearing housings 1 are being fitted, the edges should be chamfered to prevent the rubber rings being damaged. If the bearing seat on the support tube is worn oval then a new support tube must be fitted.

Fit the felt seals and inner rubber ring back into place as shown in **FIG 32**. Use compensating washers 4 in pairs of equal thickness and fit one of each pair and a bearing shell 3 onto the tube, as shown in **FIG 33**, so that the end play can be measured with feeler gauges. The end play should be adjusted to .01 to .02 mm (.0004 to .0008 inch) by selectively fitting the compensating washers 4. If required, the compensating washers can be lapped down by rubbing them over fine-grade emerycloth so as to set the correct clearance.

Assemble the bearing by tightening the bolts 2 in a diagonal sequence to a torque load of 2.5 kg m (18 lb ft). Move the bearing by hand and check that it moves freely without jerkiness or excessive play. Fit the rubber rings 5 back into place, making sure that they are not twisted. Grease the bearing through the grease fitting and install parts removed.

10 Removing the rear axle

When the axle is removed from the car it must be supported on a suitable stand. **The stand for removing, transporting or installing the axle should support the main weight under the differential housing but it must have supports that hold the axle tubes** approximately level. If the axle tubes are allowed to droop excessively, internal damage may be caused to the axle.

1 Jack up the rear of the car and place it securely onto axle stands. Separate and remove the rear exhaust pipes. Disconnect the handbrake cables and free the hydraulic brake lines from the brake calipers (see **Chapter 11**). Disconnect the propeller shaft from the rear axle.
2 Remove the road wheels. Remove the road springs and compensating spring (or hydropneumatic unit). Remove the front link that secures the cross strut to the axle and free the strut from the axle by pushing it rearwards, leaving the strut attached to the frame. Disconnect the lower ends of the dampers from the axle, or remove them completely.
3 The attachments of the brake hold down lever to the frame are shown in **FIG 34**. Free the attachment by removing the castle nut from under the rear seat and pulling out the bolt 4, while collecting the discs and rubber buffers.
4 Raise the axle tubes until they are approximately level and support the axle with a suitable stand. Remove the bolt 7, shown in **FIG 35**, that secures the rear axle carrier 1 to the frame. The bolt is accessible in the luggage compartment, just behind the front bulkhead. Lower the axle on the jack and remove it from under the car.

Installation:

The axle is installed in the reverse order of removal. A conical mandrel No. 111 589 00 61 installed on the carrier of the rear axle will make it easier to guide the carrier back into place. Before installing the axle, check that the carrier for the rear axle is exactly at right angles to the lefthand supporting tube when viewed in the horizontal plane. Lay a steel straightedge along the drive flange of the rear axle and use a large depth gauge to measure the dimension a shown in **FIG 35**. Set the dimension to 158±1 mm (5.22±.04 inch). Tighten the clamp bolts that secure the carrier to the axle when the dimension is correct. **If the carrier is not set correctly the rubber mountings will be under stress and will rapidly fail as well as causing a droning noise when the car is driven.**

Check that all rubber mountings and special washers are in good condition, renewing any that are defective.

11 Suspension geometry

Special gauges are essential for checking the location of the rear axle and the geometry of the suspension. The owner should not attempt to carry out any setting or adjustments but should take the car to a suitably equipped service agent.

Worn or damaged rubber mountings will affect the geometry and handling of the car and it is within the power of the owner to renew all these. It is still advisable to have the suspension geometry checked by an agent after renewing rubber mountings or carrying out major work on the rear axle.

12 Fault diagnosis

(a) Noisy suspension or rear axle
1 Lack of or incorrect grade of oil
2 Defective dampers
3 Defective mounting rubbers
4 Dirt on damper rams
5 Worn propeller shaft universal joints or bearing
6 Axle carrier incorrectly set
7 Defective differential unit
8 Worn bearings
9 Neglected lubrication

(b) Vibration
1 Check 3, 5 and 6 in (a)
2 Excessive run-out on drive shaft
3 Propeller shaft out of balance or incorrectly assembled

(c) Oil leaks
1 Defective hub seals
2 Defective pinion seal
3 Defective cuff
4 Defective seals on universal joint spiders
5 Blocked breather on rear axle
6 High oil level in rear axle

(d) Settling
1 Check 3 in (a)
2 Weak or broken road spring
3 Weak or broken compensating spring
4 Leaking hydropneumatic unit

CHAPTER 9 – FRONT SUSPENSION AND HUBS

1 Description
2 Maintenance
3 The front hubs
4 The dampers
5 The road springs
6 The torsion bar and flat spring assembly
7 The lateral strut
8 The kingpin assembly
9 The wishbones (control arms)
10 Fault diagnosis

1 Description

A general view of a typical front suspension assembly removed from the car is shown in **FIG 1**. The crossmember is attached to the frame and it also carries the rubber mountings for the front of the engine. The two independent front suspension assemblies are mounted onto the crossmember and they consist of unequal length wishbones with a steering knuckle assembly pivoting and swivelling between their outer ends. The inboard ends of the wishbones pivot vertically about bushes and pivot pins attached to the crossmember. The load and movement of each suspension is taken by a coil spring acting between the lower wishbone and the crossmember while the motion is controlled by a sealed telescopic damper acting between the lower wishbone and the chassis. The crossmember is located in the fore and aft plane by a pair of flat springs between it and the chassis. A strut locates the crossmember in the lateral direction.

A torsion bar (anti-roll bar) interconnects the lower wishbones to transfer load from the outer to the inner suspension on corners. Road holding is improved and body roll on corners decreased, by the action of the torsion bar.

2 Maintenance

1 At regular intervals grease the suspension swivel points. The individual grease points are arrowed in **FIGS 2** to **5**. At the same time, grease the steering idler (relay arm) for the steering as arrowed in **FIG 6**.
2 At longer intervals remove the wheel hubs and pack them with fresh grease after cleaning and checking the parts. Removing the grease cap and packing more grease around the outer bearing is **not** recommended as this will only force dirt into the outer bearing, leaving the inner bearing dry.

3 The front hubs

A sectioned view of a front hub is shown in **FIG 7**. The oil seal 4 acts directly onto the stub axle and in case of damage or scores to the surface on the stub axle it can be ground down, provided that the diameter does not become less than 44.4 mm (1.748 inch). A shallow return thread is cut into the surface on manufacture but this thread does not need to be recut after machining operations.

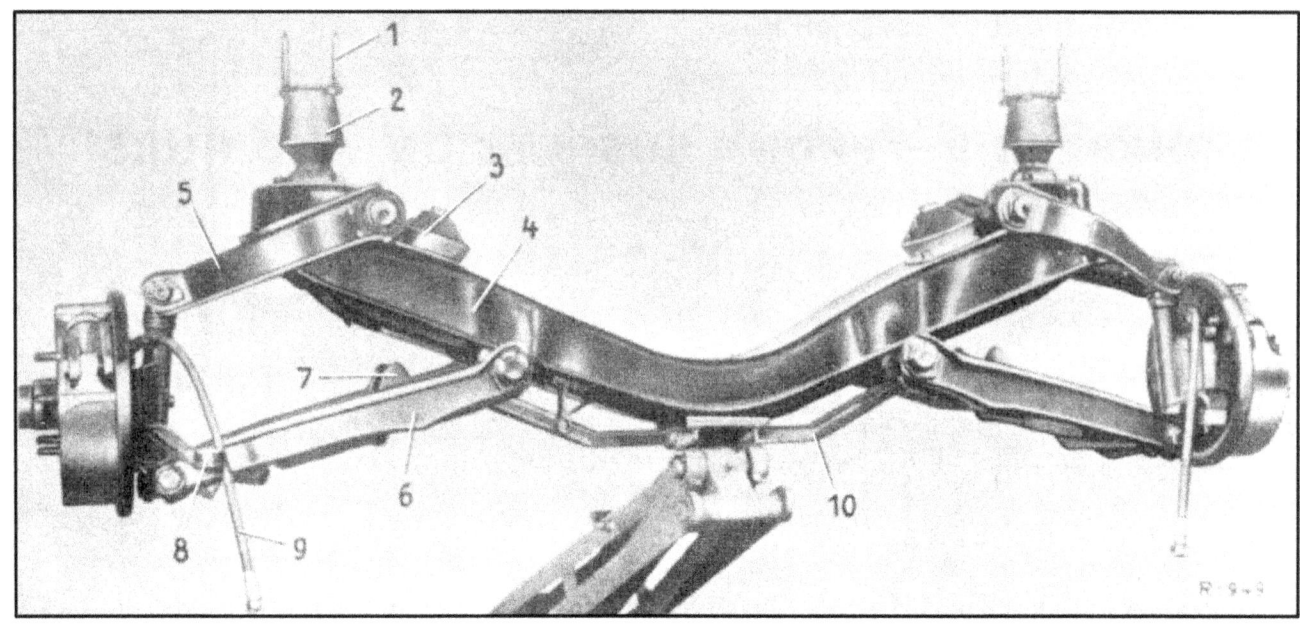

FIG 1 A general view of the front suspension removed from the car

| 1 Guide pin | 3 Rubber mount | 5 Upper control arm | 7 Rubber buffer | 9 Brake hose |
| 2 Rubber mount | 4 Front axle support | 6 Lower control arm | 8 Steering knuckle | 10 Fixture 111 589 02 63 |

Checking:

A DTI (Dial Test Indicator) should always be used to check the end float of the bearings. As a rough test, if the washer behind the adjusting nut can just be turned by finger pressure then the end float is approximately correct.

Jack up the front of the car until the road wheels are just clear of the ground. Spin each wheel in turn and check that it rotates freely without any grinding noises. Take care not to confuse noise from the brakes with that from a defective bearing. Noisy bearings either have run dry or are excessively worn.

Make sure that the wheel nuts are tight. Grip the tyre at the six and twelve o'clock positions and attempt to rock the wheel in and out while noting the play. Repeat the test with the tyre gripped at the nine and three o'clock positions. If there is excessive play in the first position only then it is caused by defective kingpin bushes, but if it is present in both cases then it is likely to be caused by loose wheel bearings. Play from wheel bearings can be removed, for testing purposes, by having an assistant apply the foot brake firmly.

The maximum play at the wheel rim caused by worn kingpin bushes must not exceed 1 mm (.04 inch), otherwise there will be excessive tyre wear. Fit new kingpin bushes to cure excessive play.

Defective wheel bearings may sound satisfactory after packing in grease around the outer bearing and tightening the adjustment nut, but they may well be damaged and on the point of collapse. For this reason the hub should be removed and the bearings visually checked.

FIG 2 Lubrication points on lower wishbone

FIG 3 Front lubrication point on upper wishbone

Removal:

1 Jack up the front of the car and place it securely onto stands. Remove the road wheel, noting that this will be easier if the wheel attachments are slackened slightly before jacking up the car. Remove the brake caliper (see **Chapter 11**). Remove the grease cap, preferably using the special impact puller No. 000 589 91 33 00.

2 Refer to **FIG 8**. Slacken the clamp bolt 13a and unscrew the adjusting nut 13. Remove the special washer 12 and check that it is undamaged, with no scores and that the sides of the washer are parallel. If the washer is damaged either have it ground down or fit a new washer on assembly.

3 Pull the hub assembly firmly off from the stub axle, **FIG 7** and collect the inner race of the outer bearing 3 as it comes free. Normally the hub should come off with hand pressure but if it is difficult, use the puller 136 589 15 33 00.

4 The inner race of the inner bearing 2 is held in place by the oil seal 4 and pulling disc 5. The best method of removal is to use a copper or aluminium drift to drive out the outer race of the inner bearing 2 so that the complete bearing, pulling disc, and oil seal are all driven out together. Otherwise prise out the oil seal and remove the pulling disc and inner race of the inner bearing.

5 The outer races of the bearings 2 and 3 can be left fitted in the hub unless they are damaged, in which case they should be evenly driven out using a drift made of soft-metal.

Cleaning and examination:

Wipe away most of the old grease and dirt using rags or newspaper. Wash the parts in fuel, paraffin or a suitable solvent to remove the remainder of the grease and any dirt. The bearings themselves should be washed separately in clean solvent to prevent them from picking up any dirt. Dry the parts with compressed air from a line or tyre pump.

FIG 5 Rear lubrication point on upper wishbone

When drying the bearings do not allow them to spin as this will cause chipping of the faces. If compressed air is not available, allow the bearings to dry in the air and dry the remainder of the parts with lint-free cloth.

Check the stub axle for excessive runout, wear, or hairline cracks, renewing the steering knuckle if defects are found.

Lightly oil the bearings with thin oil and press them back into their outer races. Oscillate the bearing under pressure to check for any roughness in operation. Roughness can be caused by dirt, so wash the bearings again before finally condemning them. If the operating face shows any signs of fretting, scoring, wear, or corrosion then the bearing is defective. Renew both bearings complete, including the outer races which are matched to the inners.

FIG 4 Lubrication points on steering knuckle

FIG 6 Lubrication point on steering idler

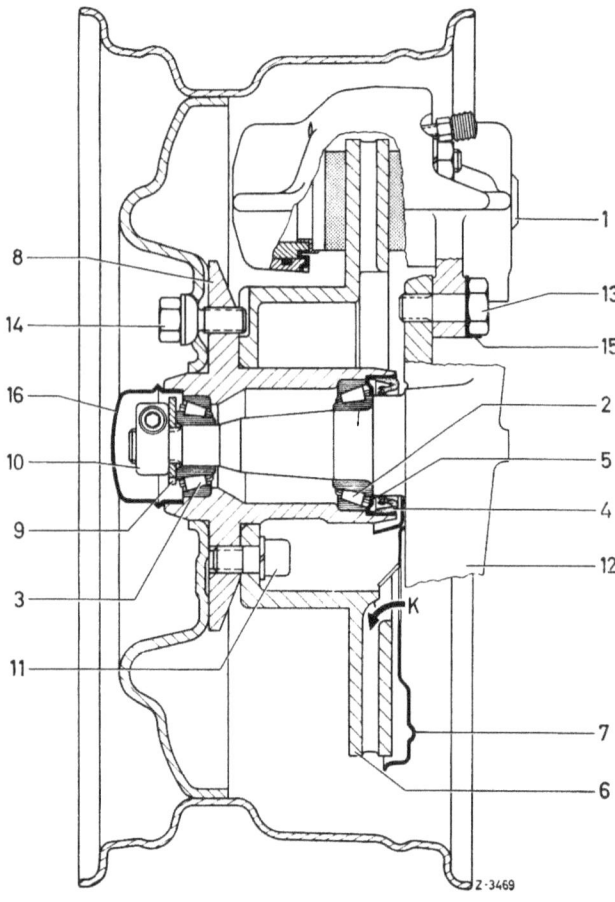

FIG 7   Sectioned view of the hub assembly

1 Brake caliper
2 Inner bearing
3 Outer bearing
4 Oil seal
5 Pulling disc
6 Brake disc
7 Cover plate
8 Front hub
9 Disc
10 Adjusting nut
11 Hex. socket screw
12 Steering knuckle
13 Hex. bolt
14 Ball flange screw
15 Lock washer
16 Grease cap
K Cooling air inlet

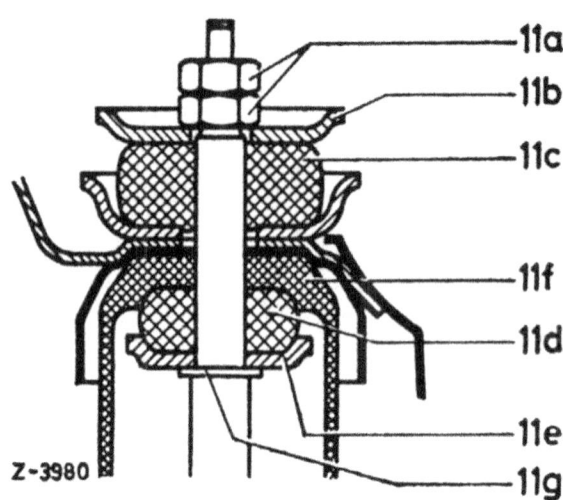

FIG 9   The damper upper attachment

11a Hex. nuts
11b Disc top
11c Rubber ring top
11d Rubber ring bottom
11e Disc bottom
11f Protective tube
11g Locking ring

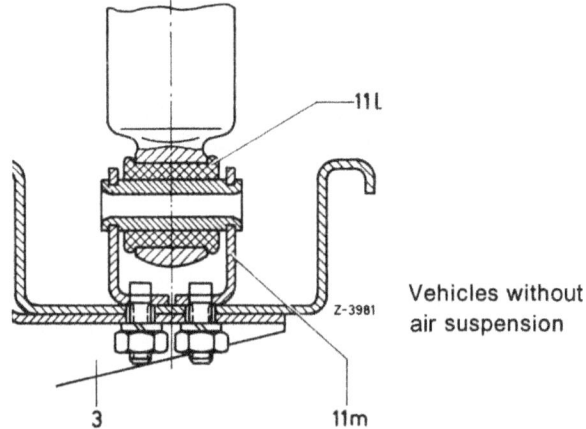

Vehicles without air suspension

FIG 10   The damper lower attachment

3 Lower control arm
11L Rubber mount
11m Fastening plate

FIG 8   The hub adjusting nut

1 Brake disc
2 Brake caliper
10 Front wheel hub
12 Washer
13 Adjusting nut
13a Clamp bolt

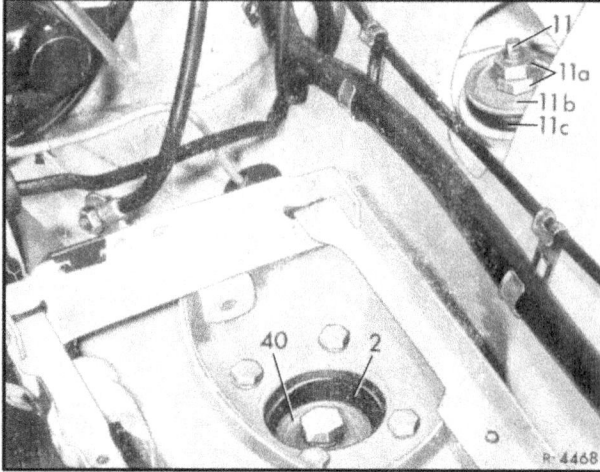

FIG 11   The access to the damper upper attachment

2 Rubber mount
40 Stop plate
11 Front shock absorber
11a Hex. nuts
11b Plate
11c Rubber ring

126

Lubrication and assembly:

If the outer races of the bearings have been removed, drive them fully and evenly back into place. A special set of tools, No. 111 589 13 61 00, is made for driving the races and oil seal back into place—otherwise use drifts made of soft-metal.

Each hub requires a total of 60 to 75 grammes of anti-friction grease for adequate and correct lubrication. Caltex Marfaco Heavy Duty 2 or Texaco are among the recommended greases. The quantity should preferably be weighed but as a rough approximation three times the amount required to fill the grease cap up to the beaded edge should be packed into the hub and bearings and the cap then filled up to the beaded edge again before installing the cap.

Pack the inner races of the bearings liberally with grease and use the remainder to evenly fill the space between the bearings in the hub.

Smear the periphery of the new oil seal 4 lightly with sealing compound. Fit the inner race of the inner bearing back into place followed by the pulling ring and oil seal.

Slide the hub back onto the stub axle and fit the inner race of the outer bearing followed by the special washer and adjusting nut. The brake caliper can be refitted at this point if desired but the grease cap 16 should be left off until after adjustment of the bearings.

Adjustment:

Spin the hub while tightening the adjusting nut 13 shown in **FIG 8**, until there is a definite resistance to turning on the hub. Slacken back the adjusting nut very slightly and give a blow with a copper mallet to the end of the stub axle to settle the parts.

Attach a DTI to the hub so that its stylus rests vertically on the end of the stub axle. Oscillate the hub backwards and forwards with a rotational movement and then pull and push it firmly in and out so that the end play of the hub can be measured on the DTI.

Turn the adjusting nut slightly and spin the hub before taking a further reading. Set the adjusting nut so that the end float of the hub assembly is correct at .01 to .02 mm (.0004 to .0008 inch). When the end float is correct, tighten the clamp bolt 13a, remove the DTI and fit the grease cap, packed with grease. Refit the road wheel and lower the car back to the ground.

4 The dampers

The damper upper attachment is shown in **FIG 9** and the lower in **FIG 10**, while the position of the upper attachment is shown in **FIG 11**.

The general details of removal, testing, and installation of the rear dampers also cover the front dampers, and **Chapter 8, Section 3** should therefore be referred to. It will be necessary to remove the air cleaner or battery when removing the front dampers.

FIG 13   View from the rear of the suspension

1	Crossmember	20	Track rod
3	Lower wishbone	21	Drag link
4	Upper wishbone	23	Idler arm
5	Steering knuckle	24	Steering arm
10	Front spring	25	Steering shock absorber
11	Front shock absorber	32	Cover plate
17	Brake hose	36	Strut

FIG 12   View from the front of the suspension

1	Crossmember	12	Torsion bar
3	Lower wishbone	18	Brake caliper
4	Upper wishbone	27	Torsion bar linkage
5	Steering knuckle	30	Eccentric bolt
6	Kinkpin	31	Flat spring
7	Steering knuckle carrier	33	Bearing bolt
10	Front spring	44	Center brake cable control
11	Front shock absorber	45	Brake lever

FIG 14   Removing a road spring

61   Special adaptor 111 589 00 63 00

127

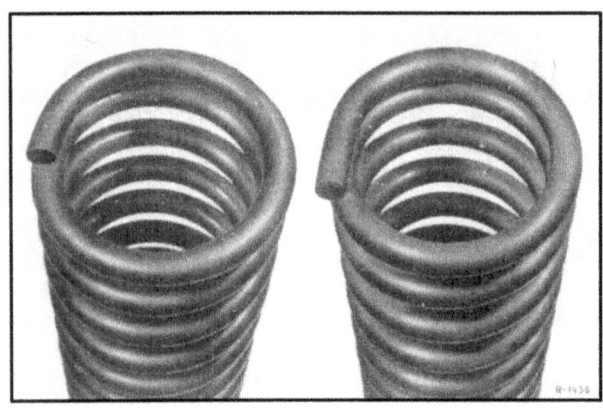

top   bottom

FIG 15 The road spring ends

5 The road springs

Two views of a suspension unit are shown in **FIGS 12** and **13**, one from the front and the other from the rear.

Care must be taken in the removal or installation of the spring as heavy pressures are involved and if the jack slips serious injury can result to the operator.

Removal FIG 12:

1 Jack up the car and set both front suspension units to the same level. Disconnect the torsion bar from the lower wishbone by removing the linkage 27.
2 Remove the outer pair of the four bolts 33 that secure the pivot to the crossmember. Support the pivot on the special adaptor 111 589 00 63 00, shown in **FIG 14**, and a strong firmly-based jack.
3 Remove the remaining inner pair of bolts 33. Carefully lower the jack so that the inboard end of the lower wishbone descends with it and the pressure of the spring 10 is relieved. When all spring pressure is off, lift out the spring 10 complete with its upper rubber mounting.

Examination:

Various springs can be fitted to alter the suspension for different uses of the car. To compensate for the different spring lengths alternative upper rubber mountings are available.

Both parts should be checked for obvious defects, such as cracks in the spring or perishing in the rubber. If it is suspected that the spring is weak it should be taken to a service agent for full checks.

Make sure that only the correct replacement parts are obtained if new parts have to be fitted.

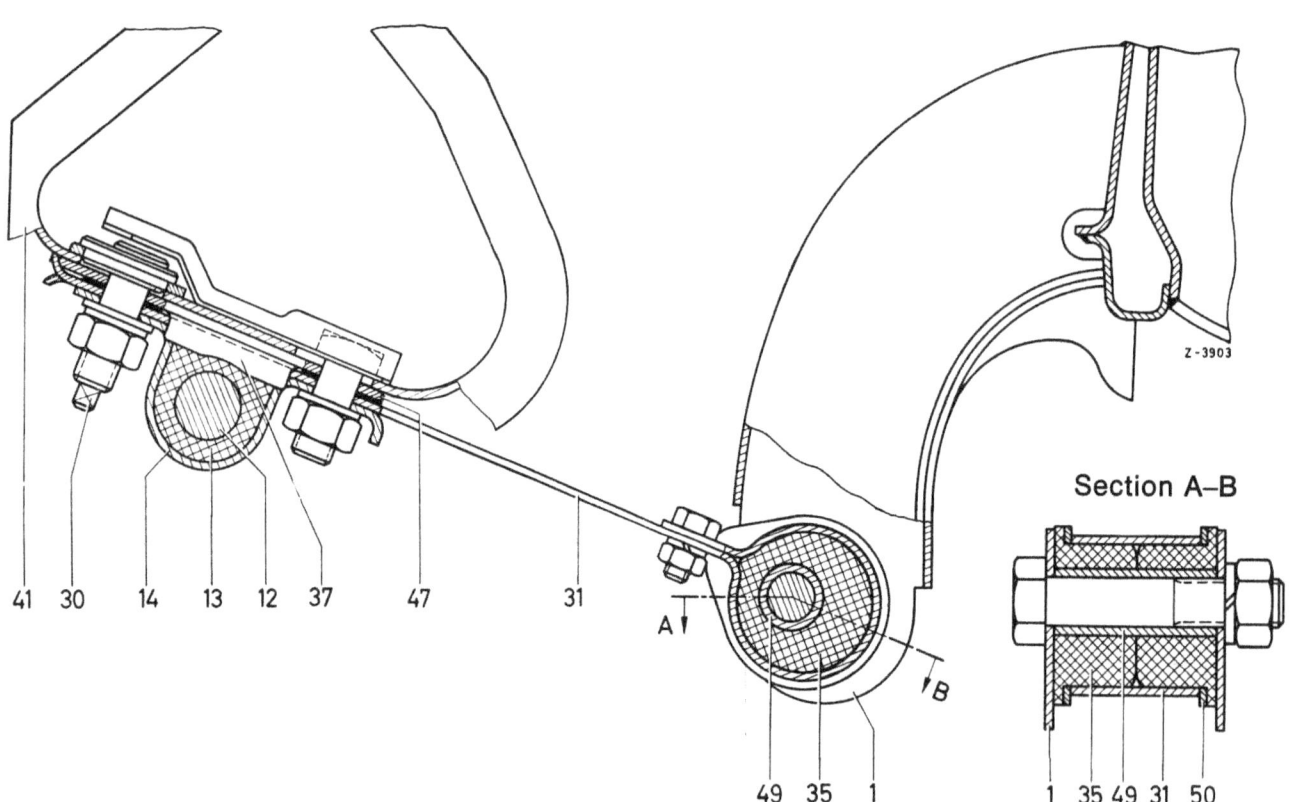

FIG 16 Attachments of the flat spring and torsion bar

1 Crossmember	14 Torsion bar holding clamp	35 Rubber mount	47 Plate
12 Torsion bar	30 Eccentric bolt	37 Lock washer	49 Spacing tube
13 Torsion bar rubber mount	31 Flat spring	41 Bracket	50 Intermediate ring

Installation:

The ends of the spring are different and are shown in **FIG 15**, so make sure that the spring is correctly installed.

1 Lubricate the rubber mounting with Talc and secure it to the upper end of the spring with a little masking tape. Fit the spring back into place, making sure that the spring end fits into the impression in the wishbone.

2 Raise the inner pivot on the jack adaptor, guiding the pivot into line with the mounting holes in the crossmember with the aid of a suitable mandrel.

3 With the pressure taken on the jack, secure the pivot with the inner pair of nuts and bolts.

The bolt heads must be fitted upwards and a washer may also be fitted under the bolt heads. A washer is fitted as standard on all models from October 1969 but it should not be fitted to earlier models on installation of the parts. Lower the jack and fit the remaining pair of bolts in a similar manner.

4 When the spring is installed, reconnect the torsion bar and lower the car back to the ground. **It is most advisable to have the suspension geometry checked by a service agent after the work has been carried out.**

6 The torsion bar and flat spring assembly

The installation of the parts can be seen in **FIG 12**. A sectioned view of the attachment to the chassis is shown in **FIG 16** and a sectioned view of the connecting linkage between bar and wishbone is shown in **FIG 17**.

The eccentric bolts 30 control the castor of the front wheels, by varying the position of the crossmember in relation to the chassis. Before removing the torsion bar or flat spring it is essential that lines are scribed across the flat springs and chassis to ensure that the parts will be installed in exactly the same position as originally.

The parts can be removed, after scribing, by taking out the attachment nuts and bolts.

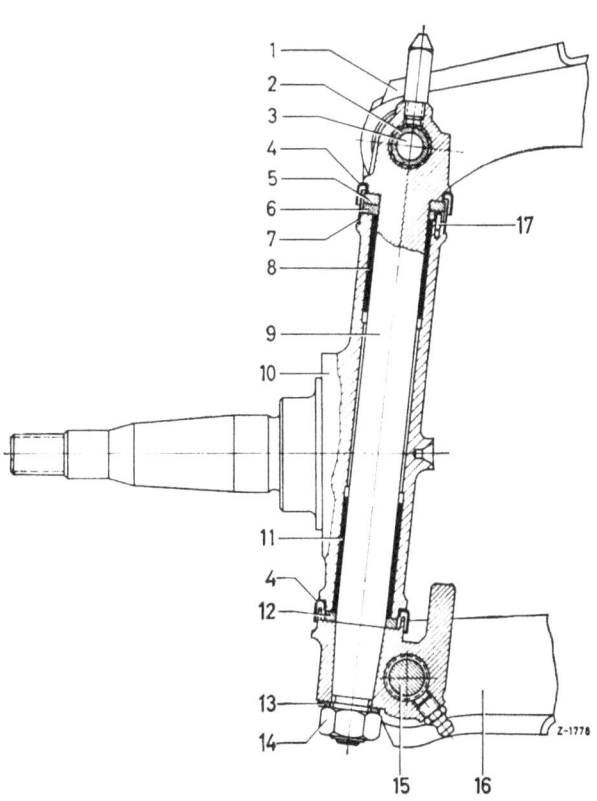

FIG 17 The torsion bar to lower wishbone link

3	Lower control arm	27a	Plate disc
12	Torsion bar	27b	Rubber buffer
27	Torsion bar connecting linkage	27c	Spacing tube
		27d	Hex. bolt

FIG 18 Sectioned view of the kingpin assembly

1	Upper control arm	10	Steering knuckle
2	Threaded pin	11	Bottom bearing bushing
3	Eccentric bolt	12	Compensating washer
4	Dust cap	13	Locking plate
5	Thrust washer top	14	Hex. nut
6	Thrust washer bottom	15	Steering knuckle carrier with threaded pin
7	Dust sleeve		
8	Upper bearing bushing	16	Lower control arm
9	Kingpin	17	Dowel pin

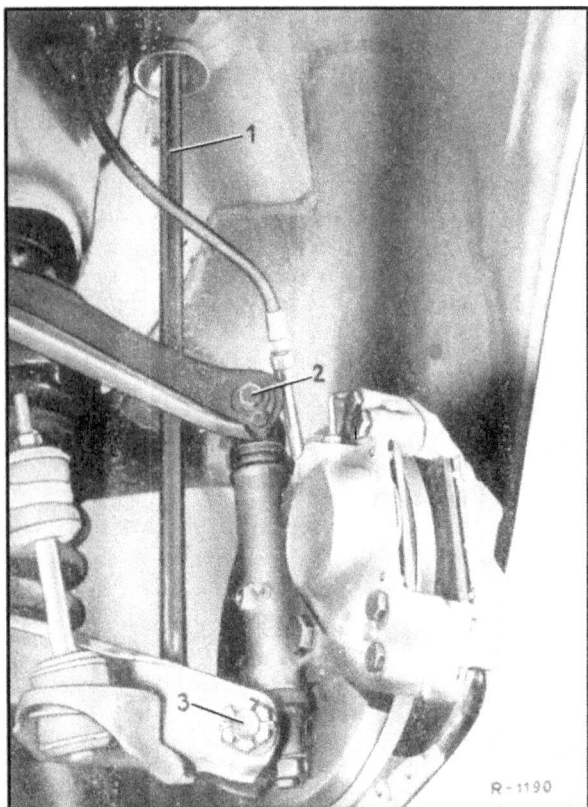

FIG 19 The kingpin assembly installed and the lower wishbone supported

1 Holding fixture 111 589 09 31 2 Eccentric bolt 3 Threaded pin

If all the parts have been removed, attach them to the chassis first. Secure the clamp bolts that hold the spring and then tighten the pivot bolt that secures it to the chassis. With the nuts that secure the brackets to the crossmember just tight, turn the eccentric bolt 30 until the scribed lines are again in alignment and then finally tighten the attachment nuts.

Before installing the parts, check that all rubber rings and mountings are in good condition, renewing them if they are defective or damaged.

7 The lateral strut

The attachments of the lateral strut 36 are shown in **FIG 13**. Renewable rubber mountings are pressed into the ends of the strut and it is made of two parts which are held clamped.

To remove the strut, take out the bolts that secure it to the bracket on the frame and the bracket on the crossmember.

Check the rubber mountings and install the strut with the clamp bolt slack. Lower the car back to the ground and check that the mountings for the crossmember to the frame are not under lateral stress, then tighten the clamp bolt on the strut.

8 The kingpin assembly

A sectioned view of the assembly is shown in **FIG 18**. The eccentric bolt 3 adjusts the camber angle of the suspension while the threaded pin 2 can be rotated by a special washer to adjust the castor angle and to even it between the two suspensions. **If the suspension has been dismantled it is most advisable to take the car to a service agent after reassembly so that the suspension geometry can be checked and adjusted as required.**

Removal:

1 Jack up the front of the car, placing it securely onto stands, and remove the road wheel. Remove the hub assembly (see **Section 3, Chapter 8**), and the damper (see **Section 4, Chapter 8**).

The brake caliper can be removed and hung out of the way or else removed with the hub after disconnecting the flexible hose (see **Chapter 11** for further details).

2 Raise the lower wishbone and support it on a jack or use the fixture 111 589 09 31 to hold it up, as shown in **FIG 19**. Remove the lock bolt, and slacken and remove the eccentric bolt 2 at the upper attachment.

3 Take off the castellated nut and remove the threaded pin 3 from the lower attachment. Disconnect the hydraulic flexible hose if required and lift the assembly out from the wishbones.

Dismantling:

The components are shown in **FIG 20**. Screw out the threaded pin 8. There should be some clearance to allow lubricant to pass through the threads and some wear is acceptable as the weight of the car will hold the parts in conjunction, allowing the play to be on the unloaded side of the threaded bolt. Free the locking plate 2 and remove the bottom nut 1. Give the kingpin a sharp upwards blow with a plastic-faced hammer to free the tapers and remove the lower steering knuckle 4, complete with compensating washer. Withdraw the kingpin from the steering knuckle and take off the washers 6.

Reassembly:

Wash all the metal parts in clean fuel and check them for wear or damage. If the kingpin bushes are worn they should be driven out, preferably with special drift 111 589 03 43 00.

Check the stub axle for signs of wear or damage. Mount it between centres and check that the maximum runout does not exceed .05 mm (.002 inch).

1 Refer to **FIG 18**. Press new bushes 8 and 11 into

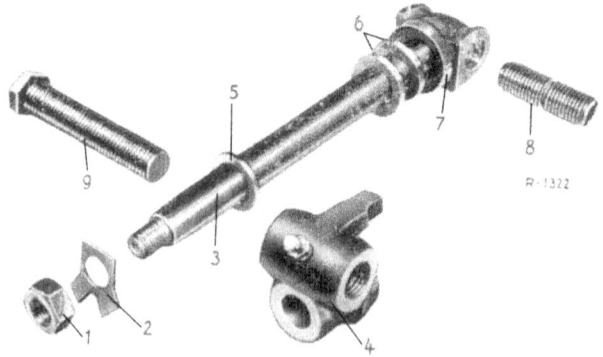

FIG 20 The kingpin components

1 Hex. nut
2 Locking plate
3 Kingpin
4 Steering knuckle support
5 Shim washer
6 Thrust washer
7 Dust cap
8 Threaded pin top
9 Threaded pin bottom

place if the old ones have to be removed. When fitting a new bush 8 into place use an old washer 6 above it as a thrust piece to protect the dowel pin 17. Line ream both bushes to an internal diameter of 20.000 to 20.021 mm (.7874 to .7882 inch), preferably using the special reamer 000 589 03 53 and taking great care to achieve an excellent surface finish.

2 Fit the lower thrust washer 6 into place so that its oil groove faces upwards and is located by the dowel pin 17. Place the upper thrust washer 5 into position and refit the dust covers 4 and dust sleeve 7.

3 Clean the tapers thoroughly and pass the kingpin back through the steering knuckle. Wipe off any grease that may have been picked up by the taper on the kingpin. Install the compensating washer 12.

4 Press on the steering knuckle onto the kingpin so that the two knuckles are accurately aligned. The only satisfactory method of aligning the knuckles is to use the fixture 120 589 01 61 which uses accurately ground pins passing through the knuckles and the jig to ensure accuracy. Fit the locking plate 13 and nut 14. Tighten the nut 14 to a torque of 9 kg m (65 lb ft) and use feeler gauges to check the end float of the kingpin in the steering knuckle. On assembly the end float should be adjusted to .05 to .10 mm (.002 to .004 inch) by selectively fitting the compensating washer 12. In service the end float may be allowed to reach .5 mm (.02 inch) before parts require renewal and the steering is affected. Lock the nut 14 when the end float has been correctly adjusted.

5 Attach the lower steering knuckle support to the lower wishbones, using new sealing rubbers. The threaded pin is fitted with its head towards the rear. Tighten the castellated nut to a torque of 9 kg m and use a new splitpin to secure it.

6 A sectioned view of the upper attachment is shown in **FIG 21**. Screw the threaded pin 7 back into the knuckle so that the pin protrudes evenly on both sides and the groove is to the front. Refit the steering knuckle to the upper wishbone using the eccentric bolt 1, setting the eccentricity of the bolt in its original direction. Use new sealing rings and make sure that the nose of the adjusting washer 4 fits into the groove of the threaded pin.

4 Refit the remainder of the parts in the reverse order of removal. Bleed the brakes if the hydraulic flexible hose as been disconnected.

9 The wishbones (control arms)

The details of the upper wishbone are shown in **FIG 22** and the lower wishbone in **FIG 23**.

If the suspension has been damaged in an accident or by 'kerbing' the wishbones should be checked by a service agent on special jigs. **Do not attempt to straighten distorted wishbones.**

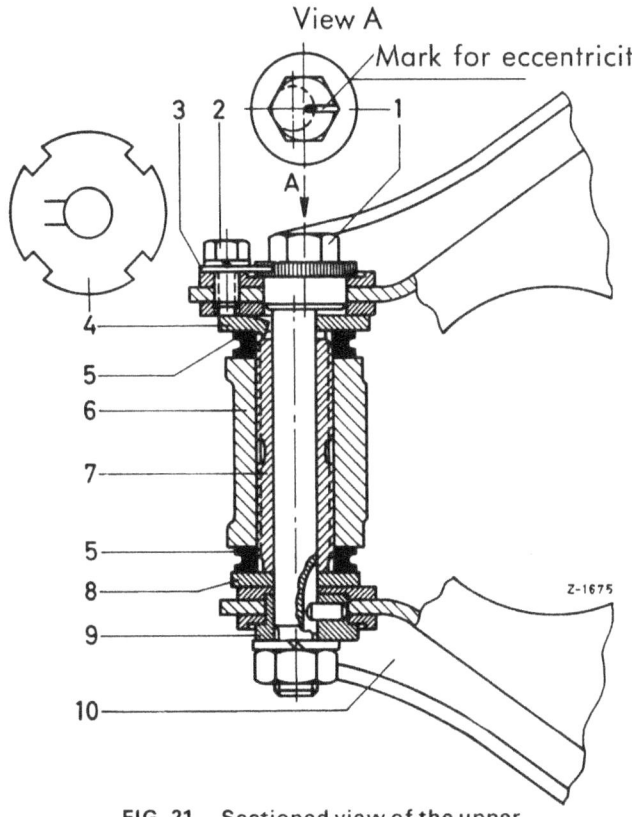

FIG 21 Sectioned view of the upper steering knuckle attachment

1 Eccentric bolt for adjusting camber
2 Hex. bolt with lock washer
3 Locking plate
4 Washer for adjusting caster
5 Rubber sealing ring
6 Kingpin
7 Threaded pin
8 Washer
9 Eccentric bushing with drive pin
10 Upper control arm

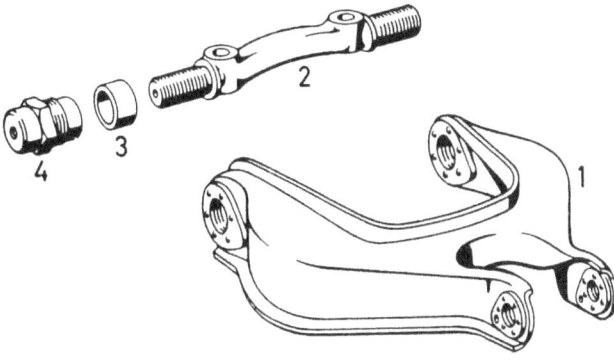

FIG 22 The upper wishbone

1 Upper control arm
2 Pivot pin
3 Rubber sealing ring
4 Threaded bushing

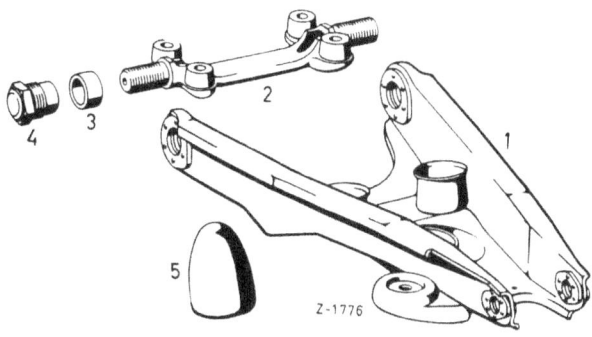

FIG 23 The lower wishbone

1 Lower control arm
2 Pivot pin
3 Rubber sealing ring
4 Threaded bushing
5 Supplementary rubber buffer

Removal:

1 Jack up the front of the car and remove the road wheels, road springs and kingpin assemblies. There is no need to remove the hub parts from the stub axle for this operation.
2 Unscrew the threaded bushings 4 that secure the wishbones. Take out the bolts that secure the pivot pins 2 to the crossmember and remove the assemblies.

Installation:

1 Fit new rubber seals onto the pivot pins 2 and refit the assemblies to the wishbones.
2 Screw in the threaded bushes 4 and tighten them to a torque load of 18 kg m (130 lb ft). Check that the pivots 2 turn freely in the wishbones and then set the pivots so that they are evenly spaced between each wishbone. A wishbone stamped with the number 31 beside the boss has an M31 thread and therefore requires a bush with similar thread. The bushes with M31 threads are identified by an annular groove below the threaded portion.
3 Attach the pivot 2 to the crossmember. Washers are fitted between pivot and crossmember and it is essential to install these into their original positions.
4 Install the remainder of the parts in the reverse order of removal. Once all parts are installed have the suspension geometry checked and adjusted by a service agent.

10 Fault diagnosis

(a) Wheel wobble

1 Unbalanced front wheels
2 Broken or weak road springs
3 Defective rubber mountings
4 Worn hub bearings
5 Uneven tyre wear or pressures
6 Worn suspension linkage
7 Loose wheel attachments

(b) Bottoming of suspension

1 Check 2 in (a)
2 Rebound rubbers worn or missing
3 Defective dampers

(c) Heavy steering

1 Neglected lubrication
2 Incorrect suspension geometry

(d) Excessive tyre wear

1 Check 6 in (a); 3 in (b) and 2 in (c)

(e) Rattles

1 Check 2 and 3 in (a) and 1 in (c)
2 Damper mountings loose or worn
3 Torsion bar broken or rubber mountings worn

(f) Excessive rolling

1 Check 2 in (a); 3 in (b) and 3 in (e)

CHAPTER 10 – STEERING

1. Description
2. Maintenance
3. Ball joints
4. The steering linkage
5. The steering wheel
6. The steering and starter lock
7. The steering coupling
8. The steering column
9. The front wheel alignment
10. The manual steering unit
11. The power steering unit
12. Fault diagnosis

1 Description

A recirculating ball steering box is fitted onto the chassis and it is driven from the safety collapsible steering column by a coupling so that the steering worm rotates with the steering wheel. The worm drives the steering shaft which has an arm splined to it. The outer end of the steering arm is connected to the steering linkage. A view of the steering linkage is shown in **FIG 1**. An idler arm (intermediate lever) 8 is fitted to the opposite end of the drag link 3 so that the drag link always is at right angles to the axis of the car. The outer ends of the drag link are connected by track rods (tie rods) 2 and 10 to the steering levers on the steering knuckles. The tie rods are adjustable so that the toe-in of the front wheels can be correctly set. A damper 5 is fitted between the drag link and a bracket. The unit damps road shocks and wheel wobble but it is not repairable and must be renewed if defective.

The ignition switch is mounted onto the steering column and it is so designed that it also acts as an antitheft device. By turning the key the steering column can be locked so that the steering cannot be turned.

The maximum steering angle of the front wheels is controlled by stops on the suspension units and additional safety stops are fitted in the steering unit. The safety stops should not come into contact during normal conditions.

If the front of the car is jacked up so that the road wheels are clear of the ground, do not spin the steering vigorously from lock to lock or the shock as the steering stops may damage both sets of lock stops.

Power-assisted steering can be fitted as an optional extra. A hydraulic pump is driven by a belt from the engine to supply the power for the system and a reservoir is fitted by the pump.

2 Maintenance

Greasing:

All the ball joints in the steering are of the sealed-for-life type and therefore do not require routine greasing. The dust boots on the ball joints should be examined at regular intervals to ensure that they are not splitting or allowing dirt to enter.

Renew the dust boots before they fail completely otherwise the complete ball joint will have to be renewed as well, as there is no method of removing dirt from the ball joint. When fitting a new dust boot, pack a little Molykote Longterm 2 grease around the ball joint.

The idler arm should be greased at the same time as the rest of the front suspension swivel points (see **Chapter 9, Section 2**).

FIG 1 The steering linkage

1 Steering arm (pitman arm)
2 Lefthand tie rod
3 Drag link (centre tie rod)
4 Hex. bolt with lockwasher
5 Steering damper
6 Bolt with nut and lockwasher
7 Strut for front axle lateral support
8 Idler arm
9 Bolt with nut and lockwasher
10 Righthand tie rod

Lubricant level in steering unit:

The unit should be filled with .3 litre (300 cc) of suitable Hypoid transmission oil on assembly.

To check the level, with the unit fitted, turn the steering until the steering nut is at the lower portion of the worm. On models with lefthand drive, turn the steering to full left lock and on righthand models turn it to full right lock. Remove the filler plug from the cover and use a depth gauge to check the oil level. When correct, the level should be approximately 40 mm (1.6 inch) below the bore in the housing.

Power steering:

At regular intervals check the fluid level in the reservoir, as shown in **FIG 2**. Unscrew the thumb screw on top of the reservoir and remove the cover 4 with the seal 3. Check with the engine running and the system at its operating temperature. If required top up to the maximum mark 2a using Automatic Transmission Fluid of a recommended type.

If the fluid level has been allowed to fall so low that air is drawn into the system, shown by the milky appearance of the fluid, fit a length of bleed tube to the bleed screw on the power steering unit. **Make sure that the tube fits on tightly as if it comes off large amounts of fluid will be lost.** With the engine running at idle, open the bleed screw by two turns with the open end of the tube held in the reservoir.

Flush through the system, without turning the steering, until no more air comes out of the bleed tube into the reservoir. Top up as necessary to prevent more air being drawn into the system. Close the bleed screw and turn the steering from full lock to lock several times. Open the bleed screw again and vent out any air, without turning the steering. When all the air is out of the system, top up to the correct level. Make sure that the bleed screw is closed before removing the bleed tube and then refit the cover to the reservoir.

At regular intervals check the tension of the drive belt (see **Chapter 4**) and at longer intervals renew the oil filter in the reservoir.

3 Ball joints

These are fitted throughout the steering linkage to allow motions to be transmitted without excessive friction or free play. The ball joints are built into the rods or tie rod ends on manufacture and therefore the complete part will have to be renewed if a ball joint is defective.

Check for wear by having an assistant turn the steering backwards and forwards while watching for play in the linkage. Apply resistance to the movement to make it easier to spot play. At the same time as checking the ball joints for wear, examine the dust covers on all the ball joints. **It is essential that the dust covers are renewed before they actually split and allow dirt to enter.**

A sectioned view of a typical ball joint is shown in **FIG 3**. The ballpin 1 is free to revolve or pivot in the plastic

FIG 2 The power steering system reservoir

1 High-pressure oil pump
2 Reservoir
2a Max. level mark
3 Seal
4 Cover
5 Spring
6 High-pressure hose
7 Return hose

into the eyes at the ends of damper and these can be renewed if they are defective. The damper on all models is Stabilus TA 20 x 208, part number 000 463 43 32. Check that the length of the damper, when fully compressed, is 330 ± 2 mm (13 ± .08 inch).

If the car has been 'kerbed' or the suspension damaged in an accident, check the safety clearances at the damper. Connect the damper at one end only and turn the steering from full lock to full lock. Check that the maximum steering angle is limited by the stops on the suspensions and not by the safety stops in the steering unit. The damper must have a further movement of 5 mm (.02 inch) at each lock to ensure that it is not jamming at full lock.

ball socket 4, the pressure of the spring 8 preventing excessive movement of the ballpin out of the socket. The tapered portion of the pin 1 fits into a mating taper on the other member and the two tapers are then pulled tightly together by screwing down a nut on the threaded portion of the pin. A self-locking or castellated nut may be used.

Separating the ball joints often appears extremely difficult after removal of the nut as even after a short period of use the two tapers seem to weld together. **Never hammer on the end of the pin, even with a slave nut fitted to protect the threads,** as the jarring will damage the plastic ball socket 4. Special extractors are made for all the differing ball joints in the linkage and they should be used whenever possible. The extractors clamp between the members and have a bolt which is tightened down to force the tapers apart. If the special extractor is not available it is still possible to part the tapers. Unscrew the securing nut to the last few threads on the pin, so that it will prevent the parts from flying apart when the tapers free. Pull or lever the tow arms firmly apart and lay a block of metal on one side of the tapered eye. Hammer on the opposite side of the eye, using a copper-faced hammer, and the tapers will quickly free.

4 The steering linkage

A general view of the linkage is shown in **FIG 1** and the method of freeing the ball joints is given in the previous section.

The steering damper:

The damper is removed after taking out the bolts that secure it to the chassis bracket and to the bracket on the drag link. When refitting the damper, make sure that the end marked 'Rahmseittex' is nearest to the chassis bracket.

The damper cannot be tested by the owner, as special equipment is required, but it should be renewed if it is obviously defective or has physical damage such as a bent ram or dented body. Rubber mountings are pressed

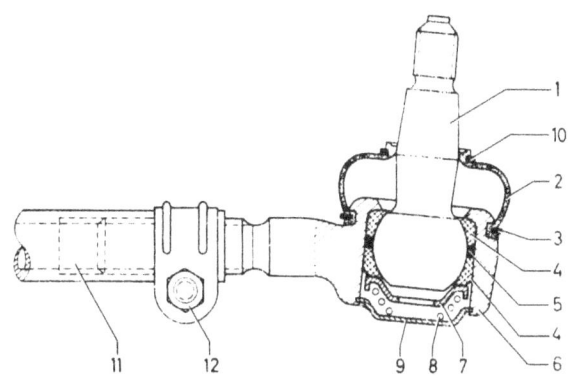

FIG 3 A typical steering ball joint

1 Ball pin
2 Dust cover
3 Wire clamp ring
4 Vulkollan socket
5 Spacer
6 Tie rod end
7 Retainer
8 Spring
9 Cover
10 Plastic clamp ring
11 Tube
12 Clamp

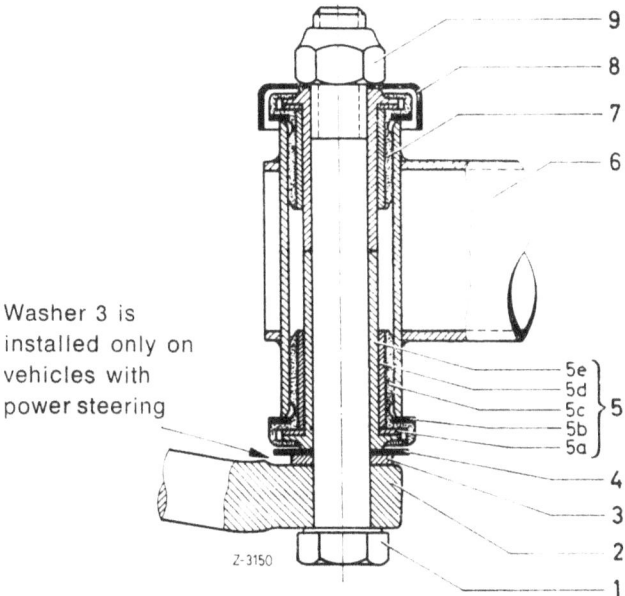

Washer 3 is installed only on vehicles with power steering

FIG 4 Sectioned idler arm bearing

1 Hex. bolt
2 Intermediate steering lever
3 Steel washer 3.5 mm (for power steering only)
4 Thrust washer
5 Lower rubber slide bearing
5a DU washer
5b Steel washer
5c Rubber bushing
5d DU bushing
5e Steel bushing
6 Journal bearing
7 Upper rubber slide bearing
8 Dust cap
9 Self-locking hex. nut

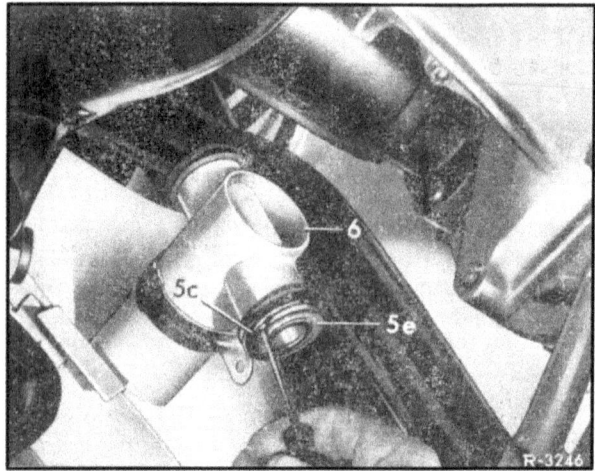

FIG 5 Removing the bearings

5c Rubber bushing   5e Steel bushing   6 Journal bearing

FIG 6 The steering wheel attachment nut

Tie rods (track rods):

The adjustment of the tie rods will be dealt with in **Section 9**. If the tie rods are removed from the linkage they must be installed back into place so that the tie rod end with the lefthand thread is on the left side, when viewed from the driving position.

Idler arm (intermediate lever):

A sectioned view through the idler arm support is shown in **FIG 4**. On later models a high-lying lever is fitted and the sectional view is exactly the same except that the lever 2 is fitted above, between the nut 9 and dust cap 8.

1 Remove the shield from around the idler arm bearing. Free the lever from the steering linkage by parting the ball joints as described in the previous section.
2 Remove the nut 9 from the assembly and take off the dust cap 8 in an upwards direction. The lever 2, bolt 1 and washers can then be withdrawn from the bearing housing 6. Remove the thrust washer 4 from the bolt.
3 Check the condition of the rubber bearings 5 in the housing. Lift the sealing lip of the rubber bushing 5c off with a screwdriver, as shown in **FIG 5**, and then withdraw the steel bushing 5e. If the rubber bushings 5c are worn or deformed, use a 12 mm ($\frac{1}{2}$ inch) diameter rod of light alloy to press out the rubber bushings, with the rod passed through the housing in each case.
4 Coat the new rubber bushings 5c with a suitable lubricant, such as white oil, and draw them back into position. The special tool 115 589 08 61 00 is made for this purpose but the tool is basically a long bolt, two washers and a nut. Grease the bushings 5e with Calypsoll AE63 or Mobilux Grease 2 and slide them back into place.
5 Position the idler arm 2 on the bolt 1 so that the offset of the lever will be upwards and the integrally cast code number will be visible from below. Secure the parts of the bearing 5 by lifting the lip of the rubber bushing back into place and insert the bolt 1 back through the bearings. Fit the nut 9 and tighten it to a torque of 12 kg m (86 lb ft) after installing the dust cover 8.
6 Refit the shield to the assembly and reconnect the lever to the steering linkage.

5 The steering wheel

The steering wheel and horn ring are mounted on a shock absorber which is in turn attached by splines to the inner steering column. The shock absorber is designed to collapse in a controlled manner when the driver is thrown forwards against the steering wheel. Usually the steering wheel is removed, leaving the shock absorber in place but when working on the column jacket, shift tube or inner column take off the steering wheel complete with the shock absorber.

Removing the steering wheel and shock absorber:

Pry out the trade mark motif from the centre of the steering wheel. Use a socket spanner and extension to remove the nut 4 shown in **FIG 6**. Make light dot punch marks on the end of the shaft and hub so that the steering wheel will be installed back into its original position. Pull the steering wheel and shock absorber off the shaft.

Install the parts in the reverse order of removal, aligning the marks so that the steering wheel will be

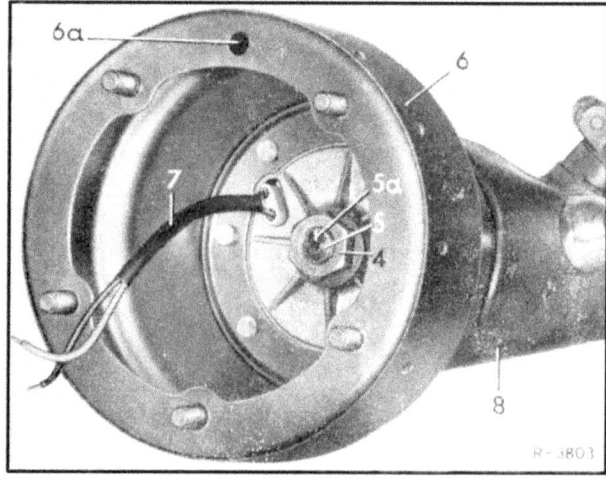

FIG 7 The slip ring cable

4 Hex. nut with spring washer   6a Assembly hole
5 Steering spindle   7 Cable for slip ring
5a Mark on steering spindle   8 Column jacket
6 Collapsible bowl

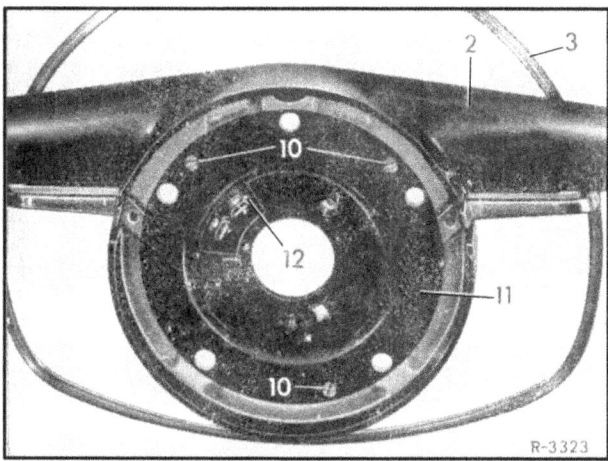

FIG 8 The horn attachments
2 Steering wheel   10 Countersunk screws   12 Contact ring
3 Horn ring   11 Centering base

correctly set. When fitting the nut 4, secure it to the socket with a piece of masking tape and then remove the tap once the nut has started.

Road test the car to check that the spokes are level when the car is travelling straight-ahead. If the spokes are not level, check the front wheel alignment (see **Section 9**). If the wheel is still not level, remove it and alter it by a maximum of two splines in either direction to set it correctly.

Removing steering wheel alone:

Pry out the motif as before. Remove the five un-unmarked nuts shown in **FIG 6**. Carefully lift the steering wheel slightly off, sufficient to gain access and disconnect the cable 7 for the slip ring from the wheel, shown in **FIG 7**. The wheel can then be fully removed.

The steering wheel is refitted in the reverse order of removal.

Dismantling the parts:

The slip ring on the bottom of the shock absorber is secured by a circlip. If the slip ring is badly burnt or corroded the circlip should be taken off and a new slip ring fitted into place. Light damage or burns should be smoothed down with a fine grade of glasspaper.

The attachments of the horn ring and centring disc on the steering wheel are shown in **FIG 8**. Take out the countersunk screws 10 and remove the centring base 11 and contact ring 12. Remove the horn ring 3. The parts are assembled in the reverse order of dismantling.

6 The steering and starter lock

The components of the lock fitted to earlier models are shown in **FIG 9** and on this type of lock the key can be pulled out when it is set to the 'Garage' position (accessories off but steering free). On later models a second type of lock, shown in **FIG 10**, is fitted to meet legal requirements. On the later type of lock the key cannot be removed when it is set to the 'Garage' position.

Each lock consists of three main sub-components; mechanical steering lock, ignition with starter switch, and the locking cylinder.

Ignition switch:

Remove the instrument cluster and the cover at the right under the instrument panel (see **Chapter 13**). Disconnect the plug from the switch and take out the screws which secure the switch 7 to the lock 1 and then remove the switch 7.

Install the parts in the reverse order of removal and check that the lock and switch operate correctly.

Early version locking cylinder:

Lift the cover sleeve 2 with a small screwdriver, as shown in **FIG 11**. Offset the end of a piece of 1.5 mm (.06 inch) diameter wire by approximately 3 mm (.12 inch) and hook the offset under the cover sleeve 2 and use the wire to pull out the sleeve, while holding the rosette 3 in place.

Introduce the piece of wire between the rosette and lock so that it presses down on the lock button 6 of the locking cylinder 5, as shown in **FIG 12**, and use the key to pull the cylinder partially out. Pull the cylinder completely out using the bent wire in the slot for the key.

The cylinder is installed in the reverse order of removal with it in the '1' position so that the locking pin engages. Push the cover sleeve back into the '1' position and check that the lock operates correctly.

Later version locking cylinder:

This is the type of lock where the key cannot be removed in the 'Garage' position.

To remove the lock, turn the key to position '1', lift the cover up as far as the key will allow and turn the key to position '0'. Withdraw both the key and the cover.

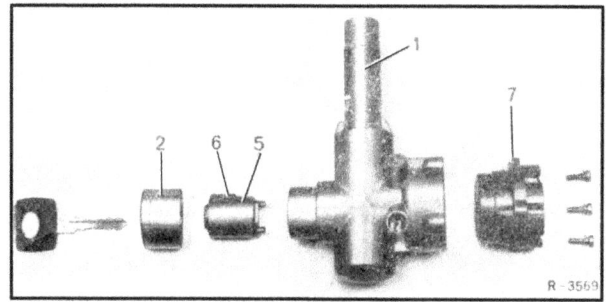

FIG 9 The components of the early steering lock
1 Steering lock   5 Locking cylinder   7 Ignition switch
2 Cover sleeve   6 Lock button

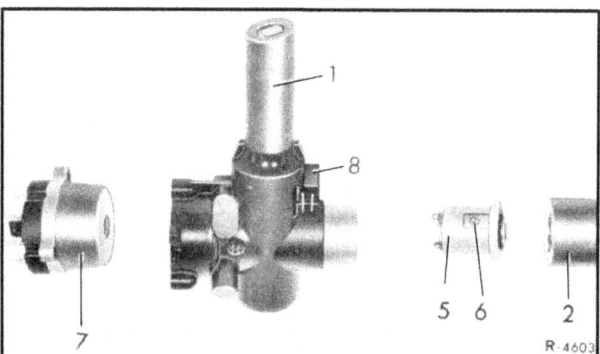

FIG 10 The components of the later steering lock
1 Steering lock   6 Lock button
2 Cover sleeve   7 Ignition starting switch
5 Locking cylinder 8 Contact switch (USA models only)

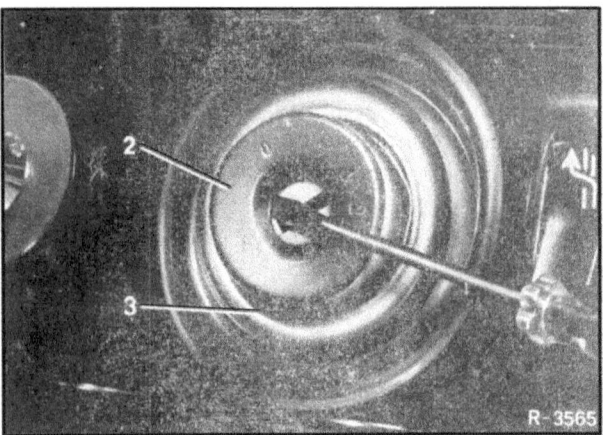

FIG 11 Prising out the cover sleeve
2 Cover sleeve   3 Rosette

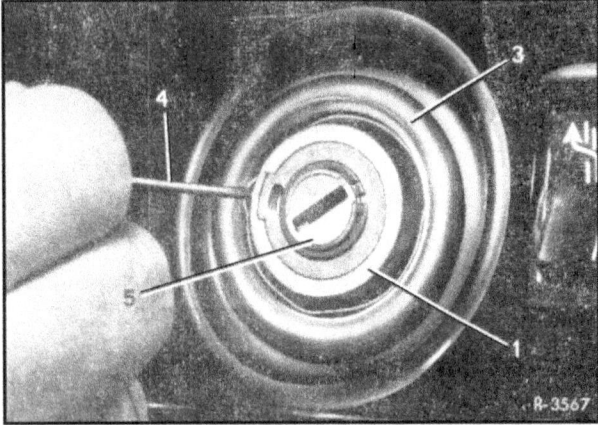

FIG 12 Pressing in the locking pin
1 Steering lock   4 Steel wire
3 Rosette   5 Locking cylinder

Insert the key again and turn it to position '1' (90 deg. right), push in the locking pin and draw out the cylinder.

Insert the cylinder with the key in place and turned to position '1' so that the lock pin engages. Turn the key to '0' and withdraw it. Place the cover over the switch, insert and turn the key, pushing the cover into position '1'. Check the operation of the lock.

Steering lock:

A view of the switch mounting is shown in **FIG 13**. Disconnect the battery and remove the instrument cluster. Free the plug from the ignition switch and put the key to position '1'. Slacken the clamp 5 and pull off the cover sleeve from the switch as described previously. On later USA models, disconnect the plug for the warning buzzer from the contact switch. Set the lock to position '1' by means of the key and use a 5 mm thick punch to press in the locking pin 7. Turn the lock and remove it from the holder 8, taking care not to damage the rosette on the instrument panel. The lockpin can only be pressed in when the switch is in the '1' position as an additional safeguard against theft. Similarly the contact switch 8 on later USA versions **FIG 10** can only be removed with the switch in position '1'.

Install the lock in the reverse order of removal and check that it operates correctly.

7 The steering coupling

The coupling shown in **FIG 14** connects the steering column to the worm shaft of the steering unit. Not shown in the figure are the hexagonal socket bolts that clamp the flanges to the shafts.

To remove the coupling, slacken the hexagonal socket bolt that secures the upper flange 7 to the steering column. Free the attachments of the steering unit on the chassis sidemember and lower the steering unit slightly, leaving it attached to the linkage. Slacken the hexagonal socket bolt that secures the lower flange 5 to the worm shaft and force the coupling off from the shaft so that it can be removed.

SL clips 1 secure the parts of the clamp together and the method of removing these is shown in **Chapter 6, FIG 1**. The clips are installed in the reverse order of removal, taking care to make sure that they are fully seated.

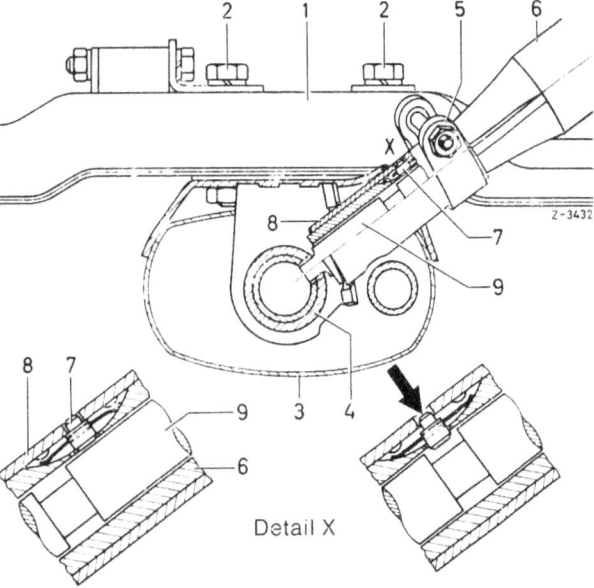

FIG 13 The attachment of the steering lock
1 Cross member   6 Steering lock
2 Bolt with washers   7 Locking pin
3 Column jacket   8 Holder for steering lock
4 Steering column shaft   9 Locking bolt
5 Fastening clamp

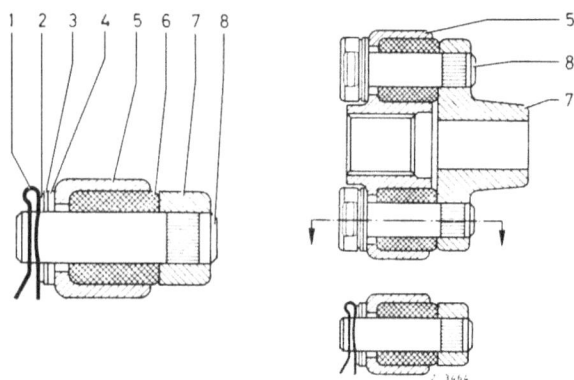

FIG 14 The steering coupling
1 SL clip   5 Lower flange
2 Steel washer   6 Bushing
3 Spring washer   7 Upper flange
4 Plastic washer   8 Bolt

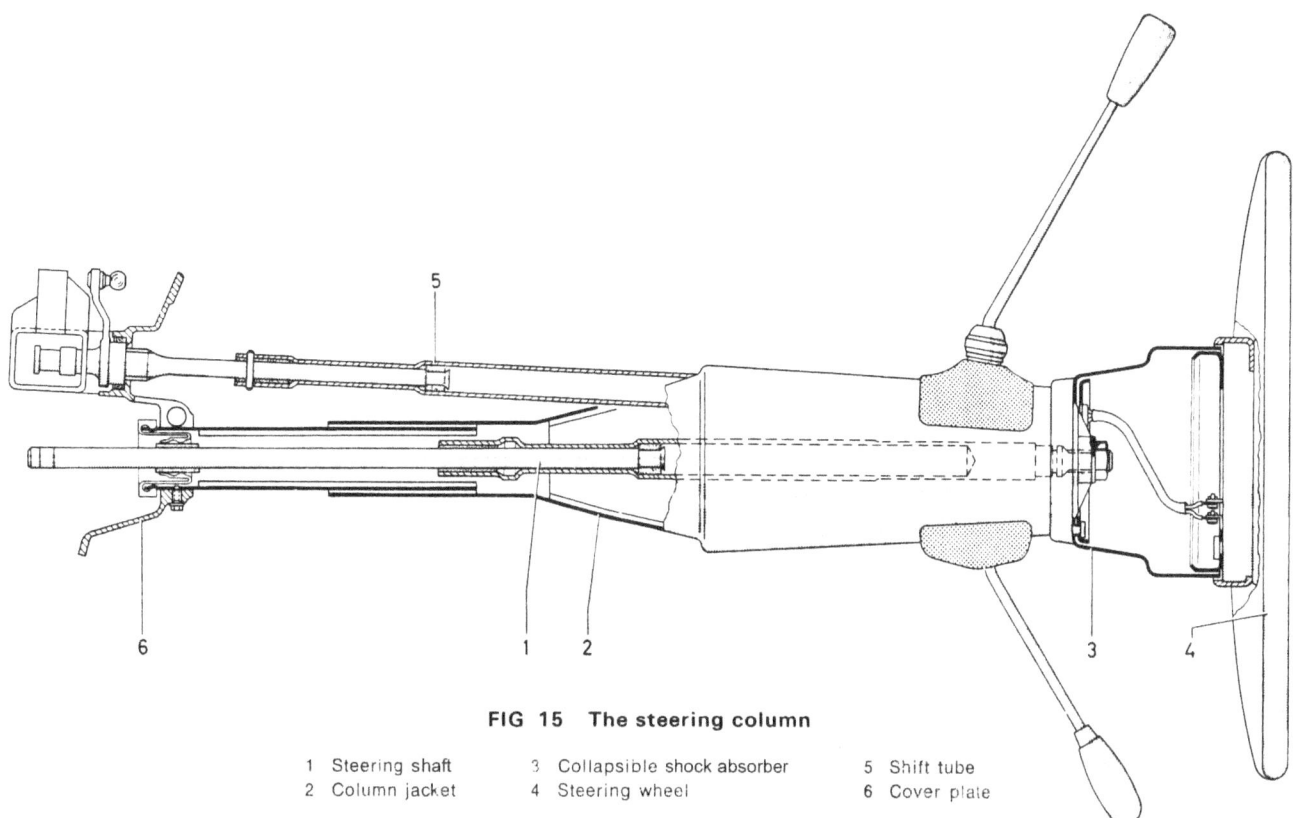

FIG 15 The steering column

1 Steering shaft	3 Collapsible shock absorber	5 Shift tube
2 Column jacket	4 Steering wheel	6 Cover plate

Remove the clips 1 from both bolts 8 and take off the steel washers 2 and spring washer 3 as well as the plastic washers 4. Pull the upper flange 7 from the lower one 5 and extract the old bushings 6.

If the flanges are damaged or the bolts 8 loose then new parts complete should be installed.

Insert new bushings 6 into the lower flange 5. Lightly grease the bolts 8 and press the upper flange back into the lower flange. Compress the two flanges between the jaws of a vice and refit the washers followed by the SL clips.

Install the coupling in the reverse order of removal and make sure that the steering unit is correctly attached to the side frame.

8 The steering column

A typical safety steering column is shown in **FIG 15**. The column itself is designed so that it will collapse together in a controlled manner under a heavy impact and this combined with the shock absorber 3 mounted under the steering wheel 4 ensures that the driver will not suffer serious injury on the steering column in the event of a serious head-on crash.

Because of the design of the steering column, force must not be used when removing or installing it. If the column is accidentally collapsed then new parts must be installed on reassembly.

When removing or installing the column a rivet of 6 mm diameter, or the special pin shown in **FIG 16**, inserted into the appropriate hole as shown in **FIG 17** will ensure that the shaft 19 is set to the correct distance, and it will also help to prevent the column from collapsing.

Removal:

Remove the instrument cluster, steering wheel and the steering column lock. Remove covers as required and disconnect the multi-pin connector for the steering column. Disconnect the shift and selector rods from the levers at the base of the steering column, if column shift is fitted. On some models it will be necessary to remove the bearing bracket and shift tube before the column can be removed. Disconnect the steering clamp from the column by slackening the clamp bolt that secures the upper flange to the shaft. Free the strap under the instrument panel that holds the column and take out the bolts that secure the coverplate to the floor board. Withdraw the column taking great care not to spread grease on the upholstery.

Refit the steering column in the reverse order of removal. Make sure that it is aligned and the attachments not strained.

Check that all parts are in the straight-ahead position. If the steering wheel is not level with the wheels straight-ahead, first check the wheel alignment (see next Section) and if this does not cure the fault, turn the shock absorber a maximum of two splines in either direction (see **Section 5**).

9 The front wheel alignment

The alignment of the front wheels should be checked after major repairs or if the wheel is run into a solid obstruction such as the kerb. If the alignment is out the tyres will wear with a characteristic feathered edge to the tread and the steering wheel spokes may not be level when the road wheels are straight-ahead.

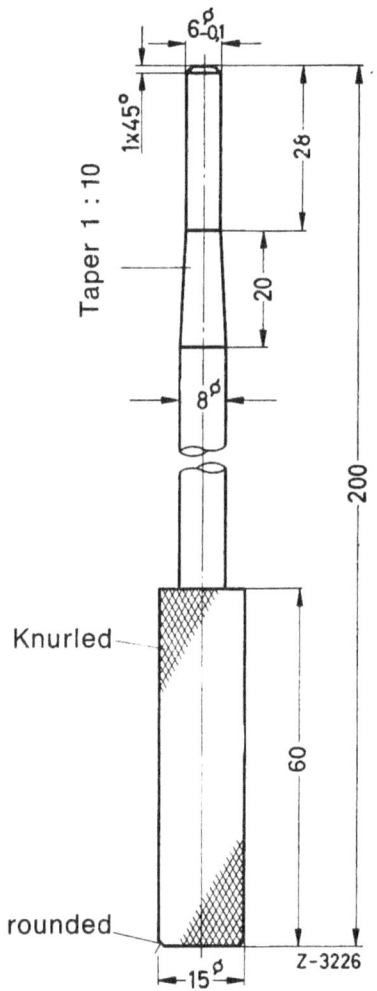

FIG 16 Locally made lockpin for the steering column

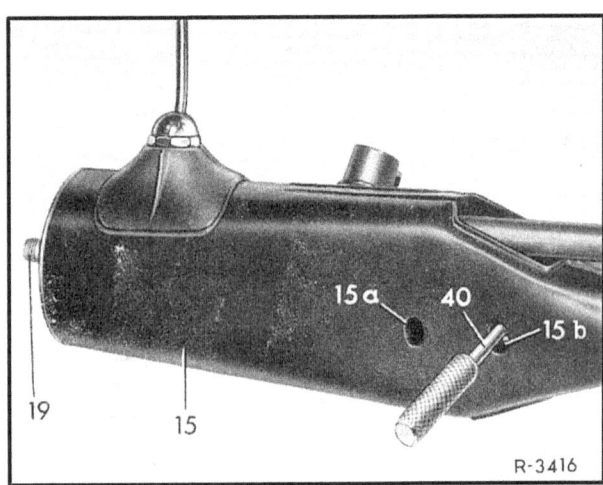

FIG 17 The lockpin fitted to the steering column

15 Column jacket
15a Inspection hole for power steering
15b Inspection hole for manual steering
19 Steering shaft
40 Lockpin

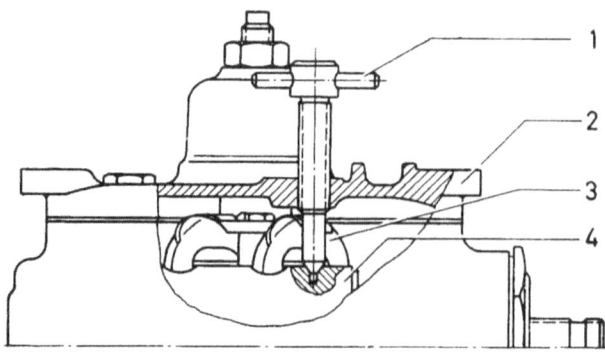

FIG 18 Locking the steering unit in the central position

1 Center position checking bolt 111 589 10 23 00
2 Steering housing cover
3 Ball guide tube
4 Steering nut

FIG 19 The steering arm attachments

19 Steering unit (power steering shown)
19a Castellated nut
20 Tie rod
21 Drag link
22 Steering arm

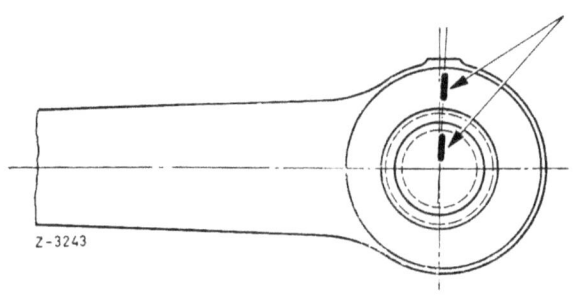

FIG 20 The steering arm alignment marks

140

It is possible for the owner to set the wheel alignment but the difficulties involved in measuring the settings as well as setting each wheel to the correct position make it well worthwhile taking the car to a service agent where the task will be quickly carried out using accurate gauges.

When setting the alignment, the steering unit should be locked in the straight-ahead position by inserting the centring bolt 115 589 10 23 00 through the hole for the filler plug and into the recess in the steering nut, as shown in **FIG 18. Do not attempt to turn the steering once the centring bolt has been fitted.** Each wheel is then set to half the correct toe-in, by slackening the clamps on the tie rods and rotating the tie rods. This ensures that the total toe-in is correct and that the wheels are both straight-ahead with the steering unit.

When setting the alignment the following points should be noted. Carry out the work on a level surface and before taking any measurement, roll the car forwards to settle the bearings. **The car must not be rolled backwards during the check and it should be loaded to its normal kerb condition.** Measure, as accurately as possible, the distance between the wheel rims at wheel centre height and in front of the wheels. Mark the points with chalk and then roll the car forward so that the wheels turn by exactly half a revolution and the marks are again at wheel centre height but at the rear of the wheels. Again measure the distance between the wheel rims. The difference between the first and second measurements will be the toe-in of the wheels.

If the owner is carrying out the work, it will be easier if some form of wooden trammel is made. The trammel should lie on the ground and have two uprights which will fit between the wheels. Nails can be used as pointers in the upright and if one nail is put into contact, the gap between the other nail and wheel rim can be accurately measured. The difference between the two dimensions is the measurement required and the length of the trammel will therefore not matter, provided that it is of a convenient length.

10 The manual steering unit

The steering should be checked for play, at the steering wheel rim, while an assistant holds the front wheels to prevent them from moving. If the circumferential play on the wheel exceeds 25 mm (1 inch) then there is excessive play throughout the system.

Check through the steering linkage, suspension ball joints, steering coupling and hub bearings for defects or wear and renew any defective parts. If after carrying out repairs the play in the steering is still excessive, the steering box itself should be adjusted. **The steering unit must be removed from the car and adjustments carried out on the bench. The steering worm must be adjusted first and then the pressure mechanism for the steering shaft.**

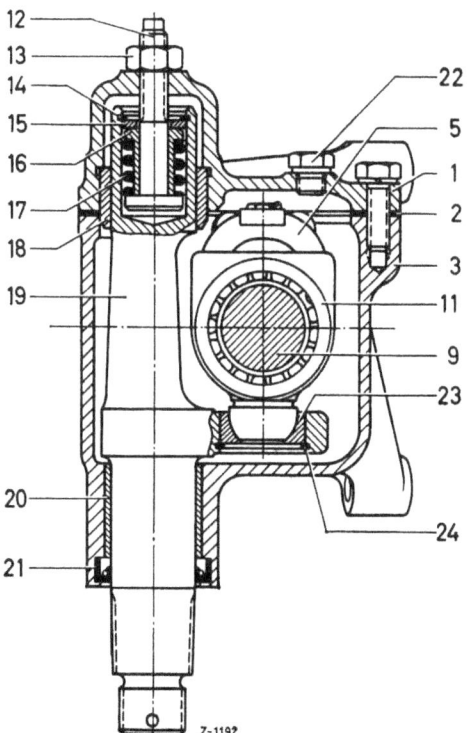
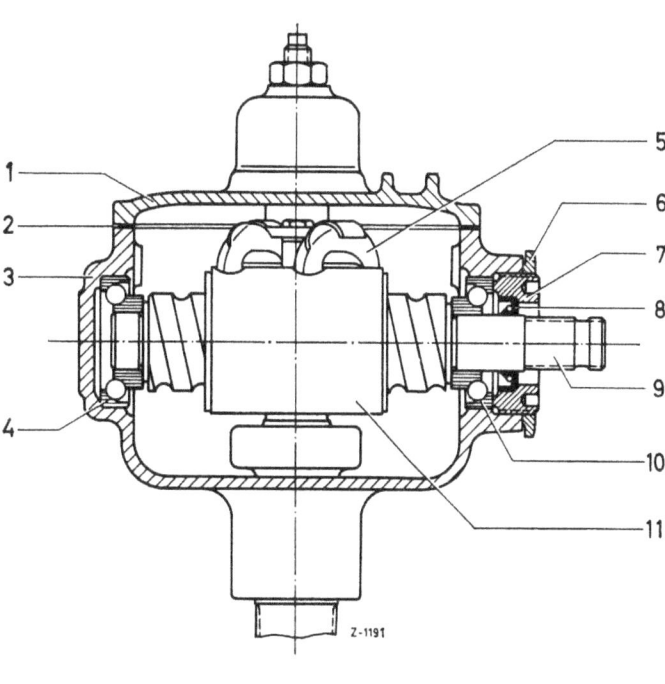

FIG 21 Sectioned views of the steering unit

1 Steering housing cover	7 Adjusting ring	13 Hex. nut	19 Steering shaft
2 Gasket	8 Grease seal	14 Snap ring	20 Lower bearing bushing
3 Steering housing	9 Steering worm	15 Thrust washer	21 Grease seal
4 Angular contact bearing	10 Angular contact bearing	16 Pressure sleeve	22 Screw plug
5 Ball guide tube	11 Steering nut	17 Compression spring	23 Ball cup
6 Hex. nut	12 Adjusting screw	18 Upper bearing bushing	24 Snap ring

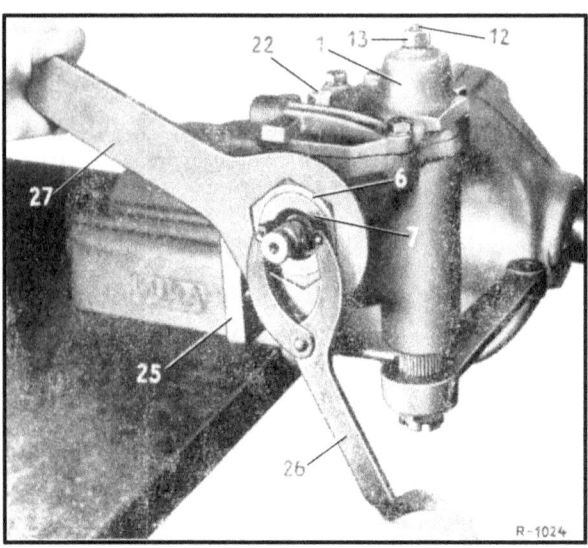

FIG 22 Adjusting the worm shaft bearings

1 Steering housing cover	22 Screw plug
6 Hex. nut	25 Assembly plate
7 Adjusting ring	26 Pin spanner 000 589 00 05 00
12 Adjusting screw	27 Special spanner
13 Hex. nut (counter nut)	180 589 03 01 00

Steering arm:

If the steering unit is being removed for exchange or servicing the steering arm can be left attached to the linkage. If the arm is to be removed with the steering unit, disconnect the ball joint that secures it to the linkage (as described in **Section 3**).

The attachments of the arm are shown in **FIG 19**. To remove the arm from the shaft, take out the splitpin and remove the castellated nut 19a. Check that there are alignment marks on both arm and shaft, as shown in **FIG 20**, and make the marks if they are not present.

FIG 23 Adjusting the steering shaft pressure block

12 Steering housing cover	25 Dial gauge
13 Adjusting screw	26 Holder for dial gauge
14 Lock nut	27 Torque spanner

It is essential to use the puller No. 100 589 04 33 00 to remove the arm from the shaft. **Hammering on the arm will transmit shocks up the shaft which will cause internal damage to the steering unit.**

Install the arm in the reverse order of removal, aligning the marks shown in **FIG 20**. Secure the arm by tightening the castellated nut 19a to a torque of 20 kg m (145 lb ft) and lock it with a new splitpin. Once the arm has been installed it is advisable to check the toe-in of the front wheels.

Removing the steering unit:

Remove the clamp bolt that secures the bottom flange of the steering coupling to the worm shaft of the unit. Disconnect the steering arm and take out the bolts that secure the unit to the sidemember on the body.

Install the unit in the reverse order of removal. The centring bolt, shown in **FIG 18** should be inserted after the unit has been turned to the correct position and it is advisable to secure the steering column with the pin shown in **FIGS 16** and **17** to prevent inadvertent collapsing of the steering column.

Once the unit is in place, check that the maximum steering angle is limited by the stops on the suspensions and not by the internal safety stops in the steering unit.

Adjustment of steering worm:

This must be carried out with the unit on the bench and not while it is fitted to the car.

Sectioned views of the unit are shown in **FIG 21**.
1 Release the pressure on the steering shaft by slackening the locknut 13 and freeing the adjusting screw 12.
2 The method of adjustment is shown in **FIG 22**. Check that the steering worm turns freely with practically no perceptible end play. If the adjustment is incorrect, hold the adjusting ring 7 with the pin wrench 26 (No. 000 589 00 05 00) and remove the locknut 6 using the special spanner 27 (180 589 03 01 00). The task will be easier if the unit is bolted to a plate 25 drilled with suitable mounting holes. Lightly coat the threads and face of the nut 6 with non-setting sealing compound and screw it back into place without tightening it.
3 Use the pin wrench to turn the adjusting ring 7 until the end float of the worm is correct at .00 to .01 mm (.0000 to .0004 inch) and fully tighten the nut 6 to secure the adjusting ring. Check that the end float has not altered while turning the nut 6 and that the worm shaft turns freely.
4 If, after adjustment, the worm does not turn freely then the unit must be dismantled for examination of the bearings and checking for internal faults.

Adjusting the pressure block:

1 Remove the adjusting nut 13, smear its threads and face lightly with jointing compound and screw it loosely back into place.
2 Remove the screw plug 22 so that it can be seen when the unit passes through the central position.

As the unit passes through the central position a light pressure point should be felt (175 to 225 kg cm (12.5 to 16 lb ft) torque required to turn the steering shaft when correctly adjusted) but there must be no actual binding.

3 Unscrew the adjusting screw 12 and tighten it down to 1 kg m (7 lb ft) against its base several times, with the unit in the central position. Loosen the adjusting screw by approximately a $\frac{1}{4}$ turn and then finally tighten it down to a torque of .5 kg m (3.6 lb ft).

4 Fit a dial indicator gauge to the unit as shown in **FIG 23** so that its stylus rests on the end of the adjusting screw and set the gauge to zero. Screw down the adjusting screw 13 for .1 to .15 mm (.004 to .006 inch) (approximately $\frac{1}{8}$ turn) and then tighten the locknut to a torque of 2.5 to 3 kg m (18 to 22 lb ft) so that the gauge returns to a reading of .03 to 0 mm (.001 to .000 inch).

11 The power steering unit

The attachments of the unit are shown in **FIG 24**. Removal is very similar to removal of the manual unit, except for the fluid hoses. Syphon out the fluid from the reservoir with a syringe. Disconnect the two hoses 2 and 3 from the unit and blank them as well as the connectors on the unit to prevent the entry of dirt. Remove the unit as for a manual unit once the hoses are disconnected. To drain the fluid from the unit once it is removed, point the connectors downwards and turn the steering worm shaft backwards and forwards.

Install the unit in the reverse order of removal. The special centring bolt should be used and the steering connector fitted as shown in **FIG 25**.

Make sure that the hoses are carefully installed so that there is no danger of them chafing. Fill the reservoir and bleed the system as described in **Section 2**. Approximately 1.5 litres of automatic transmission fluid will be required.

FIG 24 The power steering unit attachments

1 Power steering unit
2 High-pressure hose
3 Return hose
4 Elbow
5 Steering coupling
6 Clamp bolts
7 Bleed screw with rubber cap
8 Filler plug

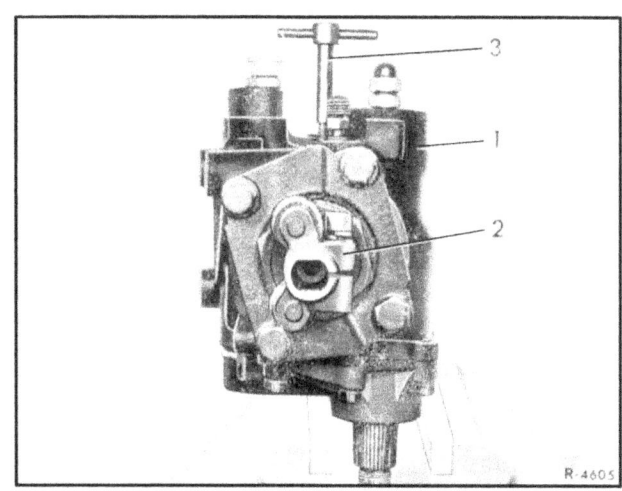

FIG 25 The steering coupling correctly set with the unit centralized

1 Power steering unit
2 Steering coupling
3 Center position checking bolt

12 Fault diagnosis

(a) Wheel wobble

1 Worn hub bearings
2 Defective or worn suspension
3 Unbalanced wheels and tyres
4 Slack or worn steering connections
5 Incorrect steering or suspension geometry
6 Defective steering damper

(b) Wander

1 Check 2, 4 and 5 in (a)
2 Front and rear suspensions not correctly aligned
3 Uneven tyre pressures
4 Uneven tyre wear

(c) Heavy steering

1 Check 5 in (a)
2 Neglected lubrication
3 Steering unit incorrectly adjusted
4 Very low tyre pressures
5 Steering tube bent or misaligned
6 Defective bearings in steering column

(d) Lost motion

1 Check 1 and 4 in (a) and 3 in (c)
2 Defective steering coupling
3 Loose steering wheel or badly worn splines

(e) Power steering grunts or drones

1 Low fluid level

(f) Power steering jerks when operated

1 Loose drive belt

NOTES

CHAPTER 11 - BRAKES

1 Description
2 Maintenance
3 Flexible hoses
4 Bleeding the brakes
5 Renewing the brake friction pads
6 Caliper removal
7 The brake discs
8 Servicing a front caliper
9 Servicing a rear caliper
10 The brake master cylinder
11 The brake force regulator
12 The brake servo
13 The Duo-Servo parking brake
14 Parking brake linkage
15 Fault diagnosis

1 Description

The braking system is designed to give excellent retardation under all circumstances and is so designed that even if components fail there will still be some braking effort left.

Disc brakes are fitted to all four wheels and they are hydraulically operated from the foot pedal. The parking brake operates a separate set of brakes on the rear wheels only, using a mechanical linkage. The parking brakes are conventional type drum brakes with shoes and linings expanding into the drum portion of the rear brake disc. Apart from a common disc and drum unit there are no other connections between the parking and service brakes.

A tandem master cylinder is fitted so that the front brakes are hydraulically independent from the rear brakes. This ensures that if a component, seal, or line fails and fluid is lost from one half of the system, the other half of the system will operate at its full efficiency, though with longer pedal travel. Floats are installed into each chamber of the master cylinder reservoir and they are fitted with a switch which closes when the float falls below a certain level. Once the switch closes it operates the warning light on the dash. The parking brake is wired into the system, as shown in **FIG 1**, for the double reason of checking the bulb in case it has blown and warning when the parking brake is applied.

A valve is fitted to limit the pressure to the rear brakes and this prevents the rear wheels from locking under heavy braking.

A vacuum-operated servo unit is fitted between the brake pedal and master cylinder unit to reduce the pedal pressure required for a given retardation. The unit is designed to fail-safe so that the brakes can still be operated if the vacuum or the unit fails, but a much higher pedal pressure will be required for the same retardation. This point must be borne in mind when towing the car as the engine will not be producing any vacuum to operate the servo.

The instructions given in Chapter 5, Section 3 should be read before servicing any hydraulic components.

2 Maintenance

Fluid level:

Regularly check the fluid level in the master cylinder reservoir (at the same time as checking the fluid level in the clutch reservoir). The positions of the reservoirs are shown in **FIG 2**. The reservoirs are made of translucent material so that the level can easily be seen without removing the filler cap. If the level is low, wipe the cap and top of the reservoir clean and remove the cap. Top up to the line on the reservoir with a recommended brake fluid (such as ATE Blue) and refit the filler cap.

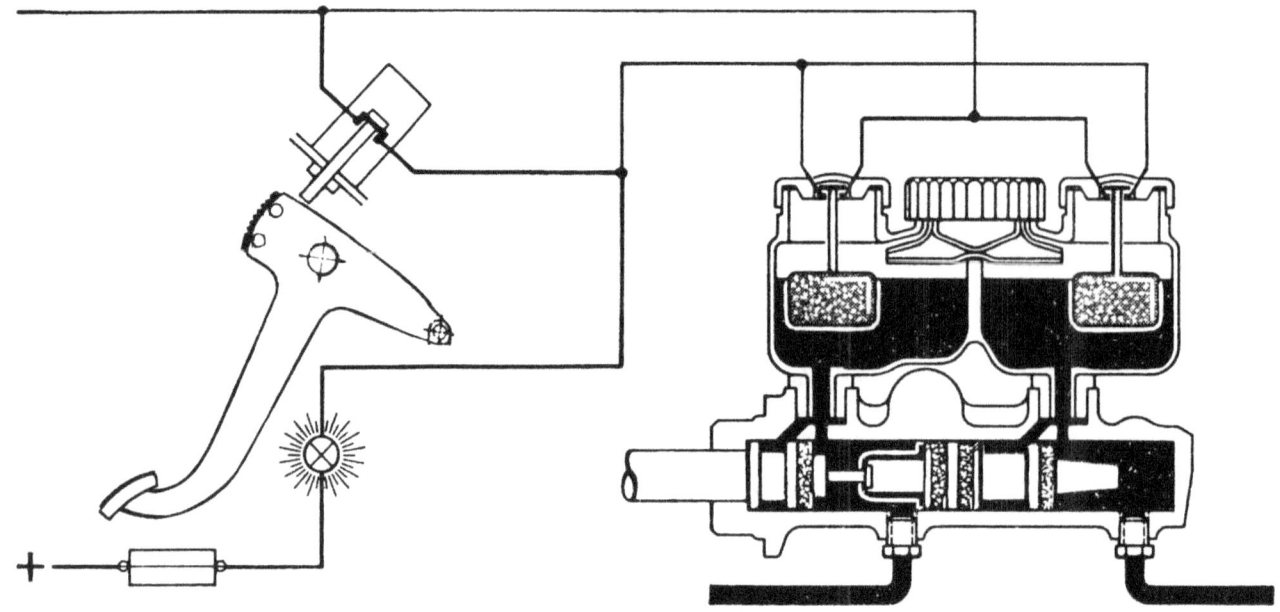

FIG 1 The brake warning light system, showing the park brake applied

There will be a slow steady drop in the level as the pads of the disc brakes wear and the only action that need be taken is to ensure that the level does not fall too far. If there is a sudden drop or the rate of use of fluid suddenly increases, this is an indication of a leak in the system. A leak must be found and rectified. Even though the two halves of the system are hydraulically independent, fluid loss from one half of the system can lead to reduced overall braking efficiency and the leak may be weeping at a weak point which fails under the stress of heavy braking in an emergency.

Do not use a fluid of the non-recommended types as some fluids will attack the material of the seals in the system, causing them all to fail with complete loss of service brakes.

Brake adjustments:

The disc brakes are self-adjusting (pump the footbrake pedal hard several times) and therefore do not need routine adjusting. However, the pads should be inspected for wear at regular intervals and renewed when the lining material is worn down to a minimum of 2 mm (.08 inch).

The parking brake must be adjusted if the park pawl can be pulled out by more than 8 of its 16 notches, or the lever on 280 SL models can be raised by more than 3 of its 8 teeth with medium force and no braking effort shows up.

The way of adjusting the parking brake is shown in **FIG 3** and the actual method is shown in **FIG 4**.

Jack up the rear of the car until the road wheels are clear of the ground. Remove one wheel attachment screw from each rear wheel. Turn the wheel until the attachment hole is positioned in the upper left direction at 45 deg. as shown. Insert a screwdriver through the hole so that it picks up in the teeth of the adjuster 21. On the left side of the car move the screwdriver upwards and on the right side move it downward, so as to rotate the adjuster until the brake shoes 20 are in firm contact with the drum portion of the disc. Turn the toothed wheel back by 2 to 3 teeth, or sufficient to free the brake, and check that the wheel rotates freely after making allowance for the drag of the axle.

Adjust both wheels, then apply the park brake by one notch and check that the park brake shoes lightly touch the drum. **The adjustments on the linkage itself are only for equalizing the cable lengths and under no circumstances should they be used for setting the parking brake.** Wear on the parking brake shoes must only be taken up as described in this Section.

Preventative maintenance:

At regular intervals check the friction linings for wear, including those for the parking brake. Loose dirt and dust should be brushed and blown out of the brake and a check made for fluid leaks or any other obvious defect. Examine all the pipelines and flexible hoses for leaks or defects. The flexible hoses should be checked for perishing or softening of the flexible portion or for chafing on adjacent parts of the car. The metal lines should be checked for corrosion or dents from stones. Renew defective pipes as the weak point may fail under the stress of heavy braking.

At intervals of three years, drain the system through a bleed nipple and flush through with at least $\frac{1}{2}$ litre (1 pint) of methylated spirits through each bleed nipple on the brakes. This treatment will clear the pipes of any sludge that may have accumulated. Remove and dismantle all the components so that they can be checked for wear or defects. Renew defective components. Assemble the remainder of the components using all new seals. Once all the parts and components have been correctly assembled and fitted, fill the system with fresh brake fluid and bleed it, as described in **Section 4.**

Care should be taken when handling the brake fluid not to spill it onto paintwork as it rapidly softens and removes paint. Hydraulic fluid makes a good substitute for penetrating oil and old fluid can be kept for this purpose. If old fluid is kept, mark the container very clearly so as to avoid any danger of it being used again in the brake or clutch system. Hydraulic fluid absorbs moisture from the air, and the moisture lowers the boiling point, which is one of the reasons for changing the fluid at regular intervals. Fresh fluid should only be stored in clean and sealed containers.

The maximum safe life of flexible hoses is five years so all the flexible hoses should be renewed after this period.

3 Flexible hoses

Hoses that show any defects such as hardening, softening, perishing, cracking or chafing should be renewed immediately. If a hose is blocked and cannot be cleared by blowing through with compressed air it must also be renewed. Do not attempt to clear blocked hoses by poking them through with wire.

Removal:

When removing or refitting a flexible hose the flexible portion must not be twisted or strained in any way.

The hose is usually attached to a bracket on the frame or suspension and the other end may be attached to another metal line in a similar manner or else screwed directly into the unit. Free the end at a bracket first. Hold the adjacent hexagonal flats on the hose with a spanner and use another spanner to unscrew the union nut that secures the metal pipe to the flexible hose. Take care that the metal pipe does not twist with the nut. Cleaning with a wire brush and lightly lubricating with hydraulic fluid will help to prevent this. Place a container under the connection to catch fluid as it drains out or empty the master cylinder reservoir before. Blank the line when it is free to prevent the ingress of dirt.

Once the metal line is free, remove the retainer and take the flexible hose end out of the bracket. The other end of the hose can then be unscrewed, allowing the flexible portion to rotate freely.

Installations:

Refit the hose in the reverse order of removal. Position the hose so that it is clear of chassis or suspension members and check that the hose is still clear when the suspension or steering moves through its full range of movement.

4 Bleeding the brakes

This is not routine maintenance and is only required when air has been allowed to enter the system during repairs and servicing, or by allowing the fluid level in the reservoir to fall so low that air is drawn into the master cylinder.

Use only fresh fluid in the system. The recommended fluid is ATE Blue Fluid but if any other brand is used it must be of the heavy-duty type and must meet the SAE J1703 Specifications.

FIG 2 The master cylinder reservoirs and installation of the brake master cylinder

1 Brake unit
2 Brake fluid reservoir
3 Tandem master cylinder
4 Cap
5 Plug connection
11 Cap
19 Vacuum hose
21 Supplementary reservoir

FIG 3 The method of adjusting the parking brake

2 Rear axle shaft
3 Screw driver
4 Brake disc
20 Brake shoe
21 Adjuster

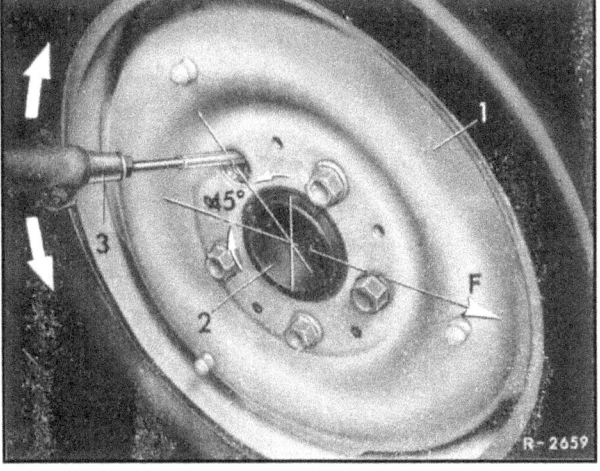

FIG 4 Manually adjusting the parking brake

1 Wheel
2 Rear axle shaft
3 Screw driver
F Driving direction

FIG 5   The shaft coverplate fitted to front brakes

1　Brake disc　　　　　10　Front wheel hub
2　Brake caliper　　　　15　Shaft cover plate
3　Cover plate

FIG 6   Driving out the pad retaining pins

2　Brake caliper　　　　17　Retaining pin
16　Cross spring　　　　30　Punch

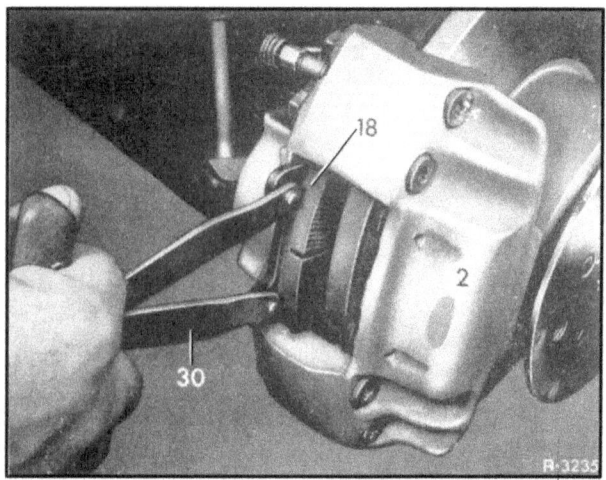

FIG 7   Pulling out a friction pad

2　Brake caliper　　　　30　Removal tool
18　Brake pad

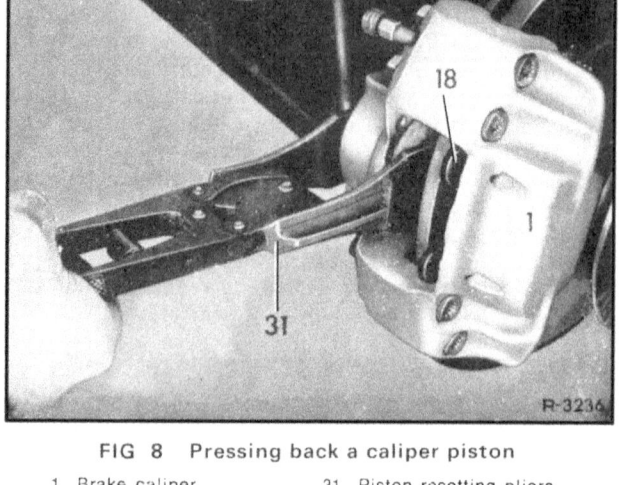

FIG 8   Pressing back a caliper piston

1　Brake caliper　　　　31　Piston resetting pliers
18　Brake pad　　　　　　　　111 589 07 37 00

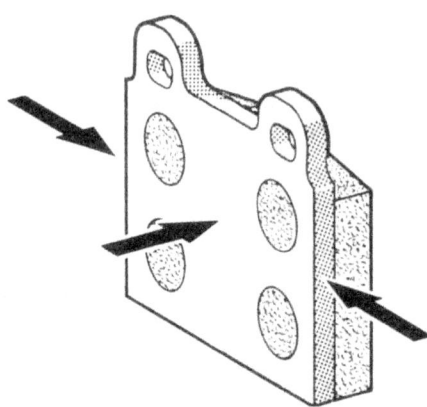

Coat brake pad on the spots indicated with Molykote-Paste "U" or "Liqui-Moly-Paste 36".

FIG 9   Surfaces to be lightly lubricated on the pads

FIG 10   The front caliper attachments

9　Brake caliper　　　　14　Lockplate
9a　Code No.　　　　　　17　Cover plate
11　Brake line　　　　　18　Bleed screw
13　Caliper attachment bolt　25　Shaft cover plate

An agent will most likely use pressure bleeding equipment to ensure that all the air is flushed out of the system and if the owner finds difficulty in removing all the air then it is advisable to take the car to an agent for pressure bleeding. For the owner, the best method of bleeding is by pumping the brake pedal to expel air and fluid from the brakes.

Before starting the bleeding operation, top up the reservoir as far as it will go without actually spilling, using fresh fluid. As the operation progresses the fluid level will fall and it must be topped up again after very few strokes to ensure that air is not drawn into the master cylinder.

The fluid that is bleed from the system should be discarded. This is particularly important for the first amount of fluid bled from each brake as it will contain particles and will also have been heated in use. Only if the fluid comes out perfectly clean from the brakes may it be used again and even so it may not be returned directly to the reservoir. Clean fluid that has been through the system should be allowed to stand in a clean, sealed container for at least 24 hours to allow all air to disperse from it.

The brakes are bled in the order of decreasing pipe runs, starting with the brake that has the longest pipe run to it. If only part of the system has been disturbed then only the two brakes of that system need to be bled, as the front and rear brakes are hydraulically independent.

Fit a length of plastic or rubber tube to the bleed nipple on the brake to be bled, after removing the rubber protective cap from the nipple, and dip the free end of the tube into a little clean fluid in a glass container. From now on an assistant will be required. Open the bleed nipple and have the assistant press the brake pedal fully down to the floor. Close the bleed nipple before the assistant releases the brake pedal. This sequence is repeated as often as is required until the fluid coming out of the bleed tube is perfectly free from any air bubbles. Close the bleed nipple and remove the bleed tube. Bleed the remaining brakes by the same method.

If, after the system has been fully dismantled the brake pedal still feels spongy after bleeding, use the car for a day or so (provided that adequate pedal pressure can be obtained) and then bleed the system again. After major work, all the components will be filled with air which turns into minute bubbles on bleeding. If the car is left for a day then these bubbles will all coalesce into larger ones which are much easier to bleed out of the system.

When the brakes have been bled, start the engine and apply heavy pedal pressure so that the system can be checked for leaks. Top up the reservoir to the correct level.

5 Renewing the brake friction pads

The brake pads must be renewed when the friction lining has worn down to a thickness of 2 mm (.08 inch) or if they have become contaminated with oil or grease.

Approved pads only must be used and they should always be renewed in axle sets, to preserve the braking balance. The same grade of linings should be used on both the front and rear brakes.

The method of renewing the pads is basically the same on both the front and the rear brakes.

On the front brakes only, remove the shaft coverplate 15, shown in **FIG 5**. On all brakes, use a suitable drift to drive out the two retaining pins 17 and remove the cross-leaf spring 16, shown in **FIG 6**.

Special tongs No. 000 589 50 63 00, shown at 30 in **FIG 7**, are made for withdrawing the old pads 18 but a strong length of cord passed through the lugs will do as well.

Remove one brake pad only and clean out the recess with a bottle brush. At the same time check the brake disc for excess dirt or deposits and if it is dirty, remove it for cleaning before installing new friction pads.

Press the piston of the caliper back into its bore, preferably with the piston resetting tongs No. 111 589 07 37 00 as shown in **FIG 8**. As the piston returns into

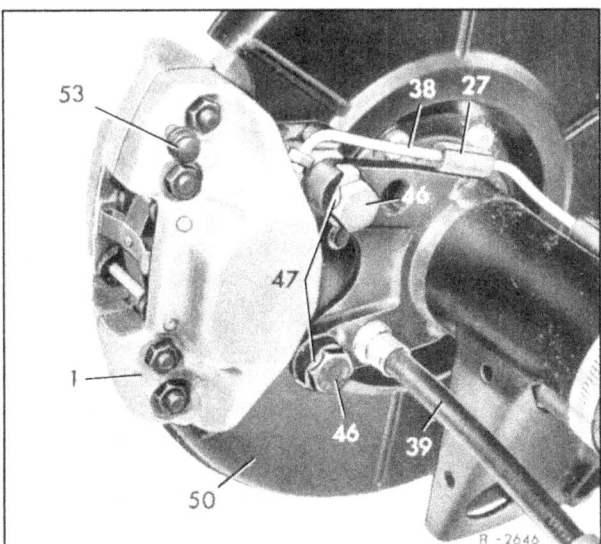

FIG 11 The rear caliper attachments

1	Brake caliper	46	Caliper attachment bolt
27	Rubber ring	47	Lockplate
38	Brake line	50	Cover plate
39	Park brake cable	53	Bleed screw

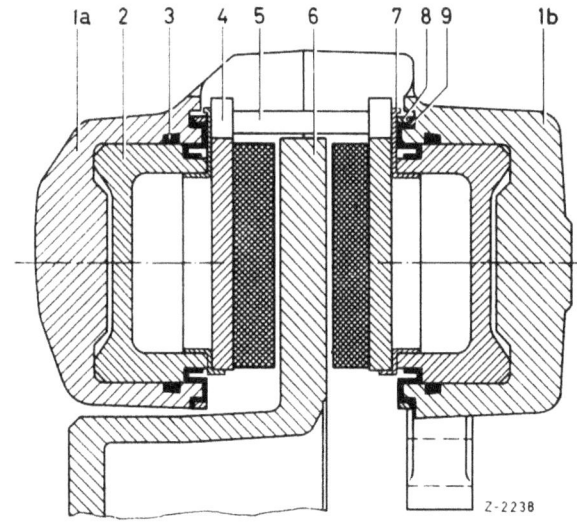

FIG 12 Sectioned view of front caliper

1a and 1b	caliper halves (not to be separated)	5	Holding pins
2	Piston	6	Brake disc
3	Piston seal	7	Heat shield
4	Brake pad	8	Clamping ring
		9	Dust cap

its bore, fluid will be forced back into the master cylinder reservoir. **Syphon out surplus fluid from the reservoir to prevent it overflowing.** Only one piston at a time is pressed in, with the other brake pad in place, as the pad prevents the other piston from coming out.

Lightly coat the surfaces of the new pad, arrowed in **FIG 9**, with Molykote-Paste U or Liqui-Moly-Paste 36 and press the pad back into position.

Renew the other pad in a similar manner. When both new pads are in place, install the cross-leaf spring and drive the retaining pins back into position to secure the parts. Fit the shaft coverplates back onto the front brakes.

Pump the brake pedal hard several times to take up the adjustment in all four brakes. If this is not carried out the brakes are liable to operate very poorly on the first normal application.

Check the fluid level in the reservoir and top up as required. **New brakes must be bedded-in otherwise the pad surface will burn to give unbalanced braking.** Slow the car several times from 80 to 40 kilometre/hr (50 to 25 mile/hr) and then allow the brakes to cool in the airflow before gently stopping the car.

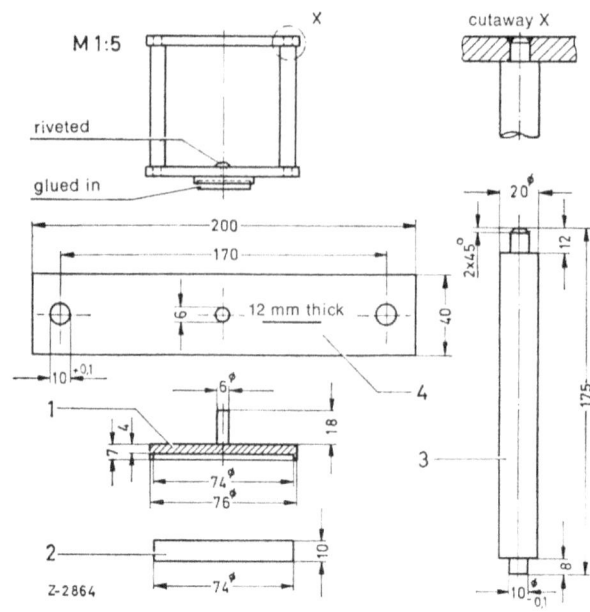

FIG 15   Dimensions of tool for refitting dust cap

1   Pressure plate   3   Connecting bolt
2   Rubber plate   4   Clamp

6 Caliper removal

On either a front or rear brake caliper, first drain the fluid out of the system. Open the bleed screw on the caliper and pump out the fluid into any suitable container through a bleed tube attached to the bleed nipple (as for bleeding the brakes but without topping up of the reservoir). Disconnect the metal line that leads to the caliper.

The attachments of a front caliper are shown in **FIG 10** and those of a rear caliper in **FIG 11**. Free the lockplates and take out the two bolts that secure the caliper to the suspension. Slide the caliper off the brake disc and remove it from the car.

Install the caliper in the reverse order of removal, using new lockplates and tightening the attachment bolts to the correct torque.

Reconnect the brake lines and then fill and bleed the system as described in **Section 4**.

7 The brake discs

In normal use the dirt and dust thrown up from the road will cause shallow concentric scores around the disc. The scores may be ignored until they reach a depth of approximately .5 mm (.02 inch). If the concentric scores exceed the stated depth, or there are radial scores, then the disc must be removed and machined down or a new disc installed in its place.

Brake discs may be machined down to obtain a smooth operating face but the work should be carried out by a specialist firm. A maximum of .5 mm (.02 inch) may be removed from the thickness of a front disc and .3 mm (.012 inch) from a rear disc.

Cleaning:

After long use a deposit may build up on the operating faces of the discs from the linings and it will be blue or grey in colour. Such deposits reduce braking efficiency and they should be cleaned off before installing new pads.

FIG 13   Bridge piece used for removing stiff pistons
1   Brake caliper   2   Piston   23   Bridge

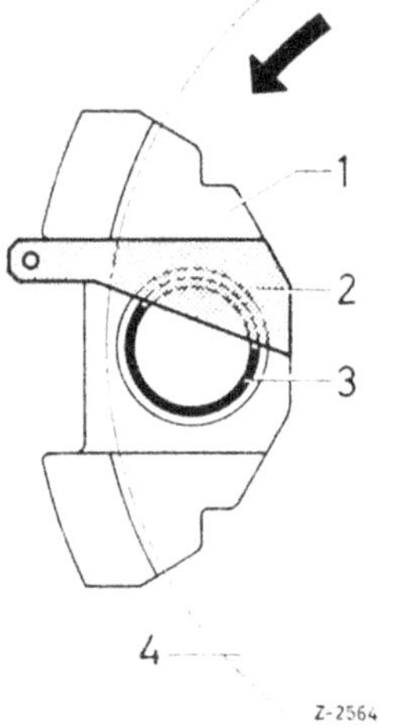

FIG 14   Setting the piston position using a gauge
1   Brake caliper   3   Piston
2   Piston gauge 001 589 30 21 00   4   Brake disc

The discs on the front brakes can be cleaned without removal of any components except the pads, but the work should then be carried out by a service agent. The friction pads are removed and special cleaning pads fitted into their place. The wheel is driven by a wheel balancing machine until the deposits are cleaned off from the disc.

This method cannot be used on the rear brakes, because the back axle would have to be driven. Instead the disc should be cleaned by softening the deposits with trichlorethylene and scrubbing them off with fine-grade emerycloth. The same treatment can be carried out by the owner to the front brake discs.

Removal of rear disc:

This can be removed once the rear wheel has been taken off and the brake caliper removed. Use a plastic-faced hammer and tap the disc gently and evenly free from the hub.

Check both the disc and drum for excessive scoring, cracks or other damage.

If a new brake disc has to be installed, be sure to remove all the protective paint from it with a suitable solvent. If the old disc is to be installed, make sure that the mating faces of disc and flange are scrupulously clean and free from any burrs. Lubricate the flange lightly with heat resistant permanent lubricant (such as Molykote Paste U) as this ensures that the disc will be easier to remove the next time it has to be taken off. Tap the disc gently back into place, making sure that the guide pin on the flange fits into the hole in the disc. Bleed the brakes after installing the caliper.

Removal of front disc:

This can only be removed after the front hub assembly has been taken off the car (see **Chapter 9, Section 23**). Mark the disc and hub so that they will be re-assembled in the same relative positions and then hold the hub in the padded jaws of a vice, so that the disc is lying horizontal. Take out the socket-headed bolts that secure the disc to the hub and lift the disc from the hub.

Clean off any protective from new discs and make

FIG 16 Installing the heat shield
1 Brake caliper
5 Holding pin
7 Heat shield
17 Fixture 000 589 49 63 00

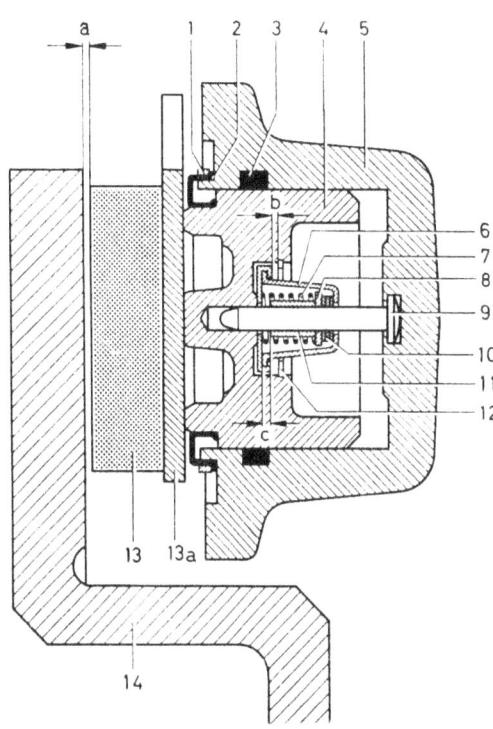

FIG 17 Sectioned view of a rear caliper

1 Clamping ring	6 Stop cap	11 Spacing sleeve
2 Dust cap	7 Compression spring	12 Locking ring
3 Piston seal	8 Spacing washer	13 Brake pad
4 Piston	9 Clamping ring	13a Base plate
5 Housing	10 Guide pin	14 Brake disc

sure that the mating surfaces of hub and disc are scrupulously clean and free from burrs before installing the disc in the reverse order of removal. Fit the hub assembly back into place and set the correct end float. Use the DTI to check the runout on the disc itself, as near to the outer edge of the operating face as possible. If the runout is excessive, try rotating the disc in relation to the hub to see if this reduces the runout and make sure that no dirt particles are trapped between hub and disc.

8 Servicing a front caliper

A sectioned view of the caliper is shown in **FIG 12**. The fluid pressure acts in the two bores so that the pistons 2 simultaneously force the brake pads 4 into contact with the revolving brake disc 6 to provide retarding action. The seals 3 distort slightly under the pressure and when the pressure is released the seals spring back to normal shape and withdraw the piston enough to give a running clearance between pads and disc. If there is excessive clearance, the piston will slide through the seal until the pad contacts the disc.

The two halves of the caliper are bolted together but under no circumstances may the two halves be separated by the owner. Only methylated spirits (denatured alcohol), hydraulic fluid or special hydraulic cleansing fluid may be used to clean the parts of the caliper. The use of any other type of solvent will rot the seals between the caliper halves.

One side of the caliper should be serviced at a time, with the other piston in place. This is because air pressure is required to remove a piston and if one piston is out, air pressure cannot be applied to the other piston. A special clamp which holds a thick rubber pad over the open bore can be made up, in which case both pistons can be removed at the same time.

If it is found that a piston has rusted into place or is otherwise impossible to remove with normal air pressure, use instead hydraulic pressure, which can be safely taken up to very high pressures.

Install the other piston, if it has been removed, and hold it in place with a bridge piece, as shown in **FIG 13**.

Reconnect the caliper to the brake system and bleed the system as described in **Section 4**. When the caliper has been bled, wrap it in rags and apply steadily increasing pressure on the brake pedal until the piston frees. Remove the heat shields before carrying out this emergency operation.

Dismantling FIG 12:

1 Remove the caliper from the car and take out the brake pads as described earlier in this chapter.
2 Pry out the heat shields 7, noting that they differ, and then use a screwdriver to pull out clamping ring 8 and dust cap 9.

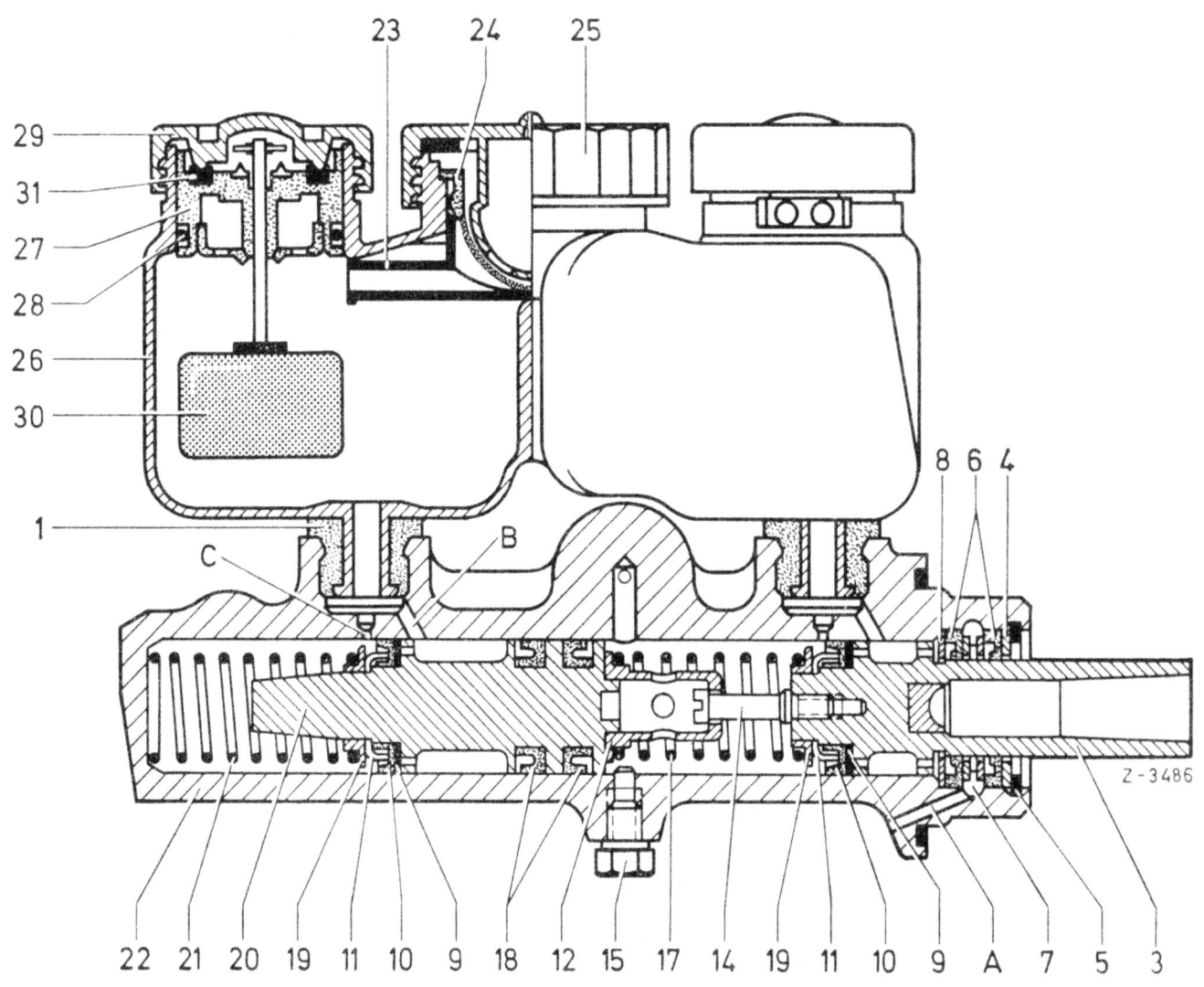

FIG 18 Sectioned view of the master cylinder

1 Reservoir plug	10 Primary sleeve	20 Piston (intermediate piston)	28 O-ring
3 Piston (plunger circuit)	11 Supporting ring	21 Compression spring	29 End cap
4 Stop washer	12 Spring supporting disc	22 Housing	30 Float
5 Locking ring	14 Conecting screw	23 Splash guard	31 Sealing ring
6 Vacuum seal	15 Stop screw	24 Strainer	
7 Intermediate ring	17 Compression spring	25 Filler cap	A Leak port
8 Bearing ring	18 Ring sleeve	26 Compensating tank	B Compensating port
9 Filling washer	19 Spring disc	27 Contact insert	C Filling port

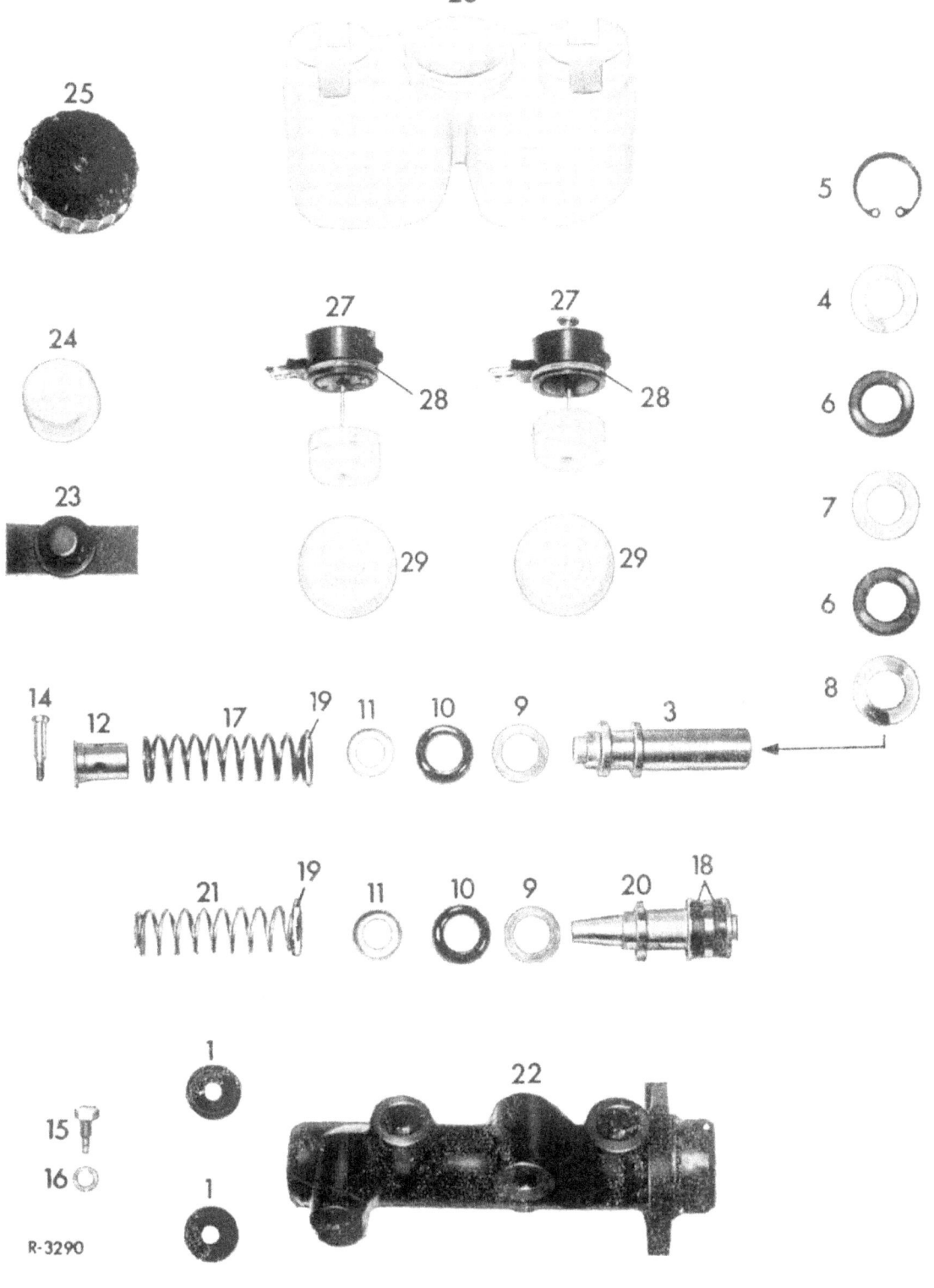

FIG 19 The components of the master cylinder

1 Reservoir plug	9 Filling washer	17 Compression spring	24 Strainer
3 Piston (plunger circuit)	10 Primary sleeve	18 Ring sleeve	25 Filler cap
4 Stop washer	11 Supporting ring	19 Spring disc	26 Reservoir
5 Locking ring	12 Spring supporting disc	20 Piston (intermediate piston)	27 Contact insert
6 Vacuum seal	14 Connecting screw	21 Compression spring	28 O-ring
7 Intermediate ring	15 Stop screw	22 Housing	29 End cap
8 Bearing ring	16 Washer (copper)	23 Splash guard	

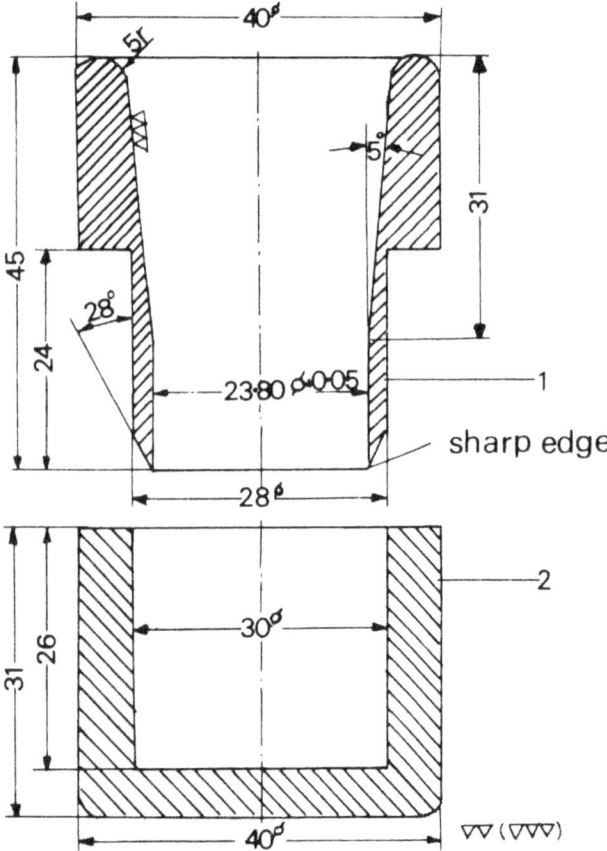

FIG 20 The assembly sleeve and its protective sleeve

3 Glue a piece of 5 mm thick rubber to the outside of one leg of the piston resetting pliers and use the pliers to hold one piston in place. Apply air pressure through the inlet of the caliper and blow the other piston out of its bore. The rubber pad will protect the piston from damage as it comes out. If a suitable clamp and seal can be made to fit over the open bore then the first piston can also be removed by applying air pressure through the inlet. If not, service one side at a time.

Cleaning and examination:

Deposits can be removed from the piston using a soft brass-wire brush or coarse cloth. **Do not use abrasives of any sort or a steel wire brush.** If the chrome surface of the piston is damaged then a new piston must be fitted on reassembly.

After cleaning with methylated spirits, examine the bore of the caliper. If the bore is scored or heavily rusted a new caliper must be fitted. Light rust or dust marks inside the bore beyond the sealing ring can be removed with polishing gloss and heavier rust marks outside the seal can be polished out using 380 to 500 grade emery-paper. A special NO-GO gauge No. 111 589 15 21 00 is mde for checking the bores and if the gauge will fit into the bore then a new caliper must be installed.

Reassembly:

1 Smear the new piston seals 3 with ATE brake cylinder paste or clean hydraulic fluid and fit them squarely back into place.

2 Insert the pistons back into the bores. The piston must be fitted with the cutout positioned using the gauge 001 589 30 21 00 as shown in **FIG 14**. The cut-out ensures that there is one-sided contact of the shoes and this helps to prevent brake squeal. Special pliers No. 000 589 36 37 00 are made for turning the piston into the correct position.

3 Position the dust cap and its clamping ring onto the collar of the caliper. A press and the special made up tool shown in **FIG 15** will then be required to press the dust cap and clamping ring back into position on the caliper. The tool is opened and passed through the caliper so that direct pressure can be applied to the clamping ring.

4 Press the heat shield back into place so that the piston projects at least .1 mm above the shield, using the fixture 000 589 49 63 00 as shown in **FIG 16**.

4 Refit the brake caliper, install the pads and bleed the the hydraulic system.

9 Servicing a rear caliper

Because the end float on the rear wheels is not under such accurate control there is a danger of the caliper pistons being pressed too far in by the wobble of the brake disc, particularly on corners. If no steps were taken an excessive amount of pedal travel would be required to take up this excess clearance.

To overcome this snag the rear brakes are fitted with a device which allows the pistons to be knocked back but then returns them to the correct clearance. A sectioned view of the device and caliper is shown in **FIG 17**. The unit may not be dismantled and if it is defective a new piston must be fitted.

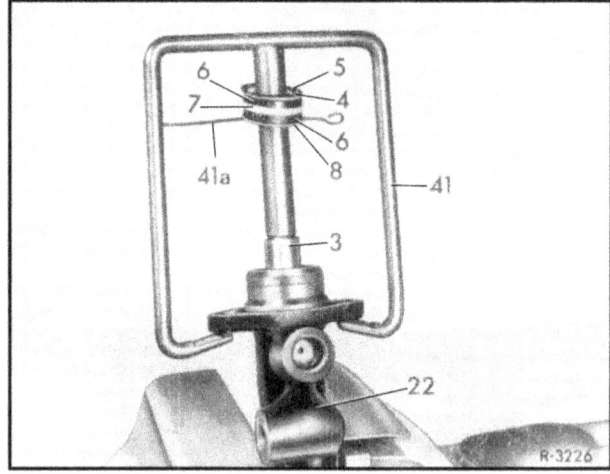

FIG 21 The tensioning drift used for reassembly

3 Piston
4 Stop washer
5 Locking ring
6 Vacuum seal
7 Intermediate ring
8 Bearing ring
22 Housing
41 Clamping fixture
41a Holding wire

When removing this type of piston a pressure of approximately 5 kg/sq cm (70 lb/sq inch) will be required to move them because of the resistance from the pin 9.

Apart from this difference the servicing of the rear caliper follows the same steps as servicing a front caliper and the same special tools are required.

10 The master cylinder

Removal:

Empty the system by pumping the fluid out through one bleed nipple on a rear axle brake and one bleed nipple on a front axle brake so that both reservoirs of the master cylinder are empty.

The attachments of the unit are shown in **FIG 2**. Hold up the lifting lugs with a small screwdriver and disconnect the two plug connections 5 from the reservoir.

Unscrew the two brake lines from the master cylinder, preferably using the special brake line spanner number 000 589 15 03 00. Blank off the lines as soon as they

FIG 22 The brake force regulator

1 Brake force regulator
2 Brake line from master cylinder
3 Brake hose to LH rear wheel
4 Brake line to RH rear wheel
5 Bracket on body/frame

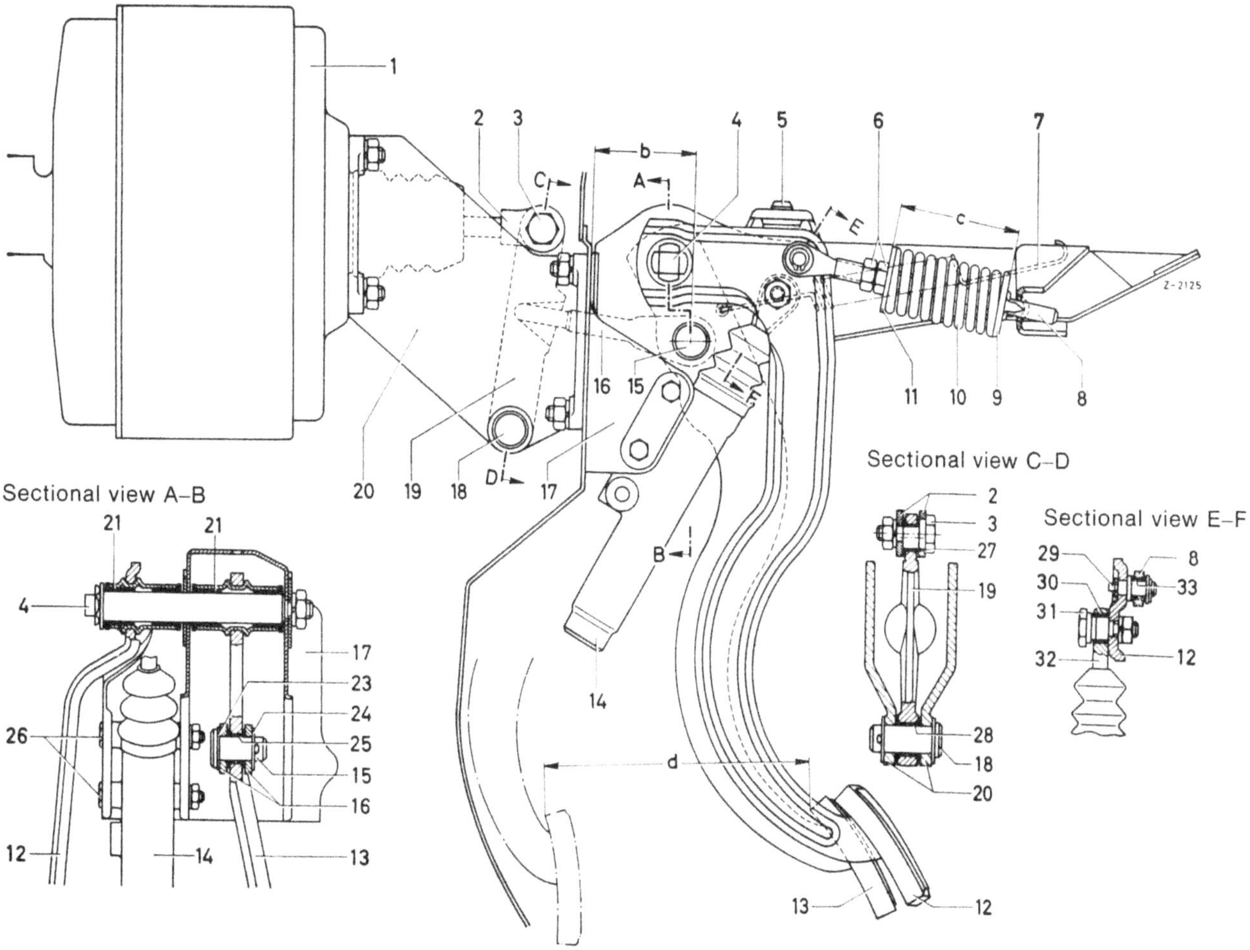

FIG 23 The service brake on the 280 SL models

1 Servo unit T 51/200	9 Spring disc	17 Bracket for pedals	26 Hex bolt
2 Piston rod	10 Compression spring	18 Flange bolt	27 Bushing
3 Eccentric adjustment bolt	11 Spring disc	19 Intermediate lever	28 Bushing
4 Bearing bolt	12 Clutch pedal	20 Intermediate flange	29 Bearing bolt
5 Clutch pedal stop	13 Brake pedal	21 Bushing for pedals	30 Bushing
6 Hex nut	14 Master cylinder	23 Spring washer	31 Adjusting screw
7 Brake pedal return spring	15 Flange bolt	24 Washer	32 Piston rod
8 Thrust rod	16 Thrust rod	25 Brake pedal bushing	33 Bushing

155

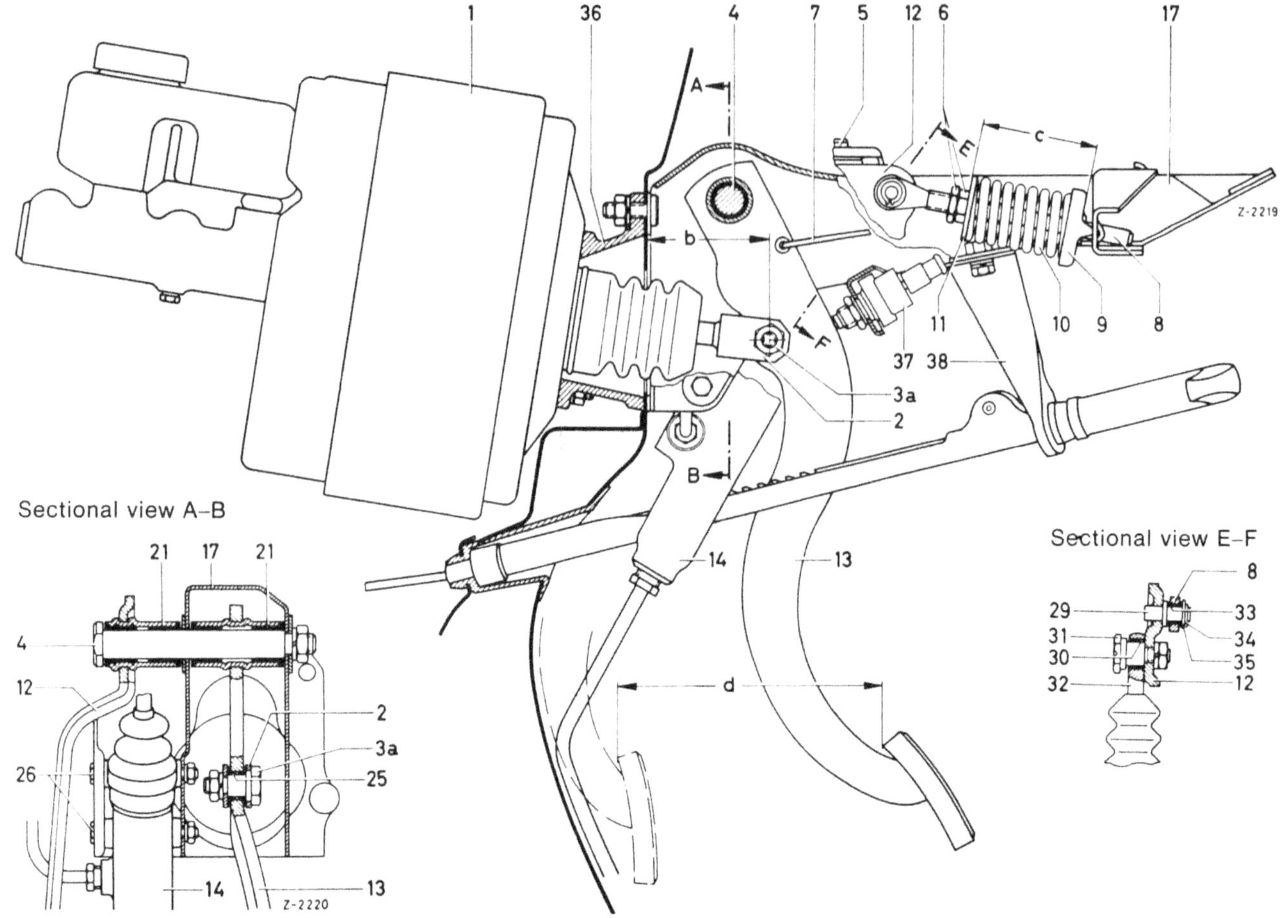

FIG 24 The service brake parts on standard models

1 Servo unit T 51/200	8 Thrust rod	17 Bracket for pedals	32 Piston rod
2 Piston rod	9 Spring disc	21 Bushing	33 Bushing
3a Eccentric adjusting bolt	10 Compression spring	25 Bushing	34 Lock ring
4 Bearing bolt	11 Spring disc	26 Adjusting screw	35 Washer
5 Clutch pedal stop	12 Clutch pedal	29 Bearing bolt	36 Intermediate flange
6 Hex nut	13 Brake pedal	30 Bushing	37 Brake light switch
7 Brake pedal return spring	14 Master cylinder	31 Adjusting screw	38 Holder for pawl rod

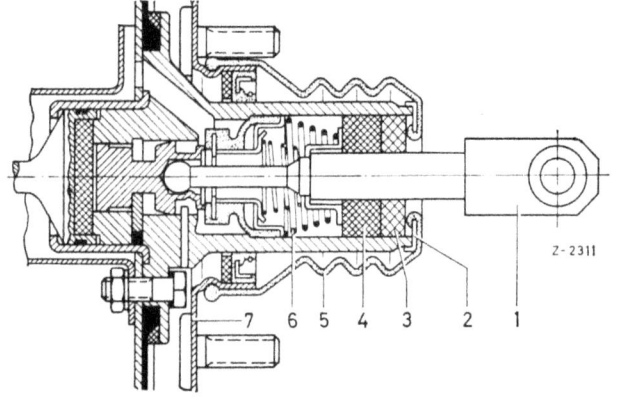

FIG 25 The brake servo air filter

1 Push rod	5 Protective cover
2 Holder for silencer	6 Control housing
3 Silencer	7 Vacuum cylinder
4 Filter	

are disconnected to prevent the entry of dirt and use rags to catch any fluid that spills.

Take off the two nuts that secure the unit to the brake servo and lift the master cylinder out of the car.

Installation:

The master cylinder is refitted in the reverse order of removal. It is essential to renew the sealing ring between master cylinder and servo to ensure that there is a vacuum tight joint.

Once the unit has been refitted, bleed all four brakes as described in **Section 4**.

Servicing the master cylinder:

A sectioned view of the unit is shown in **FIG 18** and the components in **FIG 19**. Generally the servicing follows the instructions given in **Chapter 5, Section 3**. The internal parts can be removed after taking out the lock ring 5 and stop screw 15 while pressing the pistons lightly down into the bore. The reservoir is a push fit into the tank plugs 1.

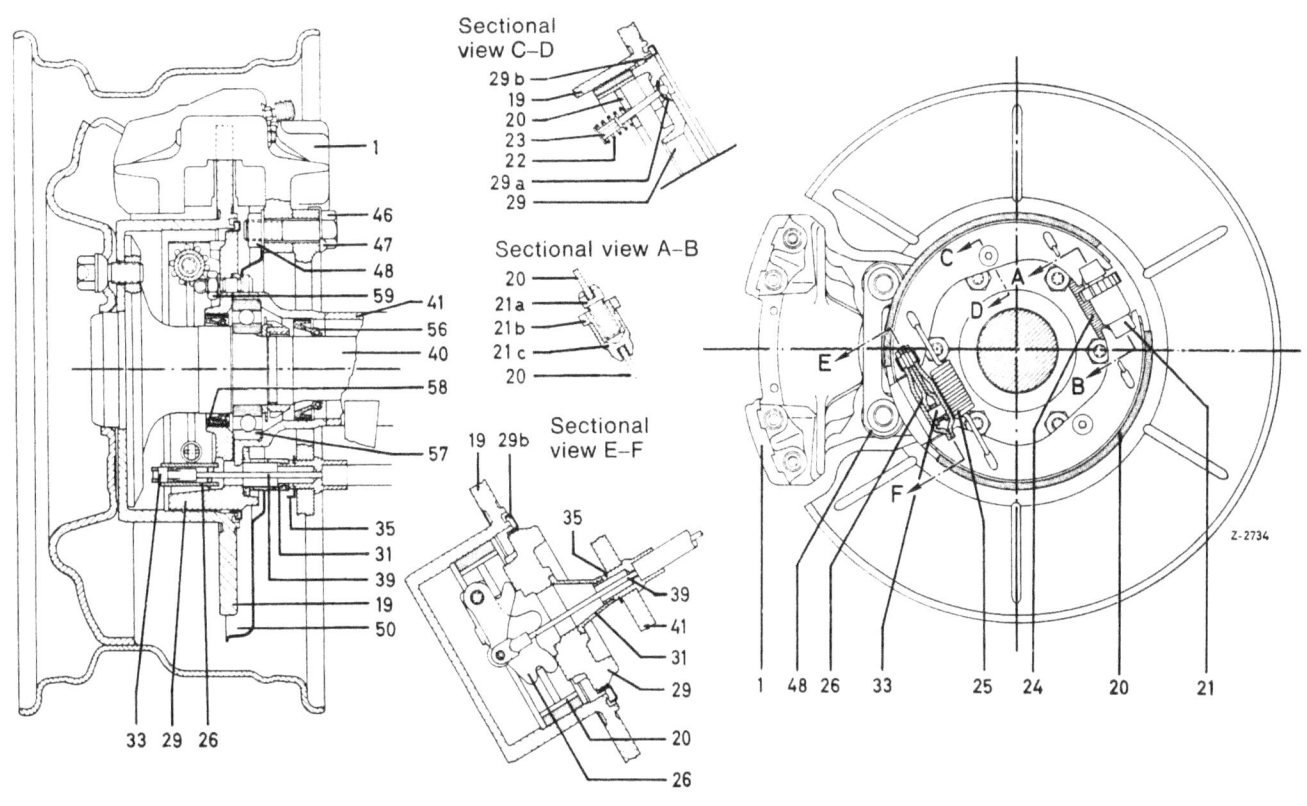

FIG 26 Sectioned views of the rear brake

1 Brake caliper	21c Thrust sleeve	29 Brake carrier plate	39 Brake cable	50 Cover plate
19 Brake disc	22 Pressure spring	29a Spring disc	40 Rear axle shaft	56 Sealing ring
20 Brake shoe	23 Clamping pin	29b Shielding plate	41 Support tube	57 Grooved ball bearing
21 Adjusting device	24 Upper return spring	31 Rubber sleeve	46 Hex bolt	58 Sealing ring
21a Thrust piece	25 Lower return spring	33 Pin	47 Lock washer	59 Fitted bolt
21b Adjusting gear	26 Expanding lock	35 KL-safety	48 Holder with weld nut	

Great care must be taken when assembling the unit because of the ease with which the seals can be damaged. The safest method is to use the assembly sleeve, shown in **FIG 20**, inserted into the bore to guide the pistons back into place. The protective sleeve shown in the figure is only used to protect the assembly sleeve from damage when it is not in use. If the sleeve cannot be manufactured or borrowed it is possible to assemble the master cylinder but extra care must be taken. The pistons and seals should be entered directly into the bore with a gentle twisting and pushing motion. **Under no circumstances should the parts be forced back into place.** A special tensioning drift, shown in use in **FIG 21**, will greatly facilitate fitting the seals, stop screw and lock ring.

11 The brake force regulator

A pressure reducing valve can be fitted into the hydraulic lines for the rear brakes. The valve does not start to operate until a pressure of 30 kg/sq cm (426 lb/sq inch) is reached in the hydraulic system but above this point it reduces the pressure proportionately to the rear brakes. This ensures that under heavy braking the

FIG 27 Removing lower return spring

20 Brake shoes	24 Upper return spring
22 Restraining spring	25 Lower return spring
23 Clamping pin	52 Spring removal pliers

157

FIG 28 Removing restraint spring

20 Brake shoes
22 Restraining spring
29 Brake carrier plate
30 Installation tool 112 589 09 61 00
40 Rear axle shaft
40a Assembly bore in rear axle shaft

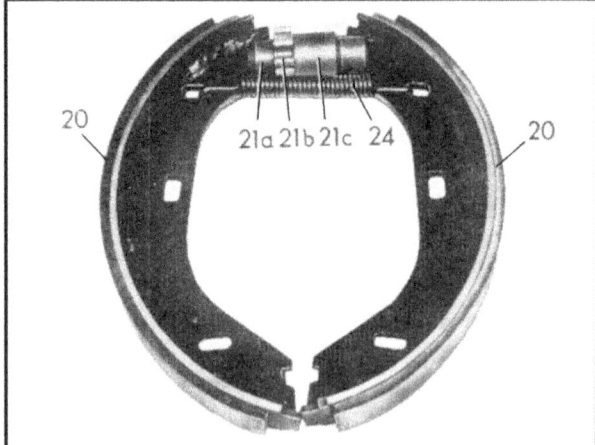

FIG 29 Brake shoe assembly removed

20 Brake shoes
21a Thrust piece
21b Adjusting gear
21c Thrust sleeve
24 Upper return spring

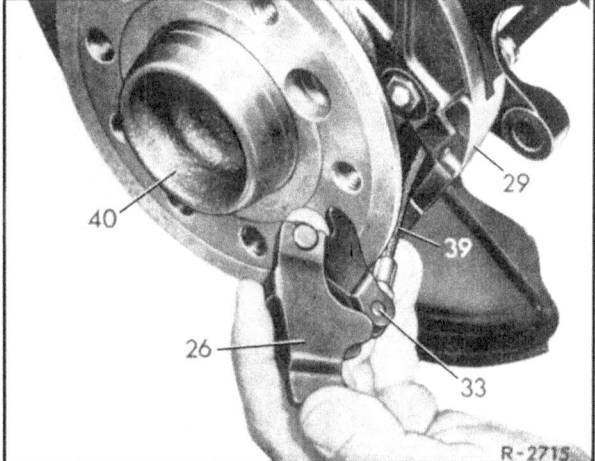

FIG 30 Freeing expanding lock

26 Expanding lock
29 Brake carrier
33 Pin for brake cable control
39 Brake cable control
40 Rear axle shaft

rear wheels will not lock. It should be noted that cars fitted with a brake force regulator have rear brake calipers with bores of 42 mm and cars without brake force regulators have caliper bores of 35 mm.

If the brake force regulator is defective it cannot be dismantled or repaired and a new unit must be fitted in its place. The attachments of the unit are shown in **FIG 22**. Once the unit has been removed and a new unit fitted, the rear brakes must be bled.

12 The brake servo

An ATE T51/200 or T51/1801 is fitted as standard between the brake pedal pushrod and the master cylinder. The position of the unit can be seen in **FIG 2**. Its attachments on the 280 SL/8 models are shown in **FIG 23** while those of all other models are shown in **FIG 24**. The eccentric adjusting bolt 3 or 3a should be set with the maximum eccentricity mark pointing rearwards so that the brake pedal travel is at a maximum, and then it should be set so that the brake pedal travel is approximately 152 mm (6 inch). The master cylinder does not require any clearance between pushrod and piston so the eccentric bolt is only used for adjusting the pedal travel.

Removal:

The unit is removed with the master cylinder attached to it. Drain the systems and disconnect the hydraulic lines to the master cylinder, as well as disconnecting the electrical leads to the switches, as described in **Section 10**. It will be necessary to free the reservoir of the clutch hydraulic system. Disconnect the vacuum line to the power unit.

On the 280 SL models take out the eccentric adjusting bolt 3 so that piston rod 2 is freed from the intermediate lever 19 (see **FIG 23**). On all other models, work from inside the car and remove the adjusting bolt 3a to free the piston rod 2 from the brake pedal 13 (see **FIG 24**).

On the 280 SL models free the unit from the intermediate flange 20 and remove it from the car. On all other models, free the intermediate flange 36 from the car and remove the unit with the flange attached, noting that two of the nuts are accessible from the engine compartment and the third one from inside the car.

Handle the unit with care as the control housing is made of brittle plastic which will shatter if dropped or mishandled.

Install the unit in the reverse order of removal. Set the correct brake pedal travel on the eccentric adjusting bolt and bleed both brake systems after the parts are in place.

Maintenance:

Maintenance is confined to renewing the air filter at intervals of 100,000 kilometres (60,000 miles). The brake servo must be removed from the car in order to change the filter. A sectioned view of the air inlet and filter parts is shown in **FIG 25**.

Pull back the protective cover 5 and remove it over the pushrod 1. Pry the holder 2 from the housing with the aid of two small screwdrivers. Withdraw the silencer 3 and filter 4 using a hooked piece of wire.

Insert a new filter, which is twice as thick as the silencer, and then insert the silencer so that slots are approximately at right angles to each other. Press on the holder and fit the protective cover back into place.

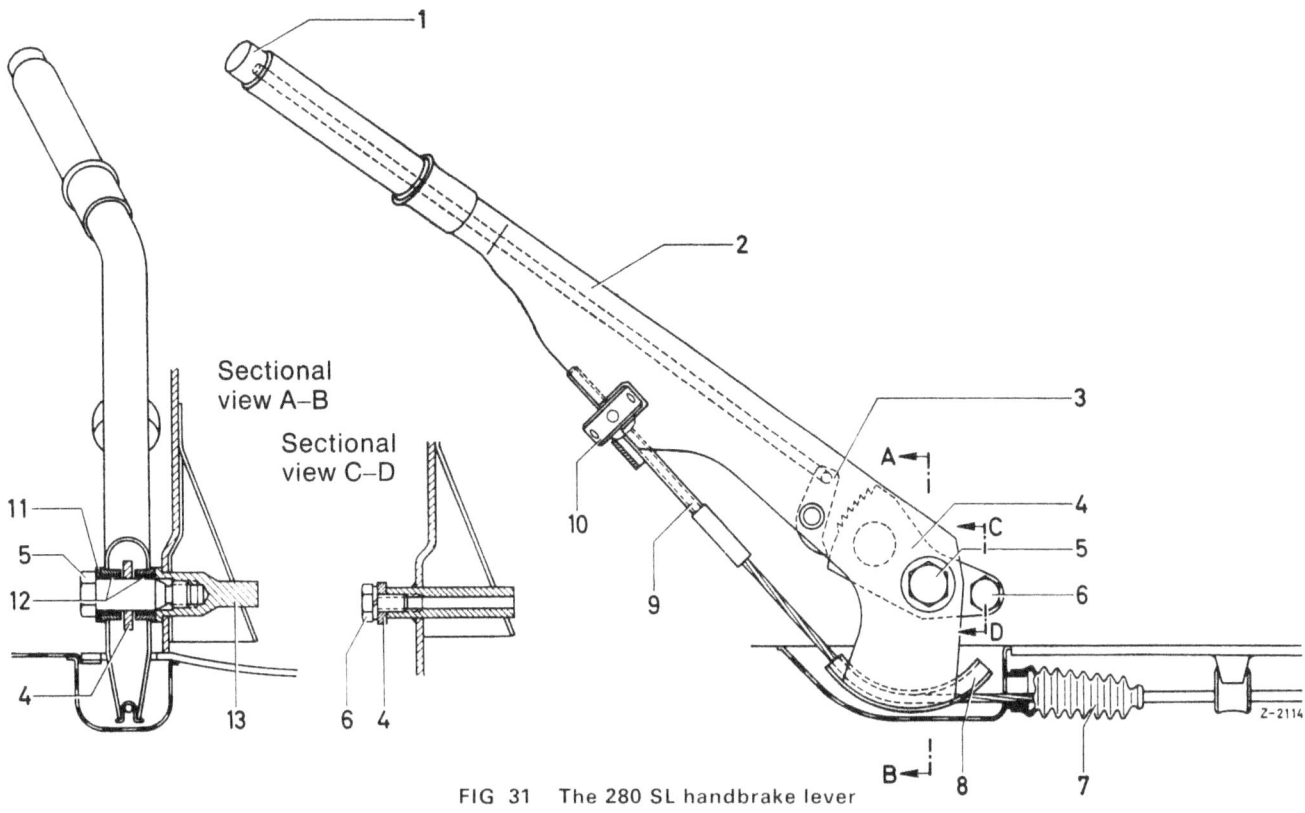

FIG 31 The 280 SL handbrake lever

1 Pushbutton
2 Hand brake lever
3 Locking pawl
4 Quadrant
5 Bearing bolt (LH thread)
6 Hex bolt
7 Rubber sleeve
8 Brake cable guide
9 Front brake cable control
10 Capstan nut
11 Washer
12 Bushing
13 Threaded member for attaching brake lever

Checking:

The action of the unit can be checked with the engine running and an assistant slowly pumping the brake pedal. When a hand is laid on the unit, the piston inside it should be felt to move and it may also be possible to hear the hiss of the air as it passes through the filter.

13 The Duo-Servo parking brake

This is the drum brake on the rear wheels which is operated by the parking brake linkage. The brake is equally effective in either direction and the shoes are designed to assist one another. Sectioned views of the assembly are shown in **FIG 26**. The adjustment of the brake is given in **Section 2**.

Dismantling:

1 Remove the brake caliper and brake disc. Take out the lower shoe return spring 25, preferably with the special pliers as shown in **FIG 27**.
2 Turn the axle shaft until the restraining springs 22 are accessible through the large hole in the flange and use the special tool 112 589 09 61 00, as shown in **FIG 28**. Push the tool slightly inwards to compress the spring and then turn it through 90 deg. so that the spring can be unhooked. Similarly remove the spring from the other shoe.

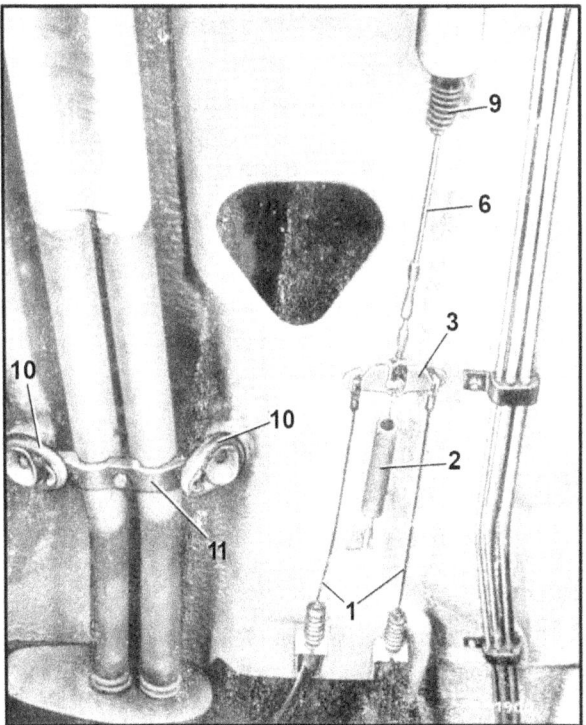

FIG 32 The 280 SL park brake linkage

1 Rear brake cables
2 Return spring
3 Compensating lever
6 Park brake cable
9 Rubber sleeve
10 Rubber ring
11 Exhaust bracket

 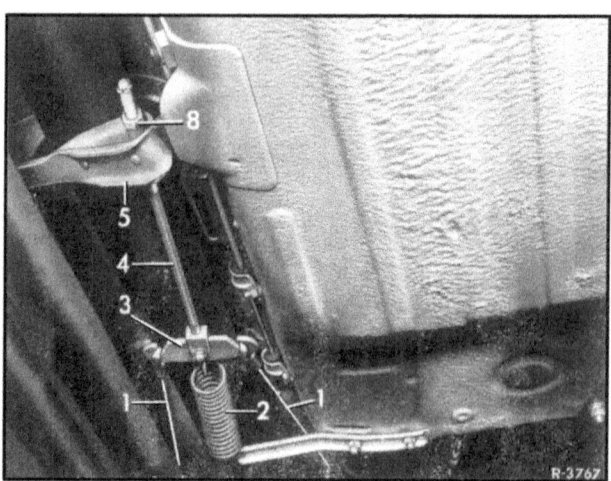

FIG 33 The lever in the standard parking brake linkage

1 Hex bolt
2 Brake lever
3 Cotter pin
4 Center brake cable control

FIG 34 The adjustment point for the standard linkage

1 Rear brake cable control
2 Return spring
3 Compensating lever
4 Clamping bolt
5 Intermediate lever
8 Hex nut

3 Pull the lower ends of the shoes apart so that they can pass over the axle shaft and the complete assembly, shown in **FIG 29**, can be removed. Take off the upper return spring 24 and remove the adjusting device 21, shown in **FIG 26**.

4 Free the brake cables from the compensating lever. Push the pin 33 out of the expanding lock 26, shown in **FIG 30**, and remove the expanding lock.

Cleaning and examination:

Check the linings and renew the shoes complete if the linings are nearly fully worn out or if they are contaminated with oil or grease. The linings must not be washed with any form of solvent.

The remainder of the metal parts can be washed with clean fuel to remove old grease and dirt. Before assembly, lubricate all bearing surfaces, pivot points and the threads on the adjuster with a suitable permanent grease, such as zinc-disulphide or Molykote Paste.

Assembly:

The brake is assembled in the reverse order of dismantling. The joint bolt on the expanding lock 26 must be fitted so that it faces upwards.

14 Parking brake linkage

The 280 SL models are fitted with a handbrake lever mounted on the floor. The compartments are shown in **FIG 31** and the linkage under the floor is shown in **FIG 32**. It should be noted, if the parts of the handbrake lever are removed from the car, that the bolt 5 has a lefthand thread.

The capstan nut 10, which can be turned using a 5 mm diameter bar, is not for adjusting the parking brakes but only for adjusting the lengths of the cables. If the cables require adjusting, slacken off the capstan nut 10 on the handbrake lever. Adjust both rear brakes as described in **Section 2**. When both brakes have been adjusted, tighten the capstan nut 10 until, when the lever is pulled up with a force of approximately 25 kg (55 lb) to the first notch, the rear wheels are lightly braked.

On all other models a pull-operated handle is fitted and this operates the brake lever 2, shown in **FIG 33**, which in turn operates the cables shown in **FIG 34**.

The nut 8 must only be used for adjusting the linkage and cables and it is not used for adjusting the parking brakes. If the linkage requires adjustment, slacken off the nut 8 and adjust the brakes as described in **Section 2**. Tighten the nut 8 until the pullrod can be pulled out by 5 to 6 teeth with moderate force, approximately 40 kg (90 lb). Check that the wheels rotate freely with the pullrod out to its first notch.

15 Fault diagnosis

(a) Spongy pedal

1 Air in the hydraulic system
2 Fluid leaks in the hydraulic system

(b) Excessive pedal movement

1 Check (a)
2 Excessively worn friction pads
3 Very low fluid level in reservoir

(c) Brakes grab or pull to one side

1 Wet or oily pads
2 Distorted or damaged brake discs
3 Brake disc running out of true
4 Worn out pads
5 Seized piston in caliper
6 Mixed pads of different grades
7 Uneven tyre pressures
8 Defective suspension or steering

CHAPTER 12 – ELECTRICAL SYSTEM

1 Description
2 The battery
3 Servicing electric motors
4 The starter motor
5 The alternator
6 The windscreen wipers
7 Fuses
8 The fuel gauge
9 The direction indicators
10 The headlamps
11 Fault diagnosis

1 Description

All the models covered by this manual are fitted with an electrical system in which the negative terminal of the battery is connected to the frame of the car (negative earth). The power for the system is produced by an engine-driven alternator and it is stored in a 12-volt lead/acid battery. The output of the alternator is controlled by a unit that regulates the current according to the demands of the system and charge of the battery. The alternator produces an alternating voltage which is then rectified by diodes to a DC current acceptable by the battery. Because of the diodes, current cannot flow in a reverse direction and therefore no cut-out is required in the system. The alternator is not self-exciting and therefore current is required from the battery to make it start to operate. A warning light is fitted into the excitation circuit and when this lamp goes out it indicates that the alternator is charging.

It is vital that correct polarity is observed and that all connections are correctly made, as reverse voltage can seriously damage the alternator and its circuit. Similarly the charging circuit must not be disconnected while the engine is running and the charging circuit should be disconnected before boost charging the battery or carrying out any arc-welding repairs to the bodywork, as induced voltages may damage the alternator.

A low-wattage test lamp, or any suitable reading voltmeter, can be used to check the continuity of circuits or to check that power is reaching a terminal. Cheap instruments must not be used for testing the performance of or adjusting components as they are incapable of measuring to the accuracy required. For accurate measurement or adjustments only high-grade, preferably moving-coil, instruments must be used.

Wiring diagrams are given in **Technical Data** at the end of this manual to enable those with electrical experience to trace and rectify wiring faults.

It must be pointed out that it is a waste of both time and money to attempt to repair components which are seriously defective, either mechanically or electrically, as they will never operate satisfactorily after repairs without specialist equipment and knowledge.

2 The battery

The battery is the most vital part of the electrical system as if it is in poor condition the performance of the remainder of the system will also suffer. Starting the engine will be difficult and may become impossible in conditions of cold or damp weather. The battery is also the component of the system that will suffer the most rapidly from neglected maintenance.

Winter conditions make hard demands on the battery as not only is the engine stiffer to turn and more use made of electrical accessories but the battery also loses

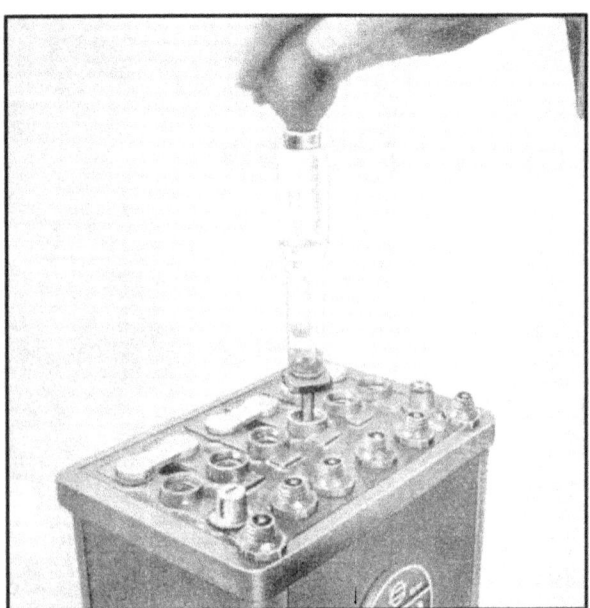

FIG 1 Testing the battery with a hydrometer

efficiency when it is cold. In extreme conditions, starting will be easier if the battery is removed from the car and stored overnight in a warm room.

The alternator gives a higher charging current at all speeds as compared to a conventional generator and it will also supply current at lower speeds. However, if the car is used for short-mileage journeys only, an occasional charging up with a trickle charger will ensure that the battery is always at full capacity.

Maintenance:

1 Always keep the top of the battery clean and dry. Wipe away any spilled distilled water and occasionally wipe the top to remove accumulations of dirt and acid. Dirt and acid will form a leakage path for the battery charge and also cause corrosion of the battery surrounds. If corrosion is found, remove the battery and wash the area with dilute ammonia or baking powder dissolved in warm water and then wash liberally with clean water. Allow the parts to dry and then protect them from further corrosion with a coat of anti-sulphuric paint.
2 Keep the battery terminals clean and tight. Wash off any corrosion with dilute ammonia followed by clean water. Oxides may be removed by careful scraping with a sharp knife or with a wire brush. Smear the terminal posts and connectors liberally with petroleum jelly (Vaseline) before reconnecting them as this will prevent further corrosion.
3 At regular intervals check the electrolyte level in the cells. Remove the vent plugs and check the level. **Do not use a naked flame or light to examine the level as the gases given off by the battery are explosive and use nothing but pure distilled water for topping up.** The correct level is approximately 5 mm (.2 inch) above the separators or the level mark.

Charging:

The best rate for charging is 10 per cent of the battery capcity, but trickle chargers may be used at a lower rate or boost chargers that give a current of up to 75 per cent of the battery capacity may also be used. Boost chargers should only be used in an emergency and then only on batteries which are known to be in good condition.

The vents should be removed and the battery charged until it gases freely. **Do not allow naked lights near a newly charged battery and avoid making sparks as the gases given off are explosive.**

A battery that is in poor condition may be partially restored by giving it several cycles of charge and discharge, using a lamp bank to discharge it and a suitable charger to charge it up again.

Storage:

Short term storage presents no problems if the battery has been correctly maintained.

If the battery is to be stored for long periods, make sure that it is fully charged and coat all exposed metal parts of it liberally with petroleum jelly. Keep the battery in a cool dry room well away from extremes of temperature, particularly frost.

At monthly intervals give the battery a freshening up charge and at every third month discharge the battery and fully charge it again. If these precautions are not carried out the plates will sulphate and ruin the battery.

Electrolyte:

Concentrated acid must never be added directly to the battery. Electrolyte of the correct specific gravity should only be added to replace spillage or leakage. Normally only distilled water should be added to replace the losses that occur in normal use. Avoid additives that are said to improve battery performance.

FIG 2 Testing the battery with a heavy-duty discharge tester

The mixing of acid and water is fraught with dangers, as large amounts of heat are given off and concentrated acid must be handled with great care. If electrolyte is required it is better to buy it ready mixed.

Testing:

The battery should normally be checked using a hydrometer, as shown in **FIG 1**. Draw sufficient electrolyte up into the instrument to ensure that the float is clear of the sides and bottom, then take the reading at eye level. Examine the appearance of the electrolyte as if it appears dirty or full of specks it is likely that the cell is defective. This will be confirmed by the cell having a different reading from all the others. If the cell has just been topped up, the battery should be charged or used for a ½ hour to ensure thorough mixing of the water and electrolyte.

The readings given by the instrument show the following indications:

For climates below 32°C (90°F):

Cell fully charged	1.270 to 1.290
Cell half-charged	1.190 to 1.210
Cell discharged	1.110 to 1.130

Replace spillage with electrolyte of 1.270 specific gravity.

For climates above 32°C (90°F):

Cell fully charged	1.120 to 1.230
Cell half-discharged	1.130 to 1.150
Cell discharged	1.050 to 1.070

Replace spillage with electrolyte of 1.210 specific gravity.

The readings given assume a standard electrolyte temperature of 16°C (60°F) and if the actual electrolyte temperature varies an allowance must be made. To convert the actual reading to standard, add .002 for every 3°C (5°F) rise in temperature and subtract it for every 3°C drop.

The battery may also be tested using a heavy duty discharge tester, provided that the intercell connectors are accessible. The method is shown in **FIG 2**. Test each cell in turn by pressing the prongs of the instrument firmly into the intercell connectors and holding them there. Do not test a battery which is known to be low in charge. If the cell is in good condition it will maintain a voltage reading of at least 1.8 volts for 10 seconds, while a poor cell will show by the rapid drop in voltage. Avoid touching the resistance portion of the instrument as it becomes extremely hot in use.

3 Servicing electric motors

All motors fitted to cars operate on the same basic principles and therefore have many design points in common. To avoid constant repetition, general instructions for motors are given in this section.

The motor part of the fuel pump fitted to fuel injection models must not be dismantled by the owner under any circumstances. If there is any defect then the pump should be taken to a service agent for repairs or exchange.

Brushgear:

Dismantle the motor sufficiently to examine the brushgear, taking care not to damage the brushes during dismantling. Check that the brushes make firm contact with the commutator and renew the brushes if they are excessively worn. Renew the brush springs if they are weak or broken. A modified spring balance can be used to check the tension of the springs. If the brushes are fitted on arms, check that the arms pivot freely.

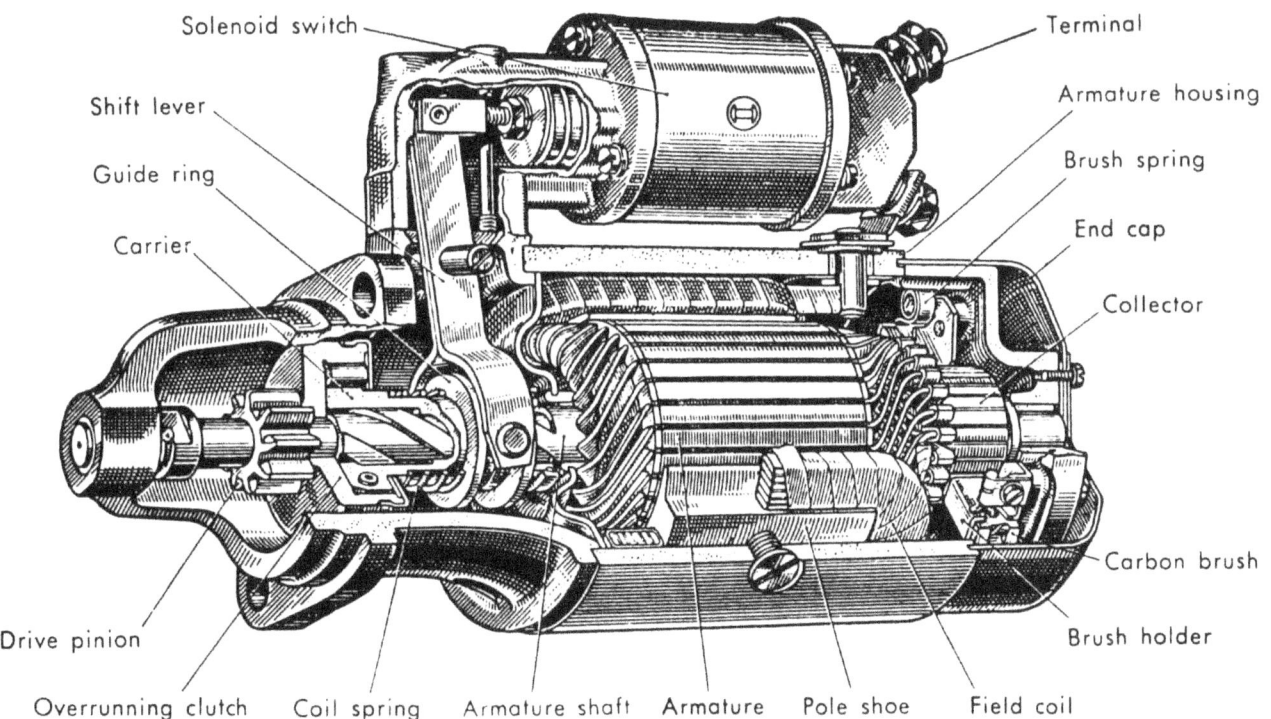

FIG 3   Sectioned view of a typical starter motor

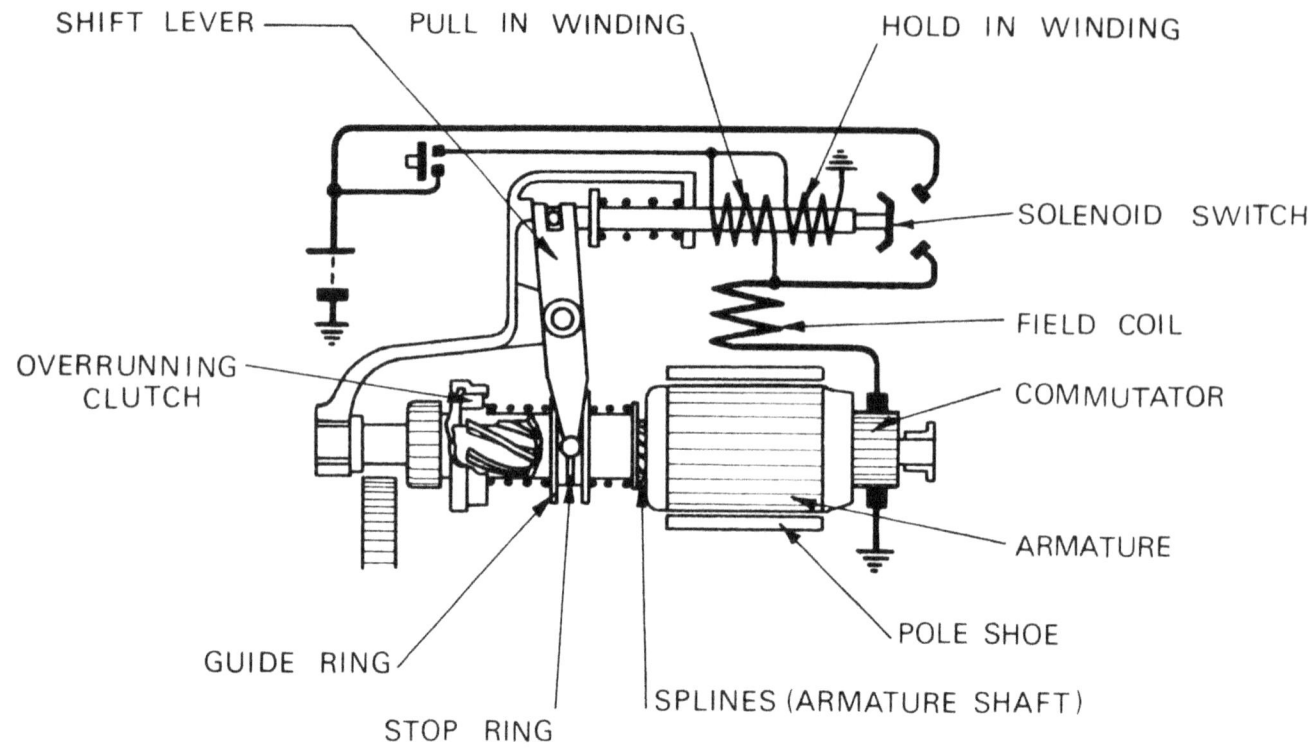

FIG 4 Typical starter motor circuit

If the brushes stick in their holders, remove the brushes and polish their sides on a smooth file. Clean the brush holders with a piece of rag dipped in fuel before refitting the brushes.

Used brushes should be refitted back into their original positions so that the bedding-in is not disturbed.

New brushes are normally supplied with the ends ground into shape. If further bedding-in is required, wrap the commutator with fine-grade glasspaper (not emerycloth) and rotate the commutator with the brushes pressing lightly against it.

Clean away all dust and dirt before reassembling the motor.

Commutator:

Normally this should have a slightly darkened but polished surface which is free from scores or burn marks. Wiping with a piece of lint-free cloth dipped in fuel or methylated spirits will be all the cleaning required in such cases. Light scores or burn marks can be polished off with a piece of fine-grade glasspaper. Never use emerycloth as this leaves particles embedded in the copper.

Deeper damage can be skimmed off in a lathe, using high speed and a very sharp tool and taking off only sufficient stock to clean off the damage. If the insulation is undercut, grind a hacksaw blade to the same thickness as the insulation and use it to squarely undercut to a depth of .6 to .7 mm (.025 to .030 inch). Take a light final skim cut using a diamond or carbide-tipped tool. If this cannot be done, then polish the commutator as it revolves with a fine-grade of glasspaper. Blow and wipe away all dust and swarf from the commutator and armature.

Armature:

Apart from cleaning and reconditioning the commutator there is very little that can be done to the armature. Special equipment is needed to check for faults in the windings, though shortcircuits may be suspected if individual commutator segments are badly burnt.

Check the armature for physical damage, such as loose laminations, segments, or wires, and also check that the laminations are not scored. Loose parts can be an indication of overspeeding. Scoring all round the laminations indicates worn bearings or loose polepieces but scoring on one side only indicates a bent armature shaft. Do not attempt to straighten or machine a defective armature. Fit a new armature if the old one is defective.

Field coils:

Some smaller motors are fitted with permanent magnets in place of field coils. Care must be taken in dismantling such motors as the armature will be drawn out with the cover and this can cause damage to the brushes.

The coils should be tested for continuity using a 12-volt test lamp and battery and the insulation should also be checked. If a resistance meter is available, use this instead to measure the resistance of the coils. Very high resistance or the lamp failing to light shows that there is a break in the winding.

On most motors the field coils can be removed by the owner. On the starter motor the polepieces hold the coils in place and the polepieces are in turn secured by large screws through the yoke. The screws are tightened to a high torque on a special wheel screwdriver and then they are staked to lock them. If the screws can be moved by an ordinary screwdriver they are too slack. For this reason renewal of field coils on the starter motor should be left to a service agent.

Cleaning:

The armature must not be dipped into solvent, but it can be wiped down with a piece of cloth moistened with fuel. The same applies to the field coils but other metal parts can be swilled in fuel to clean them. Use a small brush to remove all dirt and metal dust from crannies and crevices. Use an air-line or tyre pump to blow away loose dust and dirt.

Insulation:

After the parts have been cleaned, check the insulation. A 12-volt test lamp and battery can be used but it will be more efficient to use a neon bulb with a 110 AC volt supply. Do not use higher voltages.

4 The starter motor

A sectioned view of a typical starter motor is shown in **FIG 3** and a schematic wiring diagram is shown in **FIG 4**.

The solenoid is mounted on the starter and is activated by the starter switch. Current flows through the coil windings and the magnetic field induced draws in the solenoid plunger. This action moves the drive pinion into mesh with the teeth on the starter ring of the flywheel. Further movement of the plunger closes the contacts and allows a heavy current to flow through the starter motor for its operation. Springs are fitted to ensure that the plunger completes its travel if the teeth abut edge to edge and initial rotation of the motor then allows the gears to mesh correctly. The springs also ensure that there is some lost motion so that the current is cut off before the drive pinion is disengaged.

An overrun clutch unit can be fitted to the shaft. This ensures that there is always instant and positive drive of the motor but when the engine starts the clutch

FIG 6 The starter motor front support

1. Terminal 30 4. Hexagon head screw 7. Hexagon nut
2. Terminal 50 5. Hexagon nut 8. Holding bracket
3. Solenoid switch 6. Exhaust manifold 9. Holding bracket

releases and prevents the engine from driving the starter motor at high speed, with possible damage by centrifugal force.

Some models are fitted with brake washers on the armature shaft. These are not strong enough to affect the motor when it is under power but as soon as the current is cut off the washers bring the armature to a rapid stop. This ensures that the armature is not rotating if the engine stalls on start-up and the starter is operated rapidly.

Starter fails to operate:

1 Check the condition and charge of the battery, paying especial attention to the connectors and terminals. Dirty or loose terminals are a frequent cause of poor starting. If the battery is incapable of holding a charge, throw it away and fit a new one.

2 Switch on some lights that can be seen from the driving seat and again attempt to operate the starter. If the lights go dim the starter motor is taking current. If the lights do not go dim, listen for the noise of the starter solenoid operating. If the starter is taking current it is possible that the pinion is jammed in mesh. Engage a gear and rock the car backwards and forwards to free it. If this does not free the pinion, or the pinion jams regularly, remove the starter motor for inspection of the drive pinion, its teeth, and those on the starter ring of the flywheel.

3 If the starter solenoid is heard to operate, but the motor does not spin, short across the heavy duty terminals of the solenoid with a thick piece of metal. If the starter motor now spins freely the solenoid is defective and a new one must be fitted.

4 If the lights do not go dim, use a test lamp or voltmeter to trace through the wiring until the defect can be found. If current reaches the solenoid but it does not operate then a new solenoid should be fitted.

Removal:

Typical starter motor attachments are shown in **FIG 5**. On some models a support is fitted to the front of the motor as shown in **FIG 6**.

Disconnect the battery ground lead and disconnect the leads and cables to the starter motor. If a support is

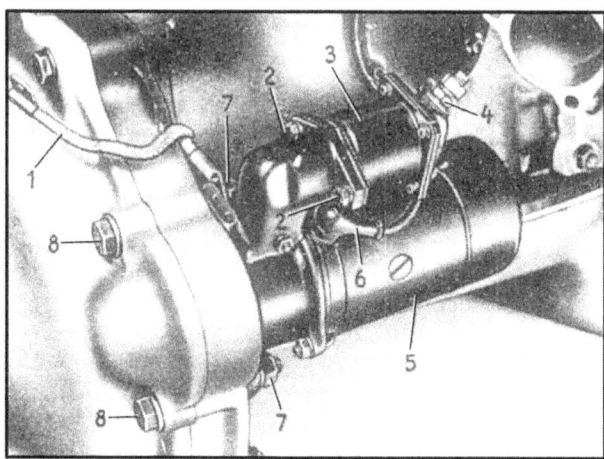

FIG 5 The starter motor mounting

1 Ground cable 4 Connecting bolt 7 Nut
2 Bolts 5 Starter 8 Bolt
3 Solenoid 6 Connecting cable

fitted to the front end, take off the nuts and bolts so that the holding bracket 8 can be removed. Take out the two bolts that secure the motor to the engine, draw the motor out of the housing and remove it from the car. On some models the upper bolt that secures the motor to the engine is only accessible from inside the car, after removing the coverplate, and then using a long extension, universal and socket.

Install the starter motor in the reverse order of removal. Evenly tighten the two bolts that secure the motor to the engine to avoid any danger of fracturing the lugs. If a front support is fitted, make sure that the two 4 mm thick packing washers are fitted between the holding bracket 8 and the engine on the studs which take the nuts 7. Do not forget to reconnect the engine ground lead.

Testing:

For full checks a test rig, meters and a torque rig are required. The test data for the motor is given in **Technical Data**.

The motor can be checked for free running without any meters. Even when running light the motor takes a heavy current, so use heavy duty leads. Clamp the motor in the padded jaws of a vice as there is considerable kick when it starts. Use the vice to hold the heavy duty lead connected to the negative terminal against the yoke of the motor. Connect another heavy duty lead to the terminal of the solenoid, or hold it firmly against the terminal of the starter motor. If the lead is connected to the solenoid upper terminal, use a separate lead to excite the solenoid. The motor should turn freely and at high speed.

5 The alternator

Fairly typical alternator components are shown in **FIG 7**. In some ways the alternator may be treated as a motor. The brushgear carries a much smaller current (excitation only) and contacts onto slip rings so there is much less likelihood of defects. The brushes should be checked for freedom of movement, wear and weak springs. Do not machine the slip rings, but if they do require more cleaning than wiping with fuel-moistened cloth they should be lightly polished with glasspaper.

When dismantling the solenoid it will be found necessary to unsolder leads. Carefully note the position of the lead, so that it will be correctly reconnected. Use a hot iron and carry out the work rapidly to prevent heat being conducted along the wire. **When soldering or unsoldering diode leads, grip the diode pin gently with a pair of pliers which will act as a heat sink and prevent heat from reaching the diode itself.**

Checking the alternator:

The charging circuit is shown in **FIG 8**. **When the excitation circuit is connected the remainder of the connections must not be disconnected while the engine is running.**

FIG 7 Typical alternator components

1 Disconnect the ground cable from the battery. Connect a suitable voltmeter between the B+ terminal on the alternator and a suitable earth or the body of the alternator itself.
2 Disconnect the red lead from the alternator B+ terminal and reconnect it with an ammeter in series (note that depending of type of alternator the ammeter will have to read up to 30 or 60 amps).
3 Connect a variable resistance of at least the same capacity as the ammeter across the battery terminals and reconnect the battery ground cable. The final connections of the sliding resistance should be left until after the engine has been started otherwise there will be an excessive drain on the battery. The circuit is shown in **FIG 9**.
4 Connect a tachometer to the engine. Start the engine and set it to run at a steady speed of 2000 to 2500 rev/min.
5 Adjust to the correct current and note the reading on the voltmeter (see **Technical Data**).

Diodes:

Diode failure is one of the more likely causes of poor, noisy, or no alternator operation. The diodes can be checked with a 12-volt test lamp and battery. When the diodes have been disconnected, connect one wire from the battery to the carrier plate and the other, through the lamp, to the diode pin. Check if the lamp lights and then repeat the test but reversing the connections. If the diode is satisfactory current will flow in one direction, and the lamp will light, but it will not flow in the other direction,

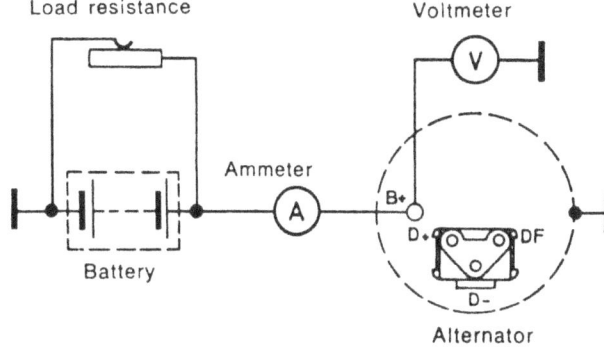

FIG 9 The alternator test circuit

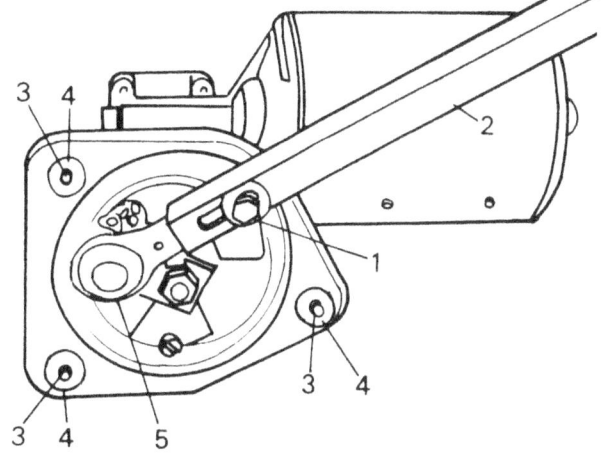

FIG 10 The wiper motor attachments

1 Pinch Bolt 4 Flexible pads
2 Link rod   5 Crankarm balljoint
3 Mounting stud

and the lamp will not light. If the lamp lights in both directions, or fails to light in either direction, the diode is defective and must be renewed.

Note that a hot iron and pliers, as heat sink, must be used when soldering or unsoldering the leads to the diodes.

6 The windscreen wipers

Motor:

The motor is removed from the engine compartment but it will be necessary to disconnect the linkage from under the instrument panel. The attachments of the motor are shown in **FIG 10**. From under the instrument panel, disconnect the link rod 2 at the ball joint from the motor crank. Do not slacken the adjusting screw 1 or the linkage will have to be reset. Remove the three nuts from the studs 3 and then remove the motor from the engine compartment.

The motor is installed in the reverse order of removal, but new sealing washers 4 should be fitted onto the studs 3.

Wiper arms and blades:

The parts and a wheel box are shown in **FIG 11**. New rubber blades can be fitted to the blade assembly 9, without having to fit a complete new assembly. The arms themselves are freed by lifting the blade of the windscreen and pressing down on the clip 11.

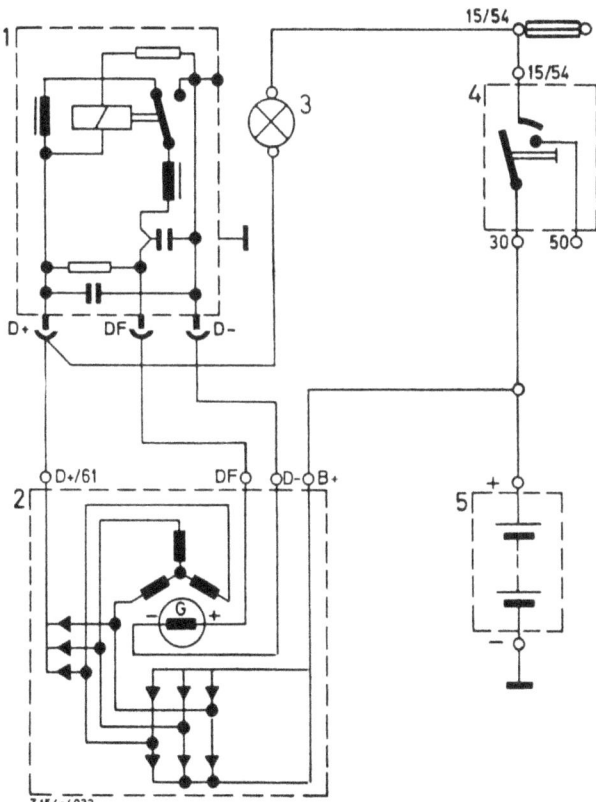

FIG 8 The charging circuit

1 Voltage regulator 4 Ignition switch
2 Alternator   5 Battery
3 Warning light

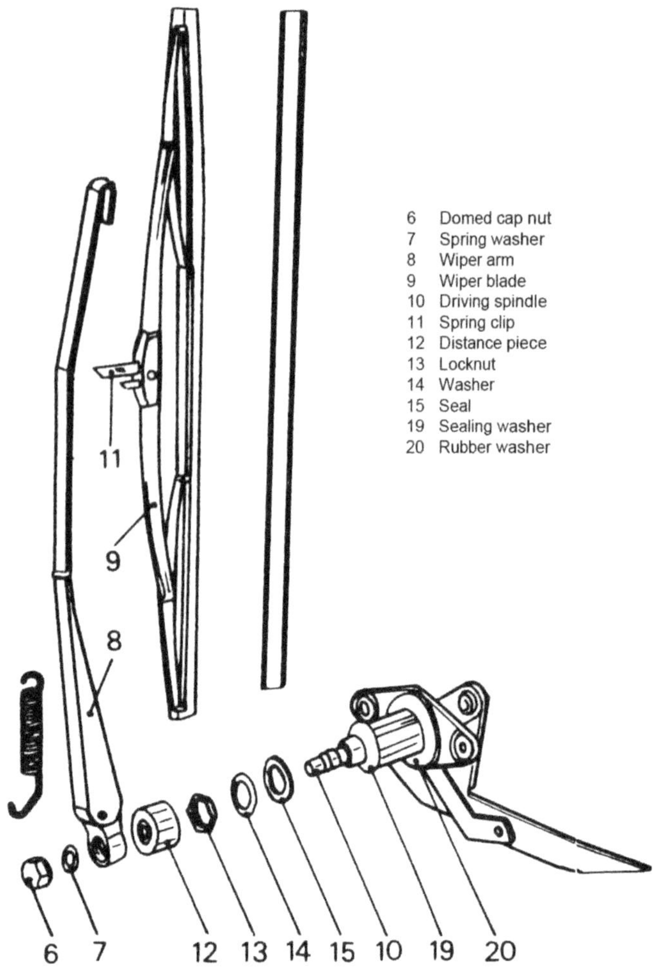

6 Domed cap nut
7 Spring washer
8 Wiper arm
9 Wiper blade
10 Driving spindle
11 Spring clip
12 Distance piece
13 Locknut
14 Washer
15 Seal
19 Sealing washer
20 Rubber washer

The arms themselves are secured to the spindles by the cap nuts 6. The spindles 10 are fitted with serrations which lock into the cone of the arm when the cap nut is tightened. New arms do not have serrations in the inner cones so that they can be set to the park position accurately with the motor switched off.

If the old arms do not park correctly, slacken the nut 6 sufficiently to partially free the arm and move the arm backwards and forwards with a wiping action until the serrations in the cone have been removed. Align the arm correctly and tighten the cap nut so that new serrations are cut into the arm.

Wheel boxes:

The righthand wheel box is shown in **FIG 11** and the lefthand one in **FIG 12**. Sufficient parts must be removed from the instrument panel to gain access, but once this has been done and the wiper arms removed, the wheel boxes can be removed by freeing the ball joints of the linkage and taking out the screws that secure them.

Install the wheel boxes in the reverse order of removal but make sure that they are accurately aligned and that the sealing washers 19 and 20 are in place.

If wipers fail to operate or operate sluggishly, disconnect the motor crank from the linkage and switch on the wipers. If the motor fails to operate still, trace back through the wiring to see if there is a fault and to check that current is reaching the motor. If the motor still operates sluggishly, there is an internal defect and the motor should be removed for strip examination. If the motor operates satisfactorily, check through the linkage for misalignment, wear or sticking.

FIG 11 The wiper arm, blade and wheel box

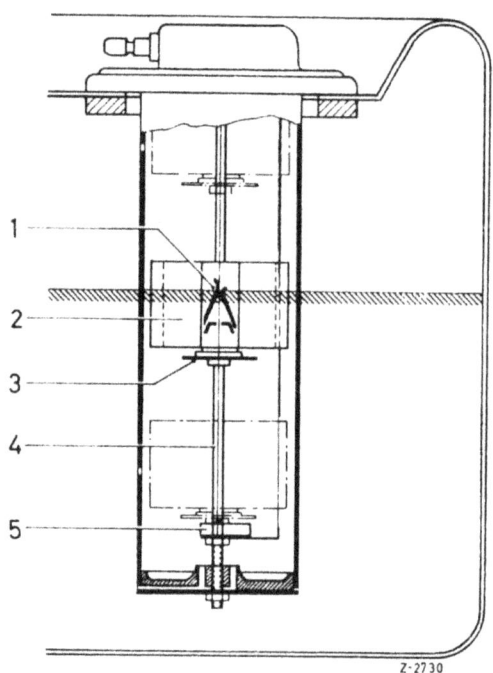

FIG 13 The fuel tank immersion tube indicator

1 Sliding contact   4 Guide and contact rod
2 Float   5 Reserve warning contact
3 Contact plate

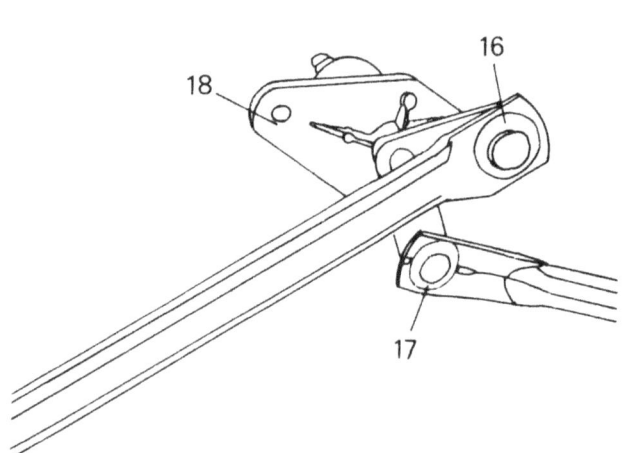

FIG 12 Wheel box attachments

16 Balljoint   17 Balljoint   18 Mounting plate

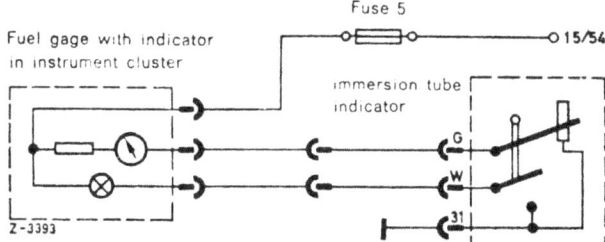

FIG 14 The fuel gauge circuit

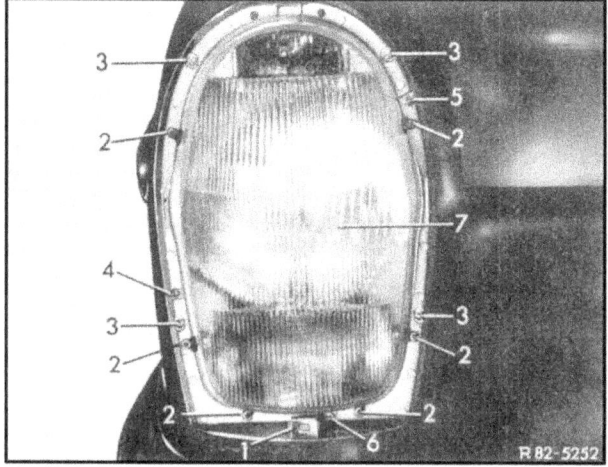

FIG 15 The headlamp attachments

1 Nut for ornamental ring
2 Swivel clips
3 Screws for lighting unit
4 Horizontal adjustment screw
5 Vertical adjustment screw
6 Fog lamp adjustment screw
7 Lens

7 Fuses

All models are well protected with fuses. If a fuse blows, check the system briefly to ensure that there is no obvious fault. Fit a new fuse of the correct rating into place and again operate the circuits protected. If the new fuse blows then there is a fault in the circuit that was live at the time, and a detailed examination must be given to it before fitting yet another new fuse. If all the circuits operate satisfactorily it is possible that the old fuse has weakened with age.

Intermittent faults can be caused by insulation that has chafed through and is making intermittent contact as the car moves or the engine shakes it. These may be quite difficult to find at times but try shaking the looms to find the weak spot.

Do not fit fuses of higher rating than called for. The fuse is designed to be the weak link in the circuit and if too large a fuse is fitted the wiring may burn out instead.

8 The fuel gauge

The immersion tube indicator is shown in **FIG 13**. The float 2 stays on top of the fuel level and moves the sliding contact 1 up and down with it. As the fuel level decreases the sliding contact moves down the guide and contact rod 4 to raise the resistance of the unit. This resistance is then measured by the gauge and the needle on the gauge also falls. When a certain level is reached, the contact plate 3 touches the contact 5 to operate the low level warning light. The circuit is shown in **FIG 14**.

If the gauge reading is faulty or erratic, first check the wiring and connections. A broken wire will lead to the gauge always reading empty and a shortcircuit will lead to it always reading full. Intermittent readings can be caused by poor insulation chafing against an earth point or a poor connection.

If the wiring is satisfactory, borrow another tank unit and connect it into the circuit, making sure that it is earthed. Carefully slide the float up and down (best with the unit on its side) and check if the gauge operates correctly. If the gauge now operates correctly the tank unit in the car is defective and must be renewed. If the gauge still does not operate, then the gauge itself is at fault. Before carrying out too many tests, make sure that the fuse has not blown.

9 The direction indicators

These are operated by a flasher unit, usually mounted under the dash.

If the flashers fail to operate or operate in an odd manner, first check all the bulbs. If necessary, remove the bulbs so that they can be visually checked.

Remove the flasher unit from its socket and use a test lamp or voltmeter to check that current is reaching the socket. **Handle the flasher unit with care as dropping it will make it defective.** Connect the terminals on the socket together with jumper leads and operate the direction indicator switch. If the lamps light correctly, but stay on without flashing, then the wiring and parts are satisfactory and the flasher unit itself is defective. If lamps do not light, check the wiring to them and their earthing. Defects can be traced to a certain part of the wiring by a process of elimination, noting which parts of the circuit operate and which do not.

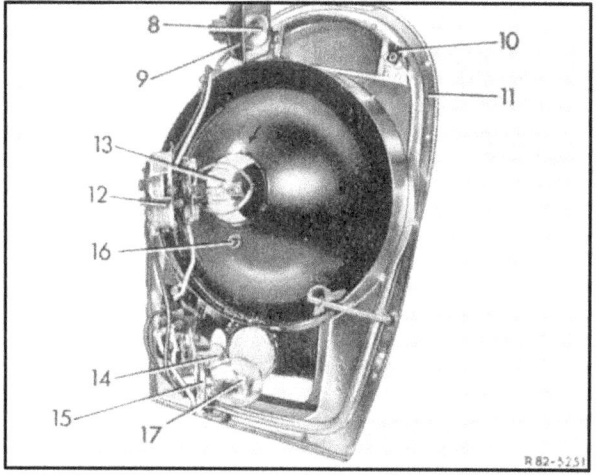

FIG 16 Rear view of the headlamp unit

8 Turn signal bulb
9 Turn signal bulb socket
10 Clip
11 Sealing frame
12 Main lamp socket and parking lamp contact plate
13 Headlamp bulb
14 Side marker bulb
15 Fog lamp bulb socket
16 Parking lamp bulb
17 Fog lamp bulb

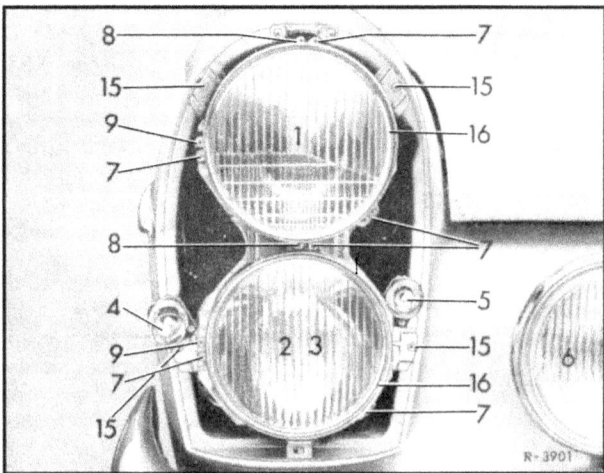

FIG 17 The halide lighting units

1 Low beam headlamp
2 High beam headlamp
3 Parking lamp
4 Turn signal bulb
5 Side lamp bulb
6 Fog lamp
7 Attachment screws
8 Vertical adjustment screw
9 Horizontal adjustment screw
15 Fastening screw
16 Rim

10 The headlamps

The attachments of the headlamps, after the removal of the ornamental ring, are shown in **FIG 15**. To remove the complete unit, for bulb changes, take out the attachment screws 3 and pull the unit out so that the connector can be disconnected. The lens alone can be removed by turning the two swivel clips 2 away from the glass, with a broad screwdriver, pulling the four-element clips slightly forwards and pressing them away from the glass. The attachments at the back of the unit are shown in **FIG 16**. Do not alter the setting screws 4, 5 and 6 (**FIG 15**) unless the beams are being set.

Twin Halogen lights can be fitted and the installation, after the removal of the ornamental ring, is shown in **FIG 17**. Either light unit can be removed after taking out the screws 7 and removing the rim 16. With the light unit out of its holding ring, slide back the cover and remove the spring clip so that the bulb holder can be taken out.

The bulbs should not be handled with the fingers or hands but should be held using clean cloth or tissue.

Beam setting:

The beam setting screws are shown in the figures and are used to alter the beam settings. The lights can be approximately aimed by standing the car squarely to and about 5 metres from a plain wall, but this method should only be used in an emergency. It is far better to take the car to a service agent where the lights can be accurately set using special equipment and it is certain that they will then meet all local legal requirements.

11 Fault diagnosis

(a) Battery discharged

1 Terminals loose or dirty
2 Insufficient charging current
3 Accessories left on
4 Insufficient mileage to recharge battery

(b) Battery will not hold charge

1 Low electrolyte level
2 Battery plates sulphated or separators ineffective
3 Electrolyte leakage from defective case

(c) Alternator output low or nil

1 Drive belt broken or slipping
2 Control box defective
3 Defective wiring or connections in charging circuit
4 Diodes failed in rectifier pack
5 Brushes excessively worn or sticking
6 Slip rings dirty
7 Weak or broken brush springs
8 Defective stator or rotor coils

(d) Starter lacks power or will not turn engine

1 Battery discharged, loose or dirty terminals
2 Starter pinion jammed in mesh
3 Defective brushgear
4 Defective commutator
5 Defective field or armature coils
6 Starter mechanically defective
7 Abnormally stiff engine

(e) Starter motor runs but does not turn engine

1 Defective overrun clutch
2 Broken teeth on pinion or ring

CHAPTER 13 - BODYWORK

1 Bodywork repairs
2 Expander clips
3 Door trim and handles
4 The door glass
5 The door locks
6 The bonnet
7 The luggage locker lid
8 The windscreen and backlight glass
9 The sliding roof
10 The instrument cluster
11 The heater
12 Air conditioning

1 Bodywork repairs

Large-scale bodywork repairs are best left to the experts. Even small dents can be tricky, as too much or injudicious hammering will stretch the metal and make things worse instead of better. Filling minor dents and scratches and then spraying with self-spraying cans of matching paint is probably the best method of restoring the finish available to the owner. It must be remembered that the paint supplied is an exact match for new paint but that the finish fades with age. Part of the original colour and gloss can be restored by using a mild cutting compound. The compound removes the top film of paint so it cannot be repeated too often.

Some models are finished in metallic paint which will give difficulties in spraying. The final appearance of the finish depends as much on the way the paint is sprayed on as on the colour of the pigments. Large areas of metallic finish should be left to expert paint sprayers.

The standard finish for all Mercedes models is a synthetic one, though some special-order cars may be finished in cellulose. **A cellulose finish must never be sprayed over a synthetic one as the synthetic paint will lift off in blisters.** Though not recommended, synthetic may be sprayed over cellulose. If there is any doubt, try a spot of paint on the car in a position where it will not show.

The appearance of the car will be improved by regular waxing, and not only is the appearance improved but the minute pinholes in the finish are filled with wax and the paint is made fully waterproof so that moisture cannot start corrosion under the paint. For the same reason, stone chips and minor scratches should be touched in as soon as possible, using matching paint and a fine brush.

It is better to spray a complete wing or panel rather than a patch, as any difference in the paint will not be so readily obvious. Before spraying an area, remove all trim from it as this will make the task easier and also improve the final appearance. Dewax the area by washing it with white spirits. If silicone-based polishes have been used, a special cleaning fluid is required to remove all traces of polish. Any small traces of polish will leave the paint pitted or cratered right down to the polish. Scuff the area lightly with a coarse paper to give a good key for the finish that will be applied.

Use a primer surfacer or paste stopper, depending on the depth of damage, to build up the damaged area so that it is just proud. Air-drying stoppers must be built up in coats, allowing each coat to dry before the next one is applied, but catalytic stoppers can be built up to the full depth as they are cured by chemical action. When the surface is hard, rub it down using 400 grade 'Wet and Dry' paper with plenty of water. If need be apply further

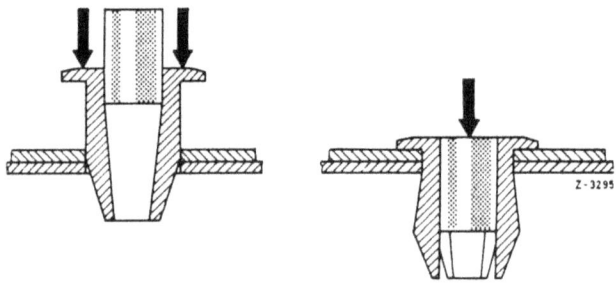

FIG 1 Expander type clips used for securing trim

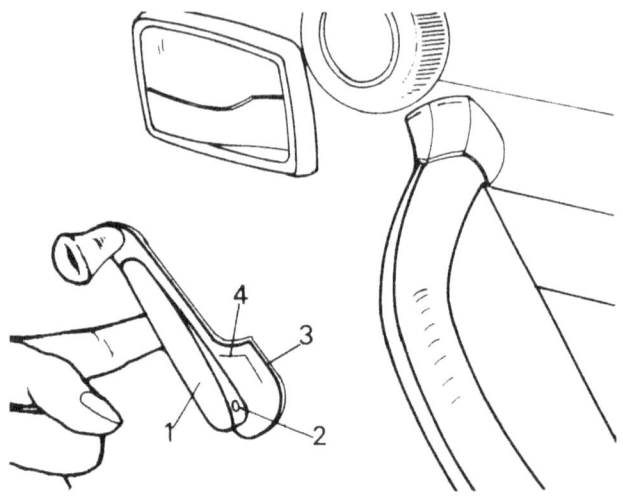

FIG 2 The window regulator handle

1 Padding 3 Plastic washer
2 Phillips head screw 4 Handle

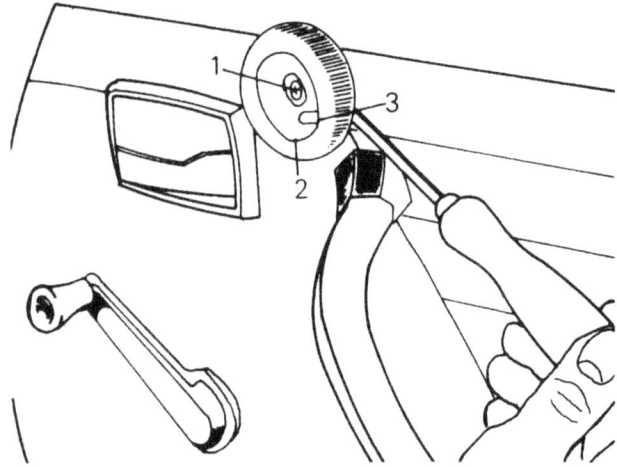

FIG 3 The vent control knob

1 Screw   2 Control knob   3 Cover plate recess

coats of stopper or filler to cover blemishes that are left. Spend plenty of time and patience in obtaining the best possible surface finish as small blemishes at this stage will stand out glaringly when the colour coat is applied and polished. When the surface is finished, wash it down with plenty of clean water and allow it to dry for a check. Fill any small blemishes and wash off any slurry that was missed on the first wash. Wipe the surface over with a proprietary 'tacky' cloth to remove any dust.

Mask off surrounding areas with newspaper and masking tape. If a complete panel or wing is being sprayed, then the paint should be applied evenly all over, spraying onto the surrounding masking to ensure that the edges are covered. If only a patch is being sprayed the paint should be 'feathered' off at the edges so that it blends smoothly with the old finish. It is better to apply two thin coats (or even more if required) rather than one thick coat which will probably run. Lightly rub down each coat when it is dry before applying the next. Do not rub down the final finish coat.

Leave the paint to dry at least overnight and then rub it down with cutting compound to remove any spray dust and to lightly polish the surface. Leave the car several weeks before applying wax polish, to allow the paint to dry and harden completely.

2 Expander clips

These are used throughout the car for securing trim, mouldings and parts. The method of fitting the clips is shown in **FIG 1**. The clip is pressed into place and the central pin is then pressed in to lock it.

To remove the clips, use a suitable drift to push the locking pin right through and then use a wooden or plastic wedge to pry out the remainder of the clip.

3 Door trim and handles

Window regulator handle:

Use a finger to press out the padding 1 in the handle, as shown in **FIG 2**. The handle can then be removed after taking out the Phillips screw that secures it.

Refit the handle in the reverse order of removal.

Control knob for ventilator:

This is only fitted to front doors. A special tool, No. 110 589 06 59 00, is made for removing the plate from the knob but a piece of stiff wire bent to shape can also be used. Insert the tool round the back of the knob, through the hole in the back indicated by the mark 3, so that the plate is pushed out, as shown in **FIG 3**. The knob can then be removed by taking out the Phillips screw 1 that secures it.

Refit the knob in the reverse order of removal.

Grip and arm rest:

Press out the cap 1 as shown in **FIG 4** and remove the screw exposed to free the grip. On the driver's door also take out the two screws that secure the arm rest so that the complete assembly can be removed.

Refit the parts in the reverse order of removal.

Remote units and lock:

Carefully pry out the recess 4 for the door catch, as shown in **FIG 5**. Take out the screw and remove the recess 3. A trim strip, secured by screws, is fitted on the panel around the door lock.

Refit the parts in the reverse order of removal.

Trim panel:

Remove all the parts so far detailed in this section. Remove the button for the inside safety lock and wind down the side window. Remove the reveal moulding in an upwards direction, starting at the end by the safety lock button. If any clips remain in the door, they should be taken out of the door and fitted to the reveal moulding before the moulding is refitted to the door.

On rear doors, remove the ashtray complete with its housing from the door.

Use a wooden wedge to free the clips at the sides and bottom of the door then lift the trim panel up so that it frees from the hook 5 shown in **FIG 6**. The trim panel is made of special plastic to withstand tropical conditions and it will break if it is bent. The side clips 6 are metal but the bottom clips 7 are of plastic and provided with a sealing surface to prevent water from entering.

Refit the parts in the reverse order of removal. If the foil 8 has been removed it must be stuck back into place.

Garnish moulding:

The exterior garnish moulding should be carefully prised up off its securing clips using a wooden or plastic wedge.

Install the moulding in the reverse order of removal but make sure that the plastic pads are fitted in place.

Weatherstrips:

The method of removing the inner or outer weatherstrips is shown in **FIG 7**, and this prevents damage to the finish on the car.

Install the weatherstrips in the reverse order of removal.

4 The door glass

Sliding glass and regulator:

Remove the door trim panel and foil from inside the door (see previous Section). Take out both screws 1, shown in **FIG 8**. Temporarily refit the handle and use it to wind the window up to the closed position. Fit a rubber wedge between the glass and the bottom of the door aperture to hold the glass up.

Remove the screws 2 and take out the window regulator mechanism. On all doors remove the screws 3.

On the front doors, hold the glass up by hand and remove the wedge. Lower the glass and free it from the screwed run channel so that it can be removed through the door aperture.

On the rear doors lower the glass, then turn it through 90 deg. so that retainer channel points towards the hinge end of the door. Free the screwed run channel and remove the inner and outer weatherstrips from the bottom of the aperture. The glass is then lifted up and out through the window aperture.

The parts are installed in the reverse order of removal.

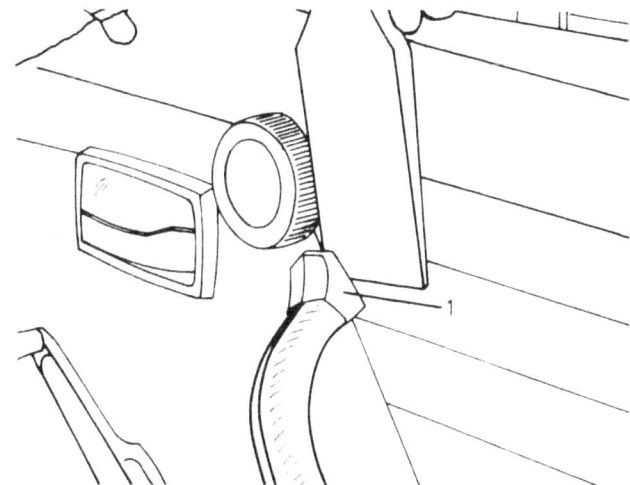

FIG 4   Freeing the cap on the grip

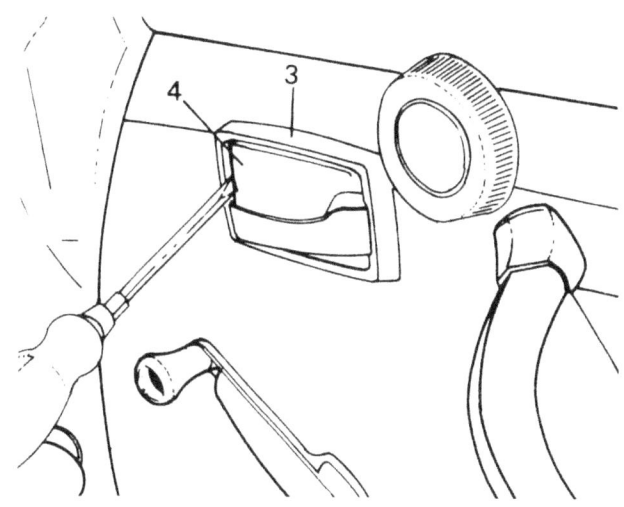

FIG 5   The door catch trim

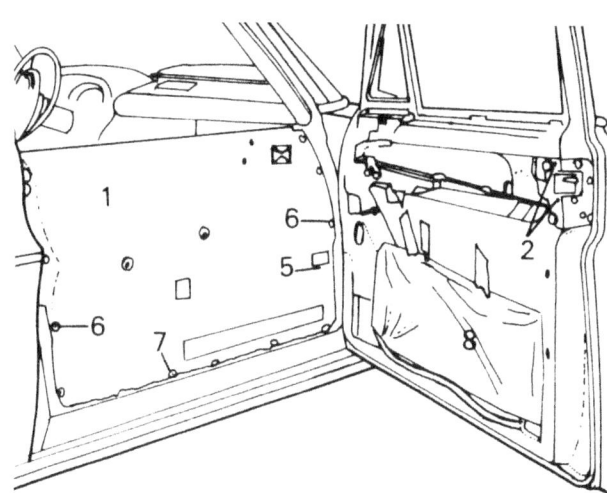

FIG 6   The door trim attachments

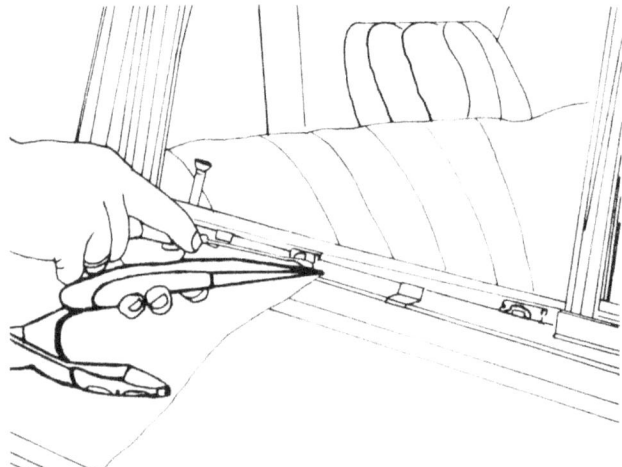

FIG 7   Removing the door weatherstrips

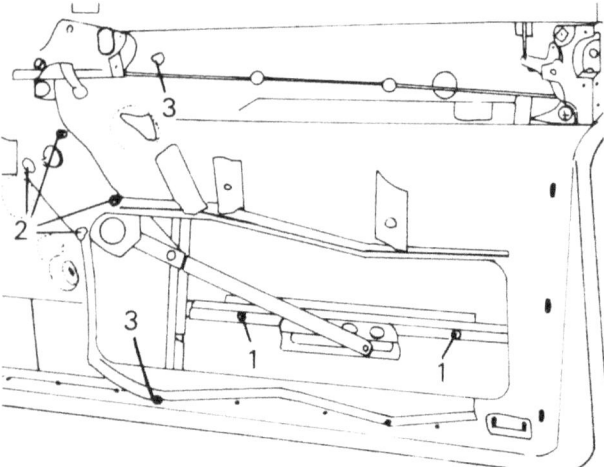

FIG 8   The window regulator attachments

1 Channel screw   2 Window regulator screws   3 Glass guide channel screw

FIG 9   The ventilator lock   (1 Shaft   2 Pinch bolts)

Ventilator:

The lock and glass are shown in **FIG 9**. To remove the lock, first take off the trim pad and door cover foil. Remove the screws 1 and 2 so that the lock can be removed through the door aperture.

The glass portion can be removed after taking out the lock and removing the external garnish moulding. Open the glass to 90 deg. and press it hard downwards so that the upper hinge pin frees.

The attachments of the ventilator frame are shown in **FIGS 10** and **11**. A plastic corner cap 5 is fitted as shown in **FIG 11**. **Do not forget to refit the cap before installing the frame.**

Fixed glass:

The attachments of the fixed glass on the rear doors is shown in **FIG 12**. Free the flexible glass run channel around the inside of the window aperture and pull down the weatherstrip. Take out the screws 1 and 2 to free the stay bar 3 and then remove the glass.

5 The door locks

Interior handle:

Remove the trim pad to gain access. The attachments are shown in **FIG 13**. Disconnect the lock spring 1 and take out the two screws 2 to free the catch.

Install the catch in the reverse order of removal but position it so that play in the linkage is just taken up before tightening the two screws 2.

Exterior handle:

The attachments of the lock and handle are shown in **FIG 14**. Normally it is possible to remove the exterior handle by taking out the screw 3 and then pressing the handle forward and out. If the handle cannot be pressed forward remove the trim panel and slacken the other handle attachment screw, accessible through the aperture 6 in the door.

Install the handle in the reverse order of removal, checking that there is a clearance of 1.5 mm on front doors and 1 mm on rear doors between the plunger of the handle and the lever on the lock. Moisten the pads to allow the handle to slide more easily.

Lock:

The attachments of a front lock are shown in **FIG 14**. The rear door lock is very similar except that it has an extra control rod attached to it and it also has a safety catch which is only accessible with the door open.

To remove the lock, disconnect the lock spring(s) 5 and take out the screws 4. The lock can then be removed.

Install the lock in the reverse order of removal.

Striker:

Shims can be fitted behind the striker plate to ensure that it is at the correct clearance from the door. To adjust the striker, slacken the bolts that secure it until it is just held in place and will not move under its own weight. Gently close the door and then pull or push against the door to position it in line with the rest of the body. Open the door carefully and fully tighten the bolts that secure the striker.

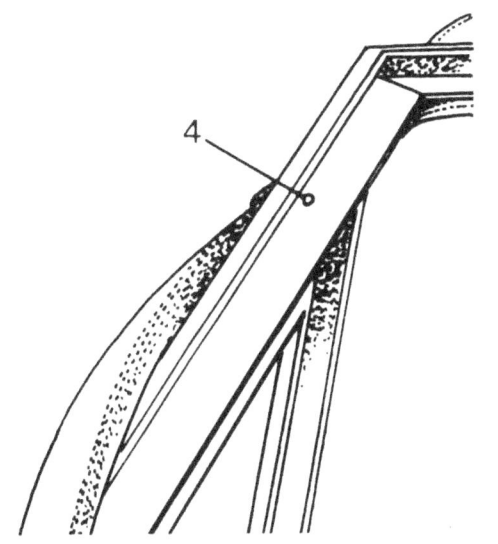

FIG 10 The upper ventilator frame retaining screw (4)

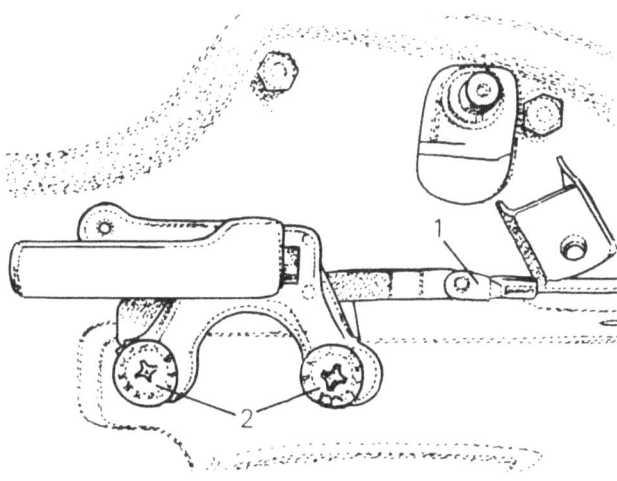

FIG 13 The attachments of the interior catch
1 Lock spring   2 Screws

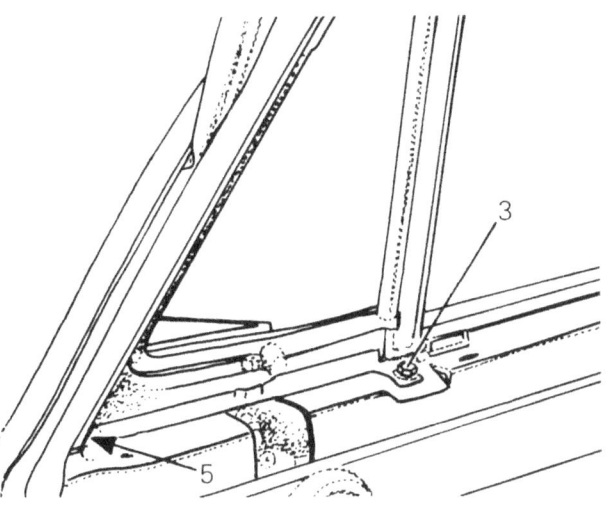

FIG 11 The lower attachments of the ventilator
3 Screw   5 Corner cap

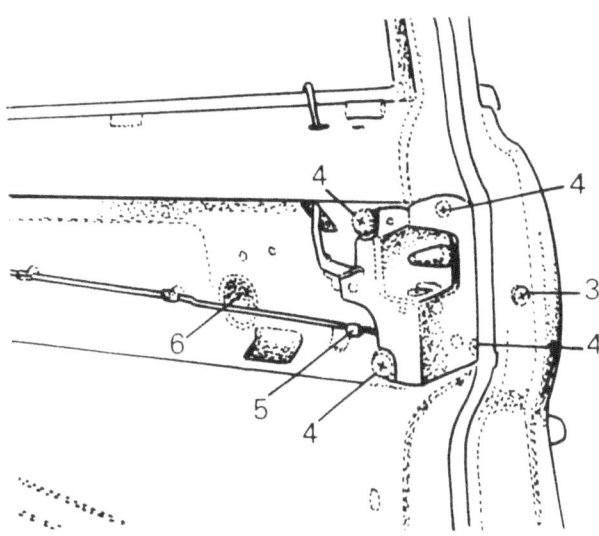

FIG 14 Door lock attachments, front door shown
3 Handle screw   4 Screw   5 Lock spring   6 Aperture

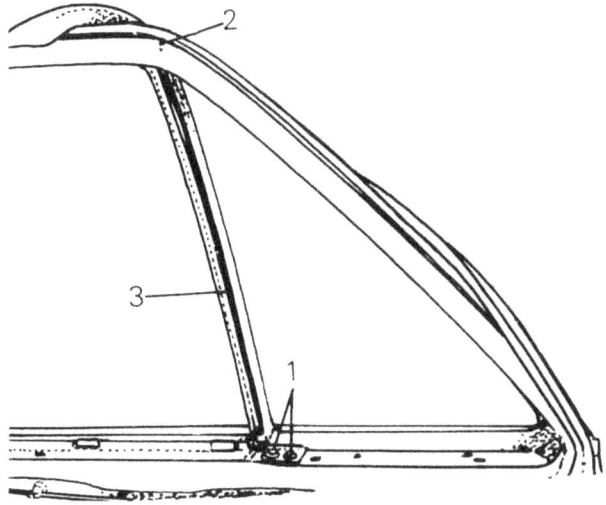

FIG 12 The attachments of the door fixed glass
1 Lower screws   2 Upper screws   3 Divider bar

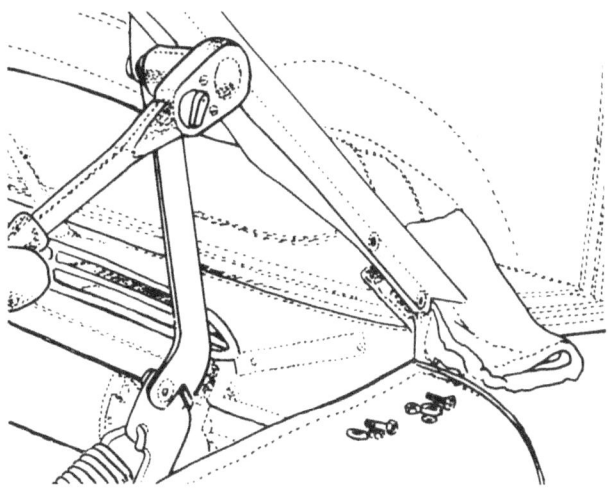

FIG 15 The bonnet attachments

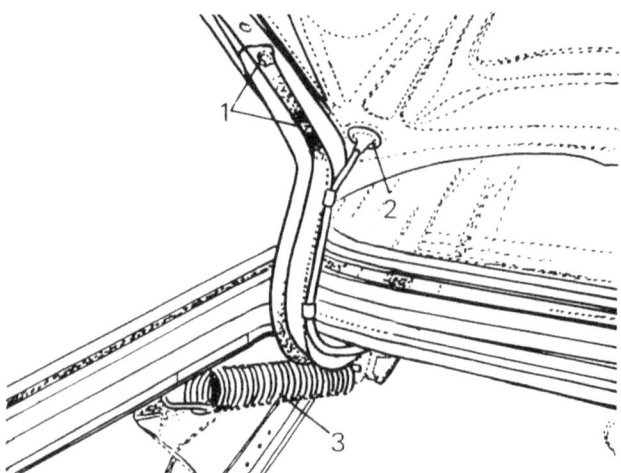

FIG 16 The luggage locker lid attachments

6 The bonnet

Typical bonnet attachment points are shown in **FIG 15**. To remove the bonnet at least one assistant is required and all areas that are liable to damage should be padded with rags. Take out the bolts that secure the bonnet, while the assistant supports it, and then lift it carefully off from the car.

The attachment holes are slotted to allow the hinge and bonnet to be positioned so that the panel aligns with the bodywork.

7 The luggage locker lid

The attachments are shown in **FIG 16**. Remove the cable together with the grommet 2 and plug from the panel and then take out the attachment screws 1. It is advisable to have an assistant to help lift off the panel, and paint areas that are liable to damage should be padded with rag.

Refit the panel in the reverse order of removal.

The luggage lid lock can be removed from inside the compartment, after taking off the coverplate, by using a socket spanner and extension to take out the bolts that secure it.

When installing the lock, make sure that the spur on the lock cylinder is pointing to the right and downwards.

8 The windscreen and backlight glass

Exterior garnish mouldings:

On the windscreen, push up the cover 1, shown in **FIG 17**, with a suitable wedge. Push aside the central cover 2, shown in **FIG 18** (on both windscreen and backlight) and then ease the garnish moulding out of the clips 3 with a suitable wooden wedge. On the backlight, open the rear door and take out the screw that secures the moulding. Remove the moulding.

The garnish mouldings are refitted in the reverse order of removal.

Interior reveal moulding:

These are secured to the frame by screws. When removing the windscreen, also remove the rear view mirror.

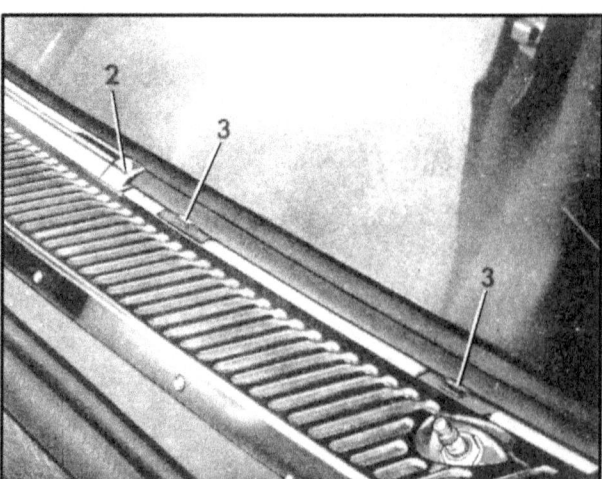

FIG 18 The centre cover on the garnish moulding

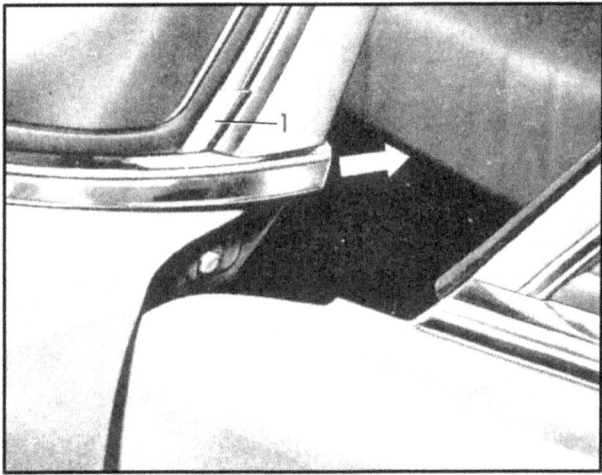

FIG 17 The side cover on the windscreen garnish moulding

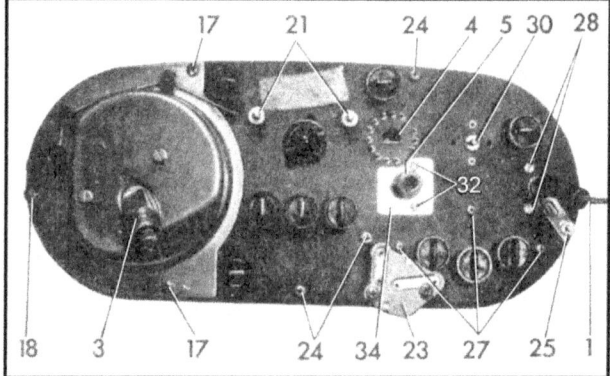

FIG 19 The instrument cluster rear view

1 Capillary tube
3 Speedometer connection
4 Multiple plug
5 Oil pressure line union
17 Bolts for speedometer
18 Nuts for speedometer
21 Nuts for electric clock
23 Dimmer
24 Bolts for contact plate
25 Nuts for contact plate
27 Screws for plate/dial combination
28 Temperature gauge screws
30 Nut for fuel gauge
32 Oil pressure gauge screws
34 Plate

Glass removal:

If the glass has actually broken and fallen out, all particles should be removed using a powerful vacuum cleaner. **It is particularly important to make sure that no particles are left in the windscreen demist system as they can be forcibly blown out by the action of the heater blower.** If in doubt, partially dismantle the heater system to remove glass.

If the glass has broken but not fallen out it will be found easier to remove if paper is stuck to either side of the glass so as to hold the particles together. Lay an old blanket over the bonnet to protect it.

If the glass has not broken, remove the mouldings and use a flat wedge to push out the lip of the weatherstrip over the flange in the aperture. When the lip is free, have an assistant outside to take the glass and press it out of the car using pressure from a padded hand or foot. Start at a corner and gradually work the glass out.

The weatherstrip is sealed to both the glass and the body so that removal will most likely damage it. To prevent leaks around the windscreen, always fit a new rubber weatherstrip when refitting the glass.

Installing glass:

Lay the glass convex side down onto a padded bench and fit the rubber weatherstrip around it. It is advisable to run a rule around the slots in the weatherstrip in case there are any points still stuck.

Coat the retaining section of the ornamental frame with soapy water and press the frame back into the weatherstrip.

Insert a greased length of cord into the slot of the weatherstrip which will fit onto the aperture flange, making sure that the cord passes all round the assembly and that there are sufficient ends free to get a grip on.

Coat the flange in the aperture with sealing compound. Accurately align the glass and weatherstrip into the aperture and press them home with slight pressure. The ends of the cords should be passed through the aperture. While an assistant holds the glass in place, grip the ends of the cords inside the car and pull them out, parallel to the glass, so that as the cord comes free it lifts the lip of the weatherstrip over the flange.

Inject sealant between the glass and weatherstrip. Wipe away surplus sealant with a cloth moistened with white spirits or fuel. Excessive solvent must not be used otherwise it will remove the sealant from behind the weatherstrip.

Install the mouldings.

9 The sliding roof

An electrically operated sliding roof can be fitted as an optional extra.

The motor for the operation of the roof is fitted into the luggage compartment. In case of electrical failure the roof can still be operated by turning the motor using a sparking plug spanner. A rubber drive is fitted between motor and gears and if the roof fails to move, this drive should be felt to see if the motor and electrical part is trying to operate. If no motion is felt then the electrical system should be checked.

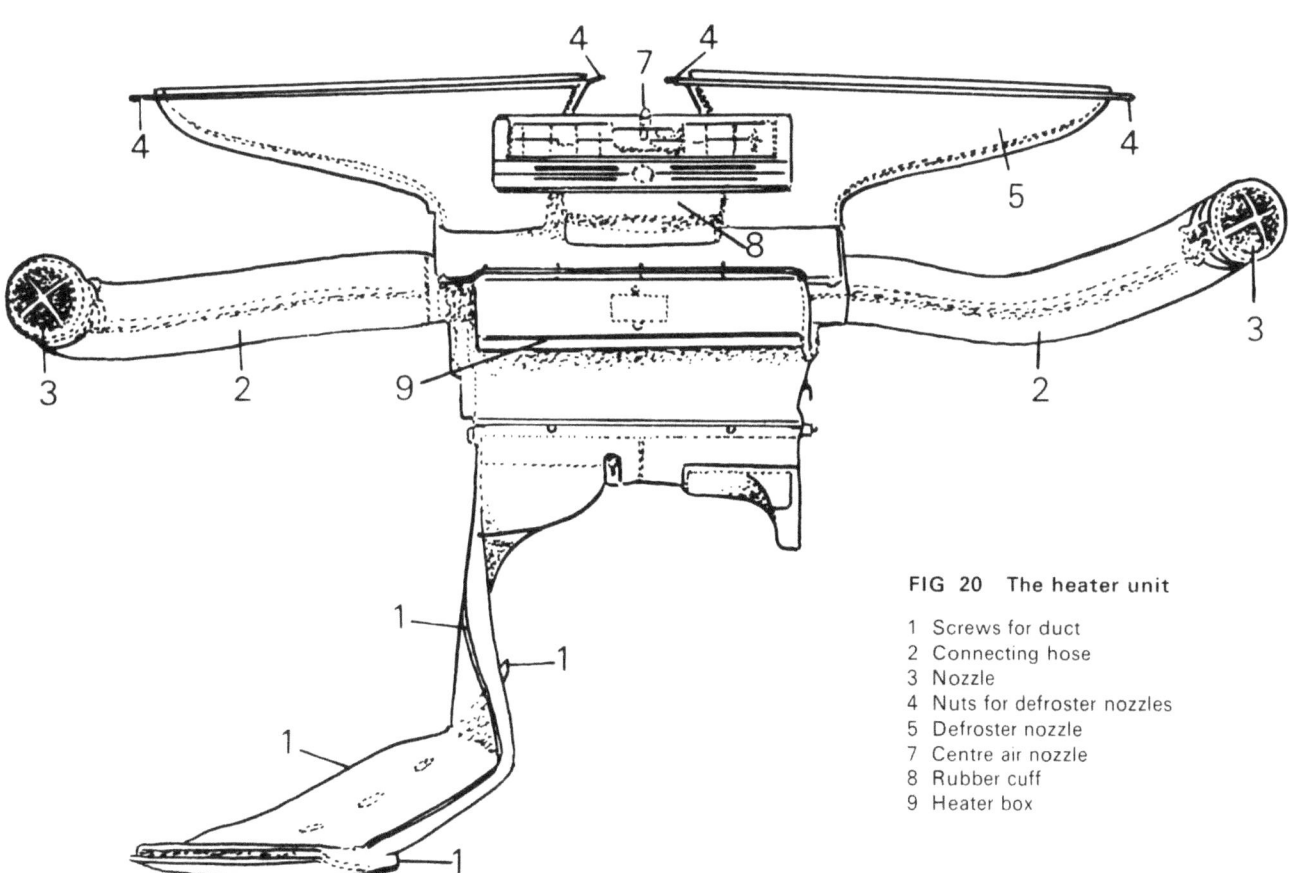

FIG 20 The heater unit

1 Screws for duct
2 Connecting hose
3 Nozzle
4 Nuts for defroster nozzles
5 Defroster nozzle
7 Centre air nozzle
8 Rubber cuff
9 Heater box

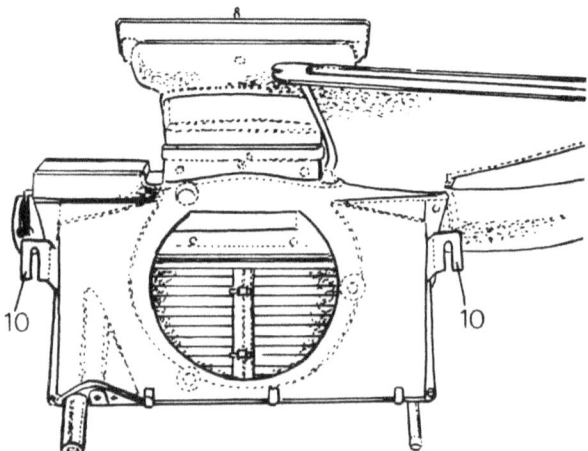

FIG 21 The heater box

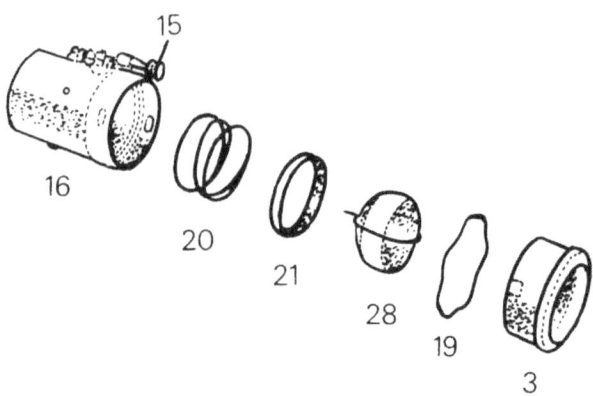

FIG 22 The heater port nozzle

3 Port
15 Handle
16 Short pipe section
19 Lockwasher
20 Spring
21 Ring
28 Nozzle

A teleflex cable operates the roof from the gears and, when free, the cable should move in its sheath with a maximum pull of 3 kg (6½ lb).

A clutch is fitted into the drive and the clutch slips when the roof reaches the end of its travel. The clutch should be adjusted so that the motor is taking a maximum of 18 amps when the clutch slips.

10 The instrument cluster

Removal:

1 Remove the temperature sensor from the cooling system and plug the orifice to prevent the loss of coolant. **Take great care not to damage or kink the capillary tube.**

2 Remove the cover from under the instrument panel. Lay pieces of rag over the steering column to save it from scratches. From behind the dash, press the instrument cluster out slightly, noting that the cluster is held in place by a rubber strip around it.

3 If a panel light is defective it can be changed at this point. Press in the holder and turn it so that it frees from the back of the cluster. Pull the old bulb out of the holder and press a new bulb back into place. Refit the holder and secure the instrument cluster back into place.

4 A rear view of the instrument cluster is shown in **FIG 19.** Disconnect the drive cable from the speedometer and disconnect the oil pressure pipe from the back of the gauge. Pull out the multiple-pin plug 4.

5 Carefully withdraw the instrument cluster, feeding the capillary tube through and **taking great care not to kink or damage it.** If the capillary is damaged a complete new temperature gauge, sensor and tube must be fitted.

The instrument cluster is refitted in the reverse order.

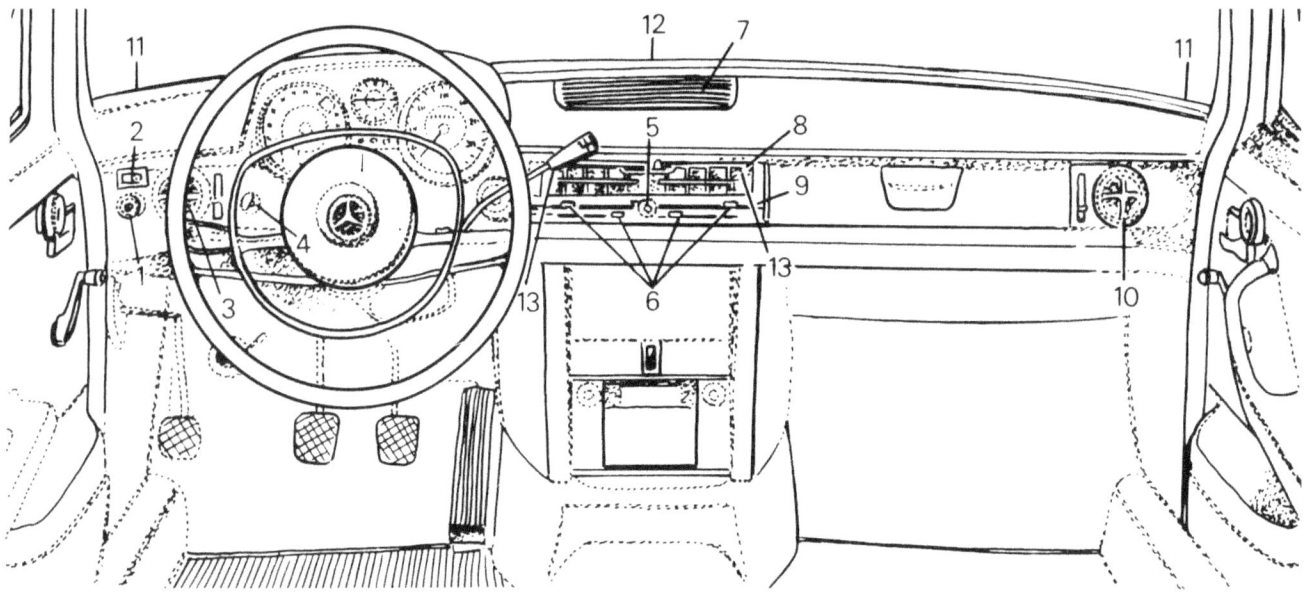

FIG 23 The instrument panel

1 Park brake release knob
2 Rear compartment light switch
3 Heater port
4 Light switch
5 Heater blower switch
6 Heater control handles
7 Loudspeaker grille
8 Centre heater air nozzle
9 Escutcheon
10 Heater port
11 Outer retaining nuts
12 Centre retaining nut
13 Centre nozzle retaining screw

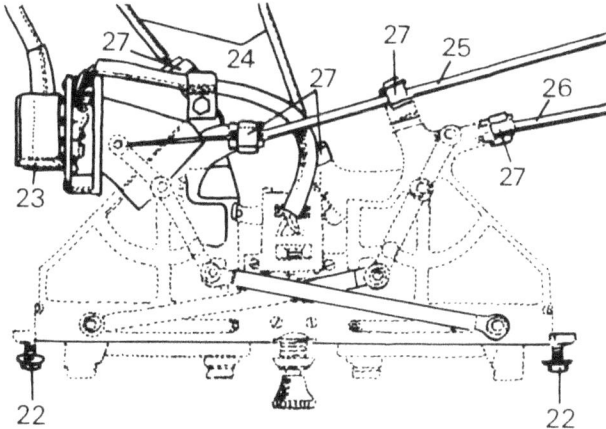

FIG 24 The heater control unit

22 Attachment screws
23 Plug
24 Water valve cable
25 Lower air flap cable
26 Upper air flap cable
27 Clips

11 The heater

The heater unit is shown in **FIG 20**.

Heating duct:

Remove the centre support and take out the screws 1 so that the duct can be removed.

Install the duct in the reverse order of removal.

Right defroster nozzle:

This can be removed after taking out the cover under the instrument panel and removing the glove box. Disconnect the hose 2 from the nozzle 3. Take off the nuts 4 and remove the nozzle 3.

Refit the nozzle in the reverse order of removal.

Heater box:

Drain the cooling system and disconnect the two heater hoses at the rear bulkhead in the engine compartment. Remove the heater duct to the rear compartment, and take out the right defroster nozzle.

Remove the other cover from under the instrument panel. Remove the two nuts that hold the supporting brackets 10, shown in **FIG 21**, and take out the screw that secures the bracket to the transmission tunnel. Reach through the glove box aperture and free the rubber cuff 8 (**FIG 20**) from the casing.

Detach the ball joint on the flap linkage of the centre air duct. Remove the lefthand side fixing nut of the instrument panel from the top of the dash. Free the Bowden cables from the righthand side of the heater box.

Hold the instrument panel up by lifting the lefthand nozzle and ease the heater box out of the rubber grommets in the scuttle then remove it towards the right.

Once the heater box has been removed, the blower unit can also be taken out after removing the three screws that secure it.

The parts are installed in the reverse order of removal. If the blower motor assembly has been taken out, use new Terostat washers on the screws that secure it to prevent water leaking into the car.

Heater ports:

The parts of a port are shown in **FIG 22**. Disconnect the hoses 2 (**FIG 20**) and pull out the handle 15. Hold the port and turn the short pipe length 16 slightly to free the parts so that they can be removed.

Install the parts in the reverse order of removal.

Centre air nozzle:

The attachments of the instrument panel and centre air nozzle are shown in **FIG 23**.

Remove the heater blower knob and escutcheon 5. Take out the screws 13 and pull off the handles 6. Remove the grille for the radio speaker 7. Reach through the opening for the speaker and free the rubber duct. Free the ball joint from the linkage of the flap actuating mechanism. Free the bolts to the control unit.

Use a wooden or plastic wedge ease out the escutcheon 9 together with the centre port.

Install the parts in the reverse order of removal.

Control unit:

The unit is shown in **FIG 24**. Remove the centre air nozzle and take out the two bolts 22. Disconnect the plug 23 and the Bowden cables. Remove the control unit through the aperture for the centre port.

Install the parts in the reverse order of removal.

12 Air conditioning

This can be fitted as an optional extra. If it is fitted the temperature inside the car can be controlled to a comfortable level irrespective of the external temperature.

When an air conditioner is fitted it must be operated at least once a month. Do not advance the blower control beyond the first notch to prevent the blast of cold air being a nuisance in the cold season. Run the system briefly. This ensures that the revolving seal on the crankshaft and the expansion valve are lubricated.

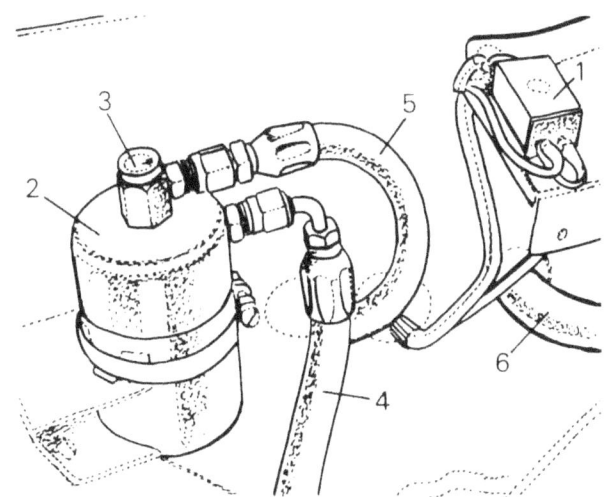

FIG 25 The air conditioning sight glass

1 Air conditioning fuse box
2 Liquid receiver
3 Sight glass
4 Hose from condenser
5 Hose to expansion valve
6 Hose from evaporator to compressor

In damp weather the air conditioning can be used to remove moisture from inside the car. Turn the heater control to Heater and set the control for the circulation through the foot space to open. With the air conditioning on, the air inside the car is drawn through the evaporator where water in the air is condensed out.

The system is charged with a refrigerant R12 which is a liquid when cool and under pressure. If the liquid is released it very rapidly turns into gas, which is heavier than air, and the heat needed chills anything that the liquid contacts. If refrigerant is spilled on the skin the treatment is the same as that for chilblains. Goggles should be worn to protect the eyes but if refrigerant does get into the eye it should be washed out with a few drops of sterile mineral oil followed by liberal use of weak boric acid solution. A doctor should be contacted immediately. The system should not be discharged in a closed space, particularly not near a garage pit, as the vapour will displace the air and though it is not toxic in itself there will be reduced oxygen and asphyxiation can therefore result. Do not carry out welding or steam cleaning operations near the system as the heat can cause the internal pressure to rise dangerously.

A sight glass, shown in **FIG 25,** should be used to check the refrigerant level. Set the belt tension (see **Chapter 4**) and with the engine running set the air conditioning to full cold. Watch the sight glass and if the system is either completely full or empty no bubbles will be seen. Check that the air into the car is being cooled, in which case the system is full. **If the system does not cool the air then it is empty and the system should be switched off to prevent damage to the compressor.**

At yearly intervals the oil level in the compressor should be checked. The compressor must be depressurized for this operation.

Any work involving the air conditioning system should be carried out at a service agent where trained personnel will work on the system.

TECHNICAL DATA

Unless otherwise stated the dimensions are given in millimetres and inches. The first figure being millimetres and the figure in brackets being inches, the metric figures are the official accurate ones and should be used in preference.

NOTE: If the owner choses to use the data that was converted from the official metric figures it is recommended that the converted figure is checked for absolute accuracy.

ENGINE

Type	6-cylinder in-line, OHV with single overhead camshaft. Water cooled with air oil cooler
Compression ratio:	
Standard:	
280 S/8	9.0:1
Remainder	9.5:1
Low compression	7.8:1
Cubic capacity	2778 cc
Firing order	1–5–3–6–2–4
Bore (nominal)	86.5 (3.406)
Stroke	78.8 (3.102)
Valve clearance	Engine cold
Inlet	.08 (.003)
Exhaust	.20 (.008)
Compression test pressure	Engine hot and throttle wide open
280 S/8 standard:	
Normal	10 to 11 kg/sq cm (142 to 156 lb/sq in)
Minimum	8.5 kg/sq cm (120 lb/sq in)
280 S/8 low compression:	
Normal	8.6 to 9.6 kg/sq cm (120 to 135 lb/sq in)
Minimum	7.2 kg/sq cm (103 lb/sq in)
Standard others:	
Normal	10 to 12 kg/sq cm (142 to 174 lb/sq in)
Minimum	8.5 kg/sq cm (120 lb/sq in)
Low compression others	As for 280 S/8
Maximum variation between cylinders	1.5 kg/sq cm (22 lb/sq in)
Crankshaft	7 main bearings, using renewable steel-backed bearing shells for all bearings
Cylinder bores:	
Standard diameter	86.500 to 86.522
Intermediate	86.750 to 86.772
First repair stage	87.000 to 87.022
Second repair stage	87.500 to 87.522
Piston play	.02 ±.01 (.0008 ±.0004)
Wear limits:	
Maximum wear	.10 (.004) across diameter
Out of round or conicity	.05 (.002)
Cylinder head:	
Height when new	84.8 to 85.0 (3.338 to 3.346)
Maximum stock removal	.8 (.032)
Maximum unevenness	.1 (.004) longitudinally 00 laterally
Valve seats	Renewable
Seat angle	45 degrees
Seat width	1.25 to 2.0 (.05 to .08)
Valve guides	Renewable

Crankcase:
- Height when new .. .. 213.1 to 213.2 (8.390 to 8.394)
- Minimum height 212.8 (8.379)
- Maximum unevenness .. .. .. .1 (.004) longitudinally
  .05 (.002) laterally

Chain tensioner spring:
- Part number 621.993.06.01
- Free length 78 (3.07)
- Text length .. .. 50 mm at 8.72 kg
- Fitted length .. .. 44 mm at 10.35 kg

Valve springs:

	280 SL/8		280 S/8, SE/8, SEL/8	
	Inner	Outer	Inner	Outer
Part No.	130.053.00.22	150.053.00.22	108.053.00.22	129.053.02.20
Outside diameter	22.2	30	22.2	33.2
Wire diameter	2.5	4.5	2.5	4.3
Free length	45	51	45	51
Test length	33 mm at 11.2 to 12.4 kg	42 mm at 34.5 kg	31 mm at 12.8 to 15.2 kg	39 mm at 36 kg
Fitted length	21.5 mm at 22.8 to 25.2 kg	30.5 mm at 85 kg	21 mm at 22.8 to 25.2 kg	30 mm at 67.7 to 76.3 kg

Valves:

All exhaust valves are sodium-cooled and care must be taken in disposing of them

	Inlet	Exhaust
Seat angle	45 deg.	45 deg.
Length	128	113.2
Head diameter	41.10 to 41.30	36.95 to 37.25
Valve stem diameter	8.970 to 8.955	10.940 to 10.918
Height of unmachined portion above seat:		
New	1.5 (.06)	2.8 (.11)
Minimum	1.0 (.04)	2.0 (.08)

Oil filter:
- Type .. .. FRAM CH-962 P.6
  Purolater PM.205 (USA—EP.178)

Oil pressure:
- Minimum .. .. .5 kg/sq cm (7 lb/sq in) at idle with engine hot. Must increase on acceleration

FUEL SYSTEM

Idling speeds: *Given in rev/min*
- 280 S/8 .. .. 800 to 900 manual shift, or automatic in N
- 280 S/8 .. .. 650 to 700 automatic in drive selection
- All others .. .. 700 to 800 manual shift, or automatic in N
- All others .. .. 700 with automatic in drive selection

Fuel pump for carburetters:
- Type .. .. APG diaphragm pump, mechanically operated
- Delivery pressure:
  - At starter speed .. .. .. .12 to .18 kg/sq cm (1.75 to 2.5 lb/sq in)
  - At idle speed .. .. .. .18 to .24 kg/sq cm (2.5 to 3.5 lb/sq in)
- Vacuum at starter speed .. .. .3 to .4 kg/sq cm (4.3 to 5.7 lb/sq in)

Fuel pump for fuel injection:
- Type .. .. Centrifugal, electrically driven
- Checked with engine stopped and minimum supply voltage of 11 volts
- Delivery pressure: *Measured in front of starting valve*
  - Line open .. .. .. .8 to 1.1 kg/sq cm (11.5 to 15.6 lb/sq in)
  - Return line closed .. .. Minimum 1.3 kg/sq cm (18.5 lb/sq in)
- Delivery capacity .. .. .. 1 litre in 15 seconds

Carburetter jets:	Primary	Secondary
Air horn K	24	28
Main jet Gg*	x 120	x 120
Air correction jet a	100**	110
Mixing tube s	4S	4N
Idling speed fuel jet g	45	—
Transition fuel jet	—	80
Idling speed air hole	1.3 mm	—
Transition air hole	—	1.0 mm
Injection quantity	.7 to 1.0 cc per stroke	—
Float needle valve	2.0	
Float weight	8.5 grammes	
Float adjustment	21 to 23 mm	
Fuel return valve adjustment	2000 rev/min	

* Main jets USA versions x 115 primary and x 125 secondary also applies to models for Sweden 1971 and on

** 90 on models for Sweden 1971 and onwards

IGNITION

Firing order 1-5-3-6-2-4

Type .. .. Normal but transistorized ignition can also be fitted

Dwell angle and contact gap:

	Standard	Transistorized
New contacts	40 ±1 deg.	30 ±1 deg.
Used contacts	35 $^{+4}_{-2}$ deg.	33 $^{+4}_{-2}$ deg.
Wear limit	32 deg.	38 deg.
Gap	.3 mm (.012 inch)	.4 mm (.016 inch)

Timing data:

Standard engines and emission control engines version 1968–69.

On these models the setting figure for stroboscopic timing is taken at 4500 rev/min with vacuum disconnected.

	Setting figure	Static		Test figures		
Engine speed	4500	Starter speed	Idling speed	1500	3000	4500
Vacuum	Without	Without	With or without	Without	With	With
Standard carburetter	**35 deg.**	2 BTDC	3 to 12 without	18 to 25	23 to 29	42 to 48
Fuel injection	**30 deg.**	8 BTDC	2 ±1 with	12 to 19	30	—
Low compression carb	**37 deg**	4 BTDC	5 to 14 without	20 to 27	25 to 31	44 to 50
Fuel injection	**30 deg**	8 BTDC	2 ±1 ATDC with	12 to 19	30	—
Emission control carb	**37 deg**	TDC	19 to 28 without	19 to 28	29 to 35	44 to 50
Fuel injection	**30 deg**	8 BTDC	2 ±1 ATDC with	12 to 19	30	—

USA models with emission control as from 1970 are set stroboscopically at 800 rev/min with the vacuum connected and ATDC

Engine speed	800	Starter speed	1500	3000	4500	4500
Vacuum	With	Without	With	With	Without	With
Carburetters	**4 ATDC**	6 BTDC	1 to 9	31 to 39	33 to 37	41 to 49
Fuel injection	**8 ATDC**	10 BTDC	0 to 5	25 to 30	—	—

COOLING SYSTEM

Normal operating temperature .. .. 70°C to 95°C

Filler cap .. .. Stamped 100, releases at 1 kg/sq cm (15 lb/sq in)

Capacity .. .. 10.6 litres, 2.4 Imp galls, 2.9 US galls

Inhibitor* .. .. Castrol 7016, Gulfcut Soluble Oil, Houghton Phosphatal, Mobil Solvac, Shell Donax C

Quantity of inhibitor .. .. .. 2.5 to 5 cc per litre (.7 to 1.5 cu/in per gall)
Antifreeze* .. .. BP Anti-Frost, Caltex Antofreeze, Castrol Antifreeze, Gulf Antifreeze and Summer Coolant

Quantity of antifreeze required to give protection:
Figure given is litres, figure in bracket is Imp. pints

14°F	—4°F	—22°F	—40°F
—10°C	—20°C	—30°C	—40°C
2.25 (4)	3.5 (6.2)	4.7 (8.4)	5.5 (9.7)

* Not full lists of all recommended but does give those that are generally available

CLUTCH

Operation .. .. Hydraulic
Hydraulic fluid .. .. Must at least meet specification SAE.70.R.3. Among recommended fluids are; ATE Blue, Lockheed HD.1, HD.12 or HD.31
Adjustment .. .. Self-adjusting (use gauge or check lever to check for wear)
Driven plate .. .. Fichtel and Sachs 228.TPD
   Part No. 002.250.16.03
Pressure plate .. .. Fichtel and Sachs M228.Sph
   Part No. 001.250.42.04

GEARBOX

Types:
  G.72 .. .. Early four-speed
  G.76/27 .. .. Later four-speed
  ZF.S.5-20 .. .. Early five-speed
  G.76/27-5 .. .. Later five-speed

Installation:
  All 280 S/8 and all other pre-1970 models .. G.72 as standard
    ZF.S.5-20 optional on all 280 S/8
  All models after May 1969, except S/8 .. G.76/27 as standard, G.76/27-5 as optional

Ratios:

Type	First	Second	Third	Fourth	Fifth	Reverse
G.72	4.05	2.23	1.40	1	—	3.58
G.76/27	3.96	2.34	1.43	1	—	3.72
ZF.S.5-20	3.92	2.215	1.418	1	.848	3.49
G.76/27-5	3.96	2.34	1.43	1	.875	3.72

AUTOMATIC TRANSMISSION

Type:
  Pre May 1969 .. .. K4A.025
  Post May 1969 .. .. KC4.025

Ratios: *K4A.025*   *K4C.025*

		K4A.025	K4C.025
First	Front and rear planetary gear trains	3.98	3.98
Second	Front, centre, rear planetary gear trains	2.52	2.39
Third	Rear planetary set	1.58	1.46
Fourth	Direct	1	1
Reverse	Front and rear planetary set	4.15	5.47

Shift speeds:

Given in kilometres/hr

Selector position	Accelerator position	1 to 2	2 to 1	2 to 3	3 to 2	3 to 4	4 to 3
K4A.025							
4	Idling	—	—	25	18	45	30
4	Full throttle	18	—	45	18	120	30
4	Kickdown	25	10	75	30	120	105
3	Idling	—	—	25	18	—	—
3	Full throttle	18	—	75	18	—	—
3	Kickdown	25	10	75	64	—	—
2	Idling	15	10	—	—	—	—
2	Full throttle	45	10	—	—	—	—
2	Kickdown	45	30	—	—	—	—
K4C.025							
4	Idling	9	—	27	20	37	28
4	Full throttle	25	5	51	20	120	45
4	Kickdown	25	16	51	42	120	125
3	Idling	9	—	32	27	—	—
3	Full throttle	25	5	71	34	—	—
3	Kickdown	26	16	71	60	—	—
2	Idling	35	5	—	—	—	—
2	Full throttle	35	19	—	—	—	—
2	Kickdown	35	30	—	—	—	—

REAR AXLE

Ratios:
  Standard:
    1st version 3.92
    2nd version 3.69
  USA versions, vehicles with 5-speed transmission, and those with 15 inch wheels:
    1st version 4.08
    2nd version 3.92
  Special versions 280 SL/8 .. .. .. 3.69

BRAKES

Type	Disc brakes on all four wheels—hydraulically operated. Mechanically operated Duo-Servo drum brakes on rear wheels only for parking
Hydraulic fluid	Must meet SAE.J.1703 specification
Adjustment:	
Disc brakes	Self-adjusting by pumping service brake pedal
Park brakes	One adjuster on each brake. Linkage can be adjusted separately but not for setting park brakes
Minimum pad lining thickness	2 (.08)
Thickness of brake disc:	
Front	12.6 (.496)
Rear	10 (.394)
Front minimum	11.6 (.457)
Rear minimum	9.4 (.370)
Calipers:	
Front	ATE.S2/57
Rear:	
1st version	ATE.M.42
2nd version	ATE.M.35

STEERING

Ratios through central position:
- Unit 19.9
- Overall 22.8

Steering unit part numbers:
- Lefthand drive 111.460.43.01
- Righthand drive 111.460.44.01

Lubricant:
- Mechanical steering .. .. .. 300 cc Hypoid transmission oil
- Optional power steering .. .. 1.5 litres ATF

ELECTRICAL SYSTEM

Polarity .. .. Negative earth
Voltage .. .. 12 volts
Starter motor:
- Type .. .. Bosch EF 12 volt 0.8 hp up to August 1968
  Bosch GF 12 volt 1.4 hp from August 1968

Test data:

	Current (amps)	Supply (volts)	Speed (rev/min)
EF 0.8:			
Free running	35 to 45	12	6400 to 7900
Loaded	165 to 200	9	1100 to 1450
Stalled	250 to 285	6	Held stationary
GF 1.4:			
Free running	50 to 70	12	9000 to 11,000
Loaded	290 to 330	9	1600 to 1800
Stalled	600 to 650	6	Held stationary

Battery:
- Capacity .. .. 55 Ah
- Acid level .. .. 5 mm above separators or acid level mark
  (note, separators are 10 mm above plates)

Alternator:
- Type .. .. Bosch K1 (RL) 14 volt 35 amp 20 or
  Bosch K1 (RL) 14 volt 55 amp 20
- Regulator .. .. RS/ADN 1/14 volt without radio suppressor
  RS/AD 1/14 volt without radio suppressor
- Alternator speed .. .. .. Engine speed x 1.95

Alternator output:

	Load current	Alternator speed
35 amp version	10	1300
	23	2000
	35	6000
55 amp version	10	1200
	36	2000
	55	6000

- Regulating voltage .. .. .. 13.9 to 14.8 volts at 28 to 30 amps

CAPACITIES

Automatic transmission:
- K4A.025 .. .. $4\frac{3}{4}$ litre — $8\frac{1}{4}$ Imp. pints — 10 US pints
- K4C.025 .. .. $5\frac{1}{2}$ litre — 9.7 Imp. pints — 11.6 US pints

Given from empty. Approximately 1 litre less for refill

Brakes .. .. Approximately .5 litre — 1 pint
Cooling system .. .. .. 10.6 litres — 2.4 Imp. galls — 2.9 US galls
Clutch .. .. Approximately .15 litre — .27 Imp. pint
  If common reservoir with brakes, approximately .8 litres for both systems

Engine:
  Crankcase only:
    Maximum $5\frac{1}{2}$ litres—9.7 Imp. pints—11.6 US pints
    Minimum $3\frac{1}{2}$ litres—$6\frac{1}{4}$ Imp. pints—$7\frac{1}{2}$ US pints
  Oil filter $\frac{1}{2}$ litre—.9 Imp. pint—1.1 US pint
  Oil cooler   .7 litre—$1\frac{1}{4}$ Imp. pint—$1\frac{1}{2}$ US pint

Fuel tank   82 litres—$18\frac{1}{2}$ Imp. galls—$22\frac{1}{4}$ US galls

Gearbox:
  G.72   1.4 litres—$2\frac{1}{2}$ Imp. pints—3 US pints
  G.76/27   1.8 litres—$3\frac{1}{4}$ Imp. pints—4 US pints
  Five-speed   2.5 litres—4 Imp. pints—5 US pints

Power steering   1.5 litres—$2\frac{1}{2}$ Imp. pints—3 US pints

Rear axle $2\frac{1}{2}$ litres—4 Imp. pints—5 US pints

Steering   .3 litre—$\frac{1}{2}$ Imp. pint—.6 US pint

Front hubs   65 to 80 grammes per hub

Inches			Decimals	Milli-metres	Inches to Millimetres		Millimetres to Inches	
					Inches	mm	mm	Inches
		1/64	.015625	.3969	.001	.0254	.01	.00039
	1/32		.03125	.7937	.002	.0508	.02	.00079
		3/64	.046875	1.1906	.003	.0762	.03	.00118
1/16			.0625	1.5875	.004	.1016	.04	.00157
		5/64	.078125	1.9844	.005	.1270	.05	.00197
	3/32		.09375	2.3812	.006	.1524	.06	.00236
		7/64	.109375	2.7781	.007	.1778	.07	.00276
1/8			.125	3.1750	.008	.2032	.08	.00315
		9/64	.140625	3.5719	.009	.2286	.09	.00354
	5/32		.15625	3.9687	.01	.254	.1	.00394
		11/64	.171875	4.3656	.02	.508	.2	.00787
3/16			.1875	4.7625	.03	.762	.3	.01181
		13/64	.203125	5.1594	.04	1.016	.4	.01575
	7/32		.21875	5.5562	.05	1.270	.5	.01969
		15/64	.234375	5.9531	.06	1.524	.6	.02362
1/4			.25	6.3500	.07	1.778	.7	.02756
		17/64	.265625	6.7469	.08	2.032	.8	.03150
	9/32		.28125	7.1437	.09	2.286	.9	.03543
		19/64	.296875	7.5406	.1	2.54	1	.03937
5/16			.3125	7.9375	.2	5.08	2	.07874
		21/64	.328125	8.3344	.3	7.62	3	.11811
	11/32		.34375	8.7312	.4	10.16	4	.15748
		23/64	.359375	9.1281	.5	12.70	5	.19685
3/8			.375	9.5250	.6	15.24	6	.23622
		25/64	.390625	9.9219	.7	17.78	7	.27559
	13/32		.40625	10.3187	.8	20.32	8	.31496
		27/64	.421875	10.7156	.9	22.86	9	.35433
7/16			.4375	11.1125	1	25.4	10	.39370
		29/64	.453125	11.5094	2	50.8	11	.43307
	15/32		.46875	11.9062	3	76.2	12	.47244
		31/64	.484375	12.3031	4	101.6	13	.51181
1/2			.5	12.7000	5	127.0	14	.55118
		33/64	.515625	13.0969	6	152.4	15	.59055
	17/32		.53125	13.4937	7	177.8	16	.62992
		35/64	.546875	13.8906	8	203.2	17	.66929
9/16			.5625	14.2875	9	228.6	18	.70866
		37/64	.578125	14.6844	10	254.0	19	.74803
	19/32		.59375	15.0812	11	279.4	20	.78740
		39/64	.609375	15.4781	12	304.8	21	.82677
5/8			.625	15.8750	13	330.2	22	.86614
		41/64	.640625	16.2719	14	355.6	23	.90551
	21/32		.65625	16.6687	15	381.0	24	.94488
		43/64	.671875	17.0656	16	406.4	25	.98425
11/16			.6875	17.4625	17	431.8	26	1.02362
		45/64	.703125	17.8594	18	457.2	27	1.06299
	23/32		.71875	18.2562	19	482.6	28	1.10236
		47/64	.734375	18.6531	20	508.0	29	1.14173
3/4			.75	19.0500	21	533.4	30	1.18110
		49/64	.765625	19.4469	22	558.8	31	1.22047
	25/32		.78125	19.8437	23	584.2	32	1.25984
		51/64	.796875	20.2406	24	609.6	33	1.29921
13/16			.8125	20.6375	25	635.0	34	1.33858
		53/64	.828125	21.0344	26	660.4	35	1.37795
	27/32		.84375	21.4312	27	685.8	36	1.41732
		55/64	.859375	21.8281	28	711.2	37	1.4567
7/8			.875	22.2250	29	736.6	38	1.4961
		57/64	.890625	22.6219	30	762.0	39	1.5354
	29/32		.90625	23.0187	31	787.4	40	1.5748
		59/64	.921875	23.4156	32	812.8	41	1.6142
15/16			.9375	23.8125	33	838.2	42	1.6535
		61/64	.953125	24.2094	34	863.6	43	1.6929
	31/32		.96875	24.6062	35	889.0	44	1.7323
		63/64	.984375	25.0031	36	914.4	45	1.7717

UNITS	Pints to Litres	Gallons to Litres	Litres to Pints	Litres to Gallons	Miles to Kilometres	Kilometres to Miles	Lbs. per sq. In. to Kg. per sq. Cm.	Kg. per sq. Cm. to Lbs. per sq. In.
1	.57	4.55	1.76	.22	1.61	.62	.07	14.22
2	1.14	9.09	3.52	.44	3.22	1.24	.14	28.50
3	1.70	13.64	5.28	.66	4.83	1.86	.21	42.67
4	2.27	18.18	7.04	.88	6.44	2.49	.28	56.89
5	2.84	22.73	8.80	1.10	8.05	3.11	.35	71.12
6	3.41	27.28	10.56	1.32	9.66	3.73	.42	85.34
7	3.98	31.82	12.32	1.54	11.27	4.35	.49	99.56
8	4.55	36.37	14.08	1.76	12.88	4.97	.56	113.79
9		40.91	15.84	1.98	14.48	5.59	.63	128.00
10		45.46	17.60	2.20	16.09	6.21	.70	142.23
20				4.40	32.19	12.43	1.41	284.47
30				6.60	48.28	18.64	2.11	426.70
40				8.80	64.37	24.85		
50					80.47	31.07		
60					96.56	37.28		
70					112.65	43.50		
80					128.75	49.71		
90					144.84	55.92		
100					160.93	62.14		

UNITS	Lb ft to kgm	Kgm to lb ft	UNITS	Lb ft to kgm	Kgm to lb ft
1	.138	7.233	7	.967	50.631
2	.276	14.466	8	1.106	57.864
3	.414	21.699	9	1.244	65.097
4	.553	28.932	10	1.382	72.330
5	.691	36.165	20	2.765	144.660
6	.829	43.398	30	4.147	216.990

TORQUE WRENCH SETTINGS

Engine

	lb f ft	Nm
Cylinder head bolts (cold)	72	100
(hot)	80	111
Rocker ball pivots	72	100
Connecting rod big-end cap bolts	44	61
Main bearing cap bolts	65	90
Flywheel bolts	28	39
Sump bolts	8	11
Spark plugs	25	35
Oil filter centre bolt	30	41
Oil cooler drain plug	18	25
Camshaft sprocket bolt	58	80
Fuel injection pipe unions	25	35
Crankshaft pulley bolt	150	207
Crankshaft damper socket screws	25	35
Engine rear plate bolts	36	50
Oil pump mounting bolts	36	50
Chain tensioner plug	42	58
Sump drain plug	30	41
Clutch or torque converter housing to engine	36	50
Driveplate to torque converter bolts	25	35

Fuel

	lb f ft	Nm
Fuel injection valves to cylinder head	25	35
Fuel injection pressure valve (Stage 1)	29	40
(Stage 2)	25	35
Carburettor mounting nuts	15	21

Clutch

	lb f ft	Nm
Clutch bellhousing bolts to engine	36	50
Clutch pressure plate cover bolts	25	35
Clutch slave cylinder bolts	22	30
Clutch master cylinder bolts	26	36

Manual Transmission

	lb f ft	Nm
Output flange nut	108	150
Drain and filler plug	43	60
Side cover bolts	11	15
Front cover bolts	11	15
Rear cover bolts (large)	32	45
Rear cover bolts (small)	11	15
Countershaft front and rear nuts	108	150
Mainshaft front nut	58	80
Clutch bellhousing to engine bolts	36	50

Automatic Transmission

	lb f ft	Nm
Drive plate to torque converter bolts	25	35
Output flange nut	87	120
Oil pan bolts	5	7
Torque converter housing to engine bolts	36	50

Propeller Shaft

	lb f ft	Nm
Intermediate bearing carrier bolts	15	21
Sliding sleeve nut	22 to 28	30 to 39
Flexible coupling plate self-locking nuts	30	41
Coupling flange bolts to rear axle drive pinion	32	44

Rear Axle

	lb f ft	Nm
Enclosed type axleshafts		
Differential suspension carrier upper mounting bolt	87	120
Differential suspension carrier mounting plate bolts to floor pan	32	45
Locating strut to bodyframe nuts	65	90
Locating strut bolts to differential housing	144	200
Front plate to differential housing bolts	25	35
Universal joint to side gear of differential	47	65
Left-hand axle tube to differential bolts	36	50
Differential carrier pivot bolt pinch bolt	87	120
Brake backplate bolts	18	25
Axleshaft bearing ring nut	144	200
Open type axleshafts		
Flexible mounting to differential end cover	94	130
Flexible mounting (rear) to floor pan	18	25
Front flexible mounting plate to floor pan	29	40
Front flexible mounting to differential carrier	87	120
Axleshaft to flange bolt	69	95
Differential end cover bolts	32	45

Brakes

	lb f ft	Nm
Front disc to hub bolts	82	113
Caliper securing bolts	82	113
Master cylinder mounting nuts	15	21
Fluid line unions	12	16
Master cylinder stop bolt	6	8
Vacuum line union to servo unit	22	30

Suspension & Steering

	lb f ft	Nm

Cars with king pin and bush type stub axle carrier and enclosed type axleshafts

Front suspension

	lb f ft	Nm
Shock absorber lower mounting bolt	18	25
Crossmember flexible mounting bolt	72	100
Upper control arm pivot to crossmember bolts	72	100
Lower control arm pivot to crossmember bolts	94	130
Stabiliser bar leaf springs to bodyframe	87	120
Stabiliser bar flexible mounting clamps	18	25
Control arm threaded pivot bushes	130	180
King pin lower nut	65	90
Lateral positioning rod bolts	44	60
Lower control arm to stub axle carrier bolt	130	180
Upper control arm cam bolt	32	45

Cars with king pin and bush type stub axle carrier and enclosed type axleshafts (continued)

	lb f ft	Nm
Rear suspension		
Shock absorber lower mounting bolt	32	45
Rear axle compensating spring right-hand carrier	87	120
Rear axle hydro-pneumatic strut left-hand balljoint	58	80
Rear axle hydro-pneumatic strut right-hand balljoint	87	120
Steering		
Steering box to bodyframe	43	60
Steering drop arm nut	144	200
Idler arm shaft self-locking nut	87	120
Track rod end and drag rod balljoint nuts	25	35
Steering coupling pinch bolts	18	25
Steering wheel to shaft nut	36	50
Steering wheel to hub (boss) nut	11	15
Roadwheels		
Roadwheel bolts	72	100

Cars with swivel balljoint type stub axle carriers and open type axleshafts

Torque wrench settings as foregoing except for:

	lb f ft	Nm
Lower control arm bearing cam bolts	87	120
Upper control arm bearing bolts	44	60
Front wheel bearing clamp pinch bolt	10	14
Steering arm to stub axle carrier bolts	58	80
Upper and lower control arm swivel balljoint nuts	58	80
Suspension rear link to rear axle carrier	87	120

Lubrication points—280SL/8 engine and running gear.

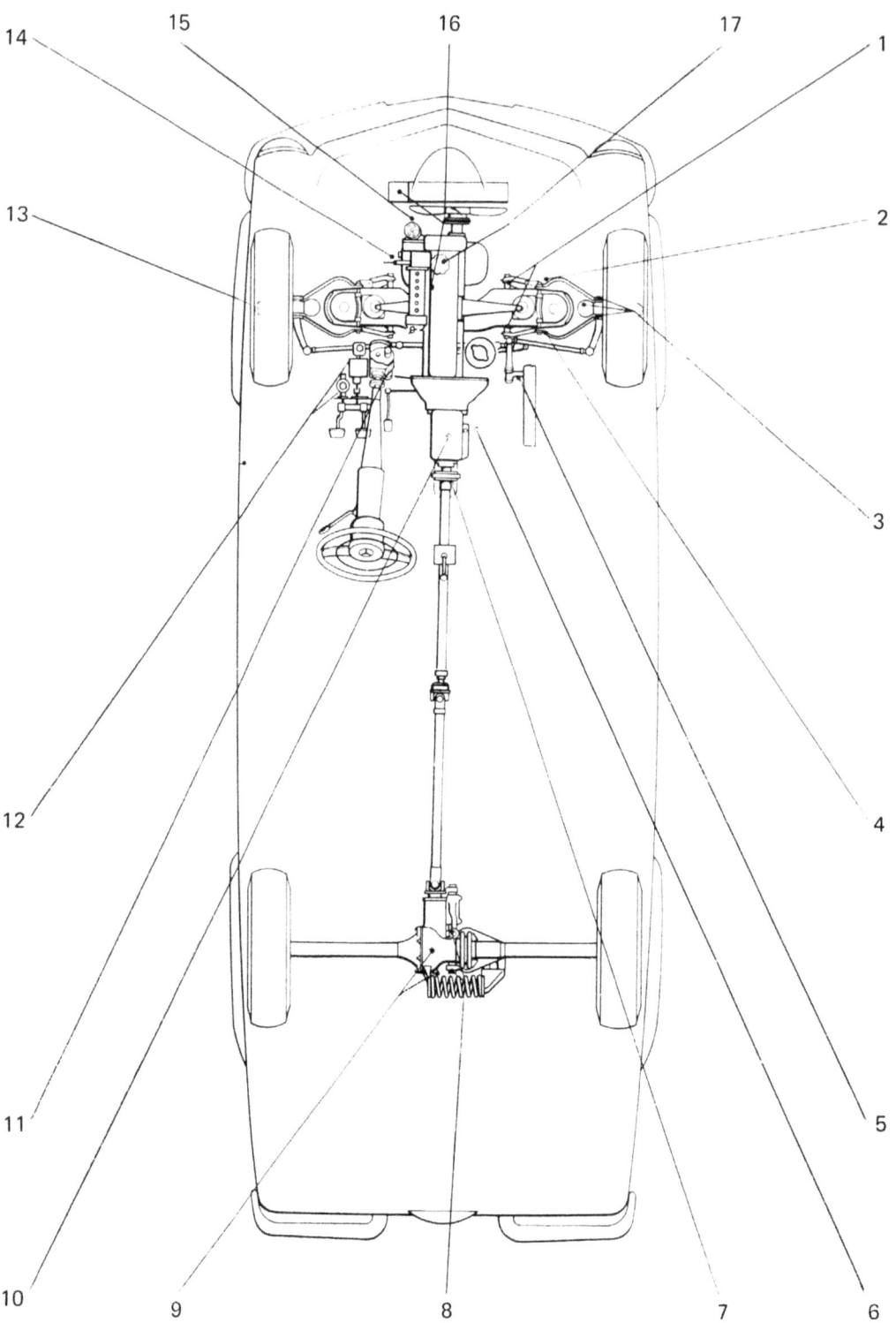

1. Lower wishbone—right and left
2. Front upper wishbone—right and left
3. King pin—right and left
4. Rear, upper wishbone—right and left
5. Intermediate steering arm (unless sealed)
6. Manual transmission oil fill plug
7. Front universal
8. Rear axle grease fittings
9. Rear axle oil drain and fill plugs
10. Manual transmission oil drain plug
11. Steering box oil fill plug
12. Brake and clutch reservoirs
13. Front wheel bearings
14. Engine oil dipstick
15. Distributor felt
16. Crankcase drain plug and oil cooler drain plug
17. Engine oil fill cap

Lubrication points—280SL/8 engine and running gear.

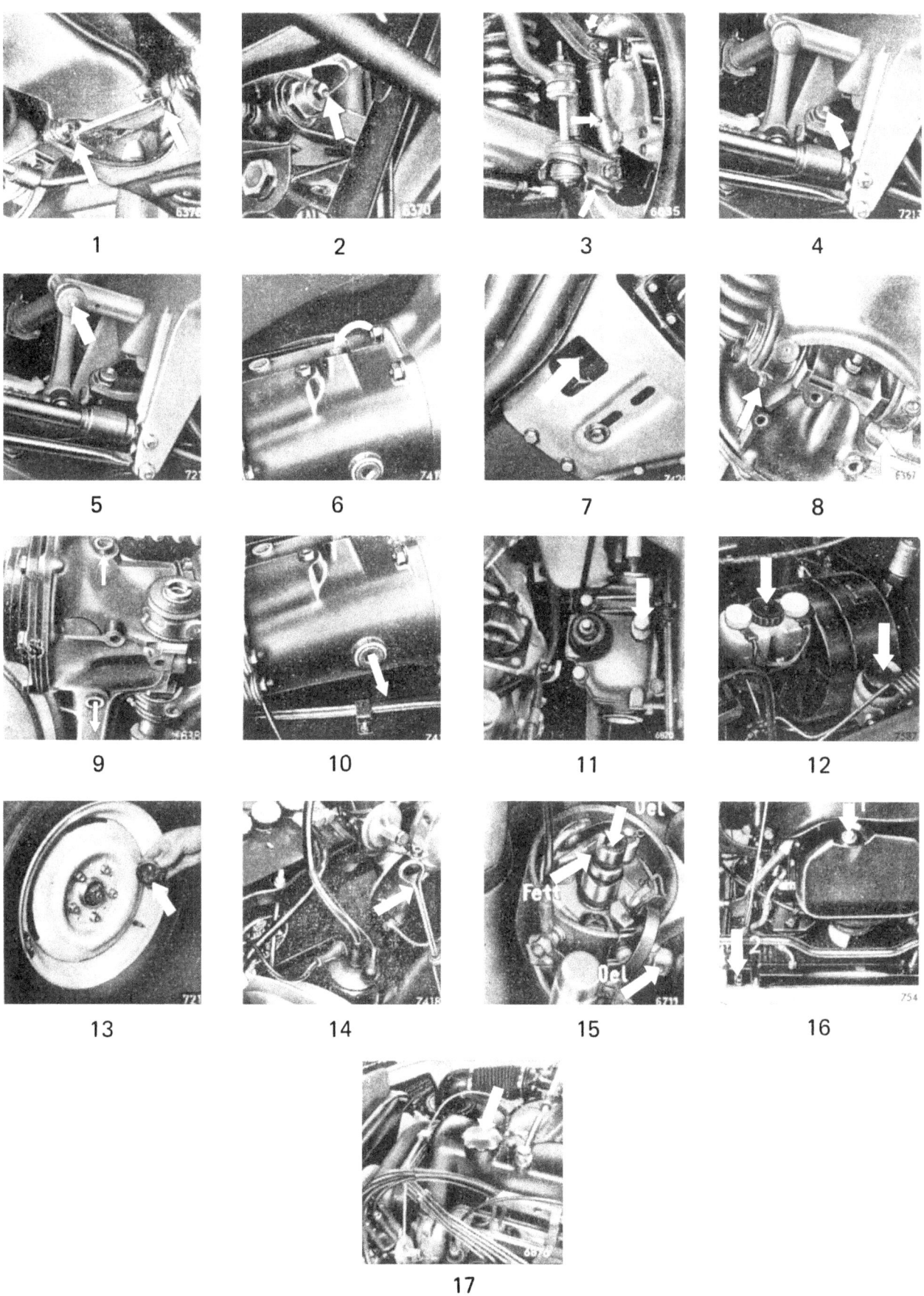

Lubrication points—280S/8, 280SE/8, 280SEC/8 engine and running gear.

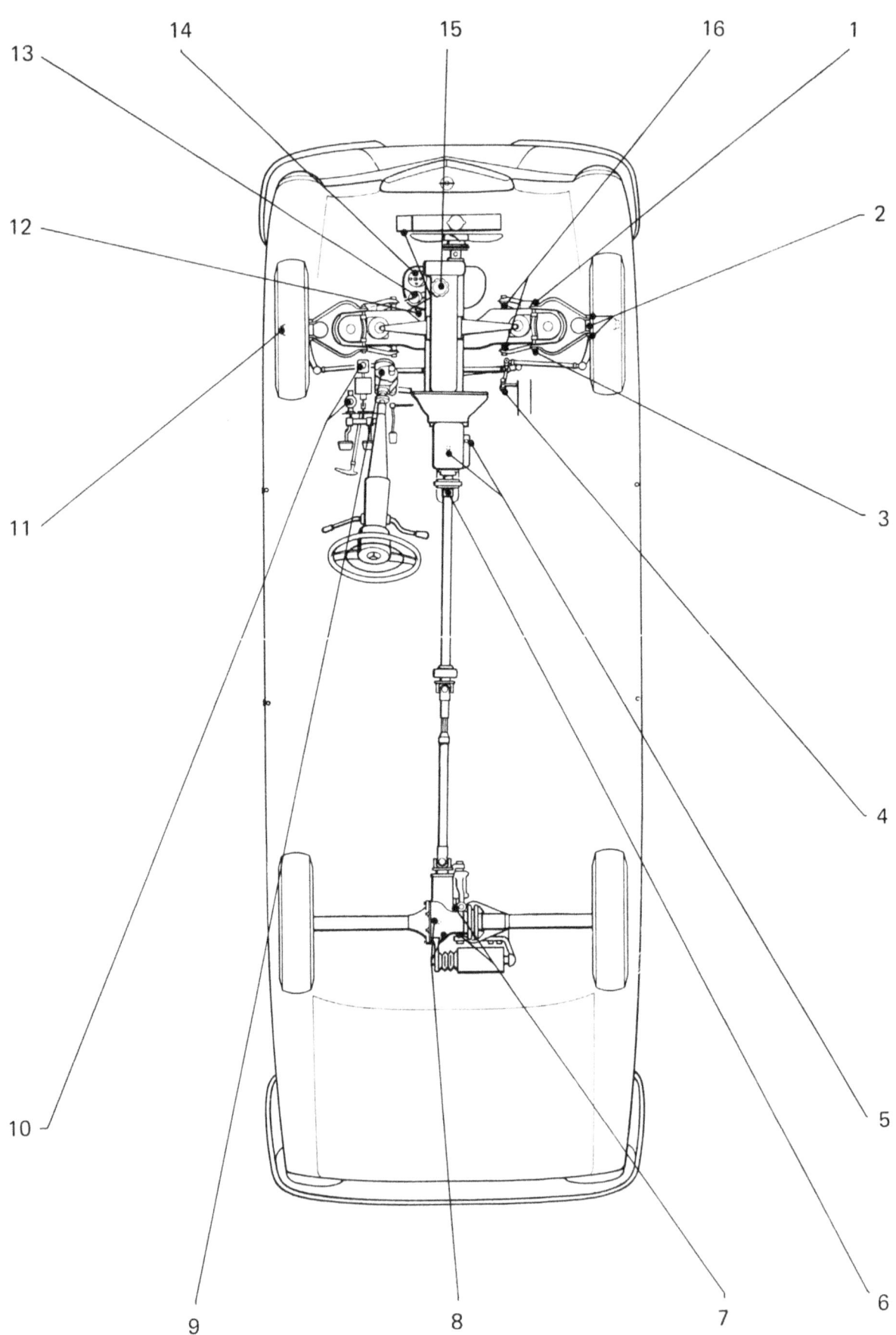

Lubrication points—280S/8, 280SE/8, 280SEC/8 engine and running gear.

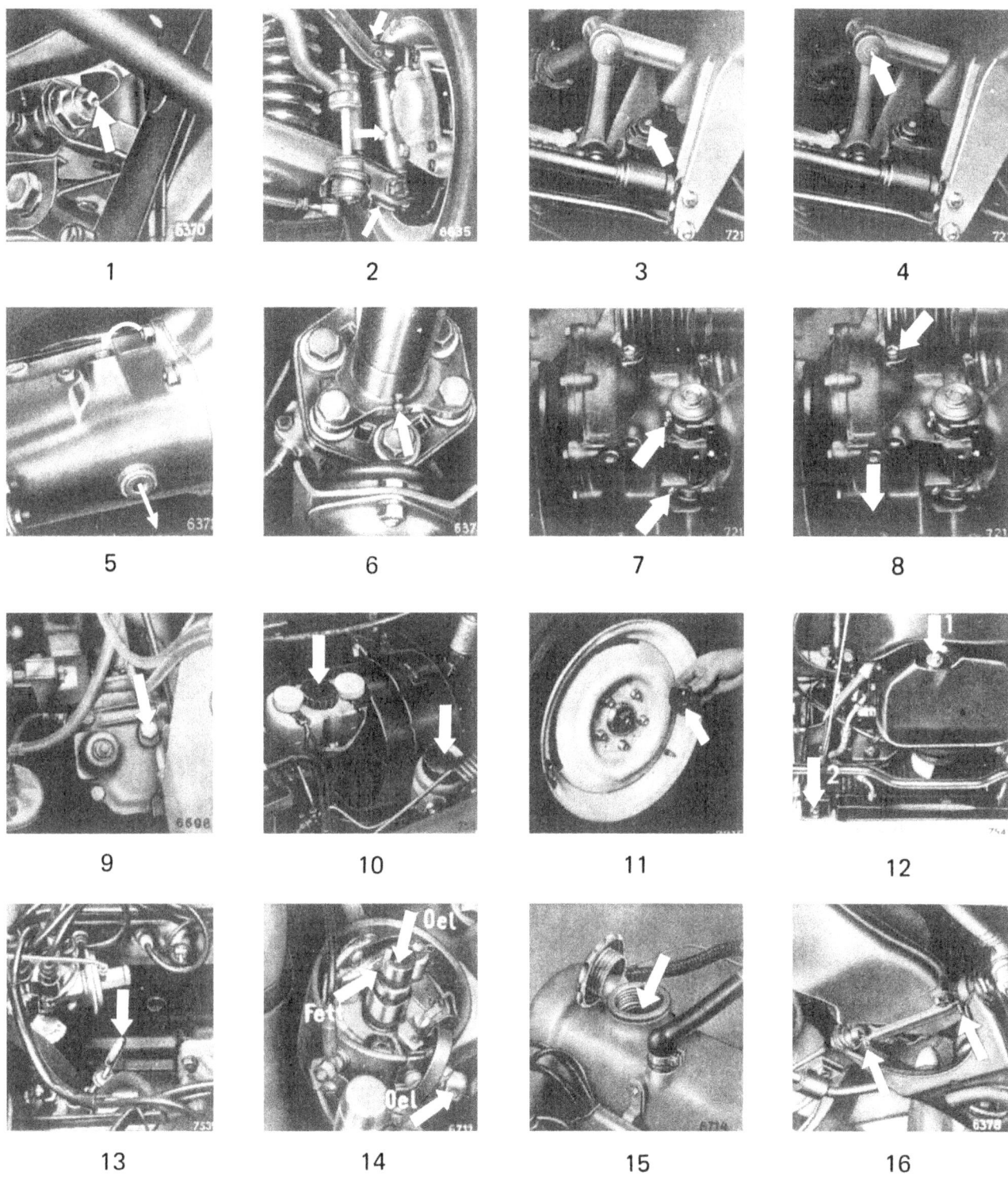

1. Front, upper wishbone—right and left
2. Steering knuckle—right and left
3. Rear, upper wishbone—right and left
4. Intermediate steering rod bearing
5. Manual transmission oil drain and fill plugs
6. Front universal
7. Rear axle grease fittings
8. Rear axle oil drain and fill plugs
9. Steering box oil fill plug
10. Brake and clutch reservoirs
11. Front wheel bearings
12. Crankcase oil drain plug and oil cooler drain plug
13. Engine oil dipstick
14. Distributor cam felt
15. Oil filler cap
16. Front, lower wishbone—right and left

280SL with transistorized ignition

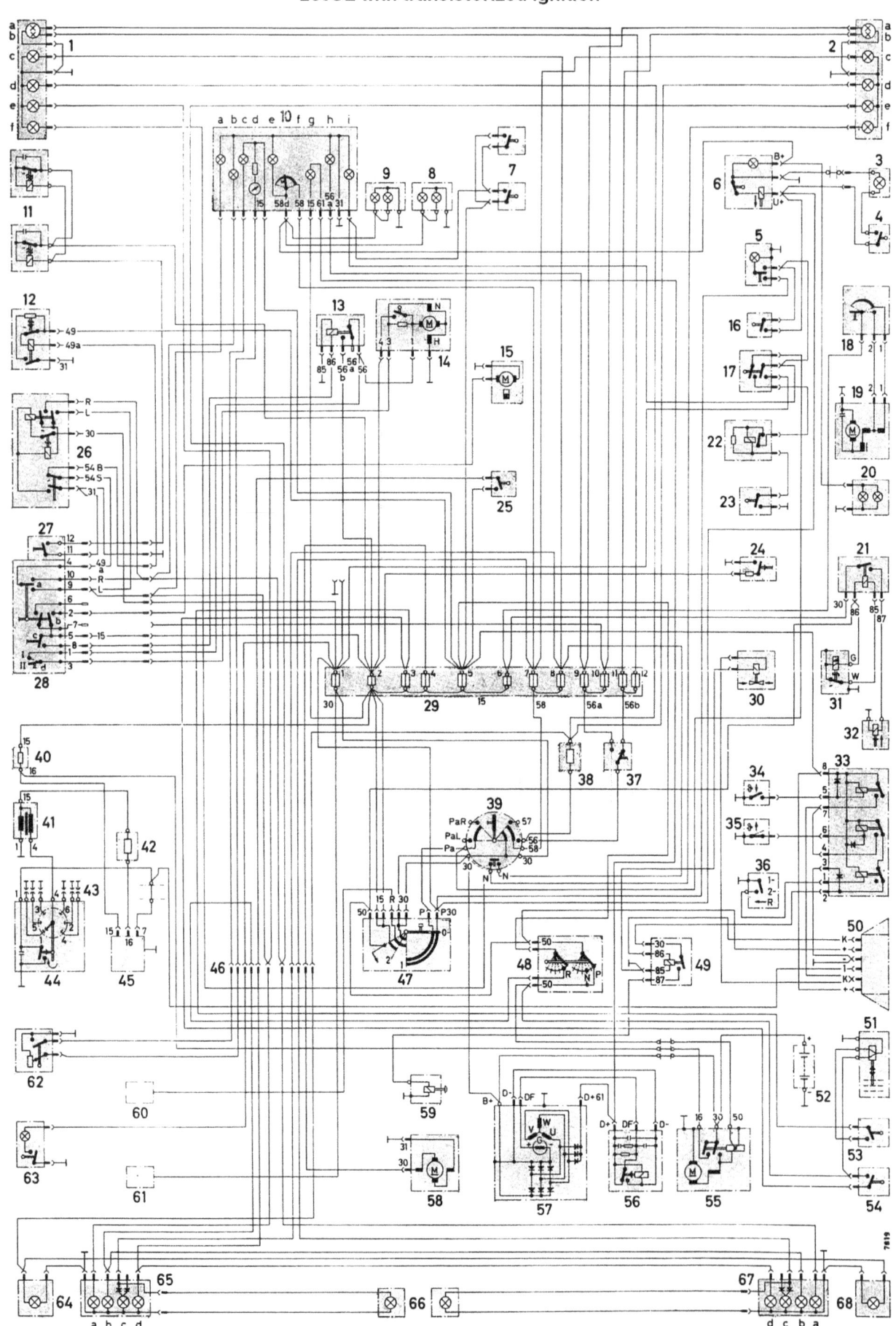

280SL with transistorized ignition

1	Light assembly (left side)	29	Fuses
2	Light assembly (right side)	30	Two-way valve
a	High beam	31	Thermotime switch
b	Low beam	32	Magneto for starter valve
c	Parking light	33	Relay box
d	Side marker lights	34	Thermo switch 100° C
e	Turn signal light	35	Thermo switch 17° C
f	Fog light	36	Hydraulic switch
3	Glove compartment and reading light	37	Dimmer switch
4	Switch for glove compartment light	38	Fuse box for side marker lights
5	Entrance light and switch	39	Headlight switch
6	Electric clock	40	Series resistance 0,4 Ω
7	Brake fluid level warning light control element	41	Ignition coil
8	Speedometer light	42	Series resistance 0,6 Ω
9	Revolution counter light	43	Spark plugs
10	Instrument cluster	44	Distributor
a	Turn signal light indicator, left	45	Switched unit for transistorized ignition
b	Turn signal light indicator, right	46	Plug connection for rear light wiring harness
c	Low fuel level warning light	47	Ignition starter switch
d	Fuel gauge	48	Starting lock and back-up light switch
e	Instrument lighting	49	Contact breaker relay
f	Instrument lighting rheostat	50	R. P. M. switch
g	Alternator charge control light	51	Idle increase solenoid
h	High beam indicator	52	Battery
i	Brake fluid level control light	53	Kick-down switch
11	Dual tone horns	54	Venturi control unit switch
12	Sending unit for turn signal light	55	Starter
13	Relay for wiper motor	56	Voltage regulator
14	Windshield wiper motor	57	Alternator
15	Windshield washer pump	58	Fuel feed pump
16	Door contact switch, right	59	Shut-off solenoid
17	Door contact switch, left	60	Radio (optional)
18	Heater blower switch	61	Antenna (optional)
19	Heater blower motor	62	Fuel gauge sending unit
20	Lighting of heater control levers	63	Trunk light
21	Relay for starter valve	64	Side marker lights (left side)
22	Warning buzzer	65	Rear light unit (left side)
23	Theft protection warning buzzer switch on steering lock	a	Turn signal light
		b	Back-up light
24	Cigar lighter	c	Tail light and side light
25	Stop light switch	d	Stop light
26	Hazard warning light transmitter	66	License plate light
27	Horn ring	67	Rear light unit (right side)
28	Combination switch	a	Turn signal light
a	Turn signal light switch	b	Back-up light
b	Windshield washer switch	c	Tail light and side light
c	Windshield wiper switch	d	Stop light
d	Windshield wiper speed control switch	68	Side marker lights (right side)

Wiring diagram 280SL/8 (fuel injection)

1	Lighting unit, right
2	Lighting unit, left
a	High beam
b	Low beam
c	Blinker light
d	Parking light
e	Fog light
f	Side light
3	Glove compartment and reading light
4	Switch for glove compartment light
5	Heater blower switch
6	Electric clock
7	Entrance light and switch
8	Speedometer light
9	Revolution counter light
10	Instrument cluster
a	Blinker control light, left
b	Blinker control light, right
c	Fuel reserve warning
d	Fuel level indicator
e	Instrument light
f	Regulating resistor for lighting
g	Charging control light
h	High beam control light
i	Parking brake and brake fluid level warning light
11	Dual tone horns
12	Heater blower motor
13	Lighting, heating control
14	Door contact switch, right
15	Door contact switch, left
16	Windshield wiper motor
17	Relay for wiper motor
18	Direction signal transmitter
19	Luggage boot light
20	Relay for starter valve
21	Relay for rich mixture
22	Windshield washer pump
23	Brake light switch
24	Back-up light switch
25	Cigarette lighter
26	Horn ring
27	Socket
28	Fuses
29	Combination switch
a	Blinker switch
b	Headlight flasher switch
c	Windshield washer switch
d	Windshield wiper switch
e	Switch for wiper speed
f	Plug connection, steering column switch
30	Series resistance
31	Electromagnetic starter valve
32	Thermo time switch
33	Solenoid for rich mixture

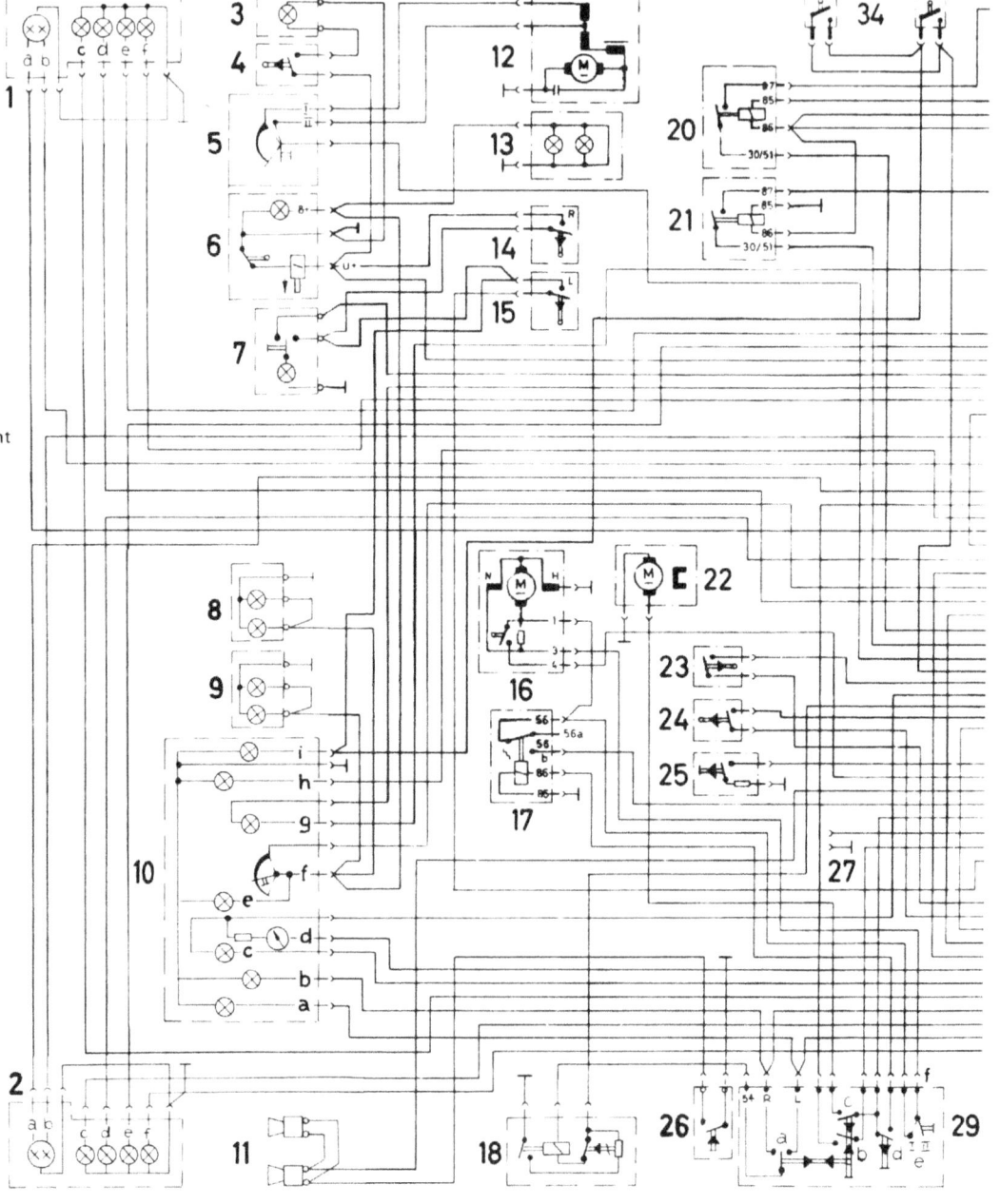

Wiring diagram 280SL/8 (fuel injection)

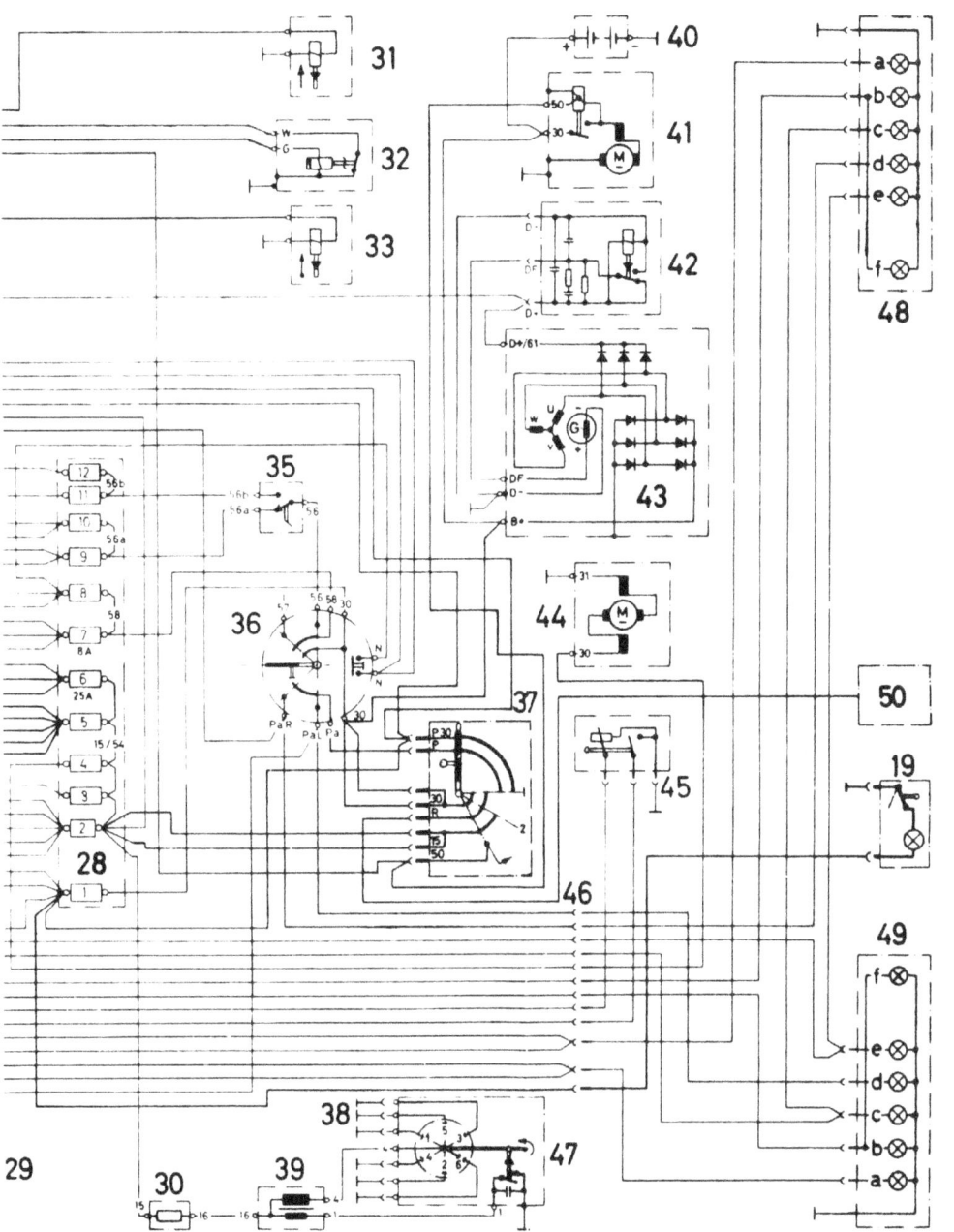

34	Brake fluid level warning light control element
35	Dimmer switch
36	Rotary light switch
37	Ignition starter switch
38	Spark plugs
39	Ignition coil
40	Battery
41	Starter
42	Voltage regulator
43	Generator
44	Fuel feed pump
45	Transmitter for fuel gauge
46	Plug connection tail light leads
47	Distributor
48	Tail light, right
49	Tail light, left
a	Flasher light
b	Tail light
c	Back-up light
d	Side light
e	Brake light
f	License plate light
50	Radio (optional)

Wiring colour code

bl	=	blue
br	=	brown
el	=	ivory
ge	=	yellow
gn	=	green
gr	=	grey
nf	=	natural
rs	=	pink
rt	=	red
sw	=	black
vi	=	violet
ws	=	white

Example:
Wire designation 1.5 gr/rt
Basic colour gr - grey
Identification colour rt = red
Wire cross section 1.5 = 1.5 mm^2

Wiring diagram 280S/8 (carburettor)

1	Light assembly, left
a	Main beam
b	Dipped beam
c	Turn signal light
d	Parking light and side light
e	Fog light
2	Light assembly, right
a	Main beam
b	Dipped beam
c	Turn signal light
d	Parking light and side light
e	Fog light
3	Supplementary fan
4	Supplementary fan relay
5	Brake fluid control switch
6	Parking brake indicator light
7	Combined instrument
a	Turn signal indicator, left
b	Turn signal indicator, right
c	Fuel reserve warning light
d	Fuel gauge
e	Electric clock
f	Instrument lighting rheostat
g	Instrument lighting
h	Charging indicator light
i	Main beam indicator
k	Service and parking brake indicator light
8	Horn two-tone
9	Series resistor for blower motor
10	Blower motor (air intake)
11	Control unit, lighting (heating and ventilation)
12	Blower switch (air intake)
13	Wiper motor
14	Foot-operated windscreen washer pump
15	Glove compartment light switch
16	Glove compartment light
17	Thermostatic switch 212°F (100°C)
18	Solenoid valve on automatic transmission
19	Auxiliary fuse box for electric blower
20	Thermostatic switch, desiccator
21	Cigar lighter
22	Hazard warning flasher (electr.)
23	Horn ring
24	Combination switch
a	Turn signal switch
b	Headlight flasher switch
c	Hand dipper switch
d	Windscreen wiper switch
e	Windscreen wiper speed switch
25	Carburettor heater socket, rear
26	Exhaust emission control relay
27	Thermostatic switch 149°F (65°C)
28	Stop light switch
29	Fuses
30	Kickdown switch
31	Starter lock-out and reversing light switch
32	Carburettor heater socket, front
33	Blower switch (air conditioner)
34	Electro-magnetic coupling of air conditioner compressor
35	Air conditioner relay
36	Blower motor
37	Auxiliary fuse box for air conditioner
38	Temperature switch
39	Lighting turn switch
40	Starter/ignition switch

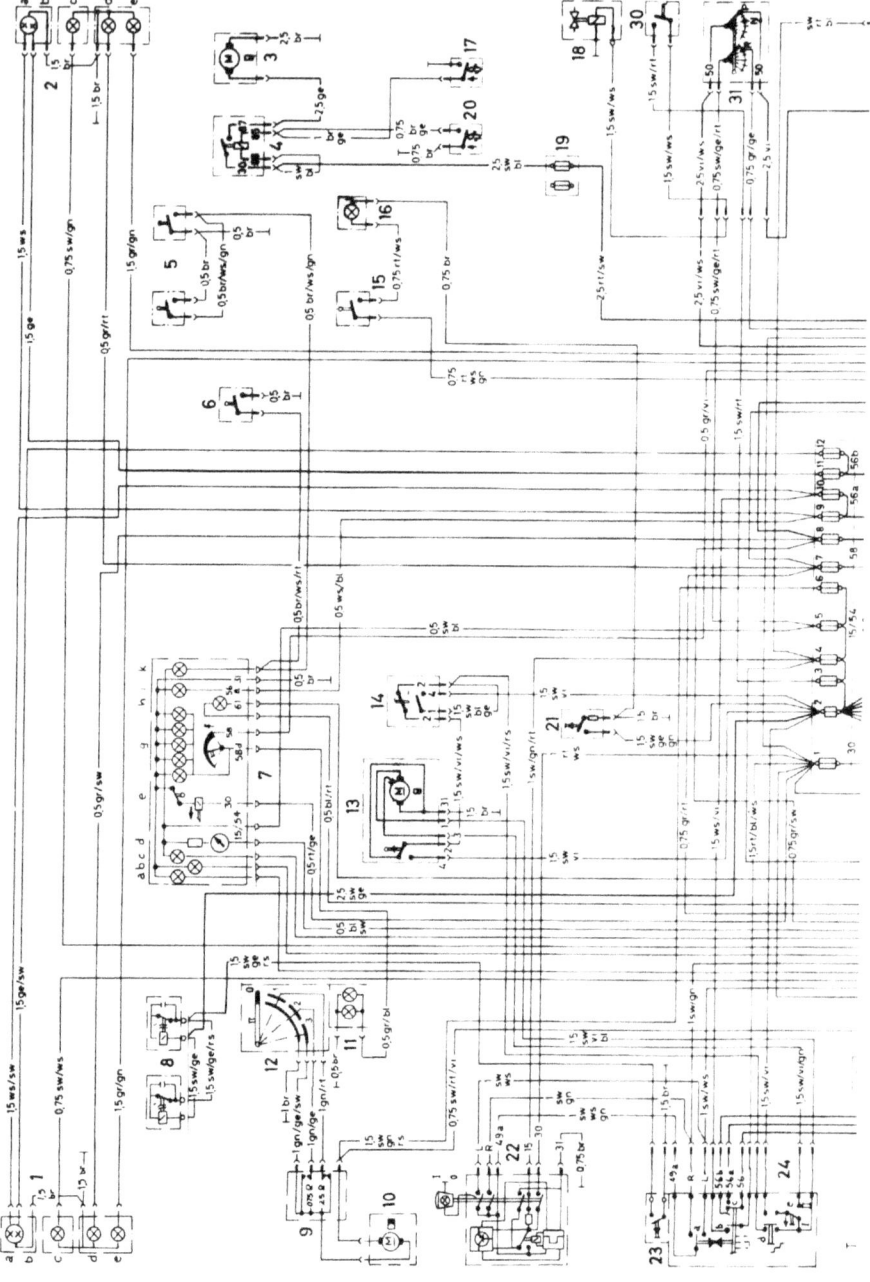

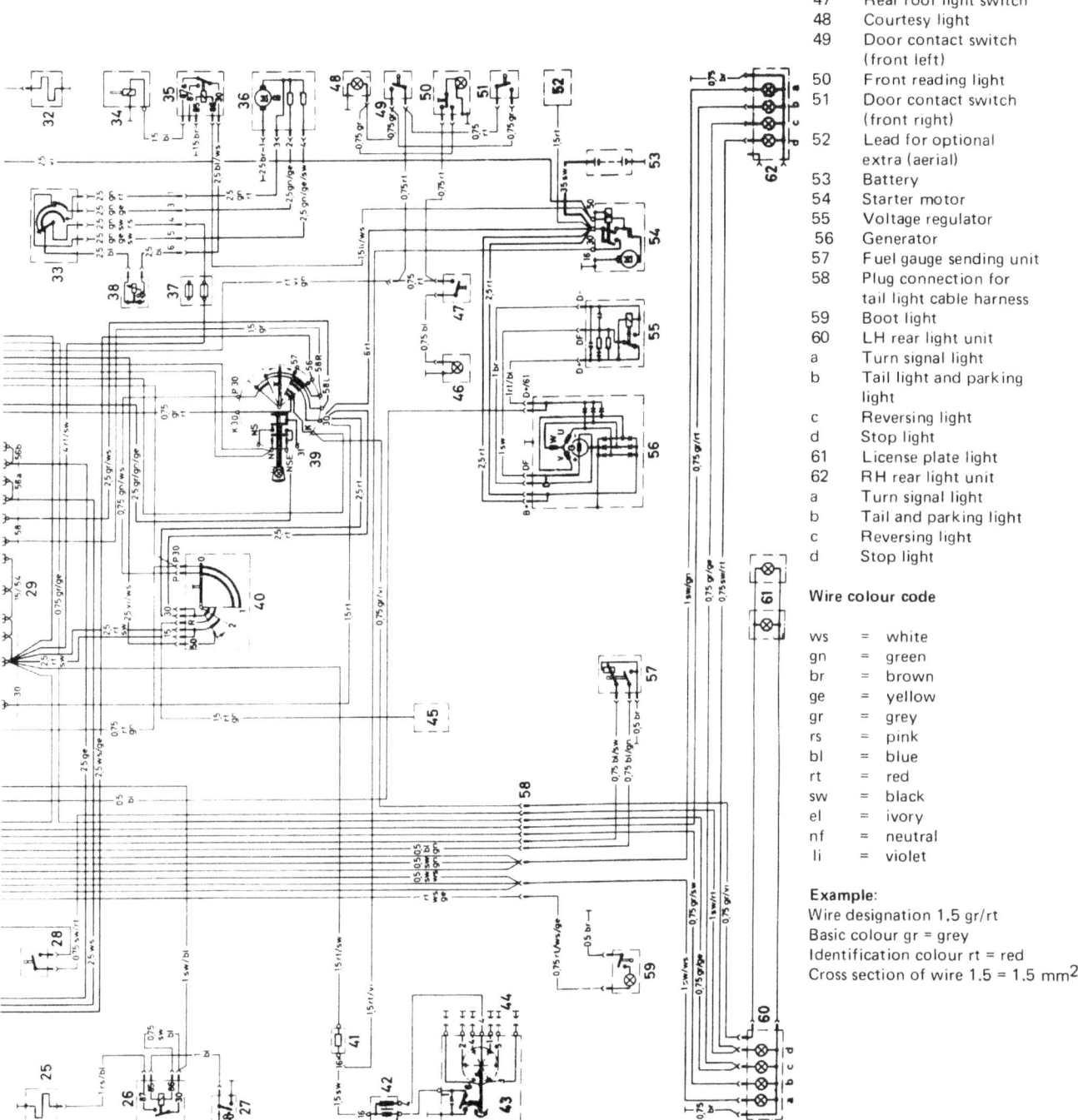

Wiring diagram 280S/8 (carburettor)

41	Series resistor
42	Ignition coil
43	Distributor
44	Spark plugs
45	Lead for optional extra (radio)
46	Rear roof light
47	Rear roof light switch
48	Courtesy light
49	Door contact switch (front left)
50	Front reading light
51	Door contact switch (front right)
52	Lead for optional extra (aerial)
53	Battery
54	Starter motor
55	Voltage regulator
56	Generator
57	Fuel gauge sending unit
58	Plug connection for tail light cable harness
59	Boot light
60	LH rear light unit
a	Turn signal light
b	Tail light and parking light
c	Reversing light
d	Stop light
61	License plate light
62	RH rear light unit
a	Turn signal light
b	Tail and parking light
c	Reversing light
d	Stop light

Wire colour code

ws	=	white
gn	=	green
br	=	brown
ge	=	yellow
gr	=	grey
rs	=	pink
bl	=	blue
rt	=	red
sw	=	black
el	=	ivory
nf	=	neutral
li	=	violet

Example:
Wire designation 1,5 gr/rt
Basic colour gr = grey
Identification colour rt = red
Cross section of wire 1,5 = 1,5 mm^2

Wiring diagram 280S (carburettor)

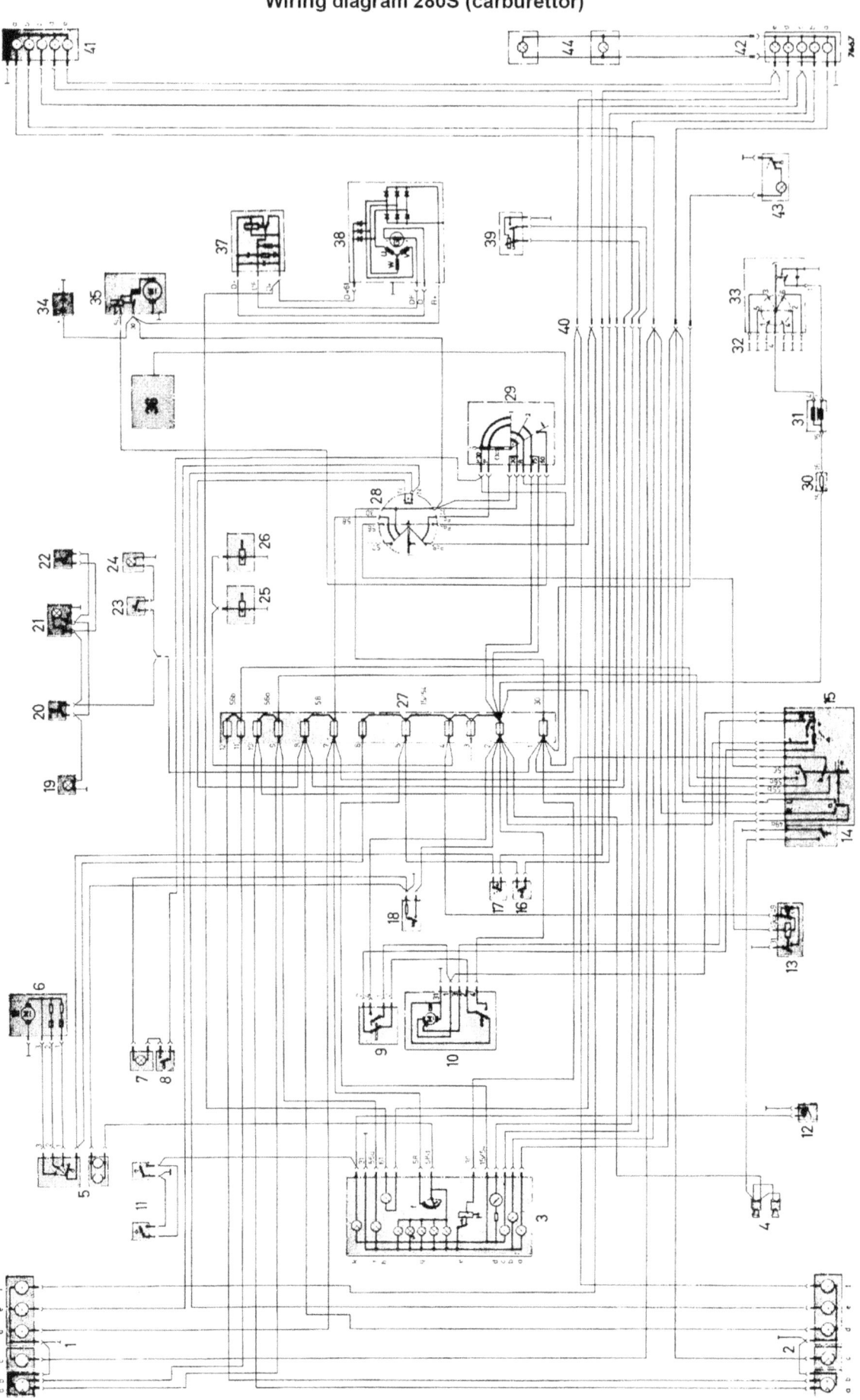

Wiring diagram 280S (carburettor)

1	Light assembly (right side)	16	Back-up light switch
2	Light assembly (left side)	17	Stop light switch
a	High beam	18	Cigar lighter
b	Low beam	19	Entrance light
c	Turn signal light	20	Courtesy light switch, left front door
d	Parking light	21	Reading light
e	Fog light	22	Courtesy light switch, right front door
f	Side light	23	Switch for dome light
3	Instrument cluster	24	Dome light, rear
a	Turn signal light indicator, left	25	Automatic choke, rear
b	Turn signal light indicator, right	26	Automatic choke, front
c	Low fuel level warning light	27	Fuses
d	Fuel gauge	28	Headlight switch
e	Electric clock	29	Ignition starter switch
f	Instrument lighting rheostat	30	Series resistance
g	Instrument lighting	31	Ignition coil
h	Generator (alternator) charge warning light	32	Spark plugs
i	High beam indicator	33	Distributor
k	Parking brake and brake fluid level warning light	34	Battery
		35	Starter
4	Dual horn system	36	Power lead for optional equipment (radio)
5	Heater blower switch		
6	Heater blower motor	37	Voltage regulator
7	Glove compartment light	38	Alternator
8	Switch for glove compartment light	39	Fuel gauge sending unit
9	Windshield washer foot pump	40	Rear light unit wiring harness connecting plug
10	Wiper motor		
11	Brake fluid level warning light control element	41	Rear light unit (right side)
		42	Rear light unit (left side)
12	Parking brake warning light control element	a	Turn signal light
		b	Tail light
13	Sending unit for turn signal light	c	Back-up light
14	Horn ring	d	Side light
15	Combination switch	e	Stop light
a	Turn signal light switch	43	Luggage boot
b	Passing flasher switch	44	Licence plate light
c	Headlight dimmer switch		
d	Windshield wiper switch		
e	Windshield wiper speed control switch		

Wiring diagram 280SE/8 & 280SEL/8 (fuel injection)

1. Lighting assembly, left
   a. Main beam
   b. Dipped beam
   c. Turn signal light
   d. Parking light and side light
   e. Fog light
2. Lighting assembly, right
   a. Main beam
   b. Dipped beam
   c. Turn signal light
   d. Parking light and side light
   e. Fog light
3. Electric fan (optional extra, air conditioning)
4. Relay for electric fan (optional extra, air conditioning)
5. Brake fluid control switch
6. Parking brake indicator light switch
7. Instrument cluster
   a. Turn signal indicator, left
   b. Turn signal indicator, right
   c. Fuel reserve warning light
   d. Fuel gauge
   e. Electric clock
   f. Rheostat for instrument lighting
   g. Instrument lighting
   h. Charging indicator light
   i. Main beam indicator
   k. Service and parking brake indicator light
8. Two-tone horn
9. Blower switch (control system)
10. Series resistor
11. Blower motor
12. Lighting for control system
13. Windscreen wiper motor
14. Foot-operated windscreen washer pump
15. Starter valve solenoid
16. Glove compartment light switch
17. Glove compartment light
18. Thermostatic switch for dehydrator (optional extra, air conditioning)
19. Thermostatic switch 212°F (100°C)
20. Solenoid valve for automatic transmission
21. Auxiliary fuse box (optional extra, air conditioning)
22. Thermostatic switch
23. Cigar lighter
24. Hazard warning flasher switch (electronic)
25. Horn ring
26. Combination switch
    a. Turn signal switch
    b. Headlight flasher switch
    c. Hand-operated dipper switch
    d. Windscreen wiper switch
    e. Windscreen wiper speed switch
27. Brake light switch
28. Fuses
29. Kickdown switch
30. Starter lock-out and reversing light switch
31. Relay for starting valve
32. Idle speed increase solenoid (optional extra, air conditioning)
33. Blower switch (optional extra, air conditioning)
34. Temperature switch (optional extra, air conditioning)

Wiring diagram 280SE/8 & 280SEL/8 (fuel injection)

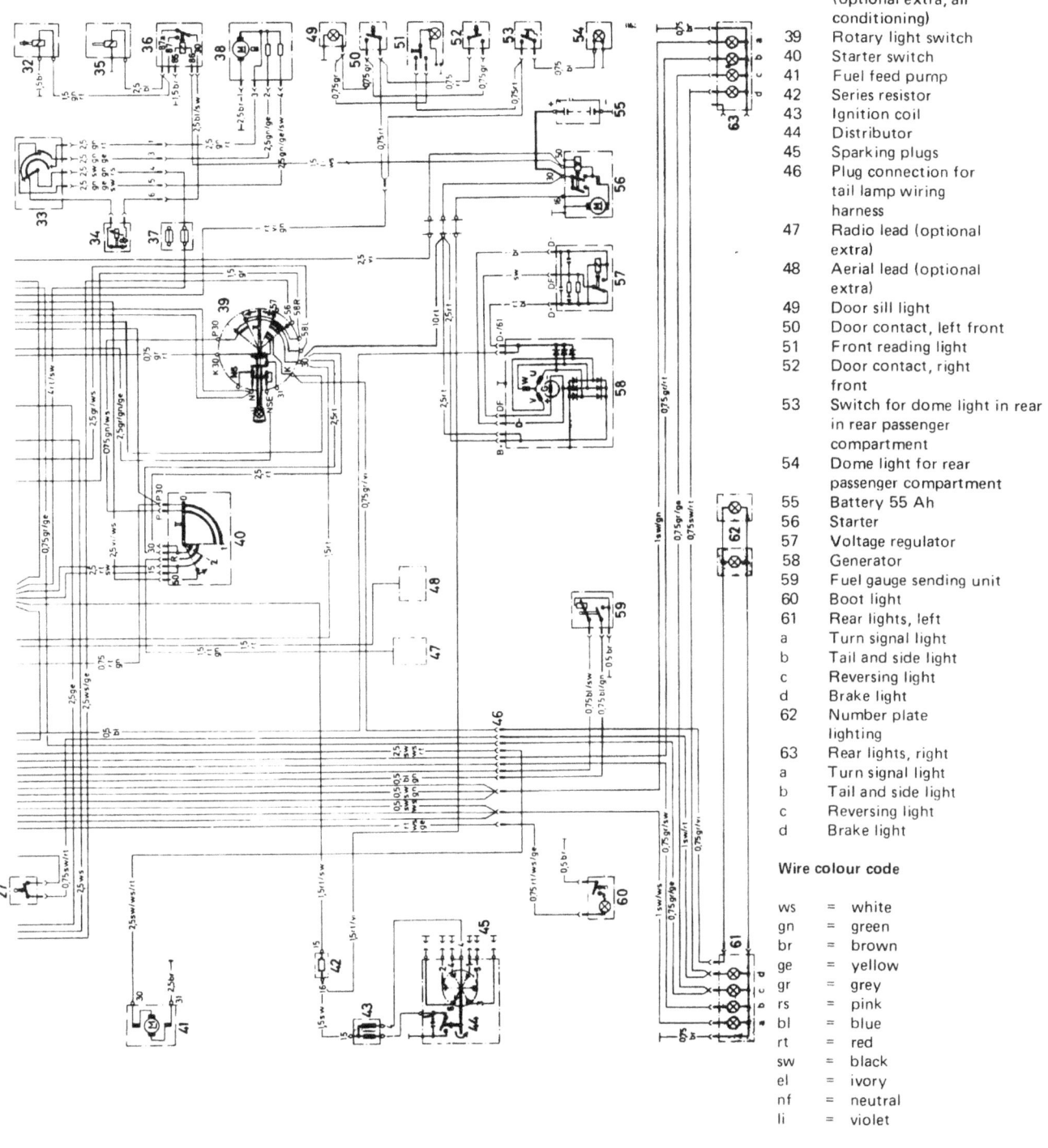

35	Magnetic coupling for refrigerant compressor (optional extra, air conditioning)
36	Relay (optional extra, air conditioning)
37	Additional fuse box (optional extra, air conditioning)
38	Blower motor (optional extra, air conditioning)
39	Rotary light switch
40	Starter switch
41	Fuel feed pump
42	Series resistor
43	Ignition coil
44	Distributor
45	Sparking plugs
46	Plug connection for tail lamp wiring harness
47	Radio lead (optional extra)
48	Aerial lead (optional extra)
49	Door sill light
50	Door contact, left front
51	Front reading light
52	Door contact, right front
53	Switch for dome light in rear in rear passenger compartment
54	Dome light for rear passenger compartment
55	Battery 55 Ah
56	Starter
57	Voltage regulator
58	Generator
59	Fuel gauge sending unit
60	Boot light
61	Rear lights, left
a	Turn signal light
b	Tail and side light
c	Reversing light
d	Brake light
62	Number plate lighting
63	Rear lights, right
a	Turn signal light
b	Tail and side light
c	Reversing light
d	Brake light

Wire colour code

ws	=	white
gn	=	green
br	=	brown
ge	=	yellow
gr	=	grey
rs	=	pink
bl	=	blue
rt	=	red
sw	=	black
el	=	ivory
nf	=	neutral
li	=	violet

Example:
Wire designation 1.5 gr/rt
Basic colour gr = grey
Identification colour rt = red
Cross section of wire 1.5 = 1.5 mm^2

Wiring diagram & test circuits for the 1972 280SE with emission control

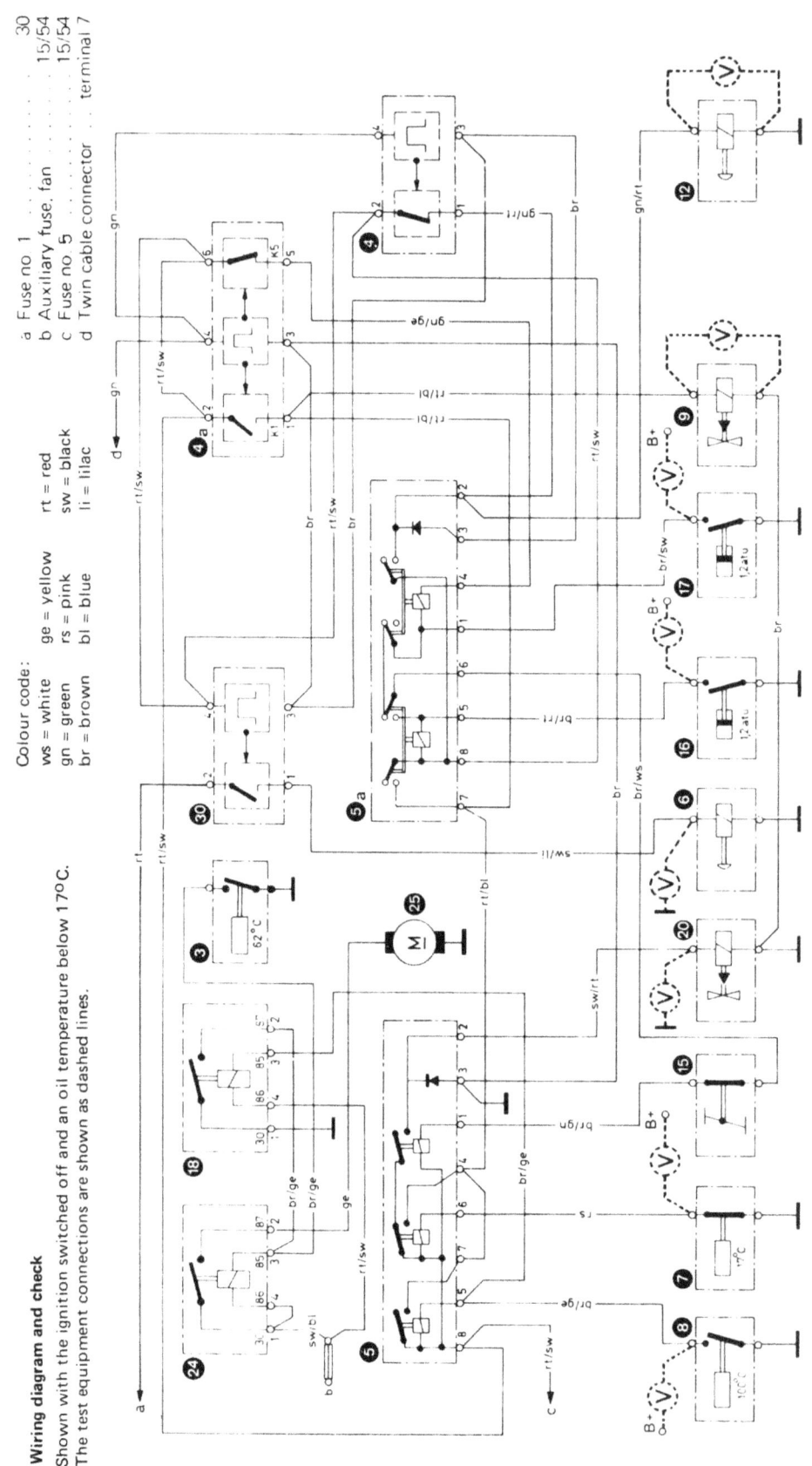

206

VELOCEPRESS MANUALS – AUTOMOBILE BY MAKE

ALFA ROMEO GIULIA WORKSHOP MANUAL 1300 TO 2000cc 1962-1975
ALFA ROMEO GIULIA TECH MANUAL CARBURETED CARS FROM 1962
ALFA ROMEO GIULIA TECH MANUAL FUEL INJECTED CARS FROM 1969
ALFA ROMEO GIULIETTA & GIULIA 750 & 101 SERIES 1955-1965 WSM
AUSTIN-HEALEY SPRITE & MG MIDGET WORKSHOP MANUAL 1958-1971
BMW 600 LIMOUSINE FACTORY WORKSHOP MANUAL
BMW 600 LIMOUSINE OWNERS HAND BOOK & SERVICE MANUAL
BMW 2000 & 2002 1966-1976 WORKSHOP MANUAL
BMW 2500, 2800, 3.0 & BARVARIA WORKSHOP MANUAL
CORVAIR 1960-1969 WORKSHOP MANUAL
CORVETTE V8 1955-1962 WORKSHOP MANUAL
FERRARI HANDBOOK ROAD & RACE CARS (SERVICE/SPECS) 1948-1958
FERRARI 250GT SERVICE & MAINTENANCE by JIM RIFF 1956-1965
FERRARI 250GT & 250GTE FACTORY PARTS AND REPAIR MANUALS
FIAT 500 FACTORY WORKSHOP MANUAL 1957-1973
FIAT 600, 600D & MULTIPLA FACTORY WORKSHOP MANUAL 1955-1969
JAGUAR E-TYPE 3.8 & 4.2 SERIES 1 & 2 WORKSHOP MANUAL
JAGUAR MK 7, 8, 9 & XK120, 140, 150 WORKSHOP MANUAL 1948-1961
MERCEDES-BENZ 280 SERIES 1968-1972
METROPOLITAN FACTORY WORKSHOP MANUAL
MGA & MGB OWNERS HANDBOOK & WORKSHOP MANUAL
MG MIDGET TC, TD, TF & TF1500 WORKSHOP MANUAL
PORSCHE 356 1948-1965 WORKSHOP MANUAL
PORSCHE 911 2.0, 2.2, 2.4 LITRE 1964-1973 WORKSHOP MANUAL
PORSCHE 911 2.7, 3.0, 3.2 LITRE 1973-1989 WORKSHOP MANUAL
PORSCHE 912 WORKSHOP MANUAL
PORSCHE 914/4 & 914/6 1.7, 1.8, 2.0 LITRE 1970-1976 WSM
TRIUMPH TR2, TR3, TR4 1953-1965 WORKSHOP MANUAL
VOLKSWAGEN TRANSPORTER, TRUCKS & WAGONS 1950-1979 WSM
VOLVO 1944-1968 ALL MODELS WORKSHOP MANUAL

VELOCEPRESS TECHNICAL BOOKS - AUTOMOBILE

HOW TO BUILD A FIBERGLASS CAR
HOW TO BUILD A RACING CAR
HOW TO RESTORE THE MODEL 'A' FORD
MASERATI OWNER'S HANDBOOK
PERFORMANCE TUNING THE SUNBEAM TIGER
SOUPING THE VOLKSWAGEN
SOLEX CARBURETORS (EMPHASIS ON UK & EU AUTOMOBILES)
SU CARBURETORS (EMPHASIS ON UK AUTOMOBILES)
WEBER CARBURETORS (EMPHASIS ON ALFA & FIAT)

VELOCEPRESS BOOKS & GUIDES - AUTOMOBILE

COMPLETE CATALOG OF JAPANESE MOTOR VEHICLES
FERRARI 308 SERIES BUYER'S AND OWNER'S GUIDE
FERRARI BROCHURES AND SALES LITERATURE 1968-1989
FERRARI SERIAL NUMBERS PART I - ODD NUMBERS TO 21399
FERRARI SERIAL NUMBERS PART II - EVEN NUMBERS TO 1050
HENRY'S FABULOUS MODEL "A" FORD
MASERATI BROCHURES AND SALES LITERATURE

VELOCEPRESS BOOKS – AUTO RACING

CARRERA PANAMERICANA - MEXICAN ROAD RACE (BOOK OF)
DIALED IN - THE JAN OPPERMAN STORY
VEDA ORR'S NEW REVISED HOT ROD PICTORIAL

(continued)

VELOCEPRESS MANUALS – MOTORCYCLE BY MAKE

AJS 1932-1948 SINGLES & TWINS 250cc THRU 1000cc (BOOK OF)
AJS 1945-1960 SINGLES 350cc & 500cc MODELS 16 & 18 (BOOK OF)
AJS 1955-1965 SINGLES 350cc & 500cc (BOOK OF)
AJS 1957-1966 FACTORY WSM - ALL SINGLES & TWINS
ARIEL UP TO 1932 (BOOK OF)
ARIEL 1932-1939 PREWAR MODELS (BOOK OF)
ARIEL 1933-1951 (WORKSHOP MANUAL)
ARIEL 1939-1960 4 STROKE SINGLES (BOOK OF)
ARIEL 1958-1964 LEADER & ARROW FACTORY WSM & PARTS LIST
ARIEL 1958-1964 LEADER & ARROW (BOOK OF)
BMW R26 R27 (1956-1967) FACTORY WORKSHOP MANUAL
BMW R50 R50S R60 R69S (1955-1969) FACTORY WORKSHOP MANUAL
BMW R50/5 R60/5 R75/5 (1969-1973) FACTORY WORKSHOP MANUAL
BRIDGESTONE 90 SERIES FACTORY WSM & PARTS CATALOGUE
BRIDGESTONE 175 SERIES FACTORY WSM & PARTS MANUAL
BRIDGESTONE 350 SERIES FACTORY WSM & PARTS CATALOGUES
BSA SERVICE SHEETS MASTER CATALOGUE ALL MODELS 1945-1967
BSA BANTAM D1 TO D7 1948-1966 FACTORY SERVICE SHEETS MANUAL
BSA BANTAM ALL MODELS FROM 1948 ONWARDS (BOOK OF)
BSA BANTAM D14 FACTORY SERVICE MANUAL
BSA DANDY FACTORY WORKSHOP MANUAL (COMPILATION)
BSA SINGLES & V-TWINS UP TO 1926 inc. 1927 SUPPLEMENT (BOOK OF)
BSA SINGLES & V-TWINS UP TO 1930 (BOOK OF)
BSA SINGLES & V-TWINS UP TO 1935 (BOOK OF)
BSA SINGLES & V-TWINS 1936-1939 (BOOK OF)
BSA C10, C11 & C12 1945-1958 FACTORY SERVICE SHEETS MANUAL
BSA OHV & SV SINGLES 250-600cc 1945-1959 (BOOK OF)
BSA C15 & B40 1958-1967 FACTORY SERVICE SHEETS MANUAL
BSA OHV & SV SINGLES 250cc (ONLY) 1954-1970 (BOOK OF)
BSA B31, B32, B33 & B34 1945-60 FACTORY SERVICE SHEETS MANUAL
BSA OHV SINGLES 350 & 500cc 1955-1967 (BOOK OF)
BSA M20, M21 & M33 1945-1963 FACTORY SERVICE SHEETS MANUAL
BSA TWINS A7 & A10 1948-1962 FACTORY SERVICE SHEETS MANUAL
BSA TWINS A7 & A10 1948-1962 (BOOK OF)
BSA TWINS A50 & A65 1962-1965 FACTORY WORKSHOP MANUAL
BSA TWINS A50 & A65 1962-1969 (SECOND BOOK OF)
DOUGLAS 1929-1939 PREWAR ALL MODELS (BOOK OF)
DOUGLAS 1948-1957 POSTWAR ALL MODELS FACTORY SHOP MANUAL
DUCATI 160cc, 250cc & 350cc OHC MODELS FACTORY SHOP MANUAL
HONDA 50cc ALL MODELS UP TO 1970 INC MONKEY & TRAIL (BOOK OF)
HONDA 90cc ALL MODELS UP TO 1966 (BOOK OF)
HONDA TWINS & SINGLES 50cc THRU 305cc 1960-1966 (BOOK OF)
HONDA TWINS ALL MODELS 125cc THRU 450cc UP TO 1968 (BOOK OF)
HONDA C100 50cc SUPER CUB O.H.C. 1959-1962 FACTORY WSM
HONDA C110 50cc SPORT CUB O.H.C. 1960-1962 FACTORY WSM
HONDA 50-65-70-90cc O.H.C. SINGLES 1959-1983 WSM
HONDA 100-125cc SINGLES CB/CD/CL/SL/TL 1970-1984 FACTORY WSM
HONDA 125-150cc TWINS C/CS/CB/CA 1959-1966 FACTORY WSM
HONDA 125-160-175-200cc TWINS 1965-1978 WORKSHOP MANUAL
HONDA 250-305cc TWINS C/CS/CB 1961-1968 FACTORY WSM
HOHDA 250-350cc TWINS CB/CL/SL 1968-1973 FACTORY WSM
HONDA 250-360cc TWINS CB/CL/CJ 1974-1977 FACTORY WSM
HONDA 350F & 400F 4-CYLINDER 1972-1977 FACTORY WSM
HONDA 450cc TWINS CB/CL 1965-1974 K0 TO K7 WORKSHOP MANUAL
HONDA 500cc & 550cc 4-CYL 1971-1978 FACTORY WORKSHOP MANUAL
HONDA 750cc SHOC 4-CYL 1969-1978 K0~K8 WORKSHOP MANUAL
INDIAN PONYBIKE, BOY RACER & PAPOOSE ILL PARTS LIST & SALES LIT

VELOCEPRESS MANUALS – SCOOTERS BY MAKE

BSA SUNBEAM SCOOTER WORKSHOP MANUAL 1959-1965
BSA SUNBEAM SCOOTER 1959-1965 (BOOK OF)
LAMBRETTA 1947-1957 ALL 125 & 150cc MODELS (BOOK OF)
LAMBRETTA 1957-1970 LI & TV MODELS (SECOND BOOK OF)
NSU PRIMA 1956-1964 ALL MODELS (BOOK OF)
TRIUMPH TIGRESS SCOOTER WORKSHOP MANUAL 1959-1965
TRIUMPH TIGRESS SCOOTER (BOOK OF)
VESPA 1951-1961 (BOOK OF)
VESPA 1955-1963 125 & 150cc & GS MODELS (SECOND BOOK OF)
VESPA 1955-1968 GS & SS (BOOK OF)
VESPA 1963-1972 90, 125 & 150cc (THIRD BOOK OF)

VELOCEPRESS MANUALS – MOPEDS & MOTORIZED BICYCLES

CYCLEMOTOR (BOOK OF)
NSU QUICKLY 1953-1963 ALL MODELS (BOOK OF)
PUCH MAXI N & S MAINTENANCE & REPAIR (3 MANUAL COMPILATION)
RALEIGH MOPEDS 1960-1969 (BOOK OF)

J.A.P. ENGINES 1927-1952 & MOTORCYCLES 1934-1952 (BOOK OF)
MATCHLESS 1931-1939 ALL MODELS 250cc THRU 990cc (BOOK OF)
MATCHLESS 1945-1956 350 & 500cc SINGLES (BOOK OF)
MATCHLESS 1955-1966 350 & 500cc SINGLES (BOOK OF)
MATCHLESS 1957-1966 FACTORY WSM - ALL SINGLES & TWINS
NEW IMPERIAL ALL SV & OHV FROM 1935 ONWARDS (BOOK OF)
NORTON 1932-1939 PREWAR MODELS (BOOK OF)
NORTON 1932-1947 (BOOK OF)
NORTON 1938-1956 (BOOK OF)
NORTON 1945-1963 MODELS 16H, Big4, ES2, 19 & 50 WSM'S & PARTS
NORTON 1955-1963 MODELS 19, 50 & ES2 (BOOK OF)
NORTON 1948-1970 DOMINATOR TWINS FACTORY WSM'S & PARTS
NORTON 1955-1965 DOMINATOR TWINS (BOOK OF)
NORTON 1960-1970 TWIN CYLINDER FACTORY WORKSHOP MANUAL
NORTON 1970-1975 COMMANDO 850 & 750cc FACTORY WSM
NORTON 1975-1978 MK 3 COMMANDO 850 cc FACTORY WSM
PANTHER 1932-1958 LIGHTWEIGHT MODELS 250 & 350cc (BOOK OF)
PANTHER 1938-1966 HEAVYWEIGHT MODELS 600 & 650cc (BOOK OF)
PENTON-KTM-SACHS 1968-1975 100cc & 125cc WORKSHOP MANUAL
RALEIGH MOTORCYCLES 1919-1933 (BOOK OF)
ROYAL ENFIELD 1934-1946 SINGLES & V TWINS (BOOK OF)
ROYAL ENFIELD 1937-1953 SINGLES & V TWINS (BOOK OF)
ROYAL ENFIELD 1946-1962 SINGLES (BOOK OF)
ROYAL ENFIELD 1948-1963 500cc TWINS FACTORY WORKSHOP MANUAL
ROYAL ENFIELD 1952-1963 700cc TWINS FACTORY WORKSHOP MANUAL
ROYAL ENFIELD 1956-1966 250cc CRUSADER & 350cc NEW BULLET WSM
ROYAL ENFIELD 1958-1966 250cc & 350cc SINGLES (SECOND BOOK OF)
ROYAL ENFIELD 1962-1970 INTERCEPTOR WSM'S & PARTS (Compilation)
RUDGE 1933-1939 (BOOK OF)
SACHS 1968-1975 100cc & 125cc ENGINES WSM & M/CYCLE PARTS LIST
SUNBEAM 1928-1939 (BOOK OF)
SUNBEAM 1946-1957 S7 & S8 (BOOK OF)
SUZUKI 50cc & 80cc UP TO 1966 (BOOK OF)
SUZUKI T10 1963-1967 FACTORY WORKSHOP MANUAL
SUZUKI T20 & T200 1965-1969 FACTORY WORKSHOP MANUAL
SUZUKI TWINS 1962 ONWARDS 125-500cc WORKSHOP MANUAL
TRIUMPH 1935-1949 SINGLES & TWINS (BOOK OF)
TRIUMPH 1937-1961 SINGLES SV & OHV 250cc-600cc + TERRIER & CUB
TRIUMPH 1945-1955 PRE-UNIT 350cc, 500cc & 650cc TWINS WSM No.11
TRIUMPH 1945-1959 TWINS (BOOK OF)
TRIUMPH 1956-1969 TWINS (BOOK OF)
TRIUMPH 1956-1962 PRE-UNIT 500cc & 650cc TWINS WSM No.17
TRIUMPH 1957-1963 UNIT CONSTRUCTION 350-500cc WSM No.4
TRIUMPH 1963-1974 UNIT CONSTRUCTION 350-500cc FACTORY WSM
TRIUMPH 1963-1970 UNIT CONSTRUCTION 650cc FACTORY WSM
TRIUMPH 1968-1974 TRIDENT T150 & T150V FACTORY WSM
TRIUMPH 1971-1973 650cc OIL-IN-FRAME FACTORY WSM
TRIUMPH 1973-1978 750cc BONNEVILLE & TIGER FACTORY WSM
TRIUMPH 1979-1983 T140, TR7 & TR65 FACTORY WSM
VELOCETTE 1925-1970 ALL SINGLES & TWINS (BOOK OF)
VELOCETTE 1933-1952 MOV-MAC-MSS RIGID FRAME FACTORY WSM
VELOCETTE 1954-1971 MSS-VENOM-THRUXTON-VIPER FACTORY WSM
VILLIERS ENGINE UP TO 1959 INC. 3 WHEELERS (BOOK OF)
VILLIERS ENGINE UP TO 1969 (BOOK OF)
VINCENT 1935-1955 (WORKSHOP MANUAL)
YAMAHA 1961-1967 YA5 & YA6 (WORKSHOP MANUAL & ILL PARTS LIST)
YAMAHA 1971-1972 JT1 & JT2 (WORKSHOP MANUAL & ILL PARTS LIST)

VELOCEPRESS MANUALS - THREE WHEELER'S

BOND MINICAR THREE WHEELER 1948-1967 (BOOK OF)
BMW ISETTA FACTORY WORKSHOP MANUAL
BSA THREE WHEELER (BOOK OF)
RELIANT REGAL THREE WHEELER 1952-1973 (BOOK OF)
VINTAGE MORGAN THREE WHEELER (BOOK OF)

VELOCEPRESS TECHNICAL BOOKS – MOTORCYCLE

1930'S BRITISH MOTORCYCLE CARBS & ELEC COMPONENTS (BOOK OF)
1930'S BRITISH MOTORCYCLE ENGINES (OVERHAUL & MAINTENANCE)
1930'S BRITISH MOTORCYCLE GEARBOXES & CLUTCHES (BOOK OF)
CATALOG OF BRITISH MOTORCYCLES (1951 MODELS)
LUCAS ELECTRONICS BRITISH M/CYCLES REPAIR & PARTS (1950-1977)
MOTORCYCLE ENGINEERING (P.E. Irving)
MOTORCYCLE ROAD TESTS 1949-1953 (Motor Cycle Magazine UK)
SPEED AND HOW TO OBTAIN IT (Motor Cycle Magazine UK)
TUNING FOR SPEED (P.E. Irving)
WIPAC (COMBO) MANUAL NUMBER 3 + M/CYCLE & SCOOTER MANUAL

www.VelocePress.com

www.ingramcontent.com/pod-product-compliance
Lightning Source LLC
Chambersburg PA
CBHW080734300426
44114CB00019B/2587